What's Left?
Who's Left?

The Layman's Handbook

for

Estate Property Management

with Accounting Records

- and -

Survivor's Guide

to

Personal and Financial Well-Being

Teresa Pedicino

Information and Accounting Records for
Estate Administrators, Trustees, and Surviving Spouses

Tristus Publishing Company

PLEASE READ THIS

This publication is designed to provide useful, accurate, and authoritative information with regard to the subject matter covered. But please be aware that laws and procedures are constantly changing and are subject to differing interpretations. This book is sold with the understanding that neither the author nor the publisher are engaged in rendering legal, accounting, or other professional advice. Therefore, neither the author nor the publisher of this book make any guarantees regarding the outcome of the uses to which this material is put. If you are confused by anything you read here, or if you need more information check with an expert. If legal or other expert assistance is required, the services of a competent professional should be sought. The ultimate responsibility for making good decisions is yours.

Published by: *Tristus Publishing Company*
P.O. Box 26268
Tamarac, FL 33320-6268

Library of Congress Catalog Card Number: 96-90816

ISBN 0-9652846-0-3

Printed in the United States of America

10 9 8 7 6 5 4 3 2 1

First Edition

Acknowledgements

The Author and Tristus Publishing Company wish to express their gratitude and appreciation to Kathleen Gaglias, Jim Jollie, Anthony Natale, and Vince Palumbo for their unending editorial patience. And to Elisa Jorgensen and Jme Palacio for their help with the cover.

Many Thanks to the following professionals for their patience and invaluable knowledge, experience, comments, and advice: Peter Cardone, C.P.A.; Nicholas Natale, L.U.T.C.F., Reg. Rep.; Marsha Malcom, G.R.I. Broker; Ann Villany, Estate Sales; Howard Harms, Mover; Ralph DeMarco, MSW, LCSW, B.C.D.; Gwelda Lorenz, RN,BSN,MA; Larry Gaglias, General Contractor; Ken Jorgensen, Building Inspector; Harold Malcom, Insurance Agent, Property and Landscape Protection Specialist.

We are particularly indebted to Suzan Herskowitz, Esq., for her thorough reading of, and extensive comments on, various drafts of the manuscript.

Finally, the author would like to acknowledge those who provided insight into the practical use of this book, while it was being written, and thus express both love and heartfelt thanks to Joanne Gugliotta, Yolanda Villani, Mary Marcel, and Rose Spindler.

Dedication

This book is dedicated to my parents, Ann and Charles, who left a legacy of love, and without whose unequaled faith, inspiration, and support this book would never have been possible.

Table of Contents - Chapters

xi

Table of Contents - Chapters

Quick Reference

TABLE OF CONTENTS - RECORDS

ASSETS

LIABILITIES

MISCELLANEOUS

INTRODUCTION

The main purpose of this book is to assist you in settling the affairs of a person who has died. This purpose is accomplished, first through explanations of the terms and tasks you may be faced with; and, second, by providing a comprehensive accounting system, which when properly used, will afford fingertip access to the information you will need when completing the tax and accounting requirements of the Estate.

Whether you are a professional administrator, an accountant, a relative, or a friend of the deceased person, this book will work with you in completing your duties in an orderly and easy manner. For those who are involved for the first time in settling the affairs of another, we have defined various terms as they are encountered. You will soon become very familiar with these terms.

Throughout the book you will be informed about the options available to you in dealing with each aspect of the Estate. This information is presented to direct you to those aspects of each item which you may want to consider, depending upon your individual situation. It is not our intention to give legal, financial, or other professional advice or attempt to tell you how you should personally handle any situation. This must be your own decision, depending on your own ability, experience, and the circumstances with which you are dealing.

Throughout the book, we suggest you seek professional help as needed in your particular circumstances, because no book could possibly cover all the current laws of every state. Additionally, situations can vary so much no book could address them all. There are, however, six safe-guards to Estate settlement, which, unlike laws and regulations, never change. These six safe-guards constitute the only advice we give in this book. The following advice may save you trouble in the future.

1. Never send a document to an agency or institution until it is requested. Your first contact, preferably in writing, should only advise the agency or institution of the death, explain what you want to accomplish by the contact, and request information and forms necessary to accomplish your purpose.

2. Make a copy for your records of each document (Insurance Policy, Stock Certificate, Medical Bill, etc.) before you deliver it, either by mail or in person, to any agency or institution.
3. Make or request a copy of every document you sign for your records.
4. Always sign your name with your title in relation to the Estate, if you have one.
5. When you **Distribute** (give) the property in the Estate to the Beneficiaries, be sure you leave sufficient funds in the Estate to pay all outstanding debts and taxes.
6. **Do not distribute** anything to <u>anyone</u> until you are sure he or she is the proper person to receive it.

The sixth item of advice can be the most important. By following this advice, you can avoid discontentment, discord, and possibly a lawsuit. Unfortunately, it seems no matter how close and agreeable family members usually are, the premature giving of property to one person can often cause great discord among the Beneficiaries and Heirs. **Beneficiaries** are the people entitled to receive a gift or benefit from the Estate. **Heirs** are people entitled by law to inherit property if the decedent does not leave a Will, or other device, to pass property at death. In reality, once a person takes possession of an item or money, it is almost impossible to get it back.

The time to settle a dispute is before someone actually takes possession of the disputed item. Discuss disputed items with the Beneficiaries and try to come to an agreement on who will receive what. Or, if no agreement can be reached, shared ownership and possession, with a written agreement, may be acceptable to all. The agreement may provide for each interested Beneficiary to keep the item for a specified period and then pass it on to the next on a rotating schedule. If the parties involved cannot reach an agreement, the matter is brought before the Court for a hearing and decision.

No matter what the decedent planned or who he or she wanted to receive what; when all the Beneficiaries reach an agreement, they can redistribute the Estate any way they want. This redistributing should be approved by the Court. To prevent problems later, all major decisions regarding the disposition of property should be discussed with all Beneficiaries. Since our society is so mobile, the most opportune time to have everyone present to discuss major issues is when the family is gathered for the Funeral or Memorial Service. (Although some family members may be unwilling or too distraught at that time.) Use the "Beneficiaries Decision Record" on page R-43.

Entering A Vacated Residence

If the residence of the decedent is empty, before you enter it decide who, if anyone, will enter the residence with you. If the residence is damaged, see Chapter 11, "Protection and Repair of Real Property" before you enter. You may consider having a trusted friend or uninvolved relative accompany you. This person can verify, if necessary at a later date, what you have found. If you choose to allow Beneficiaries or Heirs into the residence, do not allow removal of anything unless all Heirs or potential Beneficiaries agree to let that person have it. Then be sure you write a receipt for the item and have the recipient sign it on the spot. The receipt should include the value of the item, to allow for future deduction of the value from the Beneficiary's cash share of the Estate, or payment of the value to the Estate, as applicable. You may wish to use the "Tangible Personal Property Inventory and Sale Record" on page R-2, or the "Estate Distribution Record" on page R-30 for this purpose.

When the Residence is Occupied

If the home is occupied, ask the occupant(s) not to remove any property themselves or give anything to anyone until they have checked with you. Remember, even things you may consider worthless, may have sentimental value to family members and, unfortunately, the deceased person may have promised the same item to more than one person. See Chapter 10, "Distribution and Sale of Personal Property," for the appropriate time for relatives and Beneficiaries to take possession of personal property. If the home is occupied by a surviving spouse, protect him or her by not allowing anyone to take anything. The surviving spouse is often not in a psychological condition to make even a simple decision. He or she may be easily manipulated into giving away items, and later regretting the action. See Chapter 22, "Dealing With The Grief."

Note: Since terms are explained where they appear in the text; there is no Glossary included in this book. To find the definition of a word: look for the word in the index; the first or second reference to that word will include the definition. The word is presented in bold type where it is defined.

We sincerely hope this publication will prove helpful to you and your loved ones.

HOW TO USE THIS BOOK

Chapters

This book was written as a reference book. If you read the "Introduction," you have already noticed references to other chapters for more information. This will continue throughout the book. This publication is designed to provide currently accurate and useful information about most aspects of property management for an Estate. On the day a person dies, everything he or she owns becomes a separate legal entity known as the **Estate**. The information given in each chapter is solely for the purpose of education, to acquaint you with the subject matter. This hopefully will permit you to make an informed decision in each circumstance. You should not rely upon this book for legal, tax, or other professional advice. You should clearly understand that the laws of each state are different, and could never be contained in any one book. Additionally, federal and state laws are continually being changed. Therefore, you should make certain you have current and accurate information before making any final legal or financial decisions. This is the reason professionals, such as attorneys and accountants, are engaged. It is their job to stay abreast of current law and use this knowledge to serve their clients.

We present this as a reference book, which means when a circumstance arises, you can go to this book and read the applicable chapter to gain a working knowledge of the subject. For instance, if the decedent left a Will, read Chapter 2, "Wills and Probate" and Chapter 4, "Wills and Trusts Compared." Before contacting the bank where the decedent has a checking account, read Chapter 7, "Property Transfer Breakdown." We suggest that you acquaint yourself with the "Table of Contents — Chapters." You will then know what subjects are covered, and you can go directly to that chapter for information when it is needed. Of course, we have no objection to you reading the entire book.

Throughout the book, the reader is referred to various organizations, associations, and government agencies. With the ever increasing popularity of the Internet, many of these have gone online. Use your major online index to find their home pages or Web sites. The Federal Web Locator is a listing of Web addresses for government agencies, go online to *http://www.law.vill.edu/fed-agency/fedwebloc.html*

Records

Regardless of how the property in the Estate is titled or how it will be transferred to the Beneficiaries, all the property of the Estate must be inventoried, valued, taken possession of, maintained and protected, and eventually transferred to the new owners of the property. All of this requires record keeping, and good record keeping is the best way to defend yourself against an accusation of mismanagement. This is especially true if the Estate must be Probated. See Chapter 2, "Wills and Probate." Before Probate is over, the Court may require a formal accounting for every dime that has come into and flowed out of the Estate. Even if Probate is not required, records must be kept for the taxing authorities. The forms we have including should help you to keep track of Estate property, income, and debt payment. You can use them not only to record amounts received or spent, but also to record any correspondence you send or receive. These forms also provide a standardized accounting system, so if more than one person is involved in administering the Estate, coordination is easier. They also allow an accountant, attorney, or Successor Administrator to quickly and easily review the financial status of the Estate. Further, the more work professionals have to do to perform their jobs, the higher the fee they will charge. Therefore, good record keeping can save you money, because the professionals will not have to hunt for the information they need to complete their work.

The records are located at the back of this book. Each is for a specific type of property, expense or income. They may seem overwhelming at first; however, they are really not difficult to use. As you deal with each item of property, debt, income or expense, review the list of records in the "Table of Contents — Records" for the appropriate record. Tear out the record and make sufficient copies of it to suit your needs. Because you may have to make additional copies of the same form later, do not write on the original records. If you choose the correct record for the item, you will easily be able to follow the headings and fill in the proper information. We suggest these records also be used to record correspondence regarding that aspect of the Estate as it is sent or received. You can ignore the columns and just write across the sheet to enter the nature of correspondence. Reading the appropriate Chapter will also assist you in understanding what information is requested on the form. To make your job easier, we suggest you use the following accounting system for all matters concerning the Estate. The accounting system we have provided offers a double entry system for income and expenses. This means that any money received by the Estate and all money paid by the Estate is recorded on two different records. One entry is made on a record titled for the source of income or receiver of an expense. You will note that each income and expense record has two columns, labeled "Source of Funds" and "Deposited To." These are reference columns to the second entry, which is made on the "Cash Flow Record," on page R-28. This record is used if funds are deposited to, or withdrawn from, accounts owned by different people or entities. The purpose for this is to clearly show whether the funds of the decedent, the Estate, or the Administrator were affected by the transaction. Although the "Cash Flow Record" looks like a check book record, funds from a credit card or cash can also be entered as appropriate. The important thing is not what form the funds took, but whose funds were increased or decreased. If you faithfully make entries on the records as you go along, you will save yourself a lot of backtracking, reviewing, and confusion when the information is needed. For a suggested filing system for the Estate papers and these records, see Chapter 7, "Property Transfer Breakdown."

WHEN A PERSON DIES

When a Person Dies at Home

When a person dies at home, the first thing to do is have the person pronounced dead. If death has occurred as a result of natural causes, contact his or her attending physician. If the person was under the care of Hospice, call them instead of the doctor. When death is the result of injury or violence, or the physician cannot, for whatever reason, pronounce, call your local emergency number and request the police and paramedics. The paramedics will check for life signs and the police will complete the appropriate forms. If the death was violent or suspicious in nature, the coroner's office will be called to take charge of the body. If the paramedics are convinced the death was a result of natural causes, you can call the Funeral Director or Crematorium to pick up the remains. You do not have to go with them. However, if burial will take place within 24 hours or you plan on cremation, you should advise the Funeral Director not to embalm the body, or this service may be performed automatically. Once a service is performed, you will be responsible for paying for it.

Arranging for the Disposition of the Remains and Memorial Services

Usually the next of kin arranges for the services and disposition of the remains. However, this may become the job of the Administrator of the Estate even before appointment. Regardless of who makes the arrangements, it is important that any directions left in a Will are carried out. Although most attorneys do not put funeral arrangements in a Will because it may not be immediately accessible, every effort should be made to find the Will, if one exists. For more information see Chapter 7, "Property Transfer Breakdown," <u>Opening the Safe Deposit Box</u>. Also, look for any pre-arrangement contracts and Cemetery Deeds. If the arrangements become your decision, be mindful of the assets of the decedent. You may end up paying out-of-pocket for the funeral if assets of the deceased are not sufficient to cover them. Listings of organizations, societies, pre-need and service providers can be found in the Yellow Pages under the headings CASKETS, CEMETERIES, CREMATION SERVICES, FUNERAL DIRECTORS, MAUSOLEUMS, and MONUMENTS. The Funeral Director may be willing to accept, and wait for, the proceeds of a life insurance policy for payment. If this is the method of payment you choose, be sure to bring the policy and proof of its current value. Otherwise, you will have to pay for the services in cash, by check, or with your credit card, if acceptable. The Funeral Director will order certified copies of the Death Certificate for you. Usually, 6 to 12 copies will be enough. If you need more, you can order copies from the State's Department of Vital Statistics. See Chapter 20, "Locating Missing Beneficiaries," for requesting information. Most states prohibit institutions and agencies from accepting a photocopy of a Death Certificate as proof of death. Therefore, in most cases, they will only accept a certified copy of the Death Certificate issued by the state where the death occurred and was registered, and bearing the state's watermark.

Tidbit: Some cemeteries will replace damaged or destroyed monuments, gravestones, or markers only if they were purchased through or from it. So, it is wise to check with the cemetery before purchasing a stone through an independent monument manufacturer or vender. Additionally, cemeteries have restrictions regarding the type of markers it permits, as well as rules regarding how the markers may be set.

Tidbit: The Federal Trade Commission (FTC), under the Funeral Rule, requires Funeral Directors to release price lists showing the charge for every item and service offered, and to provide pricing information over the phone, which is essential for comparing costs. The FTC also prohibits Funeral Directors from misrepresenting the legal necessity for embalming, or requiring a casket for direct cremations.

When you make arrangements for the disposition of the body, you may have to provide a lot of personal information. Use the questionnaires on pages R-35 through R-38, which correspond to the following titles:

Information Needed About the Decedent for the Death Certificate:

Full Name: <u>First - Middle - Last</u>   **Maiden Name:** <u>Last</u>
Date of Birth: <u>Month, Day, Year</u>   **Place of Birth:** <u>City & State</u> or <u>Foreign Town & Country</u>
Legal Residence at Time of Death: <u>Street Address, Apartment Number, City, County, State, & Zip Code</u>
Length of Residence: <u>How long at this address?</u>   **Social Security Number:** ____-____-_____
Location When Death Occurred: <u>Street Address, Apartment Number, City, County, State, & Zip Code</u>
Name of Mother: <u>First - Middle - Last</u>   **Maiden Name:** <u>Last</u>
Place of Birth: <u>City & State</u> or <u>Foreign Town & Country</u>

Date of Death: <u>Month, Day, Year</u> **-Or- Current Residence:** <u>City & State</u> or <u>Town & Country</u>
Name of Father: <u>First - Middle - Last</u>   **Place of Birth:** <u>City & State</u> or <u>Town & Country</u>
Date of Death: <u>Month, Day, Year</u> **-Or- Current Residence:** <u>City & State</u> or <u>Town & Country</u>
Decedent's Marital Status: <u>Single, Married, Divorced</u>
Name of Spouse: <u>First - Middle - Last</u>   **Maiden Name:** <u>Last</u>
Place of Birth: <u>City & State</u> or <u>Foreign Town & Country</u>
Date of Death: <u>Month, Day, Year</u> **-Or- Current Residence:** <u>City & State</u> or <u>Town & Country</u>
Marriage: Date: <u>Month, Day, Year</u>   **Place:** <u>County & State</u> or <u>Town & Country</u>
If Decedent was a Veteran: Years of Service: From_____ To_____ **Branch:** <u>Army, Navy, Etc.</u>
Education: <u>Last Grade Completed</u>
Occupation: <u>Current Occupation</u> or <u>Past Occupation and Retired</u>

Memorial or Funeral Arrangements:

Bring all pre-arrangement contracts, cemetery deeds, and associated papers.
Funeral, Cremation, or Memorial Services at: <u>Name of Funeral Home, Memorial Garden, Church, Etc.</u>
Address: <u>Street Address, City, State, and Directions, if needed.</u>
Interment At: <u>Name of Cemetery or Place of Scattering</u>
Address: <u>Street Address, City, State, and Directions, if needed.</u>
Religious Ceremonies: <u>Name of Church or Synagogue and Name of Clergy.</u> (The Funeral Director will usually arrange.)
Military Honors: Bring a copy of decedent's **DD-214** (military discharge papers). (The Funeral Director will usually arrange for a flag to be draped over the coffin or folded near the urn; as well as complete or provide applications for Veterans' burial benefits, if requested.) For more information see Chapter 7, "Property Transfer Breakdown," <u>Veterans Administration.</u>
Religious, Professional, or Fraternal Organization Ceremonies: Schedule with organization. (The Funeral Director will usually arrange.)
Disposition of the Remains:
- Casket with burial in the ground or above-ground in a mausoleum.
- Cremation with the ashes put in an urn or plastic box container and placed in a Columbarium, Mausoleum, or buried in the ground; or the ashes may be scattered on land or sea.
- Calcination (A dehydration process using inert heat, rather than flame, to achieve the same result as cremation.)
- Donation of the Body to a Medical School for research.

Special Instructions for the Service:
- Hours of Visitation
- Music
- Religious Service or Bible Readings

Items to be Brought to the Funeral Home, if the Casket will be Open:
- Clothing:

Woman	Man
Dress or Suit with blouse or scarf	Suit with shirt
Slip	Tie and matching pocket handkerchief
Bra, Panties or Girdle	Under Shirt and Under Shorts
Shoes and Nylons	Shoes and Sox
Face Makeup and Nail Polish	Belt

- **General:**

    A Recent Photograph of the deceased person
    Glasses
    Dentures
    Hearing Aid
    Other Prosthetic Devices
    Wig or Hairpiece
    Jewelry (Good jewelry should not be left with the remains.)

Tell the Funeral Director what items are to be returned to you. See Chapter 10, "Distribution and Sale of Personal Property," for information regarding donation of personal prosthetic items.

Optional Information for Memorial Book or Obituary:

Obituary to be Printed in: Name(s) of Newspaper(s)
Survived By: List all relatives who survive the decedent and wish to be named. Include the following information for each person:
Name: Mr., Mrs., Ms., Dr., etc., First and Last **Relationship:** Child, Brother, Sister-in-law, Etc.
Current Residence: City & State or Town & Country
Membership in Religious, Professional or Fraternal Organizations: List all Organizations to which the decedent belonged.
Memorial Gift Preference: Flowers or Donations to a Charity or Organization. Include Name and Address where donations can be made.
Education: High School and/or Colleges and Universities attended, list date of graduation and degree received.
Military Record: Dates and Places of enlistment and discharge, promotions, ranks, and commendations received. Outfit name and number.
Cause of Death: Injury or Illness which resulted in the death. Length of illness.

Achievements:

This can be a narrative or an outline and would include:
Any information the family wishes to include concerning the person's achievements in his or her occupation, organization affiliation, charitable work, or with his or her family. The newspapers will usually have an obituary already prepared for individuals who have achieved a degree of fame in the community, nation, or world.

For more information see Chapter 28, "Estate Planning for a Surviving Spouse," Pre-Need Planning.

Use the "Funeral and Related Expense Record" on page R-21.

WHEN A PERSON DIES

Complaints about Funeral Homes or Cemeteries

If a problem has occurred with the services provided by a Funeral Director or Funeral Establishment, discuss your dissatisfaction with them. If this does not result in a satisfactory resolution of the problem, contact:
- The State Board of Funeral Directors and Embalmers or the professional regulation agency (the licensing and regulatory agency for Funeral Directors and Funeral Homes in you state);
- The National Funeral Directors Association provides a third-party dispute resolution program. Write to the Funeral Service Consumer Arbitration Program (FSCAP), at 11121 W. Oaklahoma Avenue, Milwaukee, WI 53227, (414) 541-2500, or call the Funeral Services Consumer Assistance Program's Hotline at (800) 228-6332;
- Cemetery Consumer Service Council provides a dispute resolution program for problems with a cemetery concerning maintenance, gravemarkers, or financial difficulties. It also provides information about Cemetery practices and rules upon request. Write to the Cemetery Consumer Problems Council, P.O. Box 2028, Reston, VA 22090, or call (703) 391-8407;
- The State Funeral Directors Association;
- Local Better Business Bureau;
- The Consumer Protection Office of the county.

Notification of Interested Parties

Go through the decedent's phone book to be sure you notify everyone who may wish to attend or participate in ceremonies. Be prepared to give the times and places of the ceremonies. To save time, you can network your calls. Ask each family member to call specific other family members. Ask one key employee of a current or previous employer to notify fellow employees at the work-place. Ask one member of an organization to notify the other members of the organization. Be sure you note who will be notified by others, so you do not duplicate calls. For other considerations see Chapter 7, "Property Transfer Breakdown," Miscellaneous.

Airline Bereavement Discounts

Many airlines have a discount pricing policy for passengers who are flying to the bedside of a seriously ill relative or to the funeral of a close relative. When an immediate flight must be arranged, contact your travel agent or the airline's reservations office. Explain the situation and ask for the requirements for a bereavement discount. Usually the requirements include showing proof of the reason for your travel. The discount is usually 50 percent off the regular non-discount fare. It is available to immediate family members. The airline will verify the information you provide. See Chapter 7, "Property Transfer Breakdown," Airlines. Immediate relatives of current or retired airline employees, or their spouses, may be able to fly free of charge, except for taxes. Call the involved airline and explain the situation.

Emergency Application for a Passport

In an emergency, your local Passport Office can issue a passport while you wait; but, you must have all the required documents with you. To avoid delay, call the office and ask what documents are required. These will include:

- Proof of U.S. citizenship (either a certified birth certificate or naturalization certificate);
- Two photos taken within the past six months (These must be two inches square, either in color or black and white, with a plain white background. Do not wear head covering unless required by your religion.);
- Proof of identity (This should be a document with your photo and signature.);
- A completed application, Form DSP-11. (These are available at the agency, at designated Post Offices, or in some states, from the clerk of the county courts.);
- Your airline tickets;
- Other:_____

_____;

- Contact the Centers for Disease Control and Prevention's 24-hour hotline (404) 332-4559, for an updated recorded message about requirements and recommendations for international travel immunizations. You must have a touch-tone phone to select from the menu.

When you receive your passport, sign it and make two photocopies; one to carry with you, separate from the original; and the other to leave in a safe place at home. If you lose your passport abroad, immediately notify the local police authorities. Get a copy of the police report and take it to the U.S. Embassy or Consulate. They can help you get a new passport.

Acknowledgements

It is appropriate to send cards acknowledging the expressions of sympathy, between a week and ten days after the services, or the expression of sympathy is received. Use the "Acknowledgement Record" on page R-41. Usually cards are:

- Not necessary for people close enough to be thanked in person.
- Sent to all people who send letters, telegrams, or gifts (flowers, charitable donations, etc.).
- Not necessary to acknowledge sympathy cards, but use your own judgement.

WILLS AND PROBATE

Transferring Property

When a person dies, someone must take responsibility for paying the decedent's debts, transferring his or her remaining property called the **Estate**, to the decedent's survivors, and paying required taxes. If a person left <u>legally</u> <u>valid</u> instructions for how this is to be accomplished and who is to perform the work involved, the person is said to have died **Testate**. The formal legal devices used to leave these instructions are "Wills" and "Trusts." But there are also many other informal but valid property-transfer devices which can be used. If a person dies without leaving instructions (whether formal or informal) for disposition of <u>all</u> his or her property, or, the instruments he or she chose to use are declared <u>invalid</u>, the person is said to have died **Intestate**. In this chapter we will discuss Wills and Probate. Trusts are explained in Chapter 3, "Trusts." A comparison and more information about Wills and Trusts are presented in Chapter 4, "Wills and Trusts Compared." Other informal but valid property-transfer devices are discussed in Chapter 5, "Property Ownership."

Wills

"Will" and "Last Will and Testament" mean the same thing. A **Will** is a plan, usually expressed in a formally prepared document, by which a person can direct that his or her debts be paid, and what is to be done with his or her remaining property, and with his or her remains after death. A Will has no power or effect until a person is deceased or declared legally dead. The person making the Will can be called a **Testator** (male), **Testatrix** (female), **Legator** (male), or **Legatrix** (female). We will use the term "Testator." The Testator **gives**, **legates**, **bequeaths**, or **devises** his or her property through a Will. The property which is given can be called a **gift**, **legacy**, **bequest**, or **devise**. We will use the word "gift" or "property." The person, institution, or organization who is the recipient of the gift, can be called a **Beneficiary**, **Legatee**, **Distributee**, or **Heir**. We will use the term "Beneficiary." The differences in wording are due to the statutory use of words.

A Will usually names a person or organization to receive the balance of the property covered by the Will, called the **Residuary Estate**. The **Residue of the Estate** is what is left after payment of all claims or debts, expenses, taxes, all other specified gifts (including property in a valid formal Trust or other valid informal property-transfer designation) have been made; and property which cannot be given because an identified Beneficiary has predeceased or is barred from inheriting. The residue is given to the **Residuary Legatee** or **Residuary Beneficiary**.

The Will may include directions for appointment of a **Guardian of the Person**, for minor children or other dependents who need this care, and may provide for the establishment of a Trust and appointment of a **Financial Guardian** or **Property Guardian** for the Trust. The Will may name the people or institutions, who will serve in these guardian positions or leave appointment up to the Court. For more information, see Chapter 3, "Trusts."

The Will may also include general, or very precise, information as to what the decedent wishes to be done with his or her body. This may include his or her desire for how a funeral service is to be conducted, the existence of pre-paid or pre-planned programs, whether or not he or she wishes to be cremated, and where the body is to be buried or the ashes placed or spread; or possibly, the desire to donate the body to a medical school. Because this type of instruction may be included in the Will, it is important that a Will be read as soon as possible after the death occurs.

In the Will, the Testator may designate an individual, professional, or an institution, to carry out his or her instructions. Depending upon the state where the Will is executed this person can be called an **Executor** (male), **Executrix** (female) or **Personal Representative** (this term is being adopted in some states). If more than one person or institution (or a combination) is named, they are called **Co-executors/trix** or **Co-Personal Representatives**, in which case, both must usually sign all documents. If the decedent failed to name someone to execute the Will; died without a valid Will; or if the named executor (and named successor executor) failed or refused to qualify, dies, resigns, becomes incapacitated and failed to settle the Estate, the Court appoints an **Administrator** (male), or **Administratrix** (female), to complete settlement of the Estate. In any case, the Judge is the one who ultimately approves who will administer the Estate, although the Court will usually approve the person named in the Will. To avoid confusion, in this book we will refer to anyone who handles the affairs (Estate) of a deceased person as the **Administrator**. Because the administration of an Estate is an ongoing process, Administrators receive a fee for their services. The Administrator is bound by law to act according to ethical and legal standards. Further, the Administrator can be found personally liable for fraud or mismanagement of the Estate. For this reason most states require the Administrator be bonded; however, the Testator may state in the Will that the Administrator need not be bonded. For more information see Chapter 15, "Hiring an Attorney."

All Wills, with rare exceptions, are **Revocable** documents, which means they can be changed by the Testator at any time before his or her death. When the person dies, the Will becomes **Irrevocable** or unchangeable. The exception is when two, or more, people (usually husband and wife) execute a separate written agreement making their Wills irrevocable. In this circumstance neither party can change his or her Will without the written consent of the other. When one party to the agreement has died, he or she, of course, cannot give consent. So the survivor cannot change his or her Will. The survivor's Will is effectively irrevocable. This occurs very rarely and in fact, may not always be upheld as valid.

Valid Will

In order for a Will to be valid, and therefore, binding, the form it takes must conform strictly to the formal requirements set forth by the laws of the individual's state of residence. The form most likely to be deemed valid is a Will drawn up by an attorney (licensed in the state where the decedent resided), and signed in the presence of witnesses. However, under certain circumstances, other forms of Wills may be considered valid depending upon their acceptability in each state. These include a **Holographic** (handwritten) Will, or a **Nuncupative** (oral) Will, which are sometimes accepted if made during the last illness or under battlefield conditions, and made in the presence of witnesses; a Pre-printed, Fill-in-the-blanks, Check-the-boxes Will form, if authorized by state law; or Video Taped or Filmed Will, which usually must be backed up by a formally executed Will. Wills executed by an illiterate or blind individual should have been read to the Testator at the time of signing by a Notary Public or other disinterested person. Further, a Will may be declared invalid, if something in the Will has been erased, crossed out, or in any way corrected. Therefore, laws in all states require that any changes to a Will be made either through executing a new Will, or adding a Codicil to the existing Will. A **Codicil** is a supplement or addition to a Will, which adds to, modifies, changes, or takes something from the original Will. In many instances if the Will is invalid, so is the Codicil. If a Will is voided, the property passes under the **Laws of Intestate Succession** of the state where the property is located, and a judge will decide who administers the Estate, and who becomes the guardian of minor children or other individuals requiring care. Similarly, if all the Beneficiaries of the Will are deceased when the Testator dies, the Testator is considered to have died intestate.

The Laws of Intestate Succession may conform to the **Uniform or Simple Probate Code**, a Federal guideline, which provides a model for states, in drafting their own probate laws. It reflects divorces, second marriages, and multiple sets of children. Intestate Succession Laws are also used when a person who, under law, is entitled to a portion of the Estate, and has been found to be **Pretermitted** (not mentioned or otherwise provided for in the Will). Without a Will, the laws of the state in which a person resided, on the date of death, will determine who receives his or her property. See Chapter 5 "Property Ownership." Lovers, friends, and companions have no intestacy rights. Although these laws may vary, the following is a sample of the way distribution may be made.

If a person dies intestate, and is unmarried, and with no surviving lineal descendants (legitimate children or grandchildren), the surviving parents will receive the decedent's real and personal property. If neither parent survives, then the brothers and sisters will receive the property in equal shares, one share for each brother or sister. If no parents, brothers, sisters, or descendants of them, survive the decedent, the Estate will be divided equally, one-half to the decedent's maternal relatives, one-half to paternal relatives, in the following order of priority as to each side of the family: to the surviving grandparents; if neither grandparent survives, in equal shares to uncles and aunts, one share for each aunt or uncle; and, if no maternal relative or no paternal relative survives, the entire Estate will go to surviving relatives on the other side of the family in the order stated. If no surviving relatives can be found, the Estate will go to the state, called **Escheat,** in which the decedent resided. This is the general rule of succession. Your state may differ.

Probate

The word **Probate** means to prove. During Probate, someone, usually the Administrator, proves that the Will was validly drawn-up, signed, and witnessed. When the decedent leaves property through a Will, or dies Intestate, the Estate must be **Probated**. Probate is a formal process governed by state law and supervised by Judges in the Probate Division of the Court System. The primary Probate proceedings take place in the county and state where the decedent resided. However, if the decedent owned real property (see Chapter 5, "Property Ownership") in another state or country, another Probate proceeding must take place there. This is called an **Ancillary Probate or Proceeding**. Usually, an **Ancillary Administrator** is appointed to administer that Probate. In most cases, the primary Administrator named in the Will also obtains Ancillary Letters to administer the out-of-state property. However, if the Administrator named in the Will is unwilling or there is no Will, the Court will appoint an Ancillary Administrator. Probate is the process by which the Court oversees the administration of the Estate, and assures the property in the Estate is properly delivered to the Beneficiaries, either according to the wishes of the decedent, as set forth in the Will, or according to the Intestacy Laws of the State. The Probate process includes court costs and document filing fees, in addition to the fees for the Administrator and attorney.

Probate begins when the Will or Intestate Estate is presented to the Court. In most cases, filing with the **Clerk of the Court** which handles Probate starts the process. This is usually within the County Circuit Court System and may be called the **Surrogate**, **Orphan's**, **Chancery**, or **Probate Court**. The phone number of the Probate Court can be found in the Blue or White Pages under the name of the county. If you cannot find a listing, call the county's information number, or the phone company's information line (usually 411). Probate is a lengthy process because of all the paperwork involved and the need to wait for Court approval of each step. However, the Court in return extends its protection to those involved in settling the decedent's affairs and distributing the property. During the Probate process:
- The authenticity and validity of the decedent's Will (if any) is established;
- An Administrator is approved (if a Will), or appointed (if no Will), and **"Letters of Administration"** or, in some states, **"Letters Testamentary"** (the legal document that empowers the Administrator to act on behalf of the Estate) are issued;

■ Prenuptial or postnuptial agreements are reviewed to ascertain if they are a valid waiver, which were entered into freely and with full disclosure of the facts. If they do not conform to validity requirements of the state, they may be set aside;

■ The Administrator is supervised and assisted, if necessary, to identify or locate, take possession of, and protect or maintain the Estate's assets or property. If someone is holding Estate property and refuses to surrender it, the Judge should be notified. The Court can order the sheriff to accompany the Administrator when recovering the property;

■ Supervises the Administrator's inventory and valuing of all property in the Estate by requiring periodic accountings. The first accounting of the Estate is required at a specified time after appointment, typically 8 or 9 months, and every 6 months thereafter. Depending upon the law, circumstances, and the complexity of the Estate, the first accounting can be the only and final accounting;

■ Property is sold as necessary to get cash for distribution to Beneficiaries or for payments to creditors;

■ The debts of the Estate are identified and paid. Anyone not making a claim within a prescribed time is barred from making a claim later. Ideally, any disputed claims can be resolved by the Administrator. However, if an equitable decision cannot be made, Probate provides a ready-made Court procedure for resolving creditors' claims faster than by normal lawsuit. Creditors who are notified (usually through publication of an ad in a prescribed publication) about the Probate must file their claims promptly with the Probate Court, often within four or six months of the filing of the Petition for Probate. If creditors do not make their claims within the allotted time, they are cut off, and need not be paid. If no Probate occurs to cut off creditors' claims, all the deceased person's property remains liable for the decedent's debts and any death taxes. Probate allows the Beneficiaries to take their property free of anxiety about future creditors' claims, by assuring a clear title to real estate and other assets;

■ Debts owed to the Estate are collected;

■ Income due the Estate, such as rents, dividends, and interest is received;

■ Tax forms are completed and taxes paid;

■ All Beneficiaries are identified and located, and designation is made concerning who inherits what property. If a Beneficiary has changed his or her name since the document was written, he or she must supply proof of marriage, divorce, or court ordered name change;

■ Disputes among the Beneficiaries about the disposition of property are settled. When Beneficiaries agree on how to divide the Estate, and the deceased person has left valid documents, the Administrator's job can go smoothly. However, problems can arise when the Beneficiaries are fighting over particular pieces of personal property. It is up to the Administrator to evaluate the situation and make reasonable decisions to handle the disputes in the most efficient manner possible. See the "Introduction" for more information. If the Beneficiaries cannot be brought to agreement, then the Administrator asks the Judge to decide;

■ Trusts are set up as required by the Will or state law;

■ The Court may authorize limited amounts of cash to be given to the surviving spouse and children for necessary family expenses. However, the Court may require a bond to protect the Estate;

■ The Court approves the amount of funds to be left on deposit in the Estate account for the purpose of paying any remaining debts or taxes due from the Estate;

■ Finally, after approval is granted by the Court, the property is distributed according to the Will (if any), or the Laws of Intestacy, to the Beneficiaries.

Simplified Probate Proceedings

Most states provide a simplified process, through the Probate Court, to settle the Estate of a person who dies leaving very little property. To find out whether or not the Estate qualifies, contact the Clerk of the Probate Court by phone or in person. Be prepared to give the Clerk an estimate of the total value of the Estate, what types of property were owned (bank accounts, real estate, car, etc.), and how each is titled (see Chapter 5, "Property Ownership"), the family situation of the decedent (This includes a list of immediate relatives, and a good idea as to whether they are in agreement about the division of the property. You may wish to use the "Family Tree Record" on page R-33.), and, if there is a Will, be prepared to give the Clerk the original. If the Estate qualifies, the Court will appoint someone to administer the Estate by awarding "Letters of Administration" or "Letters Testamentary."

States vary in what they consider a small Estate, from a limit as low as $5,000 up to about $60,000. If the Estate qualifies, the Clerk will require the person requesting appointment as the Administrator (whether through choice or as named in the Will) to file certain documents. Depending upon the circumstances, these may include an application or petition to act as the Administrator, a certified copy of the Death Certificate, the original Will (if any), a Small Estate Affidavit, and/or a Petition for Family or Summary Administration. If the forms are not available through the Clerk's office, they can usually be found at a legal stationery store. Be sure to ask the Clerk exactly which documents you need. Also, be sure you understand who must sign each paper and whether or not the signatures must be **Notarized.** (Signed before a Notary Public. It is not the concern of the Notary to know the contents of the documents being witnessed.) In some cases, approval documents may have to be signed by all named Beneficiaries and every person who may have a claim on the Estate under the Laws of Intestacy (called Heirs at Law). The Clerk should be able to advise you about how these laws apply in your particular situation. If there is a Will, it must be admitted to Probate to determine its validity. After all the required paperwork is properly completed and submitted, and a hearing attended (if required), the Court will issue the Letters of Administration, or similar document, allowing the Administrator to transfer the decedent's property, and giving authority to divide the Estate among the Beneficiaries entitled to it. The Administrator may be required to submit to the Court a complete record of how the property was distributed, after which the Judge will enter an order discharging the Administrator. Under a Simplified Administration, the deceased person's Estate and the people receiving Estate Property may remain liable for claims by the decedent's creditors for a period of time after the date of the decedent's death. Proceedings by the creditor must be filed within that period of time, which may be as much as three years. Publication of an appropriate notice in a local newspaper may reduce the period in which creditors can file claims but is not guaranteed. Be aware that some states do not permit Administrators to act without an attorney, but, contact the Court before contacting an attorney to find out.

Among the alternatives to Probate available in some states, is an **Affidavit Procedure**. Where permitted, all Beneficiaries must agree and there must be no State Inheritance or Federal Estate Tax due. Another possible alternative is the **Community Property Petition** which is a simple form that can be prepared by a surviving spouse, who is entitled to the property of a deceased spouse, either under a Will or by Laws of Intestate Succession (if there is no Will). The petition is filed with the local Probate Court which sets a hearing date. Notice of the hearing must be given to certain people, including all Beneficiaries named in the Will. The hearing is held and the property is ordered transferred to the surviving spouse, unless someone contests the Petition, which is very rare. Most surviving spouses can handle the process without an attorney.

Division of Labor in a Formal Probate Proceeding

Probate includes a lot of interaction with the Probate Court, most often through completion and submission of state prescribed documents and, in some cases, actual Court appearances. This is usually the domain of the attorney hired to handle the Probate. See Chapter 15, "Hiring An Attorney." It is normally the domain of the Administrator to provide information, sign documents, and deal with the property aspects of the Estate. Each state and, in some cases, the individual court district, has regulations regarding whether and when an attorney is required to represent the Estate. Some states allow the Administrator to handle all transactions, and the Court Clerk will be very cooperative and helpful. However, many states require an attorney for all but the simplest, or limited value, Estates. If full or formal Probate is necessary and the Court allows the Administrator to represent the Estate, there are many books in libraries and bookstores to guide the layman through the complex Probate procedure. Keep in mind that the Administrator is responsible for acting in the best interest of the Estate, and can be held personally responsible for losses that result from his or her actions or inactions and can be removed from the position by the Court.

The purpose of this book is not to advise you about how to bring the Estate through the Probate process. Its only purpose is to disclose the duties of the Administrator in dealing with the property of the decedent. Whatever you decide, time is of the essence because most states require the Will be entered into Probate within a short period of time after the death, often as little as ten days. Therefore, if you have determined the need to hire an attorney for the Estate, you should retain counsel's services as soon as possible after the death. If asked, the attorney, or someone counsel hires, can handle all aspects of the Estate. However, the attorney will charge more and probably ask that the Administrator, who does nothing but sign papers as they are presented, receive a lower fee. An alternative for an Administrator who is too busy to handle matters personally, is to hire professionals to do all the work of the Administrator, while remaining involved in decisions about disposition of the Estate. For example: the financial and legal matters may be handled by a bank trust department or private trust company. Remember that these services may be quite costly.

The first action the person who is named as the Administrator in a Will or, if there is no Will, either the person who is willing to accept responsibilities of the Administrator or the surviving spouse, should do, is call or visit the Clerk of the Probate Court of the county where the decedent resided. The Clerk can usually determine if formal Probate proceedings are necessary or if the Estate is eligible for an abbreviated Probate procedure and, if you need an attorney to handle the Estate. Advise the Court Clerk of the basic circumstances of the Estate, including:

- An estimate of the total value of the Estate;
- Whether or not the deceased person left a Will;
- The value of the property included under the Will, and the value of property subject to other property transferring devices;
- The relationship of the Beneficiaries to the decedent; and
- If the property includes real estate.

If all property is jointly held, with right of survivorship, or names an individual (not the Estate) as a Beneficiary, and no documents are required from the Court to transfer ownership of the property . . . it is not necessary to enter the Will into Probate. However, if the Will was registered with the county when it was drawn up, that agency should be notified of the death. For transfer document requirements, see Chapter 5, "Property Ownership," and Chapter 7, "Property Transfer Breakdown."

Visiting the Attorney - Getting Started

On the first visit to the attorney you have chosen to hire, you should bring the following documents and information. However, do not delay your visit because you do not have all of these items; they can be supplied later.

- The original of the Will, if there is one;
- An estimate of the total value of the Estate;
- All papers relating to any real estate owned by the decedent and, if possible, a decision as to whether this property will be transferred to a Beneficiary, or sold;
- Two or more certified copies of the Death Certificate (if you have received them);
- A copy of the obituary notice, if one was published;
- The names and addresses of all Beneficiaries named in the Will. (If there is no Will, a list of the names and addresses of all potential Beneficiaries and a family tree to show how they are related. You may want to use the "Family Tree Record," on page R-33, for this purpose.);
- The names and addresses of the witnesses to the Will, if you have them. (Often the witnesses were employees at the law office where the Will was executed.); and
- All title documents to personal property, if you want the attorney to handle everything.

After reviewing the Estate, the attorney should draw up a contract for services. The contract should specify the services the attorney will provide and the cost of the services, as well as a list of the costs of filing documents and court fees. Sign it only if you are satisfied with the terms of the contract and are sure you want to hire that particular attorney. See Chapter 15, "Hiring an Attorney" for more information. In all cases there should be a clear understanding as to the exact division of the duties the attorney will be expected to perform and the tasks the Administrator will handle.

Two weeks to a month after this initial meeting, the attorney will probably call you to come in and sign some documents. If you do not hear from the attorney, call and ask for a progress report. During this time, the attorney should have prepared the documents necessary to initiate the Probate and appoint an Administrator. During this time, the Administrator should be taking a complete inventory of all the property in the Estate and the debts owed by the Estate, unless there is a possibility that someone will object to the appointment.

Among the documents the attorney may request the prospective Administrator to sign on the second visit are: the **Petition for Administration** or **Petition for Letters Testamentary** (as appropriate to the state), **Formal Notice of Petition for Administration**, if required, waiver of bond or application for bond, and any other waivers or consents appropriate to the situation. At this time, the Attorney will need to know how many certified copies you will need of the **Letters of Administration** or **Letters Testamentary** (which will give the Administrator the legal right to act for the Estate). This can be determined by the number of institutions you will have to deal with to transfer the property of the decedent. The attorney can help you estimate the number. (For the average Estate, twelve should be enough.) Reviewing Chapter 7, "Property Transfer Breakdown" should help you make this determination.

If the Will is not **self proving** (an affidavit signed by the testator and witnesses and signed and notarized by a notary public is attached to the Will), an **Oath of Witnesses** to the Will must be obtained. The attorney will contact the witnesses to the Will, to testify to the signing of the Will and/or Codicil, or the attorney may ask the Administrator to contact them. If the witness(es) has predeceased, an appropriate relative or business associate must be found to testify to the authenticity of the deceased witness's signature. If the witness lives out of town, and the Court requires a personal appearance, the Estate must pay to have the witness present.

When all the appropriate documents are complete, the attorney will submit them to the Court along with the original of the Will, (if there is a Will). The Judge will sign an **Order Admitting Will** (if there is a Will) and the Letters of Administration or Letters Testamentary, if the Court approves of the Administrator. The Attorney will mail the certified copies of the Letters of Administration or Letters Testamentary to the Administrator. These empower the Administrator to begin administering the Estate.

After the Probate is approved, the attorney will send a **Notice of Administration** to all Beneficiaries named in the Will (if there is one) and all possible Heirs (if there is no Will) of the possibility of inheritance and who has been appointed to Administer the Estate. This notice affords the Beneficiary or Heir the opportunity to approve or object to the Will, Administration, or Administrator. The Notice of Administration may also be mailed to creditors and other interested parties, so they can submit claims against the Estate. The attorney will also publish a Notice of Administration in appropriate newspapers.

After this, the attorney completes, and presents to the Court, the mountains of paperwork that must be completed in order to comply with state laws, all with multiple deadlines and requirements. These may include one or more inventories of the Estate and documentation of the actions the Administrator has taken to settle the affairs of the decedent. You can use the "Estate Summary" on page R-29. The attorney will occasionally meet with the Administrator to get a financial update of the Estate and to have him or her sign documents. The attorney will also review contracts, claims against the Estate, transfer property titles if necessary, and provide expert assistance in the actual management of the Estate. When all the debts of the decedent have been paid and the Court is satisfied that everything is in order, the Judge will authorize distribution of the property in the Estate to the Beneficiaries and dismiss the Administrator. See Chapter 7, "Property Transfer Breakdown" for help with transfers and you can use the "Estate Distribution Record" on page R-30.

Summary of the Duties of the Administrator

- Locate and read the Will. If it is not with the decedent's legal papers in the home, check with the decedent's attorney, trust company, or bank (some banks store patrons' Wills in its vault), or look in the decedent's safe deposit box. If it is in a sealed safe deposit box, see Chapter 7, "Property Transfer Breakdown," Opening the Safe Deposit Box. Ask the spouse, a relative, trustee, or a friend where the Will can be found. Remember, it is the last Will that counts, an older, revoked Will is not valid.
- Retain an attorney, as appropriate. Although some states do not require an attorney to Probate a Will, having one is recommended for all but the simplest Estates. Good legal advice is one of the greatest preventive measures an attorney can provide. Services may be costly but can save lots of time and headaches.
- Present the original Will, a certified copy of the Death Certificate, and copy of the obituary notice (or a sworn copy, depending on the individual requirements of the particular state) to the Probate Court either in person, or through an attorney. If applicable, choose between a Formal or Simplified Administration.
- List the names and addresses of all persons who are entitled to share in the Estate. And, if the decedent died Intestate, all persons who may be eligible to inherit.
- Execute the appropriate documents required by the Court to admit the Estate into Probate and issue the certified copies of the Letters of Administration or Letters Testamentary. These "Letters" empower the Administrator to begin administering the Estate. With them the Administrator can draw out deposits, have stock transferred, and carry out any action in connection with the Estate.
- Post Bond to act as the Administrator, unless stipulated in the Will that Bond is not required. Even if the Administrator is not required to be **Bonded**, you may choose to purchase one, if you in any way fear the Heirs will cause trouble somewhere along the way. Trouble can come from any interested party who questions the Administrator's judgment, and can include such accusations as overpaying professionals, selling property for less than it is worth, or not insuring a home which is destroyed by whatever means during Probate. For other possible problems see Chapter 4, "Wills and Trusts Compared." A **Bond** is an insurance policy, purchased from an insurance company, guaranteeing that a person will honestly carry out his or her duties and that a certain amount of money will be paid to those injured if

the insured does not. The premium for a Bond is usually ten percent of the face amount of the Bond.

- Ascertain the assets and liabilities of the Estate.
- Send a **Notice of Administration** to all Heirs and Beneficiaries by Certified Mail. You can save mailing time by finding and reading the Will as soon as possible after the death and getting necessary probate forms signed while the Beneficiaries are in town for services. This is especially important because families are so scattered. While the Beneficiaries are together is also a good time to discuss any problems they have with the Will, and take home items they have been either named to have, or Heirs have agreed in writing to give (saves shipping). The discussion may also include making decisions about selling the decedent's home and whether or not a business should be continued
- Take action to notify all interested parties of the death, and make appropriate arrangements with them to carry out the duties of Administering the Estate. For more information see Chapter 7, "Property Transfer Breakdown." As you contact each agency, make a list of when each legal or tax form is due, so you don't miss a deadline. You may want to use our "Quick Reference Calendar" on page R-31, for this purpose.
- The Court requires complete and accurate accounting of all assets, liabilities, and distributions to Beneficiaries of the Estate. Be sure to keep records as you go along.
- All of the Estate's assets are appraised for a **"DATE OF DEATH"** value. Refer to Chapter 9, "Valuing Property" for more information. Hire a professional appraiser if required by the Court.
- Identify all property as "Probate" (all property transferred under the Will or Laws of Intestacy), or, "Non-Probate" (trusts, jointly-owned property, insurance proceeds left to a specific Beneficiary, pensions with a specific Beneficiary, bank and other accounts with a specific Beneficiary, etc.). See Chapter 3, "Trusts" and Chapter 5, "Property Ownership."
- Keep a record of all property, including non-probate property, to examine the tax consequences to the Estate. We, of course, recommend using our record sheets for this purpose.
- Do not transfer Trust property to the Estate. Instead deliver it directly to the named Trustee. The Power of Appointment as Trustee, in a Trust, gives the legal authority to decide who shall receive the property and transfer it to them.
- Carefully examine all claims and bills against the Estate as to their validity, amount, and correctness. If valid, pay the claim. If you cannot determine validity or correctness present it to the Court for decision. Obtain vouchers for every bill and claim paid.

Determining Domicile

Domicile is the term used for an individual's **Legal Residence**. A person's domicile is largely a matter of intent. It is the place where a person has his or her true, fixed, and permanent home, to which, whenever he or she is absent, he or she has the intention of returning. In most cases, domicile is not an issue; the majority of people have only one residence. However, when a person owns more than one residence, or has recently moved from one state to another, one state must be determined as the domicile. It is necessary to determine domicile because Estates are distributed and taxed according to the laws of the state where a person has his or her domicile at the time of death, not where he or she happens to be residing when he or she died. Because state laws vary, "Legal Residence" can affect the surviving spouse's marital ownership rights, his or her legal claim to a share of the Estate and homestead rights. It can also affect intestate succession, who may act as the Administrator, and the amount and type of taxes due to each state.

In most cases, the state or country of domicile is where the decedent lived most of the time, worked, or where he or she considered his or her permanent residence to be. This may be indicated by where the person's vehicles are registered, and the state to which the person pays taxes, as well as where the person is registered to vote, was licensed to drive, and the address on important documents. Some states specify a length of time of physical presence or residence in the state to qualify for domicile. Occasionally, a person will file a **"Declaration of Domicile"** with the local Circuit Court of the state he or she is leaving to renounce residence and another "Declaration of Domicile" in the new state to establish residence there. If it is not clear which state was the legal residence of the deceased person, consult an estate attorney or contact the Secretary of State, located in the state's capital, for each involved state. The Secretary of State can advise the Administrator of the legal residency requirements for the state. If domicile is not clearly established and there is a choice: check the income and estate or inheritance tax laws in the involved states and pick the one with the most advantageous tax requirements.

TRUSTS

A formal **Trust** is a distinct legal entity. It is created when a Trust Agreement is executed. The person(s) establishing the Trust can be known by various names, including **Settlor**, **Grantor**, **Creator**, or **Trustor**. We have chosen to use the term "Grantor" in this book. The Trust Agreement names a **Trustee** or **Co-Trustees**, and usually a **Successor Trustee** (to take over in the event of the incapacity, failure, or death of the Trustee). The job of the Trustee is to hold, invest, and administer the property placed in the Trust. The Trust becomes effective when property is formally (legally) transferred to the Trustee or Trust. The property is then known as the **Trust Corpus**. The Trust document includes instructions as to how the property is to be managed and outlines when and how the income or property will be distributed. Generally the Trustee's powers are limited to those set forth in the Trust Agreement. These may be either broad and discretionary, narrow and limited, or somewhere in between. Actually most Trusts have a clause that any powers allowed by law, but not specifically stated, are included. A Trust also names Beneficiaries to benefit from and/or receive the Trust property. Naming Beneficiaries makes a Trust a **Probate Avoidance Device**, which means that the property in the Trust cannot be left to another in a Will and is transferred to the Beneficiaries outside of Probate.

Types of Trusts

General Information

Formal Trusts can be designed to fit almost any need. Trusts afford many options and can serve a variety of purposes. In addition to avoiding Probate, they can also be used to protect property for particular Beneficiaries, or to pay, save on, or avoid estate taxes.

With the incidence of divorce and establishment of step-families rising, Trusts are becoming more common as a way for the grantor to ensure that his or her property eventually goes to his or her children and not to the grantor's step-children. Trusts can be used to protect property and provide income for a Beneficiary, who under the state's laws, or in the opinion of the grantor, is unable for any reason to handle his or her own financial affairs. These Trusts can last for a few years or for generations. They are considered **Managerial Trusts** because they can continue for an extended period of time and require ongoing management. The Trustee (if not the grantor) of an ongoing Trust usually receives a fee for his or her services. This fee is considered "reasonable compensation" and is fixed by the laws of each of the fifty states. The aspect of ongoing management distinguishes these Trusts from a **Pass-thru Trust** whose only purpose is transferring property to Beneficiaries outside of Probate. The Trustee of a Pass-thru Trust usually does not receive a fee. However, if the trustee is a bank or trust company, it will always receive a fee.

Probate avoidance should not be confused with tax avoidance. Even though trust property is not included in the "Probate Estate," it may be included in the "Taxable Estate," unless the Trust was specifically set up to avoid estate taxes. It is wise to have the Trust reviewed by a tax expert to determine whether or not the property must be included in the taxable estate. Remember, state and federal tax laws are very complicated and are always subject to change.

We can only give you basic information because of all the varieties that can be obtained by Trusts. The only way to be sure of the terms of each Trust is to read the document carefully. If you are not sure of any aspect in the Trust, or how to handle it, you should have the document reviewed and explained by the attorney who drew up the Trust or another attorney who is familiar with Trusts. Having the document reviewed by a professional will also assure you that it conforms to the laws of the state as a qualified probate avoidance device. The attorney will also assess the possibility, though rare, of it being subject to contest. This may be especially necessary if the Trust document is a standardized form from a stationery store or if a lot of changes were made in the document. Although there are unlimited variations of the terms of a Trust, there are only two categories of Formal Trusts, namely "Irrevocable" and "Revocable."

Irrevocable Trusts

A Trust is **Irrevocable** if the grantor gives up all rights to ownership and control of the property placed in the Trust and appoints someone else to be the Trustee. This means that the grantor cannot terminate, revoke, or change in any way (except in very extreme, narrowly defined circumstances) the terms of the Trust. Irrevocable Trusts are inflexible. Property cannot be removed from the Trust and Beneficiaries cannot be changed by the grantor (even if there is a change in relationship, such as a divorce). If properly executed according to IRS requirements, an Irrevocable Trust is considered to be a completed gift. As such, it may be subject to federal and, in some states, gift and/or income taxes. However, the Trust property is then considered removed from the Estate, usually avoids death and estate taxes, and enjoys immunity from the grantor's creditors because it is not part of the grantor's property.

Revocable Trusts

On the other hand, a Trust is **Revocable** when the grantor keeps some or all of the control over the property placed in the Trust. With a Revocable Trust the grantor can change the terms of the Trust anytime while he or she is alive. The grantor can add or remove property, maintain total control over the property, change the Beneficiaries, be the Trustee, or change the Trustee. A Revocable Trust has the advantage of providing for the grantor's needs in the event of incapacity. (A Trust can be used the same as a Durable Power of Attorney. See Chapter 28, "Estate Planning For A Surviving Spouse.") A Revocable Trust becomes Irrevocable upon the death of the grantor, or the death of the last of the grantors, if the trust is not terminated prior to the death of the initial grantor, or grantors, if there are more than one. Since this type of Trust is revocable, it is not a true gift. Therefore, it is not subject to gift taxes, but is included in the taxable estate, so it does not avoid death or estate taxes. A Revocable Trust is not immune from the grantor's creditors, so sufficient funds should be held in the Trust until all just debts and taxes are paid. After the grantor dies, his or her creditors usually must file a claim or be barred.

Sub-Trusts

Both Revocable and Irrevocable Trusts can contain **Sub-Trusts**. A Sub-Trust is a separate Trust within the original Trust, to provide for management of the property, assigned to the sub-trust, for the Beneficiaries. Upon the death of the grantor or the last of the grantors, Sub-Trusts become Irrevocable. A Sub-Trust is usually established for a minor child or other Beneficiary, who, either under law or by the grantor, is determined to need the financial protection provided by a Trust.

Generational Trusts

A Trust can be set up for any length of time the grantor desires. Some Trusts can last for generations before the Trust is ended and the property is distributed. This type of Trust usually provides for what is called a **Life Interest**, or **Life Estate**, or **Life Beneficiary**. Life Interest means a survivor is left the use of the property during his or her lifetime, as well as receiving the income from the property in the Trust, but never becomes the legal owner of the property and therefore cannot sell it. When the survivor, who benefited from the life interest dies, the property passes to whomever the grantor specified. Both Revocable and Irrevocable Trusts can provide for the surviving member of a couple to receive a life interest. These Trusts can be known by various names. For example a **Marital Life Estate Trust**, can also be known as an **A/B Trust**, **Spouse Bypass Trust**, **Exemption Trust**, **Spousal Life Estate**, or similar designation. These Trusts can be used by any couple, married or not. The property in the deceased member's Trust is a legally separate entity from property of the surviving member. This makes two sets of books or records a requisite. This type of Trust is designed to save on or reduce estate taxes by preventing the survivor from owning all the property belonging to both members of the couple. In addi-

tion, if a couple is married, and the Trust meets with IRS requirements, it is called a **"Q-tip"**
Trust ("Qualified Terminal Interest Property Trust"), and may avoid estate taxes.

A good example of the use of life interest is a **Generation-skipping Trust** which leaves
the bulk of the Trust property to the grandchildren of the grantor. The spouse of the grantor receives a life interest in the property, for as long as he or she lives, as the **Life Beneficiary**. After
that spouse's death, their child would receive a life interest and be called the **Second Life Bene-**
ficiary. The grandchildren are specified in the Trust to receive the distribution of the property
upon the death of the Second Life Beneficiary and are called the **Remaindermen**. This Trust can
reduce but not entirely avoid taxes depending upon the value of the Trust.

Revocable Living Trusts

A popular Probate Avoiding Trust and, therefore, the one you are most likely to encoun-
ter is called a **Revocable Living Trust**. As described above, this Trust is established when a
Trust document, or contract, is signed by the grantor(s) and becomes effective when the grant-
or(s) transfers property to the Trust and appoints a Trustee to manage the property. The grantor
transfers property to the Trust by changing the titles of property such as real estate, stocks, bank
accounts, etc., to the Trustee or the Trust. Property which does not have a title document, such as
jewelry, household furnishings, etc., are listed in the Trust to include them as Trust property or
transferred by other written document to the Trustee. Commonly, the grantor of a Living Trust
maintains control of the Trust property by naming him- or herself as the Trustee, and his or her
spouse as Co-Trustee. In this case a **Successor Trustee** is named to take over Trust management, and to distribute the property to the named Beneficiaries upon the grantor(s) death(s) in
the same way a Will names an Administrator. Unlike a Will, a Living Trust is settled without a
court proceeding; it is private and the assets are not frozen. Usually the Successor Trustee also
has the power to take over Trust management in the event the Trustee or Co-Trustees become
incapacitated. Because of this feature, the Trust takes the place of having a Durable Power of Attorney and is effective, since a Living Trust usually has all or most of the grantor's property in it.
Be aware that a Durable Power of Attorney does not control Living Trust property. The grantor
can change the Trustee at any time, as well as changing the Beneficiaries. The Trust can be revoked at any time, and the property taken back by the grantor. If the Trust still exists when the
grantor dies, it becomes "Irrevocable" and no changes can be made. The Trust property is then
distributed, outside of Probate, to the Beneficiaries, according to the terms of the Trust Agreement. The Successor Trustee usually does not receive a fee simply for distributing the Trust
property; however, if management of the Trust is ongoing, the Trustee is compensated.

Additional Aspects of Trusts

Trusts can also be funded in different ways, depending on the financial and family circumstances of the grantor. Another way to provide for children from a previous marriage is to

set up an Irrevocable **Life Insurance Trust**, and transfer ownership of a life insurance policy into it. An Irrevocable Life Insurance Trust may also be established by owners of large Estates to provide funds to pay estate and death taxes. The reason for putting the insurance policy into an irrevocable Trust, is that currently death benefits aren't usually subject to income taxes, but if the decedent owns the policy, the IRS considers it part of the Taxable Estate.

Other forms of Trusts that use a life interest are the **Spendthrift Trust**, which is set up by the grantor to protect Beneficiaries from squandering their inheritances. And a **Charitable Trust,** which is established when the grantor sends money to a charity on the condition that the property is to be held in a Trust with a guaranteed life interest for the grantor. The charity is the Beneficiary. Upon the death of the grantor, the Trust becomes irrevocable and the charity receives the property in the Trust.

Back-Up Wills

In addition to executing formal or informal Trusts, a wise person also executes a back-up Will to provide a means of transferring property not included in the Trust to Beneficiaries. The Will covers property which the grantor forgot to include in a Trust; small bank accounts or other property thought too insignificant to include in the Trust; and property received shortly before death, such as an inheritance, a settlement from a law-suit, or winnings from last week's lottery.

Testamentary Trusts

The Trusts we have discussed so far are called **Inter Vivos Trusts**, which simply means the Trust was created while the person was alive. However, this is not the only method used to establish a Trust for the management of property left to a child or other Beneficiary who is unable to handle his or her own finances. Instead of an Inter Vivos Trust, the decedent may choose to leave instructions in his or her Will for a Trust to be established for the sake of a Beneficiary. A Trust established under the terms of a Will is called a **Testamentary Trust**. The testator's Will instructs the Administrator, instead of transferring property directly to the Beneficiary, to transfer certain property indirectly to a Beneficiary, by placing it in a Trust. This Trust can include any of the provisions for Beneficiaries available if the Trust was created inter vivos. Whether the Trust is created inter vivos or testamentary, the property manager is called a **Trustee** or **Successor Trustee;** unless the terms of the Trust conform to the "Uniform Transfers (or Gifts) to Minors Act" (if adopted in your particular state), in which case the property manager is called the **Custodian**.

Note: Although property which passes to a Beneficiary in a Trust is non-probate property; property put in a Trust established through a Will is included in the Probate Estate.

29

Guardianships

The State's Uniform Gifts (or Transfers) to Minors Act requires an adult to act as manager of a child's property. The Custodian distributes income for the support and maintenance of the child, but retains title until the child reaches the age (ranging from 18 to 25) specified by the particular state's law, at which time the child receives the remaining property free and clear. The decedent may also have chosen, instead of establishing a Trust, to simply name a **Property Guardian** and **Alternate Property Guardian** in the Will to supervise a minor child's property until he or she turns 18. Even if the decedent established a Trust, a property guardian may be designated as a back-up for property not left in the Trust.

In the event that no provisions were made by the decedent to provide for management of the property of a Beneficiary, who under the laws of the state requires a **Financial Guardian** or **Property Manager**, the Court will order a Trust to be set up, appoint a guardian, and require Court supervision of the Trust. Beneficiaries requiring a property manager include: minor children, individuals who have been declared legally incompetent; disabled or impaired individuals (of any age) who will need care all their lives; and any individuals, who for any other reason, are impaired and cannot inherit outright. While Trustees named in a Trust Agreement or Will enjoy the discretionary powers granted to them in the Trust and relative freedom from Court control, property guardians named in a Will, or appointed by the Court, have very limited discretionary power and are required to submit frequent and burdensome reports to the Court. The records in this book would be of significant help in filing these reports. It is the job of the Administrator to set up Testamentary or Court ordered Trusts, and arrange for guardianship of finances, with the approval of the Court.

In addition to having a financial guardian, a minor child, left with no legal parent (biological or adoptive), must also have a **Guardian of the Person** appointed to take charge of the orphaned child and provide personal care for him or her. The minor is called a **Ward**. The guardian of the person can be named in a Will or other legal document. In the absence of a directive left by the deceased person, or if the original named guardian has died, becomes ill or unsuitable, a guardian will be appointed by the Court. In any event, a personal guardian doesn't actually become the legal guardian until approved by a Court. The Judge has the authority to name someone other than the parents' choice, if the Judge believes it is in the "best interest of the child." The Court will also hear objections, presented by family and friends, to the person chosen by the parents, or suggestions, if no one was named by the decedent. If this situation presents itself, it is usually best to give custody to one person, instead of a couple. So, if the couple breaks up, there is no need for another guardianship hearing. If there is more than one child, a single guardian may be appointed for all the children, although each child may have a separate guardian. Since the child usually lives with this guardian, appointing separate guardians for each child results in siblings being separated. This, in turn, can cause further problems for children who are already in emotional turmoil because of the loss of the parent(s). Once a guardian is confirmed by the Court, it is the job of the Administrator to arrange for the guardian to take charge of the child(ren). The Administrator should make it clear to the child and the person who cares for the child immediately following the death, that nothing is permanent until the Court says it is. For more information see Chapter 23, "When a Child is Orphaned."

To avoid confusion, in this book we will refer to anyone who manages the property of someone else as the "Trustee." The Trustee is usually named in the Trust or Will. However, if no Trustee was named, or the Trustee refuses to accept the Trust, or, having accepted it, is later removed, the Probate Court will name a Trustee to carry out the terms of the Trust set forth by the deceased person. The Court will not let the Trust fail, or be invalidated, for lack of a Trustee.

The property left to a minor child is held in a **Children's Trust** or **Minor's Trust** until he or she achieves the age, specified in the Trust or by law, for the property to pass to him or her outright. Minors can only own a small amount of property outright in their own names. The legal limit, usually $2000 to $5000, varies by state. Any amount above this limit must be supervised by an adult. The reason for this is that a minor's signature or agreement to contract is not legally binding. They may not be able to sell stocks or real estate, owned outright or jointly with an adult, without a court order. They also cannot make purchases of big ticket items, such as a car or furniture, because the vendor will not accept their signatures. An exception is a minor who is considered **Emancipated** under the particular state's laws. Commonly the grounds for emancipation are marriage, military service, or "factual independence" (determined by court order which may be granted if the minor is one or two years from becoming a legal adult, as defined by the laws of the state, usually 18 years of age). Additionally, insurance companies will not pay death benefits to a minor Beneficiary until a Trustee is in place. Some states require the Trustee for a minor to be bonded.

In order to insure that a disabled or impaired Beneficiary remains eligible for government aid, some people choose to disinherit the child and make a gift to another family member or friend, with instructions that the funds be used to care for the disabled individual. This is done instead of setting up a Trust for the Beneficiary. There can be problems with this approach. Primarily, the recipient is under no legal obligation to comply with the decedent's instructions. Should the recipient die, there may be no, or improper, provisions to care for the disabled person. In addition, there could be disadvantages in income and gift taxes for the person who received the property. If this is the case, consider discussing with this Beneficiary the advisability of seeing an attorney, who is an expert in drafting **Special Needs Trusts**, and discussing establishing a Trust for the benefit of the disabled individual.

A Special Needs Discretionary Trust should be designed to:
- Maintain eligibility for federal and state assistance benefits the individual might be entitled to receive;
- Provide secure management of the assets for the benefit of the individual;
- Assure that the individual will have a friend to give advice and support ordinarily provided by a parent; and,
- Arrange, as much as possible, for a lifetime of adequate health care, room and board, and entertainment of the disabled person.

If the assets are not sufficient to make a Trust feasible, consider using the funds to purchase a life insurance policy payable to a Trust.

The Court can appoint a guardian for any person who believes he or she is not qualified or comfortable managing his or her own finances. This is called **Voluntary Guardianship**. This Trust is established when the Beneficiary, acknowledging his or her inability or lack of desire to deal with his or her own finances, files a petition with the Court, to request the appointment of a legal guardian. A judge can void voluntary guardianship after hearing from two witnesses that a guardian is no longer needed.

On the other hand, a Court may order **Involuntary Guardianship** for a Beneficiary. In this case a **Guardian** (sometimes called a **Conservator**, **Curator**, **Committee**, **Fiduciary**, or **Tutor**) is appointed to make decisions for another person, called the **Ward**. Involuntary Guardianship can be sought by any "interested" party who believes the Beneficiary is unable to handle his or her own affairs. An "interested" party can be the Administrator, a relative, friend, or the Court itself. The "interested" party, who is usually represented by an attorney, files a Petition with the Court (usually the Probate Court) for a hearing to determine the Beneficiary's competency and the need for "Legal Guardianship." A written notice is then sent by the Court to the prospective ward to inform him or her of the Petition for Guardianship and the date, time, and place of the competency hearing. If the individual does not want a guardian, he or she can attend the Hearing, with or without an attorney and object. Very often the prospective ward is appointed an attorney by the Court for the hearing (unless the person hires his or her own attorney). However, in most states, the proceedings will go forward whether or not the Beneficiary is present at the hearing. At the hearing, evidence is presented to the Court that either proves or disproves the claim that the person can't make decisions. Witnesses may testify for either side. Some states require only the testimony of family and/or friends, while others require a specific number of doctors to testify that the person is incompetent. If the Judge, after testimony is presented, agrees that the person is incompetent, a guardian is appointed. The guardian may be given either limited responsibilities or full control over all decisions. In some states, in addition to making financial decisions, the guardian may also be given power over personal decisions, such as where the ward will live, whether the ward can marry or divorce, travel, make major purchases, or even vote. Guardians are supposed to notify the Court of major expenditures and decisions, and receive permission before carrying them out. Guardianship procedures can be costly, both monetarily and in human terms, because of the devastating effect, on the ward, of being labeled incompetent.

Trusts for Pets

So far we have discussed the property management and, in some cases, the physical care, of human Beneficiaries. Now we'll give a little time to pets. Instructions may be left by the decedent as to who should care for a pet and for sufficient funds to be set aside to provide for its care. Some set up a Trust for the life of the Trustee (not of the pet), by which a certain amount of money is set aside for the support of the animal. Finally, if no provisions were made by the decedent, it may be left up to the Administrator to arrange for the care and maintenance of the pet and making financial arrangements with the caregiver, selling the animal, or arranging to have the animal put down. Many states consider provisions in Trusts and Wills regarding pets as unenforceable. Problems are avoided if the decedent made arrangements with someone willing to care for the pet.

The Trustee

Upon the death of the grantor, the Trustee's written authority to transfer property directly to Beneficiaries or indirectly to a Trust set up for a Beneficiary, is in the Trust Agreement. The Trust Agreement is presented in the same manner as the Letters of Administration or Letters Testamentary, issued by the Probate Court, to transfer the title of property. Just as with a Probate Estate, the Trustee obtains several certified copies of the Trust and Death Certificate. The Administrator then presents a certified copy of the Death Certificate and a copy of the Trust Agreement, along with proof of his or her own identity, to financial institutions, brokers, and government offices, etc., who either have possession of, or will be involved in the transfer of the Trust property. These institutions are familiar with Trusts and how they work, so you should not have a problem. If any title documents must be prepared to transfer Trust property to the Beneficiary, the Trustee prepares them or hires a professional to prepare them. No Court or other administrative action is required.

A Trustee can be an individual, professional, trust company, or bank. The same individual or company may be both the Administrator of the Estate and Trustee of a Trust created by the Estate. In this case, the Administrator must first settle the Estate and make the distribution of the Trust property to him- or herself as Trustee, as he or she would to any other Beneficiary. After being discharged as Administrator, he or she then starts his or her duties as Trustee. If a Managerial Trustee is also the Administrator of a Probate Estate, he or she is entitled to both a fee as Administrator and a fee as Trustee.

Duties of a Trustee

The Trustee's job begins when the Trust papers are completed, a Federal Fiduciary Identification number is obtained from the IRS and, if necessary, from the state, for the Trust (see Chapter 7, "Property Transfer Breakdown") and the Administrator transfers property to the Trust after Probate, or directly from a parent Trust. Some lawyers recommend transfer of title into the name of the Trustee. Others suggest it is better to transfer title into the Trust's name, because the Trustee may change, but the Trust name remains the same throughout the Trust's existence. The Trustee's responsibilities include:

- Collecting and inventorying all financial and other valuable papers, including: notes, policies, stocks, bonds, mortgages, deeds, and contracts, all of which should be placed in a safe deposit box titled in the name of the Trust or Trustee(s). Trust property should be titled in language similar to this: "Don Doe, as Trustee for Fred Brown." If there are Co-Trustees, all accounts and property should be in joint names, and all signatures should be required to execute any transaction. This provides a system of checks and balances.

- At a minimum, the Trustee must use such care and skill in administering the Trust as a person of ordinary skill and prudence would exercise. This means knowing your limitations and hiring professionals when indicated to help manage the Trust property. Although Trustees are usually not held liable for faulty judgment, they can be held personally liable for reckless or careless management.

- Trustees may manage investment real estate themselves or employ a real estate property manager. See Chapter 11, "Protection and Repair of Real Property." Trustees can make necessary minor repairs on their own. However, to protect themselves against personal liability, Trustees may want to, or be required to, obtain the Court's approval for major capital expenditures for repairs or renovations, or before selling a home or other real estate.

- The Trustee may choose to manage securities investments alone or with the assistance of a broker, financial planner, investment adviser, or trust company. See Chapter 14, "Investment Brokers and Brokerage Accounts" and Chapter 17, "Financial Planners." Administering and conserving an investment fund is the principal business of a trust company. Its investment advisers devote their entire time to the business of making investments and are in close touch with market conditions. In any case, the Trustee should review any proposed investment and maintain final approval before any investment item is bought or sold.

- The Trustee must retain all documents and maintain complete and accurate accounts or records of the Trust property. Upon request, the Trustee must provide them to the Beneficiaries, Remaindermen, and the Court.

- The Trustee is responsible to collect any claims, and hire an attorney if necessary. If the claims become uncollectible, the Trustee may be personally liable.

- Annual income and other tax returns are required for each Trust. The Trustee may have the tax returns prepared by a professional, but should review them for accuracy before filing and make sure they are filed in a timely manner. Since tax returns are the responsibility of the Trustee, the Trustee can be held personally liable for any penalties or fines imposed for improper or untimely filing. See Chapter 16, "Tax Preparation and Tax Preparers."

- Disburse Trust money to provide for the Beneficiary according to the terms in the Trust Agreement or, if not specified, in the discretion of the Trustee, or by court order.

Choosing a Trustee or Guardian

If it is necessary for a Court to establish a Trust and\or appoint a guardian, the Administrator of the Estate may be asked for suggestions. In this case, consider answers to some or all of the following questions as they apply to the situation. We have tried to present the major considerations. However, they should be viewed as a guideline and are not all inclusive. There are as many variations as there are people, and it would be impossible for us to anticipate all situations.

Keep in mind that the Court must set up the Trust according to the laws of the state, and the Judge may have his or her own choice of Trustee.

■ Consider who should act as Trustee. The choice need not be a financial expert but should be an adult who is trustworthy and intelligent enough to know when professional help is needed, has the ability to find a good professional, and evaluate the advice received. Be mindful of the age of the individual or individuals being considered, especially if the Trust is expected to continue for a prolonged period of time. If a decision on a suitable individual cannot be made, such as a caring family member or friend (including yourself), consider a trusted attorney, business confidant, bank, or trust company. Be aware that these professionals often will not accept management of a small Trust, or if they do accept a small Trust, the fee may be excessive. Because professionals involve themselves only with finances, they do not provide personal support to the Beneficiary. A Trust may also have more than one Trustee, called Co-Trustees. Co-Trustees may also be appointed in any combination of individuals and/or professionals. Be sure to ask your choice for Trustee, before submitting the name to the Court, to be sure the individual or institution is willing to accept the responsibility.

- Is it important that the Trustee knows and cares about the Beneficiary so he or she can provide emotional support to the Beneficiary?_____

- How long is the Trust expected to last?

  ◆ For the life of the Beneficiary_____

  ◆ Until the Beneficiary is age_____

  ◆ Until the Beneficiary petitions the Court for control_____

- Should there be one Trustee or Co-Trustees?_____

- If Co-Trustees, what combination is most desirable?

  ◆ Two friends or family members?_____

  ◆ One friend or family member and one professional (Attorney, Bank, or Trust Company)?_____

  ◆ Two professionals (Attorney and Trust Company or Bank)?_____

- Choice for Trustee is:_____

- Choice for Co-Trustee is:_____

- Alternate:_____

- Should the Trustee(s) be bonded, even if not required by law?_____

■ After evaluating the short- and long-term needs of the Beneficiary or ward, including present and future living arrangements, education and employment opportunities; decide how the Trustee can make the financial goals possible. Consider the following questions, keeping in mind they must conform with the confines of state law.

- How much discretion should the Trustee have in administering the Trust?

  ◆ Total, partial, none_____

- ◆ List specific limitations:_____

  _____

  _____

  _____.

- How closely should the Trustee be monitored by the Court?

  - ◆ All transactions and expenditures_____

  - ◆ Only for major expenditures_____

- What can the Trustee spend without further Court approval?

  - ◆ All or what portion of yearly income?_____

  - ◆ Some, all, or none of the principal?_____

- If some of the property must be used for support, who should decide in what order the property will be sold? _____

- At what age, if ever, should the remaining property be transferred to the Beneficiary, outright — free and clear?_____

- For a minor, to whom shall the Trustee pay the income?

  - ◆ Remaining parent or legal guardian_____

  - ◆ Court appointed guardian for the minor's person_____

  - ◆ School or college_____

  - ◆ Beneficiary_____

  - ◆ Other_____.

WILLS AND TRUSTS COMPARED

SIMPLE OR COMPLEX

An Estate can be very simple or very complicated. There are many variables and often problems are not readily apparent. Ease of settling an Estate depends on the individual circumstances of the decedent's financial status, the size and complexity of the Estate, how property was held, the number and type of Beneficiaries, and the extent of estate planning done by the decedent. As you have probably already gathered, the more agreeable Beneficiaries are and the more specific the instructions left by the decedent, the easier the Administrator's job will be; and settling of the Estate will go smoothly. However, if instructions are not clear or not in compliance with state law, if Beneficiaries are feuding, or if another situation complicates the Estate, the Administrator's job can be a nightmare. Based on the individual situation, the Administrator must decide when and to what extent professional help is needed. There are no hard and fast rules to cover all situations.

Whatever "Estate Planning" the deceased person did or didn't do, it is now your job to take over the Estate and manage it, either according to the wishes of the decedent or the laws of the state. What it boils down to is a small mound of forms and keeping track of filing deadlines and other procedural technicalities. The name of the game is good record keeping. The forms in this book were designed to help keep track of that mound of paperwork and standardize the accounting system. This is a plus if more than one person is involved in administering the Estate, by making coordination easier. It also facilitates takeover of Administration if, for any reason, the Administrator is unable to complete the Estate's settlement.

While reading this chapter; think about your own situation. Consider carefully the size and complexity of the Estate, as well as, the personalities of the Beneficiaries and/or Heirs, problems which may arise, and the amount of time you have to spend on administration of the Estate. Then decide whether or not you are willing to be the Administrator.

Features Common to Both Wills (or Intestate Probate) and Trusts

■ Both designate Beneficiaries. The individuals or institutions receiving the property of the deceased person;

■ Both designate an Administrator, and usually an Alternate Administrator if, for any reason, the designated Administrator cannot or will not serve;

■ Both require the Administrator to locate, identify, and inventory the deceased person's property;

■ Both require appraisal of certain property, see Chapter 9, "Valuing Property";

■ Both require **Disbursement** of funds to satisfy all legal debts, which means money paid out by the Administrator for debts, including funeral expenses, assessments, charges, inheritance taxes, and other expenses;

■ Both may specify which assets are to be used to pay debts, or the Administrator may have to decide which assets to use;

■ Both provide for **Distribution** of Estate property, which means the transfer of the remaining property to the designated Beneficiaries by preparing new ownership documents;

■ Both can be attacked by a lawsuit. The challenger must prove the Estate Plan is a result of someone's illegal act, such as forgery or fraud; or the decedent was underage, under duress or pressure, undue influence or persuasion at the time the document was executed (signed) or revoked; or because of either physical or mental incapacity did not understand the nature and consequences of the document, the nature and extent of his or her property, or who should be entitled to it;

■ Both can be declared invalid or void. This occurs when the document does not comply with the technical requirements of the state, such as a document not bearing the required number of witnesses or being otherwise improperly witnessed; or, if something on the face of the document has been erased, crossed out, or in any way corrected (this most often applies to a Will); or was executed in a manner not recognized in the state; or, although legally valid when made, was later revoked;

■ Both require the Estate to bear the cost of contests and the Administrator to defend them;

■ Both require that decedent's income taxes be filed and paid for income received during the tax year(s) prior to death, just as the decedent would have been required to file if alive;

■ Both can have provision for a Trust for Beneficiaries who are minors when they inherit or for any other reason require their finances to be protected by a Trust, and for compensation of the person administering the Trust;

■ Both are subject to death taxes and/or inheritance taxes. A possible exception is a qualified Irrevocable Trust;

■ Both can be the named Beneficiary of and receive: benefits payable on death from insurance policies or the balance of I.R.A. or Keogh accounts;

■ Both forbid the Administrator from making a profit from the Estate. Administrators cannot buy or sell Estate property on their own behalf unless the transaction is made in good faith, and at a fair price. This is part of the **"Fiduciary"** responsibility which is imposed upon anyone who takes financial responsibility for any other person or legal entity. It means Administrators must always act, to the best of their ability, in the "best interest of" the Estate. See Chapter 10, "Distribution and Sale of Personal Property."

■ Both (except Irrevocable Trusts) can be changed while the grantor is alive, but become irrevocable upon the death of the grantor and cannot be altered.

Differences Between Wills and Trusts

- A Will must go through a formal public court proceeding called Probate and becomes a matter of public record, while a Revocable Trust becomes operational at death to transfer the decedent's property privately to the Beneficiaries;
- Because of the complicated paperwork, a typical Probate takes a year or more before property is distributed to the Beneficiaries, while distribution of the property in a Living Trust usually is completed in a matter of weeks;
- The Administrator of a Will usually receives a small percentage of the Estate as compensation for his or her services, while the Administrator of a Trust does not receive compensation unless there is ongoing management of Trust property, such as in a Children's Trust, or the Trust Agreement directs compensation for distribution;
- Because of the length of time it takes to settle a Probate Estate, the Estate becomes a separate, taxable, legal entity in order to report income generated by the Estate during the period of administration: from the date of death until the final distribution. In contrast, because the property is quickly transferred to the Beneficiaries under a Revocable Trust, there is rarely a need to establish such an entity; usually any interim earnings can be reported on the Beneficiary(ies)'s tax forms.

Possible Complications and Problems of Estate Settlement

- If the decedent recently moved from a community property state to a common law state or vice versa, because right of ownership may change, see Chapter 5, "Property Ownership";
- A spouse (husband or wife) who is disinherited or left less than provided by state law, without a properly executed prenuptial or postnuptial agreement, may have a right under state law to a specified portion of the Estate. Most states mandate that spouses receive a specific portion of the Estate. If the state has adopted the Uniform Probate Code the amount is set on a sliding scale of as much as 50 percent of the couple's combined property, depending on the length of the marriage;
- A child, progeny, or **Issue** (a legitimate or adopted child of a marriage or grandchild) who is not mentioned in the Will or Trust, and is not specifically disinherited, may have a right under state law to a portion of the Estate, as would a child born or adopted after the death or before the decedent had a chance to include them; the Laws of Intestacy would decide the share. (Usually, an out-of-wedlock child inherits through the mother and not the father, unless paternity is legally established or the father marries the mother.);
- Anyone who unlawfully caused the death cannot inherit;
- Some felons cannot inherit;
- If the deceased made the gift **Conditional**, a stipulation or condition in the Will or Trust document stating the Beneficiary(ies) cannot inherit, unless they perform, or refrain from, a specific action. The condition is not always enforceable or valid;
- If the property is specifically given to be used for an illegal purpose;
- If a large portion of the Estate is left to charity;
- If the Estate does not have sufficient funds to pay cash gifts, **Abatement** (reduction of gifts) may be necessary, made according to state law or Will instructions;

39

■ If a specific item of property, designated to be given to a specific Beneficiary, was disposed of prior to the death or cannot be found, the Beneficiary gets nothing.

PROPERTY OWNERSHIP

An individual can only gift property he or she owns and cannot give away property that under law, belongs to another person. Therefore, it is important to determine what is, and what is not, the decedent's property. Of course, if the person owned all the property in his or her name alone; called **Sole Ownership** or **Fee Simple**, there is no question of ownership. However, if the person was married, even if separated, at the time death occurred, there are factors which must be considered in order to determine the ownership of the property. Let's look at the effect of marriage on the ownership of property.

The Effect of Marriage on Ownership

In a marital relationship, the laws of the state or states in which the decedent resided determine who owns what. These ownership laws fall into two basic categories: Community Property and Common Law. Currently, Arizona, California, Idaho, Louisiana, Nevada, New Mexico, Texas, Washington, and Wisconsin, have Community Property Laws (to be sure check IRS tax laws or state statutes); all other states are considered Common Law. The information we provide is a basic guideline to determine ownership of marital property because each state has volumes to define every nuance of the statutes pertaining to property ownership. If you have any question as to the ownership of property, research the state's statutes yourself, or consult an attorney. Of course, in most cases, technical property ownership rules are not a worry if a deceased spouse has left all or most of his or her property to his or her lifelong partner. However, problems can arise when there is a late life or common-law marriage. If a common-law marriage is involved, the laws of the state where the common-law marriage started, as well as the laws of the state in which the decedent resided at death, must both be taken into consideration. Some states recognize common-law marriage and others do not. Additionally, the circumstances under which a common-law marriage is defined vary from state to state. If a question regarding a common-law marriage is involved, we strongly recommend seeing an attorney. To help you determine which state's law may apply, see Chapter 2, "Wills and Probate," Determining Domicile.

Community Property States

In **Community Property** States all marital assets are held in common. In other words, with a few exceptions, each spouse owns equal half shares of all marital property. Generally, in community property states all employment income and pensions earned and all property acquired by either spouse during the course of the marriage is considered property held in common. The exceptions can include property acquired before a marriage, while the married couple resided in a non-community property state, during a permanent separation, or received as "separate property" by inheritance or gift to one spouse during the marriage. If kept separate, it is usually considered separate property. The income from separate property may or may not be considered community property depending on state law.

There are no restrictions on how each spouse gives away (disposes of) his or her half of the community property or his or her separate property. Normally, a surviving spouse has no "rights" to receive any of the deceased spouse's property nor can creditors seize the surviving spouse's separate property because of the deceased spouse's debts.

Common Law States

In **Common Law** States, there is no rule that property acquired during a marriage is owned by both spouses. The ownership of property is determined by whose name is on the title slip, deed, or other legal ownership document, regardless of who paid for it or how or when it was acquired. If there is no title document to the property, the person whose income or property is used to pay for it, owns it. As a result, in a one income marital relationship, all property would belong to the earning spouse unless that spouse chooses to put title in both names or in the spouse's name alone.

To protect a surviving spouse from being disinherited and winding up with nothing after the spouse's death, most common law states give a surviving spouse legal rights to a certain portion, usually one-third to one-half, of the deceased spouse's Estate. A spouse who is left less than the portion provided by the state's law, may choose to accept what was left to him or her, or to request the minimum share he or she is entitled to receive under state law. This share is called **Dower Right** for a surviving wife, and **Courtesy Share** for a surviving husband. Courts usually will not let a flagrant injustice occur and will protect one spouse from being disinherited.

Ownership of property, in both community property and common law states can also be affected by the existence of a properly executed prenuptial or postnuptial contract, or other legally binding documents the married couple may have signed.

Common-Law Marriage

In some states, the effect of a man and woman living together, plus the satisfaction of certain other conditions, can result in a lawful **Common-Law Marriage** with virtually all the rights and responsibilities of ceremonial marriage including tax benefits and burdens, inheritance rights, property and support responsibilities, and the requirement of a formal divorce to dissolve the union. Generally, the man and woman must intend to be married, must hold themselves out as married, and be recognized in the community as such. But the criteria differ widely among those states that provide for non-ceremonial (common-law) marriage. Generally, a common-law marriage that is valid in the state where it began will be recognized in the state of domicile as well as by the Social Security Administration. This holds true even if, later, the state does not permit such marriages to be originated within its borders.

The Effect of Title Documents

Another consideration is the effect of **Title Documents**, which specify how the property is owned and define a person's right to leave property to his or her Beneficiaries. It is necessary to read the title document to determine ownership and establish in what manner the deceased person's property will be distributed.

One form of title to property is a partnership agreement clearly defining the interest of each owner in the property. It can specify the percentage of ownership. If it does not specify the percentage of ownership, the partnership is in equal amounts. If, for example, there are three partners sharing equal ownership of the property, each will own exactly one-third of the property. When a partner dies, his or her one-third share goes to that partner's Beneficiaries under the provisions of a Will, a Trust, or the State's Laws of Intestacy. This is the same type of ownership which is automatically established in a community property state in a marital relationship. Each owner is free to give his or her share by Will or Trust, unless there is a written agreement in the contract of ownership restricting choices. Common forms of this type of agreement are:
- Tenancy in Common;
- Tenancy by the Entirety;
- Partnerships; and
- Corporations.

Since these agreements do not provide for automatic transfer of ownership, the share is usually included in the Probate Estate of the deceased partner.

Another form of title to property ownership is an agreement in which ownership is shared equally and includes a right of survivorship provision. This means that upon the death of one owner, his or her share of the property is automatically passed to the surviving owner/s outside of Probate. Once property has been placed in this form of ownership, listing it in a Will or Trust has no force or effect. However, if the ownership agreement is terminated by the owners, or the other owner(s) died before or simultaneously with the deceased owner, the property is usually passed according to each party's Will, Trust or the State's Intestate Succession Laws. This is commonly called **Joint Tenancy with Right of Survivorship** (JTWRS). Joint tenancy agreements between spouses are usually deemed to be survivorship. However, if the joint tenants are not husband and wife, special language is necessary to create a survivorship tenancy.

43

Ownership with Probate Avoidance Devices

A **Probate Avoidance Device** is just what it sounds like. It permits the naming of a Beneficiary in the Title Document. The property automatically passes to the named Beneficiary without the property being included in the deceased person's Probate Estate.

The title document of the property may or may not provide for shared ownership, and specifies a Beneficiary to receive the property upon the death of the owner(s). This means that upon the death of the sole owner, or the last surviving owner, the property passes automatically, outside of Probate, to the named (designated) Beneficiary. However, if the Beneficiary(ies) died before or simultaneously with the deceased owners, the property is then passed under the provisions of the deceased person's Will, Trust, or the State's Intestate Succession Laws. This type of agreement includes Informal Trusts and Formal Trusts. Informal Trusts are usually used for single items of property and include a simple phrase indicating who will receive the property upon the death of the owner(s). Formal Trusts (see Chapter 3, "Trusts") are legal documents which usually list most or all of the property in the Estate and may include very specific instructions as to exactly when and how the property in the Trust is to be distributed to the named Beneficiaries.

The following are types of property title in which ownership is shared, with right of survivorship, or Beneficiaries are named, allowing the property to pass to the survivors outside of Probate. The property cannot be left to another, in a Will or Living Trust, unless the tenancy is terminated by the owner(s) or the Beneficiary predeceases the owner(s). See Chapter 7, "Property Transfer Breakdown" for transfer information. Upon the death of the owner(s), the property is automatically inherited by the joint owner or designated Beneficiary.

- Property which is included in a Revocable Living Trust. This Trust can be revoked as long as the person who set it up is alive. Property included in a Living Trust cannot be left to another in a Will unless the Trust is terminated by the decedent prior to death.
- Property which is included in an Irrevocable Trust. This Trust cannot be altered or revoked, except in very narrow circumstances defined by the terms of the Trust.
- Property which is held in an Informal Trust Agreement with a Beneficiary designation which can be similar to the following:
  - **"Beneficiary"** on:
    - Life Insurance Policies;
    - Pension or Retirement Plans (public, corporate, military, or private), IRA's, Keogh's, etc.;
  - **"In Trust For"** on:
    - Bank Accounts (checking, savings, or C.D.'s);
  - **"Pay-on-Death"** on:
    - U.S. Savings Bonds;
    - Totten Trusts.

Surviving Spouses

If all property is jointly held (with automatic right of survivorship) between the deceased and a surviving owner, or specifies a named Beneficiary (not the Estate), Formal Probate is not necessary. The property need only be transferred to the survivor or Beneficiary. The Beneficiary or surviving joint owner need only present a certified copy of the Death Certificate and proof of his or her own identity. "Letters of Administration" or "Letters Testamentary" are not required. We suggest you read Chapter 7, "Property Transfer Breakdown" for specific details, as well as helpful information and tips. Transfer of title to the survivor or named Beneficiary is accomplished by:

- Presenting a certified copy of the Death Certificate to the bank, broker, insurance company, etc. holding the property.

- For Real Estate submit a certified copy of the Death Certificate to the County Office of Property Records, or County Appraisers Office where the property is located. Filing the Death Certificate is proof in the property records to show chain of title. Call before you go, to ask if you need to bring any other documents, such as an "Affidavit of Death of Joint Tenant," or similar document. The affidavit is a standard legal form, available from the County Recorders Office in some cases, or in many office supply stores. The names of the forms may vary by state. If the property is jointly held, it is not necessary to have a new deed drawn up by an attorney or title company. The property can remain in joint title until it is sold. A new title will be required to transfer the property to the new owner.

  - **IMPORTANT:** When Real Property is transferred, it is usually necessary to prove that there are no death taxes due on the Estate in order to clear the title. Even if a surviving spouse is able to transfer the title without this, when he or she [or the surviving spouse's Beneficiary(ies), after his or her death] sells the property, it will be necessary to show that any death tax liabilities have been satisfied. This can be shown either by presenting a receipt from the state's revenue department for the taxes that were paid, or a tax certificate showing that no taxes were owed. In states where the tax appraiser must release the property after evaluation, this tax certificate may be issued automatically. However, if this is not the case, it is up to the surviving spouse to get the certificate. This can be done by completing a form requiring a listing of all property owned by the decedent with its value on the date of death. This form may be available from the county property records office. If they do not have the form, call the state's revenue department. If the local revenue department is not familiar with the form, ask them for the number of the office in the State Capital and call there. There is often a submission time requirement, often as short as six weeks after the death, so don't put this off. When you receive the Tax Certificate, keep it in a safe place, so it can be found when the property is sold or transferred to your Beneficiary(ies). However, the county property records office may require the Tax Certificate be filed upon receipt in the property records to prove no inheritance tax lien exists against the property, and to transfer property (homestead) tax records to the surviving owner.

- Property listed in a jointly owned Living Trust need not be transferred by the surviving joint owner because the property is owned by the Trust. However, if you wish to transfer property out of the Trust, present the Trust Agreement, along with the certified copy of the Death Certificate and your identification.

Although these transfers can be accomplished very easily, it is still necessary in most cases, to establish and keep records of not only the updated basis of the property established as of the date of death, but also the original basis. For information on basis see Chapter 9, "Valuing Property." The reason for this is that when property is held jointly, in most instances, only the basis of the decedent's half of the property is updated while the basis of the other half uses the original cost, plus additional investment (such as home improvements), to determine the basis for tax purposes when the item is sold. The "Real Property Basis, Sale, or Transfer Record" on page R-14 is ideal for recording this information.

Note: Probate avoiding methods such as Living Trusts, informal trusts, joint tenancy, or insurance can be used to pay taxes if other funds are not available; or if the surviving spouse or children make a claim against the Estate or are disinherited. The decedent's creditors may also have a claim against joint property. They may be able to legally attach property to pay the debt owed but usually can only collect from the decedent's share of the property.

If all property is jointly held, with right of survivorship, or names an individual (not the Estate) as a Beneficiary, and no documents are required from the Court to transfer ownership of the property . . . it is not necessary to enter the Will into Probate.

PROPERTY DEFINITIONS

Property can be defined by various criteria and divided into many different categories depending on the purpose for the division. When dealing with the property in the Estate, you will probably have occasion to use all of these divisions.

First - All property is defined as either **"Real"** or **"Personal."**

■ **Real Property** is called real estate. Real property includes all land whether or not it has been developed and includes everything attached to the land. It does not matter if the property is owned as a personal residence, a place of business, or for investment purposes. Real property includes all the buildings and structures on the land and their fixtures, rights to minerals or water under the land, and in the case of agricultural land, may also include tools and animals (as defined by the state where it is located).

■ **Personal Property** is every other kind of property and includes:
   - Monetary Assets, such as: cash, Certificates of Deposit (C.D.'s), checking or money market accounts, savings accounts, and precious metals.
   - Personal Assets, such as: animals, antiques, art works, clothing, collectibles, computer equipment, electronic equipment, entertainment equipment, furs, household furnishings, jewelry, musical instruments, tools (garden), tools (handyman), vehicles (motorcycles, cars, trucks, boats, planes, recreational vehicles), etc.
   - Investment Assets, such as: bonds, insurance policies, loans and notes receivable, mutual fund shares, pension funds, stocks, a share in a small corporation, partnership, or limited partnership, etc.
   - Business Assets, (if not considered part of the real estate) such as: business machines and vehicles, farm animals and equipment, manufacturing machines or office equipment; customer lists and goodwill; copyrights, patents, rights to royalties; notes, leases, and accounts receivable, etc.

Second - Property is defined as **"Tangible"** or **"Intangible."**

■ **Tangible Property** is anything that can be touched or possesses value in and of itself, such as: cash, real estate, personal items, etc.

■ **Intangible Property** is usually represented by a piece of paper which bases its value upon what it represents, such as: stocks, bonds, mutual funds, money market funds, limited partnership interests; loans, notes, and accounts receivable; and beneficial interest in a Trust.

Third - Property is divided into **"Probate"** and **"Non-probate."**
- **Probate Property** is anything that passes from the decedent to the Beneficiary(ies) under the terms of a Will or the Intestate Laws of the State.
- **Non-probate Property** is anything that is excluded from the Probate Estate through a probate avoidance device. Once property has been placed in a probate avoidance device, listing it in a Will has no force or effect. The following cannot be transferred by Will unless the named Beneficiary(ies) predeceases the owner or dies in a common accident, or the Beneficiary is the Estate:
  - All joint tenancy property which automatically goes to the surviving joint tenant;
  - All property in a formal Trust goes to the Beneficiary(ies) named in the Trust;
  - Life insurance proceeds payable to a named Beneficiary(ies), not the Estate, goes to the Beneficiary(ies) named in the policy;
  - Retirement plans, pensions, IRA's, Keogh's, etc. payable to a named Beneficiary(ies);
  - Informal bank account trusts or pay-on-death accounts where the Beneficiary(ies) designated on the account documents inherits.

Fourth - Property is defined as **"Titled"** or **"Non-titled."**
- **Titled Property** is anything that is registered or has a formal document stating who owns the property. Items of property which normally have title documents are: bank accounts, bonds, businesses, money market accounts, mutual funds, real estate, stocks, and vehicles. In addition, a title document can exist for any item. All that is required is a written document, which names or describes the item or items and declares the form of ownership of the personal property. Although it should be notarized, it does not have to be filed with any agency.
- **Non-Titled Property** includes anything that does not have a document showing ownership. A purchase receipt with the name of the buyer may or may not determine ownership. For further information, see Chapter 5, "Property Ownership."

Fifth - Property is defined as **"Liquid"** or **"Non-liquid" Assets.**
- **Liquid Assets** are things that can be readily turned into cash, even if full or desired value cannot be received for them.
- **Non-liquid Assets** are things which do not always have a ready market or immediate buyer. Almost anything can be non-liquid simply because no one wants to buy the item at the particular time. Commonly, certain intangible items are non-liquid because the contract establishing the asset sets a schedule of periodic payments or sets a date in the future when the money is to be paid.

Sixth - Property is defined as **"Capital Gain"** and **"Non-Capital Gain."**
A capital gain or (loss) is realized when an item of property is sold. The amount of gain or (loss) is the difference between the cost (or basis) of the item and the price for which it was sold. This is the reason that a basis must be established for most property in the Estate. Internal Revenue's laws are very complicated, so we will not even attempt to list all the variables involved. However, for more information on establishing basis see Chapter 9, "Valuing Property."
- **Capital Gain Property** which we are all familiar with includes real estate, stocks, and bonds; but there are many others.
- **Non-Capital Gain Property** includes cash, bank accounts, accounts receivable, insurance, etc., which are not usually sold.

PROPERTY TRANSFER BREAKDOWN

Whether you are the Administrator of a Will, Trustee, or Surviving Spouse, your job is basically the same. You need to find all the assets of the Estate, value them, protect them, and finally, sell or transfer them. The amount of help you need to complete these tasks depends upon your own knowledge, ability, time, and the circumstances of the Estate. If you are not familiar with the procedures for transferring property, we suggest you read Chapters 2 through 6, or at least the ones appropriate to your situation. They will give you a reasonable idea of the professional help you may need to settle the Estate. To keep track of the fees paid to these professionals use the "Estate Administration Expense Record" on page R-22. The professionals you may wish to contact include:

- Attorney or Paralegal — see Chapter 15, "Hiring an Attorney";
- Financial Advisers — see Chapter 14, "Investment Brokers and Brokerage Accounts," Chapter 17, "Financial Planners," and Chapter 18, "Insurance and Insurance Agents";
- Tax Advisers — see Chapter 16, "Tax Preparation and Tax Preparers";
- Property Appraisers — see Chapter 9, "Valuing Property";
- Building Contractors, Repairmen, Home Inspectors, Property Managers — see Chapter 11, "Protection and Repair of Real Property"; and,
- Real Estate Salespeople, Domestic Help — see Chapter 12, "Transfer and Sale of Real Estate."

Getting Organized

An **Estate** includes all the property owned by the decedent, minus the deceased person's debts, or **Assets** minus **Liabilities**. The Gross Estate is the market value of everything the decedent owned with no deductions for debts, plus the value of life insurance. This is the value taxes are based upon. The Net Estate is the market value of everything the decedent owned, minus any debts or encumbrances on the property. The Net Probate Estate is the net value of all property left by Will or through the Laws of Intestacy. See Chapter 9, "Valuing Property."

These are the values the Administrator must determine. It means going through and organizing all the financial papers in the decedent's home, safe deposit box, etc. We suggest you establish an Estate file box. You can purchase a box or accordion file, or use any cardboard box that fits standard size files. Then buy file folders. Use one file folder for each type of property. You can use our Record Forms as the first page of each folder, and put the documents represented on the record behind it. Documents pertaining to each company or agency should be separately paper-clipped.

As you go through the property each item must be identified as "Probate" (passed through a Will or Intestate Laws) or "Non-Probate" (Trusts, jointly-owned property, insurance proceeds left to a specific Beneficiary, pensions with a specific Beneficiary, bank and other accounts with specific Beneficiaries, etc. See Chapter 5, "Property Ownership.") If you are unsure of the classification of an item of property, consult an attorney. It is important to record all property, including non-probate property, to enable you to examine the tax consequences to the Estate and to the Beneficiaries.

Make a thorough search of the home for money and documents. Popular hiding places are the pockets of clothing, wallets, underneath or behind drawers and furniture, garbage cans, freezers, toilet tanks, stove tops, and under mattresses. Do not be limited in your search by our suggestions. Look everywhere. As you go through each section of the home, segregate the items as you list them on an inventory to avoid confusion and backtracking. Use the "Tangible Personal Property Inventory and Sale Record" on page R-2 and "Collectibles Basis Record" on page R-3, for personal property. Throughout this Chapter the appropriate record form for each type of property will be referenced.

Any income received by the Estate, which does not fit into a specific accounting record category, should be listed on the " (Miscellaneous) Income Record" on page R-12. Any expense paid by the Estate, which does not fit into a specific accounting record category, should be listed on the " (Miscellaneous) Expense Record" on page R-24. These records provide a blank line in the title, so they can be titled as appropriate to the situation.

Each entity with which the decedent had dealings must be contacted, advised of the death and ultimately instructed as to how the property is now to be titled. It is the purpose of this book and especially this Chapter, to facilitate notification and transfer. The documents required to transfer property depends upon the title of the person making the transfer. You will always need to present personal identification and:
- A Probate Administrator's authority to act are the Letters of Administration, Letters Testamentary, or Affidavit and a certified copy of the Death Certificate;
- A Trustee's authority to act is the Trust Agreement and a certified copy of the Death Certificate;
- A Surviving Joint Owner with Right of Survivorship needs only present a certified copy of the Death Certificate; and
- A Named Beneficiary needs only present a certified copy of the Death Certificate.

An accurate record should be kept of all expenses incurred by the person administering an Estate or Trust, so reimbursement can be made. Such expenses would include stamps, paper, envelopes, mailing or shipping costs, phone and transportation expenses, etc. Use the "Administrator's Expense Record" on page R-23.

Here, we present a check list. We recommend you sit down either at a computer or typewriter, or with a pen, and a supply of paper and envelopes and all the Estate documents handy. Look at the title of each segment in this Chapter. If you are dealing with that type of property, debt, or agency read through the segment. Our aim is to remind you of what you may want to request or accomplish when dealing with each entity. Then write a letter. **Never send any documents with this first inquiry.** The purpose of this first contact is to advise the agency of the death and state what you want from them, if anything, and to request forms and information so you can accomplish your purpose. Be sure to note the mailing date of the letter on the appropriate Record Sheet. When you receive the agency's response, you can follow their directions to accomplish your goal. When bills are paid, always be sure to get a voucher or statement, that the bill was paid. This can be as simple as the last statement of a credit card with a zero balance or a cancelled check. We also suggest you keep a copy of all correspondence, receipts, checks, etc. Additionally, as you contact each agency make a list of when each legal or tax form is due so you do not miss a deadline. We have included a "Quick Reference Calendar" on page R-31 for your convenience. It is important for you to remember to never sign your name on a document unless you put your title next to your name.

When you do mail the actual documents always use either Certified or Registered Mail, with a request for a return receipt. The return receipt is the sender's proof of delivery. It shows who signed for the item and the date delivered. For an additional fee, the sender can get the addressee's correct address of delivery or request restrictive delivery to a particular person at the address. Certified Mail provides a mailing receipt and a record of delivery which is maintained at the recipient's post office. This service should be used for mailing documents which have no value in themselves. If you are mailing documents which are valuable or irreplaceable, Registered mail should be used. Insure the mailing for the full amount of replacement. Photocopy each document before mailing it.

Breakdown

Opening the Safe Deposit Box

There is generally an established procedure, based on each individual state's laws and by the institution where the Safe Deposit Box is located, for gaining access to a deceased person's Safe Deposit Box. Call the institution where the box is located for specific details of the procedure to open the box. Be prepared to give them the name or names the box is registered in, the date of death, your authority for inquiring, and if you have the box key.

Tidbit: Usually a joint owner with a key can gain access immediately after death and before the bank is notified of the death.

You may be able to gain limited access before administration to get specific items, such as the Will, deed to a cemetery plot, or similar document, which may be needed before the Death Certificate and Letters of Administration, or Letters Testamentary, are issued.

- Arrange for opening of the Safe Deposit Box:
  - Some states with death taxes require banks to seal the box as soon as they are notified of the death of the owner. The contents cannot be released until the box is inventoried by a government official. In this case you will have to arrange for the tax appraiser to accompany, or meet you, at the bank. Check with the bank to find out if the box is sealed and how it can be opened. This can usually be done quickly and easily.
  - If not sealed, bring the appropriate transfer authority documents to gain access.
- Be sure to bring the key for the box with you.
- List contents as items are removed from the box; you can use the "Safe Deposit Box Inventory Record" on page R-1.
- Value the contents with the aid of an appraiser, if required by the Court, the Insurance Company, or Tax Authorities. This can be done later along with the contents of the house.
- After the contents of the box have been inventoried, usually with a bank officer or a representative of the state's taxing authority present, and a copy of the inventory has been sent to the state tax authority, you can get permission to take over the contents. The IRS may regard any cash in the box as income for the current year.
- Protect valuable items by opening an Estate Safe Deposit Box and putting them in it.

Tidbit: If you have reason to believe the decedent had a Safe Deposit Box, but you are unable to determine its location:

- Put a small ad in the State's Bankers Association's Magazine describing the problem;
- Wait for the institution to send a bill for the box;
- If the key is imprinted with the name of the company who made it, they may be able to help you;
- Contact the American Safe Deposit Association, 330 W. Main Street, Greenwood, IN 46142 or call (317) 888-1118. There is a fee. or;
- Just wait. After a state specific number of years after a box is abandoned, the bank must legally turn the contents of the box over to the State Comptroller's Abandoned Property Section. See Missing or Abandoned Property at the end of this chapter.

Post Office and Mail Forwarding

Decide what you want to do with mail sent to the decedent. If a trusted person will be in the residence, you may not want to notify the Post Office of the death, but allow them to continue delivering the mail as usual. If you want to advise them of the death and change the mailing address, the Post Office prefers notification be made in person. If this is not possible, notification must be made in writing. You can request a Postal Form 3575, change-of-address card, from your mail carrier. The form may be included in a kit with change-of-address cards you can mail to individual mailers. Call first to determine which office services the address and what documentation you need, then:

- Complete the form required to report the death.
- Request any mail addressed to the decedent be returned to the sender marked "Deceased" or request the mail be forwarded to you or the person of choice.
- If you close a Post Office Box, be sure to request a refund of any unused rental payment.
- Mail should be received in a secure mailbox and removed promptly. If expected mail is not received or delivered mail is stolen, notify the Post Office immediately, as well as the issuing agency.

Note: When forwarding is requested all mail is forwarded including catalogs and magazines. The Post Office may charge to forward these items. To avoid these charges, write to the sender and ask them to use the new address or advise them of the death and ask them to discontinue mailing. To stop a lot of the catalogs, and charitable or other solicitations, write and advise the following trade organizations of the death and request their members discontinue mailings to the decedent. Lists usually go out quarterly to members, so do not expect an immediate end to the unwanted mailings. Be sure to include all variations of the name and address as they appear on the mailing labels of catalogs, sweepstakes entries, etc.:

- Mail Preference Service, **Direct Marketing Association**, P.O. Box 9008, Farmingdale, NY 11735-9008;
- **ADVO Systems Inc.**, Director of List Maintenance, 239 W. Service Road, Hartford, CT 06120-1280;
- **TRW Inc.**, Mail Preference Service, 600 City Parkway W., Orange, CA 92668-2972;
- **Equifax Inc.**, Equifax Options Division, Name Removal Department, P.O. Box 4081, Atlanta, GA 30302-4081; and
- **Trans Union Corp.**, National Service Division, 111 W. Jackson Boulevard, 16th Floor, Chicago, IL 60604-3595.

Real Estate

Gaining Access to a Vacant Home:

- To gain access to a sealed house so you can get such things as the Will or address book (to allow you to notify friends and relatives of the death), contact the Public Administrator's office (or similar office that conducts estate tax appraisals for the state) or the local police and ask for permission to enter. Otherwise, you will have to wait to accompany the tax appraiser, or wait until the house is officially unsealed (perhaps four or more days after the death).
- If you cannot find a neighbor, friend, or relative with a key, arrange to have a locksmith meet you there.
- If the home is damaged, before entering see Chapter 11, "Protection and Repair of Real Property." Take whatever steps you and the Beneficiaries consider necessary to protect the property.

- Either enter the residence alone or with a disinterested but trusted person, or <u>all</u> the Beneficiaries and Heirs at law. **Do Not Let Anyone Take Anything.** It is wise in most cases to wait until you are sure you have, or will have, Administrative Authority before you really get into things. Ask the Clerk of the Court or your attorney when it is appropriate for you to take charge. See the "Introduction" for more information.

- Make a complete list of all contents. Our records will help you with the inventory of all personal property. Use the "Tangible Personal Property Record" on page R-2 and "Collectibles Basis Record" on page R-3.

- Value contents with the tax appraiser's help, or hire an appraiser, if required. See Chapter 9, "Valuing Property."

- Provide for the care of pets, plants, etc. See <u>Pets</u> below.

- Locate - mortgages, deeds, abstracts, lot surveys, or lease contracts. Use the "Real Estate Basis, Sale, or Transfer Record" on page R-14.

- Arrange to continue mortgage payments. You can use the "Mortgage or Rent Payment Record" on page R-15. See <u>Mortgage</u> below.

- Inspect the house, and write a description of its condition. Be specific. Take pictures of any damaged area. Use the "Maintenance and Repair Expense Record" on page R-19.

- Locate insurance policies for the house and contents — notify the insurer of the death, review the coverage for adequacy, and arrange to continue payments when necessary. See Chapter 18, "Insurance and Insurance Agents."

- Arrange for "Ancillary Administration" of property located in other states or countries, to maintain a clear claim of title to the property, arrange for care, etc.

- Be sure property taxes are paid up to date.

- If the residence is in a controlled community — check with the Condominium Association, Residence Association, etc., before renting or selling the home. This is especially important because unauthorized sale or rental can cause a foreclosure action brought by the Association. See Chapter 12, "Transfer and Sale of Real Estate."

Leased Residence

When the decedent lived in a rented apartment or house:

- Contact the landlord or superintendent and advise them of the death. If you do not have a key to the residence, ask them to admit you. The landlord will probably require some proof of your authority to enter.

- Review the lease agreement carefully. The Estate is responsible for paying the rent to the end of the term agreed upon in the lease. The Estate can be sued for breach of contract if rent payments are not made. This is true even if the residence was destroyed by the disaster which resulted in the decedent's death. However, the landlord may agree to let you out of the contract. If there is no lease agreement, you may be able to walk away. Use the "Mortgage or Rent Payment Record" on page R-15.

- Ask the landlord for permission to sublet the residence. Get the agreement in writing. Understand the terms of allowing for a sublet.

- Ask permission to conduct an estate sale. Find out any restrictions they may impose. See Chapter 10, "Distribution and Sale of Personal Property."

- Request a refund of the down-payment or damage deposit. You may have to clean the residence to claim the deposit. Be sure to review documents to determine the condition of the residence when it was first leased.
- Whether the residence is vacant or under a sublease, you are still responsible for damages. Check the insurance coverage with the agent. See Chapter 18, "Insurance and Insurance Agents."
- If there is a lease purchase agreement, decide if it is worth continuing payments and purchasing the residence to be sold or passed to a Beneficiary; or ending the contract if permitted.
- If the decedent alone leased the residence, roommates may have to get permission from the landlord to remain in the residence. A new lease agreement may be necessary to allow any person to remain in the residence.
- If the decedent was receiving a housing subsidy, contact the Subsidized Housing Authority.

Real Estate Property, other than residence, in addition to the above;

- Collect rents;
- Maintain the property;
- Make repairs;
- Obtain tenants, etc.;
- Arrange, if necessary, to hire a property management firm.

Mortgage

Locate the mortgage coupon book or evidence of direct payment withdrawal from the decedent's bank account. Be sure mortgage payments are made on time. As long as payments are being made, the mortgage company is usually not bothered about who is making them. However, if payments are missed you will not only have to catch up on the monthly payments, but will incur delinquent interest and late fees added to the loan. Additionally, if too many payments are missed, the property could be foreclosed. For more information see Chapter 12, "Transfer and Sale of Real Estate." If you know you're going to miss a payment and the problem is temporary, get in touch with the lender and explain the circumstances. Most lenders are willing to work out an interim solution such as suspending mortgage payments for one or two months. Check to be sure homeowner's insurance and property taxes, if paid from the mortgage escrow account, are current. At the appropriate time, according to the circumstances, write and notify the mortgage company of the death, who will be making payments, and whether the property will be sold or transferred.

Tidbit: If the mortgage is FHA insured, when it is paid off, the borrower may be eligible to receive a refund on part of the insurance premium. For information and possible refund write to the U.S. Department of Housing and Urban Development, Assistant Secretary, Comptroller, FHA Insurance Refunds, 451 Seventh Street, S.W., Washington, D.C. 20410 or Distributive

Shares Branch, Department of Housing and Urban Development, P.O. Box 23699, Washington, D.C. 20036. Include the FHA case number, name of the borrower, property address, your name and current address, lender's name, loan number, and loan payoff date.

Reverse Mortgage

With a **Reverse Mortgage**, the lender makes monthly or periodic payments to the borrower/homeowner. When the homeowner dies, (upon the sale of the house) the lender is paid all the cash the owner received from the loan, plus interest, and the rest goes to the Estate. For more information see Chapter 27, "Living On a Reduced Income."

- Advise the lender of the death, so loan payments will stop.
- Indicate whether the property will be transferred to a Beneficiary or sold;
- Advise the lender of the circumstances under which the loan will be repaid, and by whom.

Utilities

Contact Utility Companies (electric, gas, water, phone, alarm, cable or satellite service for television). The address and phone number of each utility is on the company's bill for service. When appropriate:

- Advise each company of the death of the customer;
- Give them your name and address and arrange for payment of current and future bills;
- Request continuation of the utilities necessary to maintain the property;
- Stop service of unnecessary utilities. (Companies usually require at least 24 hours to start or disconnect service.);
- Request a refund of the deposit when, and if, appropriate. (Refund of the deposit may depend upon the return of undamaged company equipment, such as a cable television service's converter box.) Use the "Utilities Expense Record" on Page R-16.

Tidbit: As long as utility companies are receiving payment for service, they usually are not concerned about who is making the payment. A widow may want to keep the phone service and phone listing in her husband's name.

Tidbit: If you have an unresolved problem with an electricity, gas, or water provider; contact the state's utility commission.

Home Delivery Items (Newspapers, milk, water, etc.)

- Advise the provider of the death of the customer;
- Request the deliveries be stopped, and ask how to:
  - Have the remainder of the pre-paid subscription or service delivered to another location;

- Request a refund of the value of the unused pre-paid subscription or service;
- Arrange to pay the bills for delivered items;
- Use the "_Miscellaneous) _Expense Record" on page R-24.

Magazines and Publications

Review each publication to see when the subscription expires. Then decide if you wish to continue receiving it. If appropriate, write to the company and:
- Advise the publisher of the death of the subscriber;
- Request a change of name and address for forwarding; or
- Cancel the subscription and request a refund of the unused price; or
- Request forwarding from the Post Office. They will charge extra for delivery which might make this a poor choice.

Pets

- Arrange for immediate care;
- Then look for Trust Agreements or directives in a Will. See Chapter 3, "Trusts";
- Arrange for permanent care or putting the animal down.

Tidbit: For purebreds, there are rescue services who find homes for dogs, cats, and horses. Referrals to rescue groups are available from:
- Managers of local animal shelters;
- The Humane Society of the United States, 2100 L Street, N.W., Washington, D.C. 20037, or call (202) 452-1100; or
- The American Kennel Club Library, 51 Madison Avenue, New York, NY 10010, or call (212) 696-8200.

Domestic Help

- Determine which help will be needed to maintain the property. See Chapter 12, "Transfer and Sale of Real Estate" for tax treatment of employees and other considerations;
- Contact each person and advise them of the death;
- Advise them of any future services you require;
- Arrange to pay the person or company for previous and future services. Use the "Payroll Calculation Record" on page R-17 and "Employee Expense Record" on page R-18.

Vehicle Location and Protection

- Find and add to the inventory any automobiles, mobile homes, recreational vehicles, vans, trucks, boats, or aircraft.

- Use the "Tangible Personal Property Inventory and Sale Record" on page R-2.
- Put them in a safe place, house garage or driveway, drydock, hangar, etc.
- Perform any necessary maintenance to avoid deterioration or damage.
- Find title and registration. Check with the Department of Motor Vehicles, Auto Tag Agency, or other registering authority; they can supply information about:
  - License tag renewal;
  - Title and registration transfer;
  - Replacing a lost or destroyed title;
  - Any inspection requirements and, if required, where and when the inspections are performed.
  - Use the "Miscellaneous Expense Record" on page R-24.
- If there is a car (boat, plane, etc.) loan — advise the loan company of the death, and arrange to keep up loan payments. Use the "Debts Owed By the Estate Payment Expense Record" on page R-25.
- Be sure insurance is appropriate and paid to date, and make any necessary future payments. For more information, see Chapter 18, "Insurance and Insurance Agents."
- To find out the value of vehicles — contact a bank which makes loans on these vehicles. They have what is called the Blue Book, which lists the current costs of used cars, vans, and trucks. They may also have reference books for other vehicles. If they do not, visit your local library and ask for the *N.A.D.A. Official Used Car Guide* or *Edmund's Used Car Prices*. The N.A.D.A. also provides lending institutions with the current price of boats, motorcycles and aircraft. As a last resort, if you cannot find a listing, call N.A.D.A. at (800) 544-6232. The *BUC Boat Pricing Guide* lists the prices of used boats. If you cannot find this publication call BUC at (800) 327-6929 but only for boats. Another option is to visit used vehicle dealerships that trade in the particular vehicle and ask for a quote.

Benefits

Use the "Benefits Receipt Record" on page R-11 for payments received or funds returned for all entities in this section.

Social Security Administration

Often, the Social Security Administration (SSA) is notified by the funeral director or county, when a death occurs. If SSA has been notified, the surviving spouse will usually be contacted by SSA a few days after the death. However, if you do not hear from the SSA, it is up to you to make the contact. Start with a phone call. Look in the Blue or White Pages of the phone book under the UNITED STATES listings. Advise the local Social Security office of the death and:

- If the decedent was receiving benefits, ask how to arrange for discontinuance of checks;
- Ask how to return unearned benefits. Usually:

- If payments are made by check, uncashed checks are returned;
- If the check was deposited, a check should be written to the Social Security Administration. (Wait for them to request it.); and,
- If payments are made by direct deposit, the Social Security Administration will make a direct withdrawal.

■ Ask how to have uncashed checks of earned benefits reissued in the name of the Estate, surviving spouse, or Trust, as applicable;

■ Ask what documents you will have to present to claim the one-time death benefit. (Currently $255 payable to the surviving spouse of the deceased person or to a child who has been receiving benefits on the decedent's Social Security record.);

■ Ask to make an appointment for any survivor who is already receiving benefits. Survivors should have their benefits reviewed at this time to be sure they are receiving the highest benefit they are entitled to receive.

■ Ask to make an appointment to discuss benefits for any survivor who may now be eligible to receive survivors' benefits. If you are unsure whether you should apply for benefits at this time, make an appointment with the nearest Social Security district office. You will receive, free of charge or obligation, any help you need in making a decision. Then if you decide to start receiving benefits, you will get help filling out the claim forms. Social Security gives recipients the highest benefit amount they are entitled to receive. If, because of illness or distance, you are unable to go to the Social Security office in person, you may write or telephone. Applicants should bring their social security cards and other appropriate proof with them, such as the deceased person's Social Security Card (or at least the number) and, if the deceased person was not receiving benefits when he or she died, the employment record of the decedent for the past (12) twelve months, a certified copy of the Death Certificate, as well as certified copies of Marriage Licenses, Divorce Decrees, Birth Certificates, etc. If you do not have these documents see Chapter 20, "Locating Missing Beneficiaries."

■ If the decedent was on Medicare and left unsubmitted doctor, medical service, or hospital bills, request a supply of the form "REQUEST FOR INFORMATION-MEDICARE PAYMENT FOR SERVICES TO A PATIENT NOW DECEASED" so you can request payment of the benefits and have the checks sent either to the supplier, the survivor, the Trust, or the Estate.

■ For low income survivors, ask how to obtain a Form SSA-4926 Sm, for proof of Social Security benefit amount, to present for application to receive food stamps, rent subsidies, energy assistance, bank loans, etc.

■ For more information, see Chapter 24, "Social Security, Medicare, and Medicaid."

Railroad Retirement Board

Railroad Retirement is a retirement program for railroad workers. Benefits derived from both this program and Social Security are usually combined into one check from Railroad Retirement. Despite this, both the Social Security Administration and the Railroad Retirement Board should each be notified of the death, benefits discussed and, if appropriate, application made. Refer to information booklets supplied to the recipient for the appropriate address. Or write to the Office of Public Affairs, U.S. Railroad Retirement Board, 844 N. Rush Street, Chicago, IL 60611-2092, or call (312) 751-4776.

Federal Employees

Contact the appropriate Personnel Office responsible for pensions and benefits for employees and their dependents for the decedent's federal agency. Refer to information booklets supplied to the recipient for the appropriate address. If you are unable to find information, contact the Federal Retirement Thrift Investment Board, 1250 H Street, N.W., Washington, D.C. 20005, or call (202) 942-1600. Refer to Employer below for the appropriate requests.

Veterans Administration

If the decedent was a United States Veteran, discharged under other than dishonorable conditions, the government will provide an American Flag to be draped upon his or her casket. The flag is given to the next of kin after the services. The Veterans Administration (VA) or the Funeral Director can arrange for this upon receipt of the decedent's DD-214 form (which documents the service dates and type of discharge). Do not let the Funeral Director keep the original. The Veterans Administration will request a copy of the DD-214 or the Veteran's full name, military service number, branch of service, and dates of service for any benefits requested. Funeral Directors usually also have the forms necessary to claim current benefits. If the Funeral Director does not have these forms, contact your local Veterans Administration Office. Look in the Blue or White Pages of the phone book under the UNITED STATES listings for the Veterans Administration regional office or call (800) 669-8477, or write to the Veterans Benefits Administration, Department of Veterans Affairs, 810 Vermont Avenue, N.W., Room 900, Washington, D.C. 20420, or call (202) 273-4900, or (800) 827-1000, or go online to *http://www.va.gov*

- Arrange for burial in a Veterans Cemetery if requested by the decedent or survivors. The U.S. Government will pay for the plot, a headstone, and a flag for burial, but you must arrange and pay for any other merchandise or services. The cemetery at Arlington, VA is closed to further burials and the government does not arrange for any burials overseas.
- If the decedent was receiving disability, educational benefits, or a retirement pension call or write the office who issued the checks and:
  - Advise the Veterans' Administration of the death of the beneficiary;
  - Ask how to arrange for discontinuance of checks;
  - Ask how to return unearned benefits. Usually:
    - If payments are made by check, uncashed checks are returned;
    - If the check was deposited, a check should be written to the issuer (Wait for them to request it.); and,
    - If payments are made by direct deposit, the issuer will make a direct withdrawal.
  - Ask how to have uncashed checks of earned benefits reissued in the name of the Estate, Trust, or surviving spouse as applicable.
- Request an application and instructions for claiming any burial allowances or benefits for which the veteran's service qualifies. These allowances are payable to the next of kin or the person or agency bearing the veteran's burial expenses. Currently this includes $300 ($1500, if the death is service connected) toward burial and funeral expenses, a $150 plot or interment allowance when not buried in a national cemetery, plus removal allowance if death occurs in a VA hospital.

- Request information and an application for a free headstone or marker for the veteran's grave or allowance toward its purchase. See Chapter 1, "When A Person Dies."
- If the decedent is survived by a spouse and/or other dependents (minor children or parents), the Veterans Administration may provide them with a pension.
  - Request an application or appointment to apply for Survivor's Benefits;
  - Always make a written application, so you will receive a written determination;
  - If benefits are denied you can accept the decision if you agree with it or appeal the decision to the VA if you disagree.
- If the veteran was retired, the surviving spouse and ex-spouse may be eligible to shop at the commissary or pharmacy, or take advantage of other services at certain military bases. They must have identification cards to permit them to use these facilities. Request information and an application for an identification card.
- If the decedent's life was covered by a United States Life Insurance for Veterans policy:
  - Contact the regional VA office and request a claim form or write directly to the Department of Veterans Affairs, Regional Office and Insurance Center, at P.O. Box 8079, Philadelphia, PA 19101 (for states east of the Mississippi River) or at Bishop Henry Whipple Bldg., Fort Snelling, St. Paul, MN 55111 (for states west of the Mississippi and the states of Minnesota, Wisconsin, Illinois, Indiana and Mississippi);
  - If you cannot find the life insurance policy, call the National Personnel Records Center (314) 263-3901.
- For more information request a copy of *Federal Benefits for Veterans and Dependents.* This 100-page booklet lists Veterans' centers, National Cemeteries, and benefits available to qualifying surviving spouses, children, and parents. The booklet is also available from the U.S. Government Printing Office, Superintendent of Documents, Washington, D.C. 20402 for $3.25, or credit card orders may be placed by phone call (202) 783-3238. The stock number of the booklet is 051-000-00-200-8.

Tidbit: In some cases, states have provided certain real estate tax exemptions for veterans or their widows. Your local tax authorities can assist you.

Tidbit: If the deceased was an honorably discharged U.S. War Veteran, or the wife or widow of a veteran of any U.S. war prior to and including WW1, most states provide an additional burial allowance, usually payable to the next of kin or the person paying the funeral expenses. The same papers will be required.

Tidbit: War-time Veterans of countries other than the United States, as well as their spouses, may be entitled to benefits, including pension benefits, from that country. Contact the appropriate country's embassy for information.

Tidbit: The Older Veterans Assistance Program of the DAV helps disabled veterans find assistance with transportation, nutrition, housing, home visitation, home repairs, and recreation. In addition, the DAV National Service Program assists clients in filing claims for Veterans disability compensation, pension, and death benefits, employment and training programs, Social Security disability benefits and many other programs. Write to: Disabled American Veterans National Headquarters, P.O. Box 14301, Cincinnati, OH 45250-0301 or call (606) 441-7300. Assistance is also available to complete VA forms from the local Veterans Administration or contact the service officers of your local American Legion, Veterans of Foreign Wars, Amvets, Disabled American Veterans posts, or the Red Cross.

Employer

Call the current employer as soon as possible and advise them of the death. In most cases this call should be followed by a letter.

Write a letter to notify any previous employer from whom the deceased was receiving benefits or from whom the survivor may be eligible to receive any benefits.

The initial letter is only to advise the employer of the death and to inquire about what needs to be done now. Most companies will send forms. The company will also request any legal documentation required in their reply. For more information see Chapter 25, "Employer Health and Pension Benefits." Include in the letter all applicable requests:

- Ask that any unpaid salary, accrued vacation or sick leave, pension, or other benefits be paid to the Estate, Trust, or a specific Beneficiary.
- Ask how to return unearned salary or pension benefits. Usually:
  - If payments are made by check, uncashed checks are returned;
  - If the check was deposited, a check should be written to the issuer (Wait for them to request it.); and,
  - If payments are made by direct deposit, the issuer will make a direct withdrawal.
- Ask for any forms necessary to discontinue the decedent's pension.
- Ask for any forms necessary to initiate payment of pension checks to an entitled survivor or for obtaining a lump sum distribution for a beneficiary. Before requesting a lump-sum distribution, check the IRS codes.
- Ask for claim forms for health insurance provided through the company, if there are outstanding medical bills for the decedent. Use the "Medical Bills Payment Record" on page R-20.
- Ask for claim forms for any life insurance policies issued through the company.
- Ask for forms and information regarding the continuance of health insurance for the surviving spouse and dependents. Because of the death of the money earning spouse, the surviving spouse's and dependent(s)'s insurance may be canceled. It is important to read any material from the company regarding benefits to be sure you understand what the survivors are entitled to receive.

Unions and Professional Organizations

Write a letter as a courtesy, if for no other reason, to allow publication of the death to members and to keep membership records up to date:

- Notify the organization of the death;
- Cancel membership;
- Request a refund of dues, if appropriate;
- Request any benefits due to dependents. (See Employer above, for suggested considerations.)

Unemployment Compensation

- Advise the agency of the death of the insured, either by phone or letter. The phone number and address for the local office can be found on the insured's identification card or benefit documentation;
- Ask how to arrange for discontinuance of checks;
- Ask how to return unearned benefits. Usually:
  - If payments are made by check, uncashed checks are returned;
  - If the check was deposited, a check should be written to the issuer (Wait for them to request it.); and,
  - If payments are made by direct deposit, the issuer will make a direct withdrawal.
- Ask how to have uncashed checks of earned benefits reissued in the name of the Estate, surviving spouse, or Trust as applicable.

Workers' Compensation

Workers' Compensation (also known as Workmen's Compensation) is an insurance policy most employers are required to carry which pays the medical expenses, and a portion of lost wages, for employees hurt at work, or for an injury or illness resulting from their employment. It also provides benefits to dependent survivors of workers whose deaths were related to their work. This benefit program, though paid by private insurance companies, is administered by the state. The type and amount of benefits available are determined by the laws of each state. Look in the Blue or White Pages of the phone book under the name of the STATE for the Workers' Compensation Agency. If the decedent was receiving benefits, call or write the office who issued the checks and:

- Advise the agency of the death of the insured;
- Ask how to arrange for discontinuance of checks;
- Ask how to return unearned benefits. Usually:
  - If payments are made by check, uncashed checks are returned;
  - If the check was deposited, a check should be written to the issuer (Wait for them to request it.); and,
  - If payments are made by direct deposit, the issuer will make a direct withdrawal.
- Ask how to have uncashed checks of earned benefits, reissued in the name of the Estate, surviving spouse, or Trust as applicable.
- Ask if there is a death benefit. If there is a death benefit, ask what documents you will have to present to claim it.
- If any survivor is receiving benefits, ask to make an appointment for the survivor's benefits to be reviewed at this time, to be sure they are receiving the highest benefit they are entitled to receive.
- If the death of the decedent was work related, by accident or illness, the decedent's survivors may either be entitled to benefits or to bring a lawsuit against the employer. Under most states' laws, if you accept benefits you cannot later decide to bring a lawsuit. The first step is to make sure the employer has properly filed a report of the death to the insurer. Then contact the Workers' Compensation Agency for information and advice. Often there is a time

limit for benefit application, so do not delay. Workers' Compensation Agencies suggest you contact an attorney specializing in workers' compensation law before making a claim for benefits. When you have chosen an attorney (see Chapter 15, "Hiring an Attorney"), call and ask for a free (or low cost) consultation to discuss the case. Ask what documents you should bring with you.

Government Funded Aid Programs

- If the decedent or the family was receiving benefits:
  - Advise the appropriate office of the death of the recipient, either by phone or letter. The phone number and address for the local office can be found on the recipient's identification card or benefit documentation;
  - Ask how to arrange for discontinuance of checks;
  - Ask how to return unearned benefits. Usually:
    - If payments are made by check, uncashed checks are returned;
    - If the check was deposited, a check should be written to the issuer (Wait for them to request it.); and,
    - If payments are made by direct deposit, the issuer will make a direct withdrawal.
  - Ask how to have uncashed checks of earned benefits reissued in the name of the Estate, surviving spouse, or Trust as applicable.
  - Ask if there is a death benefit. If there is a death benefit, ask what documents you will have to present to claim it.
  - If any survivors are receiving benefits, ask to make an appointment for the survivors' benefits to be reviewed at this time, to be sure they are receiving the highest benefit they are entitled to receive.
- If the death of a parent results in possible eligibility for benefits for the surviving family members; call to make an appointment, as soon as possible, to apply for benefits. Be sure to ask what documentation is necessary to prove need when applying.

Private Disability Insurance

- Advise the insurance company of the death of the insured, either by phone or letter. The phone number and address for the local office can be found on the insured's identification card or policy documents;
- Ask how to arrange for discontinuance of checks;
- Ask how to return unearned benefits. Usually:
  - If payments are made by check, uncashed checks are returned;
  - If the check was deposited, a check should be written to the issuer (Wait for them to request it.); and,
  - If payments are made by direct deposit, the issuer will make a direct withdrawal.
- Ask how to have uncashed checks of earned benefits reissued in the name of the Estate, surviving spouse, or Trust as applicable.
- If there is a death benefit, ask what documents you will have to present to claim it.

Vocational Rehabilitation

■ Advise the agency of the death of the client, either by phone or letter. The phone number and address for the local office can be found on the client's identification card or benefit documentation;

■ Ask how to arrange for discontinuance of checks, if appropriate;

■ Ask how to submit any bills the agency may be responsible for paying.

Food Stamps

■ Advise the issuing office of the death of the recipient, either by phone or letter. The phone number and address for the local office can be found on the recipient's identification card or benefit documentation;

■ Ask how to arrange for discontinuance;

■ Ask how to return unearned benefits;

■ If any dependent survivors, ask to make an appointment to re-evaluate eligibility.

Businesses

It is the duty of an Administrator to find property, value it, and protect its value. In most areas of ownership this is a simple directive. It becomes more difficult when the decedent owned all or a major share of a business. This is because the Administrator can be caught in a dilemma. Depending upon the type of business, if its obligations to customers are not met in a timely manner, the Estate can be left open to lawsuit or government fines. The solution would, of course, be to continue the business uninterrupted. But it is not that simple, because the Administrator may only continue the business if specifically instructed to do so, under the Will, in a written continuation document, or if all the interested parties give their written permission. In many cases the approval of the Court is also required. Without such consent the Administrator has no right to continue the business and will be held personally responsible for any losses resulting from their unauthorized actions.

If you are lucky the deceased owner has made specific, practical arrangements for the continuity of the business. This would include such documents as buy-sell agreements and shareholder's agreements, providing exact mechanisms for management succession, financing, stock sales, payout schemes, etc. The Court can challenge these agreements if not properly executed, so do not proceed until Court approval is received. After approval of the plan is received, share the details with bankers, lawyers, accountants, creditors, key employees, and major clients.

As you may gather, in most cases, unless a decision is made quickly, the business may fall apart and there may be nothing to continue. It is up to the Administrator to decide with the Beneficiaries and, if applicable, the co-owners, partners, and shareholders how to proceed to protect everyone's best interests. This discussion should at least result in a firm decision (get it in writing), as to whether the business should be liquidated - or - the business should be continued, so one or more of the Beneficiaries can take it over, or the company can be sold. We suggest consultation with the company's attorney or, if the company does not retain counsel, a corporate attorney. An attorney's advice may prove invaluable in this situation.

Whether or not the Administrator will continue the business, a physical inventory, appraisal of property, and an audit of the books must be done as soon as possible to determine the value of the business. The complexity of this procedure and the need for professional help depends upon the size and ownership of the business. Arrangements must also be made to protect the property from damage or theft. Because the business should have its own accounting and inventory system, we have not made records specifically for a business. However, the value should be included on the "Estate Summary" on page R-29.

Patents, Copyrights, Trademarks, Etc.

The rights to Patents, Copyrights, Trademarks, and items (inventions, books, songs, etc.) resulting from the mind of the decedent, which have not been registered, must be assigned to someone. Included in this area are residuals from work in the entertainment industry. As with all other property, the Administrator must take control of this property, value it, and protect it. Because of the complexity of the laws in this area and the many complications which can arise with these rights, we strongly suggest you consult an attorney specializing in patent, copyright, and trademark law to be sure the rights are protected. If royalties or residuals are being received, review all contracts, then write to the entity paying them, and:
- Advise the payor of the death;
  - Direct future payments be made to the Estate, Trust, or Beneficiary, as appropriate;
  - If there are uncashed checks, request information about returning them for reissue.
- Re-register the Patent or Trademark in the name of the Trust or Beneficiary by writing to the Patent and Trademark Office, 2121 Crystal Drive, Arlington, VA 22202. Call (703) 305-8341 for more information.
- Re-register a Copyright in the name of the Trust or Beneficiary by writing to the Registrar of Copyright, Library of Congress, 101 Independence Avenue, S.E., Washington, D.C. 20540-8610, call (202) 707-2905.

Income, Investment, and Financial Sources

Banks, Savings and Loans, and Credit Unions

It is the duty of the Administrator to locate all money deposited in Financial Institutions (Banks, Savings and Loans, and Credit Unions), determine the value of the accounts at the date of death, and gain control of the funds. While going through the decedent's papers, set aside all bank books, bank statements, etc. which indicate the presence of an account. Then decide what is to be done with the funds according to the way the account is titled. If funds are to be moved to another bank; to protect the funds, request either a cashier's check or wire transfer. For more information see Chapter 5, "Property Ownership," and Chapter 19, "Financial Institutions" and use the "Financial Institution Comparison Sheet" on page R-34. For accounting purposes, use the "Financial Accounts Basis and Transfer Record" on page R-4 and the "Cash Flow Record" on page R-28.

- **Locating the Funds:**
  - Look on the monthly statement, certificate, or passbook for the address of the institution.
  - If records were destroyed and accounts are unknown, send a blanket letter to all financial institutions in the area asking if the decedent has an account there. (If the decedent just moved, be sure to check with institutions around the previous address.) Wait for a monthly statement, Form-1099, or other evidence of an account to be mailed to the decedent. This is one reason mail forwarding is so important.
  - If you find evidence of an account but cannot locate the institution, call or visit the main branch of the Public Library. The librarians can check *Polks Bank Directory* and *Sheshunoff Bank Quarterly,* both of which have listings of chartered banks in the United States, including previous names.

- **Establish the date of death value of deposits.** It is not always possible to determine the exact value of the account on the date of death because of the institution's accounting system. This is not really a problem. Just be sure to make a reasonable division as accurately as you can, as close to the date of death as possible, and attribute the appropriate value and earnings to the decedent and to the Estate. The value can be established by:
  - Writing a letter to advise the institution of the death and requesting a balance for the date of death. (Many institutions will not comply with this request, so you may have to rely on the next two methods.);
  - Wait for the monthly statement to arrive for a checking, money market, or combined accounts, and note the value on, or closest to, the date of death. Be sure to keep this statement with the Estate papers;
  - Mail or bring the passbook or Certificate of Deposit to the bank and have the interest entered as soon as possible.

- **Gain Control of the Funds.** Carefully review the title on each account to determine what is necessary to gain control of the funds. You may have to wait in some states for the tax authorities to release the accounts (including joint accounts) before you can take action. Also, take care not to unnecessarily forfeit interest or incur penalties, by timing when you make withdrawals. If it is not necessary to make an immediate withdrawal, discuss the timing with the institution's representative. Although many institutions will waive penalties when the depositor dies, they may charge penalties if an instrument, such as a Certificate of Deposit is allowed to automatically renew after the death. Always call the institution first to be sure you bring the documents you need. Usually:
  - Accounts held jointly with right of survivorship, the survivor of the account can control the account automatically without any legal procedures or documents. However, the institution may require a certified copy of the Death Certificate to close the account. Now may be a good time to consolidate accounts and for a surviving sole owner to consider

adding a joint owner and/or a beneficiary to the accounts. For more information see Chapter 28, "Estate Planning for a Surviving Spouse."

- Accounts held in the <u>sole name of the deceased person with a designated Beneficiary</u> (in trust for), either:
    - ◆ The named Beneficiary can go to the institution with a certified copy of the Death Certificate and personal identification and have the funds released to him or her; or
    - ◆ The Administrator can go to the institution with a certified copy of the Death Certificate, his or her documents to act for the Estate and personal identification, and have the funds released. The Administrator can then give the funds to the Beneficiary(ies).

- Accounts held in the <u>sole name of the deceased with no individual Beneficiary designation</u> will be included in the Probate Estate. To release the funds, the Administrator must present a certified copy of the Death Certificate, his or her Letters of Administration or Letters Testamentary, or an Affidavit from the Court, and personal identification. The Administrator must also open an Estate Account, into which funds will be deposited. The Administrator may choose to open one account for each account closed, or to open one account and transfer all funds into it.

- Accounts held in a <u>Formal Trust</u>, the Trustee or Successor Trustee must present the Trust Agreement, a certified copy of the Death Certificate, and personal identification. See Chapter 3, "Trusts."

Tidbit: Where possible, do not notify the bank of the death or close the decedent's checking account until all checks expected to be sent payable to the decedent are received. Deposits can be made without an account owner's signature. This would save time and trouble because checks would not have to be returned to the issuer and be reissued in the name of the Estate, Trust, or Beneficiary. For the most part the bank employees will not ask why there is no signature and they do not want to know. Do not tell the bank about the death until you are ready to close the joint account. Usually six months after the death is an adequate period of time.

Investments - Stocks, Bonds, etc.

The duty of the Administrator is to find documents which represent investments, value the investments for the date of death, and gain control of the investments.

- **Locating and Identifying Investments:**
    - If you are not familiar with investment instruments read Chapter 13, "Basic Investment Information."
- **Establishing the Fair Market Value Basis of Investments:**
    - The updated basis of an investment instrument can be established by:
        - ◆ Finding the investment's quoted price for the date of death in the newspaper. If you cannot find it listed in the local newspaper's Business Section (these often have a limited listing of prices), check the third section of *The Wall Street Journal* (which has complete listings of investment prices). If you did not save the paper, you can find a copy at the Public Library. Be sure to keep the entire page where the investment is listed or photocopy enough of the page to show the publication date. The

Fair Market Value (FMV) of investments is the mean or median selling price (midpoint between the highest and the lowest selling price) of the instrument on the deceased person's date of death. The median price is found by using this formula: first, subtract the low price from the high price, then divide the difference by 2, then add this result to the low price. Example: 25 minus 23 equals 2, 2 divided by 2 equals 1, 23 plus 1 equals 24, which is the median price. If the investment is one that is only listed with the closing price, such as bonds, use that as the median price.

♦ An alternative method is to request that the broker write a letter to you listing the investments and their median prices for the decedent's date of death.

♦ The value of shares of a privately held company should be determined by the company's accountant.

♦ It is not necessary to determine the original basis for investments which were solely owned by the decedent.

♦ For more detailed information dealing specifically with determining the FMV of stocks, bonds, and funds, get a free copy of IRS Publication 550, *Investment Income and Expenses*.

■ **Gaining Control of the Investments:**

• When an account or investment is <u>jointly owned</u>, all that is necessary is to remove the name of the deceased joint owner and re-register the investment or brokerage account in the name of the surviving joint owner. All the surviving joint owner needs is a certified copy of the Death Certificate and personal identification.

• If the investments are registered in the name of a <u>Trust</u> or the account owner is the Trust, they can be left in the name of the Trust or Trust Account. The Trust document, plus a certified copy of the Death Certificate, and the Trustee's personal identification is all that is necessary to transfer the investments or account or change the name of the Trustee to the Successor Trustee.

• Investments or accounts which are <u>solely owned</u> are included in the Probate Estate. Therefore, it will be necessary to transfer investments first into the name of the Estate or to open an Estate Account (through which you can make trades and receive dividends), and then, when distribution is appropriate, transfer the investments to the Beneficiaries.

• Investments held in <u>Certificate form</u> can be transferred by writing to the **Transfer Agent** for each investment. The name of the transfer agent is usually listed on the certificate. If the transfer agent is not listed on the certificate, or unreachable at that address, contact the Investor Relations Department, listed in the company's current annual report, and ask for the transfer agent's name and address, see Chapter 13, "Basic Investment Information" <u>Stocks</u>, or ask a broker. Investments which are included in a formal Probate proceeding are transferred into the name of the Estate, and later into the name of the Beneficiary(ies). When the transfer agent responds, follow their directions. In the letter:

♦ Advise the transfer agent of the death;

♦ State to whom you wish to transfer the investment (Estate, Trust, Beneficiary, Surviving Joint Owner);

♦ Specify your authority to make the request (Administrator, Trustee, Surviving Joint Owner);

♦ Request information about how to transfer the investment;

♦ If applicable, inquire as to where uncashed checks made out to the decedent can be returned to be reissued;

- ◆ Request future dividend or interest payments be made payable to the Estate, Trust, or Beneficiary.
- • If you do not want to contact the Transfer Agent yourself, bring the certificates to a broker and request that they make the transfer. You will probably have to open an account with the broker. Call the broker to make an appointment before you go. Explain the situation and ask what documents and information you will need to bring to the meeting. Some brokers may charge a small fee for each investment transferred. For more information see Chapter 14, "Investment Brokers and Brokerage Accounts."
- • If the stocks are held in "Street Name," contact the brokerage where the account is held. Call the broker to make an appointment before you go. Explain the situation and ask what documents and information you will need to bring to the meeting.

In most cases the investments included in an Estate are not sold or traded, but are transferred to the Beneficiaries in a portion equal to the portion of the Estate they are to receive. In other words, if there are five Beneficiaries among whom the Estate is to be divided equally, each receives one-fifth of the amount of each investment in the Estate. For example, if there are 300 shares of IBM Common Stock, each of the five Beneficiaries would receive 60 shares. However, investments cannot be transferred to Beneficiaries with margin. Margin can be paid off with other funds or it might be necessary for the Administrator to sell some investments to clear the margin. It would be wise to discuss with the broker or investment advisor as well as the Beneficiaries which investments should be sold. The Administrator may have to make trades necessary to protect the value of the Estate. Particular attention should be paid to speculative investments which can result in vast losses. Discuss speculative investments immediately with your attorney, accountant, and broker. To record the various aspects of investment ownership and transfer, use the following records: "Investment Basis Record" on page R-5, "Investment Account Transfer Record" on page R-6, "Investment Sales Record" on page R-7, "Individual Investment Transfer Record" on page R-8, "Investment Income Record" on page R-9, and the "Investment Statement Reconciliation Slip" on page R-44.

When owners and former owners of stocks and other securities determine that they have unfairly suffered a loss due to an action, or inaction, on the part of a company, they file a **Class Action Lawsuit**. The action usually is taken on behalf of all owners or participants during a specific period of time. This group is then known as the **Class**. The records of the company named in the action are checked for members of the class, and each is mailed information about the action. At the appropriate time in the proceedings, class members are sent forms by the attorney representing the class, to be completed and returned if they wish to be included in any compensation awarded to the class. In addition to completing the forms, proof of ownership must be submitted during the time period stated in the lawsuit. Proof of ownership is either a "Confirmation" or "Statement" showing when the investment was acquired, when it was sold, or if it was still held after a particular date. If the Administrator receives papers for a class action lawsuit, it is his or her responsibility to file on behalf of the Estate or choose to be excluded from the class. This demonstrates the importance of retaining confirmations and statements. Since people who made a profit on an investment usually do not complain, we suggest you retain all confirmations and statements which would support a loss for about ten years after the purchase of the investment. These should be passed along to the Beneficiary(ies), receiving the investment, in case of future lawsuits.

Notes Held by the Decedent or Debts Owed to the Decedent

It is the duty of the Administrator to collect all debts owed to the Estate. However, the Administrator has the right to use his or her discretion in the disposition of debts due to the Estate. Each debt should be classified as hopeful, desperate, and doubtful (or a similar classification). The Administrator may be wise to discuss each note with the Beneficiaries, attorney, or Court, and obtain approval in advance before taking it upon him- or herself to forgive any indebtedness. For each debt owed to the Estate, the Administrator should contact the person or entity who owed money to the decedent, in writing, and:

- Advise the debtor of the death;
- If the debt was forgiven in the Will or Trust advise the debtor;
- If the debt is to be collected:
  - Work out a payment schedule;
  - Direct that payments be made to the Estate, Trust, or designated Beneficiary;
  - Execute a "Notice of Assignment" form to formally place title of the "Promissory Note" into the name of the Estate, the Trust, or a specific Beneficiary. Forms are available at stationary stores or from a title company;
- If loans are not paid appropriately, advise the Court;
- If the debtor files bankruptcy, decide whether or not to pursue the debt and take action accordingly.
- Use the "Debts Owed to the Estate Payment Receipt Record" on page R-13.

Tidbit: Under the Federal Debt Collection Practices Act, debt collectors:
- May only contact the person owing the debt [includes spouse, parent (if a minor), guardian, executor, or administrator], his or her attorney or consumer reporting agency.
- May leave a message on the answering machine if:
  - the to-the-caller message states that it is the debtor's phone; and
  - the message avoids unnecessary third-party disclosure.
- May not discuss the situation with the debtor's employer, neighbors, minor child, or friend who happens to answer the phone; unless that party informs the debt collector that although they are not the debtor they are familiar with the debt and are willing to discuss it or pay it.
- May call a third party to locate the debtor.
- May contact a debtor in the military through his or her military commander.
- When a consumer debtor writes to you asking that you stop contacting him or her, you must cease communications and decide whether to institute a lawsuit or forgive the debt.

Precious Metals and Numismatic Coins

- Decide if you want to sell the coins or other precious metals;
- Find a dealer who trades in them. Look for purchase documents; the company from which the coins were originally purchased will probably be the best company to deal with;
- Request a price list from at least three dealers, banks, or brokers.

71

Life Insurance Policies

Life Insurance is the quickest way for families to get money to pay funeral and living expenses. Insurance companies usually pay claims promptly. However, states that impose death taxes may prevent the insurance company from paying the death benefit if it is above a set dollar amount, until the tax officials approve. If an insurance company delays payment for any other reason, write to the insurance commissioner of both your state and of the one where the company is headquartered. Send copies of the complaint to the company. They will usually pay the money without further delay. Each state has its own Department of Insurance to regulate insurance companies operating in the state, and to deal with consumer complaints and provide general information. To encourage quick payment, some states require the company to pay interest on the policy's surrender value from the date of death or the date the company is notified of the death until benefits are paid. Be aware that the surrender value of a policy may be reduced by the amount of any loans the owner has borrowed from the cash, or surrender value, of the insurance policy. Insurance policies have always provided low interest loans and recently a growing number of life insurance companies are allowing terminally ill policyholders to collect part of their death benefits while they are still alive through a so-called "Accelerated Benefit." See Chapter 18, "Insurance and Insurance Agents."

If the life insurance policy named an individual as the Beneficiary, that Beneficiary can request payment of the policy's death benefit to him- or herself, or have the Administrator request the benefits. If the insurance policy named the Estate as the Beneficiary, the named Beneficiary predeceased the insured, or no Beneficiary was named, the benefits must be claimed by the Administrator. Begin by sending a letter to the insurance carrier.

- Include the following information and requests in the letter, as appropriate:
  - Advise the company of the death of the insured;
  - Request a claim form and any information necessary to claim the death benefit of the policy.
  - Be sure to include your status;
  - If appropriate, request a "Change of Beneficiary" form for survivors who have a life insurance policy with the same company that names the decedent as the beneficiary.
  - Request a refund of any unused prepaid premiums.
- The insurance company will send the appropriate forms and request appropriate documentation.
  - Complete the forms and return them along with the requested documentation;
  - Request a Form 712, which may be necessary for tax purposes;
- Use the "Life Insurance Proceeds and Premium Refund Income Record" on page R-10.

Tidbit: If you have reason to believe the decedent was insured but you cannot find a policy write to: The American Council of Life Insurance, Policy Search Division, 1001 Pennsylvania Avenue, N.W., Washington, D.C. 20004-2599. Request a "Lost Policy Questionnaire" and include a self-addressed, stamped envelope. When you receive the form, fill it out and return it to the Council. They will circulate it among 100 big insurers. The Council also provides a consumer hotline (800) 942-4242 and will answer questions about insurance, refer complaints to appropriate resources and, upon request, send a free copy of its brochures "A Consumer's Guide to Life Insurance" and "What You Need to Know About Accelerated Benefits."

Miscellaneous

U.S. Immigration and Naturalization Service

Mail "Green Cards" along with a certified copy of the Death Certificate to the U.S. Immigration and Naturalization Service, Records Department, 425 I Street, N.W., Room 1522, Washington, D.C. 20536. Mailing it to the INS insures that it will not end up in the wrong hands.

Supervisor of Elections

Notify the nearest office of the Supervisor of Elections of the death of the Voter, either in writing or in person. They will require the surrender of the Voter's Registration Card and receipt of a certified copy of the Death Certificate. Usually they will copy the Death Certificate and return the certified copy.

Spousal and/or Child Support

If the decedent was paying spousal or child support, notify the recipients and the Court who made the determination for support, as well as the Probate Court, and request a new determination.

If the decedent was receiving spousal or child support, notify the payor and the Court who made the determination for support, as well as the Probate Court, and request a new determination. If the person responsible for paying child support is delinquent and local authorities are unsuccessful, contact the Office of Child Support Enforcement, Department of Health and Human Services, Washington, D.C. 20447 or call (202) 401-9373 or the Child Support Hotline (800) 622-5437.

Club, Church or Synagogue Memberships

- Notify the club or organization of the death and cancel membership;
- Request refund of dues, if appropriate;
- Check for any unpaid promises of donations and handle according to the validity of claim;
- Arrange for appropriate ceremony at funeral, memorial service, or burial.

School

- If the decedent was a student, notify the institution of the death, and:

- Request a refund of some, or all, of the tuition, if applicable;
- Request the school send the personal possessions in the decedent's locker and/or dormitory room to the appropriate person, or arrange a time to collect them;
- If the decedent was receiving a student loan, contact the source of the loan.
  - If a survivor is a student, who is receiving or seeking a student loan, advise the loan source of changes in the family income due to the death.

Service Providers

As a courtesy to the people or agencies who routinely provide some service to the decedent, call or write to them and advise them of the death. Be sure to check the decedent's calendar for any appointments and cancel them. Some people you may want to include are:

- Doctors not in attendance: dentist, ophthalmologist, optometrist, dermatologist, etc.
- Personal care providers: beautician, massagist, manicurist, aide, nurse, physical therapist, etc.
- Home care providers: cleaning service, maid, lawn service, exterminator, etc. If service for the home or property is still desired, arrange for it. For information about employing domestic help, see Chapter 12, "Transfer and Sale of Real Estate."

Court or Trial Related Responsibilities of the Decedent

- If the decedent was scheduled to appear in Court as a Juror, Witness, Complainant, Respondent, or Defendant; notify the appropriate Court of the death, as soon as possible, as well as the attorney representing the decedent, if applicable.
- If the decedent was a Parolee or Probationer; notify the appropriate Parole or Probation Officer of the death.

Debts Owed by the Estate

Publish Notice to Creditors

A Will usually contains a clause directing the Administrator to pay all the decedent's just debts. To be sure this directive is carried out, when an Estate is formally probated, the Administrator or attorney for the Estate is required to publish a "Notice to Creditors." The Court will also usually require this notice for an Intestate Estate. It is a good idea for <u>all</u> Estates, whether or not they are subject to Probate, to publish this notice. Be sure to obtain and keep proof of publication from the newspaper office. Most papers send a certified and notarized copy to the attorney or

Administrator. When the notices are printed keep a section of the paper large enough to include the notice and the date of publication. The "Notice to Creditors" should be to the attention of all creditors of the decedent and include:

- Notification of the death;
- A directive to file their claims for payment against the Estate, Trust, or Beneficiary;
- Provide creditors with the name and address of the Administrator, attorney, institution, or person assuming responsibility for the debts of the decedent; and
- Advise the creditor that all claims not filed by a specified date will be barred.
- Use the "Debts Owed By the Estate Payment Expense Record" on page R-25.

Each state has its own requirements as to the number of times the notice must be published, what publications it should be placed in, the amount of time the creditors are given from the date of publication to file their claims, and how long the Administrator must wait after publication before distribution of the Estate's assets may be made. If a creditor does not file the claim within the required period, the Administrator is safe in making distribution. A creditor may file a claim after the stipulated period but the Administrator is relieved of liability. The creditor will have to follow the assets into the hands of the Beneficiaries by filing a lawsuit in either a Law or Equity Court.

As claims are filed, it is the duty of the Administrator to carefully examine them to determine their validity and correctness and to pay all valid claims from the assets of the Estate. If the validity or correctness of a claim cannot be determined, it should be presented to the Court for decision. If the Administrator refuses to pay a valid claim, the creditor may file a lawsuit against him or her. If the assets of the Estate are not sufficient to pay all claims, a certain priority must be followed as to which claims are paid and the extent of payment to each. The formula for payment varies according to the laws of the individual state.

Debit, Credit, and ATM Cards

Review the literature associated with each card. Then write to each issuing company:
- Advise the company of the death of the cardholder;
- Destroy cards bearing the deceased person's name;
- Provide the company with the name, address, and phone number of the person assuming responsibility for paying the bills, or who is to receive the debit balance;
- Compare receipts to billing statements to be sure all charges are accurate;
  - Write an objection to any charge you determine to be in error;
  - Arrange to pay the valid balance, if funds are available;
- If the card is enrolled in a protection plan, which provides for payment of the balance in the event of death, request forms for coverage payment;
- If the card provided a life insurance policy, follow company instructions to claim benefits;
- If applicable, ask to retain cards in the name of other family members or to transfer the account to the surviving spouse's name;
- If records were destroyed by fire or other disaster, wait for bills to arrive or contact one of the major credit reporting bureaus. See Chapter 27, "Living On a Reduced Income."
- Use the "Debts Owed By the Estate Payment Expense Record" on page R-25.

Doctor, Hospital, Medical Bills, and Health Insurance Policies

Whether or not there are medical bills outstanding, the Administrator should notify the Health Insurance Company of the death. This prevents anyone from making false claims on the decedent's policy. Consider the following items when you write to the company:

- Notify the insurance company of the death;
- If there are medical bills which have not been submitted for payment, request claim forms. (Often the claim forms for a deceased person are different from those used by a live claimant.);
- If payment for previously submitted medical bills is still pending, request payment of claims be made to the Estate, Trust, or Beneficiary;
- If you receive insurance payment checks made out to the decedent, inquire about returning the checks, for reissuance to the Estate, Trust, or Beneficiary;
- Request refund of pre-paid insurance premiums;
- Ask for coverage to continue for a surviving spouse and dependent children, if applicable.

Paying Medical Bills

It is the duty of the Administrator to pay all the just debts of the deceased person, to the extent there are funds available in the Estate. This includes bills for medical care received before death. Check all insurance policies for the type and extent of the coverage the decedent carried. Read all directions about claim procedures and be sure to fill out claim forms properly. This will avoid delay in benefit payments or denial of a claim.

- Review all bills for accuracy. Check hospital and outpatient clinic bills for:
  - Repeat billings for identical services performed on the same day;
  - Charges for an entire day's stay when the patient was discharged in the morning;
  - Charges for drugs, tests, supplies, services, or procedures that were never received;
  - Charges for drugs, tests, supplies, services, or procedures that were performed but were not ordered by the patient's physician;
  - If the bill has charges that you do not understand or agree with, call the doctor or hospital's billing office for an explanation.
- Establish the order of filing for medical benefits according to who is the primary payor and supplemental payor. Then:
  - Follow the companies rules for filing;
  - Be sure forms are completed properly;
  - Keep a copy of the claim and bills;
  - If the insurance company has not communicated in 30 days, send a copy of the claim and the bill, with a letter explaining the problem;
  - If the insurance company denies a claim, insist on getting a written explanation of the refusal. Review the descriptive booklet carefully and hold the company to promises made in it;
  - If you consider the explanation for the refusal of benefits confusing or unreasonable, appeal the decision. Companies sometimes deny a claim on a technicality, saying the booklet information is not complete or accurate. Unless the technicality is clearly stated in the booklet, the denial may not be legitimate. Items and conditions not covered by your policy must be clearly written and prominently displayed in your policy.

- If the benefits are denied on the appeal:
  - Call the agent who sold the policy and see if they will intervene on your behalf;
  - Put your complaint in writing and send it to the company along with copies of relevant claim forms and bills;
  - Request that the company respond to your inquiry within 10 working days;
  - Keep a date and time record of phone calls you make to the company.
- If you simply cannot get satisfaction from the company:
  - Contact your State's Department of Insurance Regulation.
  - If all else fails, see an attorney who will represent you, or go to small claims court, depending upon the amount of the claim. If the wording of the contract can be read two ways, Courts usually rule in favor of the policyholder.
- If the doctors or other medical providers to which money is owed are not aware of the death be sure to notify them. This often makes them more patient and cooperative with their billing.
  - Assure them that you will be responsible for getting their bills paid;
  - Request their cooperation by issuing appropriate bills or submitting insurance claims as required by the insurer. (Medicaid claim forms must be filed by the doctor. Doctors also must submit Medicare claim forms if you request them to do so.);
  - As soon as insurance has paid its portion, be sure to pay any balance on a bill to the provider.
- Use the "Medical Bills Payment Record" on page R-20, to track correspondence, payments, submission of forms, and, receipt of determinations and benefits.
- See Chapter 24, "Social Security, Medicare, and Medicaid" and Chapter 26, "Providing Care For A Dependent Adult Survivor," for more information.

Medicaid . . . Repayment of Benefits

If the decedent was a Medicaid beneficiary, the Estate may be held responsible for repayment of some, or all, of the benefits received under the program. Some states have instituted a "Benefit Recovery Program." Often, this is implemented by the state placing a lien on the decedent's home, which effectively prevents the Beneficiaries from selling the home without paying the lien. The state can also make claims against property held in a living trust, joint account, insurance policy, etc. **Repayment is not required until after the death of the surviving spouse.** The rules are very complicated and vary from state to state.

Bankrupt Estates

If the property in the Estate is not sufficient to pay the debts of the Estate, the Estate is bankrupt. Advise the Court of the situation. The federal government and each state has a specific formula for the order in which debts are to be paid in bankruptcy. The Administrator can elect either the state or federal exemption, whichever is more advantageous (leaving the most property to the bankrupt). The debts of the Estate are payable only to the extent that there are funds in the

Estate to pay them. The survivors are not responsible for debts beyond the value of the Estate, unless another person's name is on the lien. You should have an attorney to handle this situation. If you cannot afford an attorney, contact the local Legal Aid Society (usually called Legal Aid, Legal Assistance Foundation, or Legal Services), or the Area Agency on Aging.

Airlines

Ticket Refunds — Most airlines will give a refund, even for a nonrefundable ticket, if the reason for cancellation is due to illness, a subpoena, jury duty, or the death of a close relative. But you may need documentation.

Frequent Flyer Plans — In some cases, when a person dies, the earned miles become worthless. However, most airlines have ways to transfer the miles, which qualify passengers for free tickets or first class upgrades from the decedent's account to a Beneficiary. Contact the airline and inquire.

Emergency or Bereavement Travel Discount — Many airlines will discount the cost of tickets for travel to attend funeral or burial services, or for a personal emergency. Even if you did not mention it when you booked the flight, call the airline, explain the reason for travel and ask if you may be eligible for a refund. If you are, follow their directions for claiming the refund. See Chapter 1, "When A Person Dies," <u>Airline Bereavement Discounts</u>.

Charities

Before giving property designated by the decedent to be donated to a charity, it would be wise to check out the charity, especially if you are not familiar with the organization's name or reputation. If you can show the Court that the designated organization is not a legitimate charity or that it does not use its finances wisely, you may be permitted to donate the property to a similar but more reputable or more effective organization. Experts advise that the average charity spends 75 cents of every dollar it gets on its programs. You can get a financial statement from the charity upon request, review charity rating publications at your local library, or write to either or both of two charity watchdog agencies listed below. Both print detailed individual reports on each charity. These reports state how long each group has been in existence, describes its programs, explains how it raises funds, and provides a breakdown of how the money is spent; e.g. the charity's fund-raising, management, and program costs.

- The National Charities Information Bureau (NCIB) evaluates 300 charities. To receive up to three free detailed reports on individual charities and/or its free booklet *Wise Giving Guide*, send your request plus a self-addressed, stamped envelope to NCIB, 19 Union Square West, New York, NY 10003-3395. Call (212) 929-6300; or

- The Philanthropic Advisory Service, a division of the Council of Better Business Bureaus, offers a booklet entitled *Give But Give Wisely*, which includes tips on how to spot a bogus charity and detailed comparisons of some of the nation's best known philanthropic groups. To order, send a self-addressed, stamped envelope and $2 to the Council of Better Business Bureaus, Philanthropic Advisory Service, 4200 Wilson Blvd., Suite 800, Arlington, VA 22203. For answers to specific questions about any of the hundreds of charities, even those not listed in the booklet, call (703) 276-0100.

Unless the decedent was specific in stating what property is to be donated to the charity, the tax laws regarding charitable gifts should be reviewed before the donation is made. Then it is up to the Administrator to:

- Decide whether to give a particular piece of property, or to sell the property and donate the cash proceeds;
- Determine whether the charity will use the property for its tax-exempt purpose or sell it;
- Determine if it is a foreign or domestic organization;
- The Internal Revenue Service will tell you if the charity is a not-for-profit organization and if it is a tax-exempt organization. Call (800) 829-1040;
- Based on the above information, determine the value of the gift and to what extent it is tax deductible.
- Use the "Charitable Contributions Record" on page R-26.

Taxes

Filing Tax Forms and Paying Taxes Due

The type of tax returns that must be filed when a person dies is determined by the relationship of the surviving Beneficiaries to the decedent, the total value of the Estate, the way property was titled, whether or not the Estate is probated, and the state where the decedent resided. We are all aware of the complexity of the federal tax codes and, of course, the yearly changes made to them. The same is true for state tax laws. Therefore, we would not even attempt to explain the regulations. A surviving spouse, the Administrator, or whoever takes possession of the Estate property, is responsible for filing the appropriate tax forms. To find out what is necessary, call the Internal Revenue Service and the state's taxing authority and explain the situation, or consult an accountant, or your attorney to determine your tax responsibilities. See Chapter 16, "Tax Preparation and Tax Preparers." The list of "life events" that professionals say may necessitate help at tax time includes retirement, divorce or death of a spouse, a large inheritance, the sale of a home, business ownership, and moving from one state to another. Be sure to make yourself aware of the date when each return is due and mark them on a calendar. We have provided a "Quick Reference Calendar" on page R-31 and the "_____Taxes: Filing and Payment

Record" on page R-27. Here, we will only point out that there are three distinct categories of taxes which must be addressed:

- <u>Federal, State, County, and City Annual Income Tax Returns</u> must be filed just as they would have been by the decedent, if he or she had lived. The Internal Revenue Service suggests you locate copies of the last three years' tax returns and review them carefully.
  - If the decedent was a taxpayer, the Administrator or the next of kin must file the Individual's Income Tax Return for the year of death, and the previous year, if the decedent had not filed it before death. Be sure to make any estimated tax payment that may be required. (If the decedent recently moved from one state to another, you may have to file a return in each state.) Returns are filed according to the decedent's usual tax period.
  - Even if the decedent did not earn enough to require filing of a tax return, you should file a return to claim a refund if taxes were paid. Additional forms may be required to claim a refund.
  - A surviving spouse may file a joint return for the year of death and may be entitled to similar tax savings for following years.
  - If the decedent was a dependent, he or she can be claimed as a dependent for the entire year in which death occurred, even if he or she only lived a few moments during that year. If the deceased person was entitled to extra exemptions during life, they are still applicable after death.
  - In addition to, or instead of, an income tax, some states, counties, and cities impose taxes on particular property. These may include:
    - **Tangible Personal Property Tax** which may be imposed on property held for the production of income, such as furniture and furnishings in an office or rental apartment.
    - **Intangible Property Tax** which may be imposed on stocks, bonds, etc. See Chapter 5, "Property Ownership" and Chapter 6, "Property Definitions."
    - **Real Estate Property Taxes** which may be imposed on all real estate property. Check with the county tax appraisers office to be sure all taxes are paid up to date. Plus, in states which offer homestead exemptions, adjustments may have to be made to deductions.

- <u>Federal and State Estate or Fiduciary Income Tax Return</u> must be filed if a Probate Estate was established or for a Trust.
  - An Estate of a deceased person is a taxable entity separate from the decedent. An Estate is established the day a person dies and, generally, continues to exist until the final distribution of the assets of the Estate are made to the Beneficiaries. The income earned by the property in the Estate during the period of administration or settlement must be accounted for and reported by the Administrator or any person in possession of the property in a decedent's Estate.
  - A Trust is also a separate and distinct entity. The Trustee is responsible for filing a return for any income earned by Trust assets.
  - It is necessary to get an **Employer Identification Number** (EIN) if a Fiduciary Tax Return must be filed. A Federal EIN will be assigned upon application to the Internal Revenue Service on IRS Form-SS4. A separate EIN may be required by the state. Call, write, or visit and ask for the appropriate form. Before applying, you should consider the tax year you want to use. The tax year starts with the first day of the month the person

died, and runs for no more than twelve months. One important consideration is that banks, brokers, etc. only issue income reporting forms in January.

For a death occurring between:		Tax Year	Alternate Tax Year
January	1 through 31	1-1 to 12-31	none
February	1 through 29	2-1 to 1-31	2-1 to 12-31
March	1 through 31	3-1 to 2-29	3-1 to 12-31
April	1 through 30	4-1 to 3-31	4-1 to 12-31, etc.

- <u>Federal and State Inheritance or Death Tax Return</u> must be filed if the Estate was large enough to be subject to the tax.
  - This tax is based on the total value of all the property in the Estate, regardless of how it was titled. If the gross (total assets without any liabilities subtracted) Estate qualifies as taxable, a return must be filed even if after deductions, the value is below the taxable amount. It is the responsibility of the Administrator to file this tax return, if it is necessary.
  - The Federal Estate Taxes valuation is the fair market value on the date of death or the "optional valuation date" of six months after death. See Chapter 9, "Valuing Property," for a summary of establishing the basis (value) of property. States may have other valuation requirements. If the Estate is subject to this tax, the help of a professional is strongly suggested.
  - Since the Federal Tax on Estates is actually the "Unified Estate and Gift Tax," it is necessary for you to include amounts on Gift Tax returns filed by the decedent throughout his or her life. Currently this tax is assessed on Estates valued at $600,000 or more. This amount includes any gifts in excess of the current $10,000 limit per person, per year. When reviewing the Estate papers, look for any gifts or transfers of cash or property with a value of more than $10,000. At present there is no limit on the amount of property gifted to a <u>U.S. citizen</u> spouse. For more information see Pub-448 "Federal Estate and Gift Taxes." Some states also include gifts in their inheritance tax. State property value exemptions also vary.
  - Obtain a receipt for Federal Estate Taxes paid.

Tidbit: Look for evidence of inheritances received by the decedent within ten years prior to the death. If the property was included in the previous owner's estate tax return, the deceased beneficiary's Estate may be entitled to a tax credit.

Tidbit: IRS Publications and Forms are available by calling (800) 829-3676.
IRS Helpline provides answers to specific questions; call (800) TAX-1040.
IRS tax help, filing instructions, and downloadable forms are available online at *http://www.irs.ustreas.gov*

Consent to Transfer Form (Release from Inheritance Tax Lien)

In order to sell and, in some cases, to transfer property, especially real estate, you may be required to prove that no "Inheritance or Estate Taxes" are due on the property. This is usually done by showing a document issued by the state's revenue department, called a "Nontaxable Certificate and Receipt for Estate Tax," "Consent to Transfer," or similar name. States which freeze assets until the tax representative can appraise the Estate, may issue this document automatically if no taxes are due, or, a receipt will be issued when inheritance taxes have been paid. However, you should ask the Clerk of the Probate Court, or state's revenue department if this is, or is not, automatic. If an attorney has been hired to handle the Probate of the Estate, he or she will submit the form. In states where no taxing authority representative performs an appraisal, you should request an appropriate form from the local state's revenue department. In some states this is called a "Preliminary Notice and Report." It is a form on which you list all the assets (property owned) and all the liabilities (debts owed) of the decedent, valued on the date of death. This must usually be submitted within a couple of months of the death to avoid penalty.

Even when all property was jointly owned and the surviving spouse is able to transfer the property without this document, it would still be necessary to apply for it. In the future, when the surviving spouse or Beneficiaries want to sell real property, it will be necessary to present this certificate, showing there are no taxes due on the Estate, in order to clear the title.

Missing or Abandoned Property

All states require that after a period of time, from 3 to 10 years, abandoned property is **Escheated** (turned over to the State Treasurer or Comptroller), and the money, by law, is held in perpetuity by the state, unless or until it is claimed. Tangible property may be auctioned a few years after being turned over to the state, and a record of the proceeds kept, so the money can be claimed. In an effort to find the owner or Beneficiary(ies) of the property, the Office of Unclaimed Property (or similar designation) often publishes a list of the names of the owners of the property in local newspapers. If you have reason to believe the state may be holding property; write and ask. Be prepared to show proof that you are entitled to receive the property. The types of property which are subject to these laws are:

dormant bank accounts	uncashed checks
dormant brokerage accounts	unused gift certificates
abandoned mortgage escrow accounts	unclaimed insurance benefits
unclaimed utility deposits	unclaimed oil royalties
unclaimed rent deposits	abandoned safe-deposit box's contents
unclaimed inheritances	unclaimed securities

Unclaimed federal funds are left on deposit with the issuing agency. For example, uncashed, or undeliverable, Social Security checks are returned to the Social Security Administration. Uncashed, or undeliverable, Internal Revenue Service checks are returned to the IRS office. For unclaimed tax refunds, contact the appropriate revenue agency.

Found Money, Inc., maintains a database of 17,000,000 individuals who are entitled to money, it can be searched for free and if money is available a $10 fee will be charged to obtain details for collecting the funds, go online to *www.foundmoney.com*

BASIC CONTRACT DEFINITION

While settling the Estate, the Administrator will be signing contracts and bound by the terms of those contracts. A Will is a contract and when the Administrator signs the "Oath of Acceptance of Duties" he or she is signing a contract agreeing to abide by the terms of the Will. A Trust is a contract and by assuming the role of the Trustee, the Trustee is bound by the terms of the Trust Agreement. If real estate property is to be sold, the Administrator will be required to sign a number of contracts. Therefore, we believe it is important for you to have a basic understanding of the commitment that is made when a contract is signed. Of course, this is not intended to substitute for the advice of an attorney.

Each individual transaction and situation must be dealt with individually, according to the laws of the state where the contract is executed. Laws vary from state to state, and change with the times. It should be clearly understood that the terms of a contract can ultimately be enforced by the Courts. If one participant, known as a **Party**, breaks a promise made in the contract, he or she is said to have caused a **Breach** of the contract. If the breach cannot be settled between the contracting parties, the offended party can bring the matter to Court; where the Judge can order the party who breached the contract to pay the money damages caused by the breach or order **Performance**, which means he or she must do whatever he or she promised to do in the first place. Although a contract can be either a written or verbal agreement, it is easy to understand that a written contract would be more easily enforced. It is also reasonable to conclude that the more detailed the agreement included in the contract, the better. Therefore, it is important for the terms of a contract to be clear, precise, and without ambiguity, so the parties and, if necessary, a Judge, can tell the rights and duties of each party or who was supposed to do what and when. If no time limitation is designated, most Courts will determine what they consider, sometimes through expert testimony, a reasonable time. In any dispute, the Court will try to determine what the parties intended.

Every contract, no matter what the parties are contracting about, has four basic parts:

1. **An offer and an acceptance**: What did one person give up and one other receive?
2. **Consideration** (which may or may not involve an exchange of money) means:
   - Doing something, the party doesn't have to do;
   - Not doing something the party has a right to do; or
   - An exchange of promises.
3. **It is made between parties capable of contracting**, which means the parties must be consenting adults who have the legal capacity to enter into a valid agreement. The parties cannot be minors, or persons not mentally competent, whether the disability is alcohol or drug induced, or psychological; and
4. **Its subject matter or purpose is not illegal.**

Tidbit: Ambiguity and possible future problems can result when lines and spaces are left blank. A fill-in space on a contract, can be filled with an N/A for not applicable. A diagonal line can be drawn through any space between clauses, which is larger than the usual spaces between the paragraphs on the contract.

Tidbit: When signing a contract as the Administrator of a Will, Trustee of a Trust, Attorney-In-Fact, etc.; always be sure to write your title alongside, or beneath, your signature.

VALUING PROPERTY

Basis

Basis is the value upon which the Internal Revenue Service and state revenue authorities will base the taxes due, both for Income and Inheritance or Death Taxes. Here is a very simplified overview of the federal regulations.

- The **Original Basis** of property which is bought, is the purchase price paid for the item, including fees, postage, etc. associated with acquiring the property, plus the cost of any capital improvements.

- The **Transfer Basis** of property which was previously transferred to or from the decedent, depends upon the nature of the transfer, the type of property transferred, and the relationship of the giver and receiver of the property to each other. For specific information read IRS Publication 551 *Basis of Assets*.

- **Fair Market Value** is defined by the IRS as the price at which property would change hands between a willing buyer and willing seller.

- When a person dies, the basis of the decedent's share of property is **Stepped-up**, or adjusted upward from the decedent's **Original Cost** (plus capital improvements) to match the property's **Fair Market** value at the date of his or her death. The result of a stepped-up basis is that all capital gains liabilities disappear and death becomes the ultimate tax shelter. Often, a surviving spouse who is a joint tenant only gets a stepped-up basis for one-half the value of the property, the half owned by the deceased owner. The half owned all along by the surviving joint tenant retains its original basis. The basis of the surviving spouse's portion of shared property may be stepped-up, depending upon how the property is transferred, how it is titled, and the laws regarding community property. Basis can also be **Stepped-Down**, if the fair market value is less than the cost. The **Basis of Inherited Property** can also be determined using the fair market value on the alternate or optional date (six months after the date of death), or the value under the special use valuation method for real property used in farming or other closely-held businesses. Both these methods must be elected by the Administrator of the Estate. Professional tax advice should be obtained if these elections apply.

- The **Beneficiary's Basis** of any property received from the Estate in a distribution is the Estate's Basis of Inherited Property adjusted for any gain or loss recognized by the IRS to the Estate on the distribution. If no election was made, the Beneficiary's basis is the same as the Estate's basis of inherited property.

Note: State tax rules regarding the stepped-up basis of inherited property vary considerably. To be sure you value property properly, consult with an accountant or tax attorney or research both the federal and state tax rules yourself.

APPRAISALS

This Chapter deals with valuing tangible property. Information for valuing intangible property can be found in Chapter 7, "Property Transfer Breakdown" and Chapter 13, "Basic Investment Information."

Formal Appraisals

An **Appraisal** is done to determine the true worth of property. There are three basic ways for the Administrator to set the value of Estate property: have a professional appraiser conduct a formal appraisal; have an appraiser walk through and give an informal ballpark figure on designated items; or, the Administrator can assign an estimated value. It is the responsibility of the Administrator to decide which valuation is appropriate for each item of Estate property.

A formal appraisal need only be done on items of value (a good benchmark is $5,000 or more) and only when necessary for legal or insurance purposes. We've listed the most common reasons.

- Legal purposes for an appraisal include:
  - If there is any question as to the Federal Estate Tax liability of an Estate, (based on the current exclusion allowance), it would help to have an appraisal if there is an audit;
  - If cost basis is needed to determine profit or loss for Estate (Administrator) Income Tax purposes;
  - If an updated cost basis is needed on property to be retained by Beneficiaries to enable them to figure profit or loss on future tax returns when property is sold or donated to a non-profit organization;
  - If the property is in a state which imposes death taxes, an official appraisal is done as part of the death tax return;
  - If needed to determine the value of gifts to non-profit institutions for tax purposes;
  - If selling real estate property;
  - If specifically required by state law or the Court.

- If indicated, to avoid or defend a lawsuit brought by the Beneficiaries against the Administrator for being delinquent in the duty to competently value property which was sold;
- If required to authenticate a piece or collection of art, antiques, coins, jewelry, stamps, etc. Note: Authentication must be made by an appraiser who ranks as an expert in the particular field of the item(s);

- Insurance purposes for an appraisal include:
  - If required to evaluate property to obtain adequate replacement coverage or to protect the Estate against loss until property is distributed or sold;
  - If required to evaluate property to obtain adequate replacement coverage while items are being moved or shipped.
  - If needed to prove the value of the particular item of property if a loss occurs, if the last appraisal is out-of-date.

When a formal appraisal is done, the appraiser gives you the findings in a written, documented analysis, called an **Appraisal Report**. In order to win acceptance by the IRS, an Appraisal Report must include the following information:

- Details of acquisition, including the date, cost, cost basis, and the manner in which it was acquired;
- A detailed description of the property:
  - For an artwork, antique or collectible: background of the item, including **Provenance** (proof of authenticity); the name of the artist or artisan who created the work, its size, the medium of the work (oil, etching, marble, bronze, and so on) the artist's signature or identifying symbol; and the item's citation in catalogs, scholarly works, and so on;
  - For real estate: details of the investigation of the structure, condition, number and type of rooms, interior equipment, energy efficiency, and neighborhood;
- The date the property was completed and the character of the ownership interest;
- The written description must be supported by a photograph that is both big enough and clear enough to adequately show the property. Transparencies are often used for artworks, since they can be projected to any size;
- A statement by the appraiser that spells out in detail the procedures used to estimate the value, including the condition of the particular market at the time of the appraisal and specific references to recent sales of similar property, or analysis of comparable sale estimations;
- A clear statement of the kind of value being determined, such as: fair market, liquidation, or replacement/reproduction, etc. (For real estate the value must be the home's fair market value or "the most probable sales price.");
- The signature of the appraiser, who is responsible for its validity and objectivity;
- A statement of the professional qualifications of the appraiser.

The Appraisal Report should be understandable, descriptive, and objective. Read the report to be sure all of the above appropriate information is included. If you think the value is incorrect, don't hesitate to request a revised appraisal by the same appraiser based on more current information. Then, if you still do not agree with the appraisal, get a second opinion from another appraiser. For Estate Tax purposes the appraisal should strike a balance between the low wholesale and high retail values. Remember, when dealing with the IRS or insurance companies, nothing can beat a properly documented formal appraisal. Although the IRS training manual states

"The art of appraising and authenticating is not an exact science."; the IRS will not hesitate to challenge or reject appraisals with a gross misevaluation, or one that was not done by a qualified appraiser, and impose a penalty if the appraisal results in tax underpayment.

For more information, write to the American Society of Appraisers, P.O. Box 17265, Washington, D.C. 20041, and request any of these free publications (include a self-addressed, stamped envelope): "Information on the Appraisal Profession"; "About the American-Society of Appraisers"; "Directory of Certified Professional Personal Property Appraisers"; "ASA Principles of Appraisal Practice/Code of Ethics"; "Career Opportunities in Appraising"; "Viewpoint on the Appraisal of Personal Property" (for fine arts/antiques, jewelry, etc., collector). You may also request a current price for the *Up-to-date Professional Appraisal Services Directory.*

Master Senior Appraiser (MSA), the highest designation, Master Farm and Land Appraiser (MFLA), and Master Residential Appraiser (MRA), are designations given to members of the Accredited Review Appraisers Council (ARAC). The members have completed specific educational requirements and are experts in appraising the value of a home and property. They also agree to abide by the high code of ethics and high standards of practice of this Association. You can write to the ARAC at 303 W. Cypress Street, P.O. Box 12528, San Antonio, TX 78212, or call the ARAC at (210) 225-2897 or (800) 486-3676, and ask for a current copy of its *Membership Directory*, which is a State-by-State listing of members who are currently certified appraisers and auctioneers of real estate. You can write to the same address if you have a complaint about an appraiser. (If you know the details of recent neighboring home sales, be sure to tell the appraiser. The best appraisers welcome information on the prices of recent nearby home sales. You can be sure the appraiser will confirm the details you supply, so be sure of the accuracy.)

Informal Appraisals

If a formal appraisal is not required, you may still want to hire an appraiser to estimate the worth of less valuable items. The reason may be to enable accurate accounting to the Probate Court and state tax authorities; to determine value for equitable distribution of items to Beneficiaries; or for setting the price for sales purposes or donation to a non-profit organization. Collectibles, such as art, antiques, clothing, coins, decorative objects, and jewelry are among the most difficult to appraise because their value is based on subjective factors, including the quality of the pieces, their condition, and whether there is a market for them. An appraiser can offer a sense of how much a piece should go for if sold, as well as ensuring its authenticity. Advise the appraiser of your purpose for the appraisal.

An informal appraisal may be done in one of two ways. The appraiser may write a less structured documentation by simply making a list with a brief description of the items and an estimated value next to each; or the appraiser may just examine each item and verbally give an estimate of its worth or what the appraiser thinks you can get for it. Decide which is necessary, according to your reason for hiring the appraiser. In the latter case you can either label each item as you follow the appraiser around, or you can put the price next to the item on your inventory list. (Ask the appraiser to sign the inventory sheet.) You can use the "Tangible Personal Property Inventory and Sale Record" on page R-2 and "Collectibles Basis Record" on page R-3.

To facilitate the appraisal, set aside items to be appraised so when the appraiser comes they can be easily located and examined. If you make a separate inventory list of these items and mark the price on the list as each is determined, you will be sure the appraiser doesn't overlook an item. You may want to have all the other items of the Estate in plain view, so the appraiser can take a quick look around to see if the trained eye can pick out some valuable item you may have misjudged. It is not necessary to appraise "everyday" household furnishings, clothing and personal effects. You can set an approximate value on them yourself. It is also unnecessary to list items that are worth less than $10 on the inventory.

Whether the value of property is to be determined by an appraiser or by you, it is important to have all pertinent documents handy. While going through the deceased person's papers, look for any receipts or other documents, containing information regarding the acquisition (who paid for it, the cost, and where it was purchased), and the property (origin, description, appraisal, insurance rider, warranty or service contract). These can be very useful when making an appraisal and, in a formal appraisal, are absolutely necessary. This preparation can also save time and money.

Locating the Appropriate Appraiser

There is no federal licensing, registration or certification of appraisers. There is presently no state supervision, either by tests or regulations, of personal property appraisers. However, under pressure from the federal government, states are passing licensing laws for real estate appraisers. Currently, only about a dozen states supervise appraisers by requiring them to hold Real Estate Brokers/Salesman Licenses. They are Delaware, Florida, Indiana, Michigan, Mississippi, Nebraska, Oregon, Pennsylvania, Rhode Island, South Carolina, Texas, and West Virginia.

Although this limited licensing allows just about anyone to claim to be an appraiser, the industry does monitor itself through a number of appraisers' associations. Unfortunately, being a member of an appraisers' association does not ensure competence, but hiring a member of an association carries the benefit of knowing that the association has at least checked the appraiser's credentials. The major associations require members to pass rigid competency tests, as well as having a minimum number of years of full time appraisal experience, as is the case with designations of the Appraiser Association of America or the American Society of Appraisers, the two largest. They also insist that their members be bound by a strict code of ethics. Membership must be updated periodically by meeting requalifying requirements. Checking current status is especially important if you require a specialist in fine arts or other exacting category. All of the associations can direct you to the nearest member appraiser. Look in the White and Yellow Pages for local listings of particular associations. We have listed the main offices of some major associations in the box on page 90.

Appraisers Associations

Some well known Appraisers' Associations are listed here. There are many more for many general and specific areas of expertise.

- **Appraisers Association of America**, 360 Park Ave., S., Suite 2000, New York, NY 10016, . . . Call (212) 889-5404.
- **American Society of Appraisers**, P.O. Box 17265, Washington, D.C. 22041, . . . Call (703) 478-2228 or (800) 272-8258.
- **International Society of Appraisers**, 895 W. Pulaski Highway, Elkton, MD 21921, . . . Call (410) 392-3314.
- **Art Dealers Association of America**, 575 Madison Avenue, New York, NY 10022, . . . Call (212) 940-8590.
- **Antiquarian Booksellers Assoc. of America**, 50 Rockefeller Plaza, New York, NY 10022, . . . Call (212) 757-9395.
- **American Philatelic Society**, 100 Oakwood Ave., P.O. Box 8000, State College, PA 16803, . . . Call (814) 237-3803.
- **Gemological Institute of America**, 1660 Stewart Street, Santa Monica, CA 90404, . . . Call (310) 829-2991 or (800) 421-7250.

Finding the Appropriate Appraiser

Some individuals or firms specialize in a single category, such as real estate, art, coins, or jewelry and gems, and command higher fees because they refine their expertise to a narrowly defined field, while other appraisers are generalists, known as **Estate Appraisers**, who will give ballpark estimates on everything in a home. These evaluations are not as precise since no single individual will be thoroughly competent in every area. Before looking for an appraiser, determine the type of appraisal(s) you need, and decide which type of appraiser can best fulfill your requirements. Then you can start checking with the appropriate sources listed below to find an appropriate appraiser in your area:

- Ask dealers or museum curators about the type of object you wish to have appraised. They may know the best people to call or may take the job themselves.
- Ask at banks, S&Ls, or insurance agencies for a list of approved appraisers. When you see the same name on several lists, the person is probably a well qualified local appraiser.
- Appraisers are listed in the Yellow Pages, either as individuals or firms. Some headings to look under are APPRAISERS, REAL ESTATE APPRAISERS, COLLECTIBLES, COIN DEALERS, Etc.
- Look for an appraiser who has passed a written examination and met other qualifying criteria to receive a professional designation, such as MAI (Member, Appraisal Institute), RM (Residential Member), SRA (Senior Residential Appraiser), SREA (Senior Real Estate Analyst), ASA (Senior Member of the American Society of Appraisers), or GIA (Gemological Institute of America).

Selecting An Appraiser

Shop comparatively among your selected group of appropriate appraisers. The appraiser you choose:
- Should be unbiased and objective;
- Should not be influenced by your desires or objectives for the outcome of the appraisal;
- Should not have a vested interest in the amount of the appraisal value. If the appraiser is also a dealer who might be interested in buying some or all of the property, this should be clearly understood before the appraiser starts work. It is hard to find a personal property appraiser who is not also a dealer, but if you consider this important and you search, it can be done;
- Should charge a flat fee or hourly fee. It is considered unethical to charge a percentage of value; because consciously or unconsciously, there is a built-in bias to arrive at the highest reasonable value in order to swell the fee when a percentage is charged;
- Ask the appraiser to give you an estimate of the fee for your particular appraisal, before arranging a consultation. Fees can vary widely between appraisers, even within the same firm. Of course, the fee will be higher for greater expertise or if the appraiser has to travel a long distance to get to you;
- Ask for credentials and qualifications, such as membership in an Appraisal Society, and check claims with the organization;
- Ask if the appraiser is certified or licensed for mortgage appraisals for FHA and VA loans, if you need a real estate appraisal;
- Ask for names of the appraiser's satisfied clients. Calling them may help you feel more secure;
- Ask the appraiser to discuss his or her encounters and failure rates with the IRS, especially if the appraisal is for tax purposes. Before hiring, check with the IRS for the requirements concerning which appraisals must be performed by Certified Appraisers, and which by Licensed Appraisers;
- Ask if the appraiser carries "Errors and Omissions Insurance" to protect his or her clients.

Alternative Appraisal Methods

Appraisals are also available from over-the-telephone art and antique appraisal services. They use computer-stored information on auction sales to provide rough estimates of original objects. Of course, since they are only going by a phone description, they cannot determine the authenticity. Only an in-person appraisal can determine if you have a copy or original. Teleprai-sal, in New York, is the largest of the over-the-phone appraisers. Call (800) 645-6002 from 9:30 a.m. to 6 p.m. Have your credit card handy and expect a charge of at least $30 per item.

Major auction houses will provide a free approximate value (not for tax purposes) for a piece of jewelry, a painting, or an antique. They charge for a formal estimate for tax purposes.

You can either bring the piece in to the gallery, or mail a photocopy or photograph along with information on the object, such as the size of the work, any signature, or other documentation. Two of the major auction houses, Christie's and Sotheby's, based in New York, have galleries in other major cities and experts who travel around the country giving free appraisals. You can call them to find out where and when these estimates will be conducted or watch for announcements in the papers.

Sotheby's will also authenticate old documents, books and manuscripts. If you send a photocopy or a photograph to Sotheby's, Department of Books and Manuscripts, 1334 York Avenue, New York, NY 10021, experts will do a preliminary inspection and determine if what you have is authentic. If you prefer to call first, Sotheby's phone number is (212) 606-7000 or (800) 444-3709.

Another way to get a free appraisal is to visit antique and collectibles stores and shows. Read the labels and ask why items are priced as they are. Learn prices on items similar to your own. Many dealers are willing to provide information to help you identify your items. Take the item, or a small piece of a collection and photo of the rest, to a dealer or a large antique show. Look for dealers who specialize in such pieces and ask one or more to put a bid on the item(s). The bid may be on the low side if the dealer sniffs the potential for a bargain. Or you can pay a fee for an opinion on age and value. It's always good to get several opinions.

If you have the time and desire to investigate the price of collectibles yourself, major antique shows, and the Public Library, usually have a good selection of books, price guides, and magazines on collecting categories. There are books containing descriptions and pricing information on just about every class of collectible. Periodicals are published on the most popular collectibles. These publications usually include price lists, auction results, and dealers' and collectors' offers to buy and sell. You will find many such magazines on news-stands or in magazine stores.

For a fee, the major auction houses, such as Sotheby's, Parke Bernet or Christie's, will provide a detailed catalog of upcoming sales, usually bearing pre-sale estimates of prices. For an additional fee, the auction houses will also send a list of the actual prices paid and listing items that failed to reach the reserve price. The price list will give you an indication of what you could command for a similar work. In addition, the yearbooks of the auction houses and the *Art Price Index* (which can tell you whether a particular artist is on an uptrend, is holding stable, or is on the decline) are available in many libraries. To find other publications and associations that deal with collectibles, ask for these reference books at the library:

- *Gale Encyclopedia of Associations* (Gale Research Inc.) lists more than 20,000 associations, including addresses and phone numbers, membership directories, and newsletter information.
- *Gale Directory of Publications and Broadcast Media* for newspapers and magazines.
- *The Standard Periodical Directory* lists magazines.

DISTRIBUTION AND SALE
OF
PERSONAL PROPERTY

Once you have determined the value of personal property (See Chapter 9, "Valuing Property."); you are ready to distribute to the Beneficiaries the items they want and then sell or give away the remaining property. You may want to discuss with the Beneficiaries the best way to handle the remainder of the property. You may choose only one method of disposal or a combination. The methods you choose depend on the value of each piece of property, the amount of time you can wait to sell it, and the amount of time you have to make arrangements to sell the property. You have a number of options including:

- Consignment arrangements through an auction house, dealer, or gallery;
- Outright sale to a dealer or gallery;
- Private sale to a collector;
- Hiring an estate sale team;
- Conducting your own estate sale;
- Spending a day at the flea market selling leftovers;
- Donating some or all of it to a non-profit organization.

Being in a rush to just get rid of everything may result in the loss of thousands of dollars. Never assume an item is worthless. In the past, antiques were strictly defined as items more than 100 years old, usually handcrafted before the Industrial Revolution. But items made as recently as the 1960's have appreciated. These days, just about anything can be a collectible. On the other hand, in most cases you cannot expect to receive more than 50 percent of the estimated value. Don't expect to sell items for the retail prices except at an auction, where the appraisal may be lower than the auction value, especially if the appraiser is not an expert on rare antiques. This leaves it up to you to set aside items that may be extremely valuable. Prices depend upon condition, rarity, quality, and historical importance of the item, as well as the dictates of popular taste and economic conditions. Prices run in cycles. You may want to wait for a market upturn.

When selling artwork, antiques, collectibles, or rarities, you must always be ready to ascertain the authenticity, the expertise of the authenticator, plus previous documentation: information about previous ownership, previous expert certifications, and the sale price history.

Tidbit: Do Not try to clean collectible coins yourself. Improper cleaning can damage the coins and diminish their value.

Tidbit: A Collectible has more value when sold with the original box and packaging.

Auction Houses, Galleries, and Dealers

Major **Auction Houses** usually handle valuable (benchmark $5000 or more) pieces or collections. They often provide **Specialty Auctions** which offer only coins, only stamps, only 19th Century prints, etc. They are usually held in large cities and are attended by a good mix of dealers and collectors who are interested in those particular items. Obviously, this method of sale will usually bring the best price. A general auction, offering a mixture of items to less interested buyers, will bring lower prices. Armed with the appraisal, take snapshots of the items, send both in a letter to the top auction houses in the country. They will only accept an item they determine to be appropriate for their sales. Some have representatives in other cities who will come to the residence to make judgments. Check the Yellow Pages under the headings AUCTIONEERS and ESTATES. If you decide on an auction sale, you can expect:
- To wait several months for your category auction;
- To wait another 30 days before you receive payment;
- To pay the auction house a percentage fee, which depends on the value of the item. The more valuable the piece, the lower the percentage;
- To pay shipping and insurance charges, if applicable;
- To pay the cost of a photo in the catalog, if applicable;
- To set a minimum price, called a **reserve bid** (from 50 to 75 percent of the low estimate), below which the auctioneers will not sell the item. Otherwise, items may be practically given away to the highest bidder. The auction house's expert will provide a minimum and maximum estimate of what the piece or collection will bring;
- To pay a reduced commission to the auction house should the item fail to reach the reserve bid;
- To insure, in writing, that the artwork is protected for its value, or for restoration cost while it is in their custody (or make sure it is covered by your own private insurance);
- To permit you to review the sales receipt for the consigned work after it is sold, in order to ensure that the dealer has not taken too high a commission or paid you too little.

These same expectations may be applied to consignment to **Galleries** and **Dealers**. However, consignment to a dealer has the same disadvantages as a private sale to a collector; someone has to want the piece before you can get your money. The gallery will charge a consignment fee, which can range from 25 to 45 percent of your asking price. Most galleries have an established clientele, so if they accept your item, they believe they can sell it. Usually a gallery will resell (on consignment) any work it has previously sold, so check the purchase receipt, if you find it. Often, galleries deal with a limited number of artists and may be willing to accept a work done by one of these artists when an appropriate showing and sale is scheduled. Some galleries, and most dealers, will buy a work outright. The advantage is that this is the most liquid sale; you receive the money immediately. However, you can expect an offer to be at least 50 percent less than what the dealer will charge. Prices to dealers will almost invariably yield the lowest price. Check the Yellow Pages under the headings COLLECTIBLES, COIN DEALERS, STAMPS, etc.

There are also shops that resell used furniture, clothes, personal items, and less valuable collectibles on a consignment basis. Look in the Yellow Pages under CONSIGNMENT SERVICE. Although the expectations are basically the same as for auction sales, there is one major difference: if the item does not sell within a stated period of time, usually three months, the dealer takes ownership, instead of charging a fee and returning the item to you.

If you live in or near a large city and have a lot of midrange antiques and collectibles, or just everyday household furnishings, there are dealers and auction houses which conduct "clean sweep" buyouts, or full-service auctions (that means even the broom). If possible, go to the dealership or attend a few auctions before you do anything. Auctions are listed in the newspaper's classified section. Check in the Yellow Pages under the headings LIQUIDATORS, FURNITURE-USED, ESTATES, or AUCTIONEERS.

Some of these dealers will conduct an **Estate Sale** in the decedent's residence. If time permits, before hiring, attend one of their sales to see if it is done professionally and with dignity. These dealers are very useful when you, and all the Beneficiaries, live far away from the decedent's residence. They will go through all of the decedent's possessions for you and send you items you request, including any of the deceased person's financial papers which they find. They should:

- Remove everything from every drawer, closet, or cabinet;
- Inventory merchandise at the designated location;
- Be careful to prevent damage to, or loss of, merchandise;
- Price the merchandise (If they are not professional appraisers, they usually have some expertise in personal property valuation.);
- Do what is necessary to display merchandise in the most appealing way and condition;
- Arrange for the advertising;
- Arrange for required local government permits;
- Require a month or more before the sale will take place;
- Arrange for moving of sold furniture;
- Dispose of all remaining contents according to your wishes; by donating it to charity, arranging outright or consignment sale to a dealer (If they are not dealers themselves, they will usually know a reputable dealer.), or leaving it for you to handle;
- Charge a fee of 35 to 50 percent of the money received from the sale.

Contract For Sale

Whatever you decide to do, make sure you read, understand, and agree with, the terms of any contracts. The contract should detail the financial terms and conditions of the sale or consignment. If you are not satisfied with the contract, be sure all corrections are made in writing, or contact an attorney before you sign. See Chapter 8, "Basic Contract Definition."

Keep in mind that at a private sale, property cannot be sold for less than its formally appraised value. A private sale is one made to an acquaintance, friend, or relative of the seller, who is not competing with anyone else to buy the property, resulting in the price paid for the item being lower than the price which would have resulted from a public sale. At a public sale, property is usually sold for the highest price obtainable. A public sale is determined by notice of the prospective sale being published in a newspaper for a required number of weeks, according to the laws in your state. In large Estates, or Court Monitored Estates, all sales must be reported and ratified by the Court and may be contested for cause.

Direct Sale To Collectors

If you want to take the time to find an interested collector yourself, you can advertise through art magazines and collector magazines, which involves both a considerable expense, the time it takes a person to answer the advertisement, and then like the item enough to buy it for a price you want. When dealing with potential memorabilia or antique buyers, keep the following in mind:

- Always include a self-addressed, stamped envelope along with your letter of inquiry;
- Provide a description of the item including any lettering it has on it, the condition of the item, and a photocopy or good sketch. Indicate its shape, size, and brand name. Be as specific as possible;
- If the buyer asks you to quote a price, do so provided you have some knowledge of the item's value. If not, state this in your letter and ask the collector to make an offer;
- Never send unrequested items through the mail, unless you don't care to see them again.

CONDUCTING YOUR OWN ESTATE SALE

If you have about a month and almost nothing else to do, you may want to conduct an estate sale yourself.

Pricing and Record Keeping Suggestions:

- As you go through the personal property, list the items on the inventory sheets, assign each item a number, and prepare a label for the item, including the price and item inventory number. Remember, a good benchmark for listing on the inventory sheet is a current value of $10. Use a general heading for less valued items, such as clothes, kitchen utensils, garden tools, etc., and then approximate money received for them under each heading.
- If you use removable tags, when the item is sold you can put the tag on a piece of paper. Then, after the sale, you can match the tags to the items on the inventory records and enter

the amount received on the inventory record. Caution: using removable tags allows customers to change the tags during the sale. When the customer is paying, if the price doesn't seem right to you, check the number on the inventory sheet for the description of the item.

■ To save time, you can use different color stick-on circle labels to mark inexpensive items (without marking a price or inventory number on the label). Each color can represent a different price, for example: yellow = 25 cents, blue = 50 cents, green = 75 cents, orange = $1, red = $2, and white for individually priced items. With this method, it is necessary to make signs explaining the color coding and post them around the sale area. Or you can write the price on each circle and use color coding to tell you the type of item, such as: blue for kitchen utensils, red for clothing, etc.

■ For clothing, shoes, purses, etc., use tie-on labels, which can be twisted around a button, strap, etc. and stick the price label dot to it. Sticking a dot on fabric or leather may damage the material.

■ Toward the end of the sale (the last two hours or the last day), you may want to reduce everything to half price. A quick method of keeping track of the price reduction is to have different color sheets for half off. Prepare signs to let buyers know of the price reduction and post them at the appropriate time. If there are items you do not want to reduce, mark them with another "not reduced" color dot.

■ During the sale, you can expect customers to haggle over prices. If you choose to reduce the price of an item during the sale, be sure to mark it on the label or next to it on the paper to which you stick it. Sales can get to a fever pitch at times, so only concern yourself with keeping track of markdowns of inventoried items.

■ Go to the Salvation Army, etc. to get a feel for the prices of used furniture and clothes. Generally, for everyday household items, you can expect to receive one-third of the current selling price of a like item in the store. Clothing won't even bring that much. Collectibles and artwork may bring more.

■ You can mark the prices higher than this to give yourself room for negotiations and reductions.

Display Suggestions:

■ Make sure all items are as clean as possible to show them in their best light.

■ Display small items on a raised surface such as tables, counters, shelves, beds, or on top of boxes. Try to place every item in plain sight, grouped with items of like kind.

■ If the item is still under warranty, be sure to attach a note to the item and give the warranty papers to the new owner.

■ If you have the instruction sheet or booklet for an item, attach a note to the item and give the instructions to the new owner.

■ Have a working electrical outlet to check appliances and a lamp to check bulbs.

■ Since the sale is usually held at the residence of the decedent, you can also offer vehicles, and the residence, for sale, if you wish.

■ Keep non-sale items totally out of sight -or- mark them clearly "SOLD."

Advertising Suggestions:

■ Place ads in local papers a few days before the sale. Look through local papers to determine which would be the best for your advertisement. Look for a good number of similar ads and check the circulation of the paper for the highest number of subscribers in your local area. Be sure to mention "Estate Sale" and any large items or collections (with the price, if it is within range of similar advertised items) you are selling, the address with simple directions from a major road, and the phone number. (You can always disconnect the phone during the sale if you get too many calls.)

■ Make up flyers. List all items you think will draw buyers. Place them in local stores, beauty shops, etc., and mail the flyer to each dealer listed in the Yellow Pages that you think would be interested in some items.

■ On the starting day of the sale, put signs on lawns to direct people to the sale. Try to put signs near major roads, where they will have the most exposure. Check periodically to be sure they are still standing and readable. Psychedelic green or yellow paper, with large black lettering, is the most visible. Secure it to a piece of wood or unbendable cardboard.

Sale Day Suggestions:

■ Friday and Saturday from 8 a.m. to 2 p.m. is the most effective time. Of course, you may want to extend the days and times. Keep in mind buyers usually like to get out early.

■ If possible have one person in every room where there are items smaller than furniture to watch out for thieves pocketing items or moving price tags. Keep doors to rooms without sale items in them closed and put a "Keep Out" sign on the door. Keep jewelry in a see-through closed box or have someone to watch it. If possible, have all payments made to one person at the door. Limit the entrances, so you will not have someone walking out an unguarded exit without paying for merchandise. Even with these precautions expect some losses.

■ Be prepared to watch people subject items to rough treatment and make extremely low offers for what they'll call "your junk."

■ Have paper and a pen ready to take bids on higher priced items. Include the person's name and phone number. Be sure to let them know that if someone is willing to pay the marked price, you will sell it.

■ DO NOT accept personal checks for anything unless you know the person. Accept only cash or money orders.

■ Expect professional dealers to show up (sometimes before the sale date), to buy low for resale. Often their offers will be the best you will get, so give them some consideration.

■ Don't expect to sell all, or even most, of the items. Keep in mind that the object of the sale is to get rid of what you have. If you are too stubborn about the price, you will find you are left with a lot of merchandise.

WHAT TO DO WITH THE LEFTOVERS

Think about what you want to do with the leftovers. Your decision should depend on the quality and quantity of the items left after the sale. Some choices are:

■ Take the rest to a local flea market and set up a clearance booth.

■ Prior to the sale, call a charity who picks-up, and arrange pick-up soon after the sale. Call around and ask the local organizations what type of items they accept. Some non-profit organizations, such as Faith Farm, will accept small and large appliances for repair and resale. The Salvation Army will accept working appliances, as well as boats, campers, and cars, which it auctions once a year.

- Bring the rest to a charity collection site.
- Arrange for a dealer to buy the rest.
- Arrange for large trash pick up or, if necessary, bring items to the dump yourself.

WHAT TO DO WITH THE OTHER THINGS

Coins (damaged) —— Send mutilated coins to: The United States Mint, Coin Redemption Branch, 5th and Arch Streets, P. O. Box 400, Philadelphia, PA 19105, along with a claim letter. Send the package by registered mail, insured for the full value of the coins, and request a return receipt.

Currency (damaged) —— Send to: U.S. Department of the Treasury, Bureau of Engraving and Printing, Office of Currency Standards, Room 344, P.O. Box 37048, Washington, D.C. 20013, for information call (202) 874-4820. It redeems partially destroyed or badly damaged currency as a free public service. When currency notes are not clearly more than half of the original and/or in such condition that the value is questionable and requires special examination. If the method of mutilation and supporting evidence demonstrate to the examiner's satisfaction that the missing portions have been totally destroyed, a reimbursement check is issued. (A local bank will replace any badly soiled, dirty, defaced, worn out, or otherwise damaged currency note that is clearly more than half of the note.) The Treasury suggests that you keep the money as intact as possible by leaving it in the container (purse, box, etc.) in which it was found. Carefully pack and box it, trying not to disturb the fragments any more than is absolutely necessary. If it is brittle, pack it in cotton. Include a claim letter, with an explanation of how the damage occurred. Send it by registered mail, insured for the full value of the currency, and request a return receipt. DO NOT send coins in the same package, they may further damage the currency. If you want the money back, in the event that you can't be reimbursed, state that in the letter.

Dentures (full and partials) —— Technical Education Schools who offer dental laboratory technician classes, may welcome these for practice. Call schools in your area.

Eyeglasses and contact lenses —— The Lions Clubs International collects used glasses to pass on to the needy worldwide. Collection drop-off boxes are located in banks, eyeglass sales locations, and participating funeral homes. If you can't find a drop-off box, call the Lyons Club for a mailing address in your area. Ask information for the phone number or call (708) 571-5466. Or, mail glasses securely packaged to: New Eyes for the Needy, 549 Millburn Avenue, P.O. Box 332, Short Hills, NJ 07078, phone (201) 376-4903.

Greeting Cards (used, modern) —— Children use donated cards from any holiday or occasion to make new cards to sell in their gift shop. Cut off the greeting portion of the card, and mail the picture portions to: St. Jude's Ranch for Children, 100 St. Jude's Street, Boulder City, NV 89005-0985. To buy rebuilt cards write to St. Jude's Ranch for Children, P.O. Box 60100, Boulder City, NV 89006 or call (702) 293-3131 for information.

Hearing Aids and Devices —— The Lions Community Hearing Bank repairs and refurbishes hearing aids, then provides them to those who are financially unable to buy their own. They will send a letter for tax deduction purposes, if requested. Participating funeral directors will forward them, or you can put them in an eyeglass collection box, or call the local Lions Club for a mailing address in your area. Ask information for the phone number or call (708) 571-5466. Or, send hearing devices in a small box or padded envelope to Hear Now, 9745 E. Hampden Avenue, Suite 300, Denver, CO 80231-4923. Hear Now recycles hearing devices for low-income deaf and hard-of-hearing children and adults throughout the U.S. Or, mail children's hearing aids to Salesian Missions, Dept. HA, 2 Lefevre Lane, New Rochelle, NY 10801 for distribution through its missions in third-world nations.

Medical Equipment (wheelchairs, lift-chairs, walkers and canes, bedside commodes, etc.) —— Can be sold privately at an estate sale, through ads in newspapers, on consignment through the medical supply stores where they were bought (or they may buy them outright); or call the local office of the Easter Seal Society, and other area charities, to donate them.

S&H Green Stamps (full or partial books) —— If there is no local redemption center, call (800) HELLO-SH (435-5674) for catalog and cash redemption information, or write to: S&H National Mail Order Center, P.O. Box 5775, Norcross, GA 30091-5775.

Tableware (China or Crystal Tableware) —— If you are looking for an appraisal or to complete a set, ask for the buy price list. If you just want to sell to them, ask for the sell list. Specify pattern name or send a photocopy, sketch, or picture of the design. Write to: Replacements, Ltd., P.O. Box 26029, Greensboro, NC 27420, or call (910) 697-3000 or (800) 737-5223, (china, crystal, and porcelain collectibles); or Walter Drake China Exchange, 14 Drake Building, Colorado Springs, CO 80940, (china).

Tableware (Sterling and Silverplate Flatware, Oneida Stainless) —— If you are looking for an appraisal or to complete a set, ask for the buy price list. If you just want to sell to them, ask for the sell list. Specify pattern name or send a photocopy of the design. Write to: Walter Drake Silver Exchange, 14 Drake Building, Colorado Springs, CO 80940, or call (800) 525-9291; or Tere Hagan Flatware Matching Service, P.O. Box 25487, Tempe, AZ 85282, (also provides a repair service); or Replacements, Ltd., P.O. Box 26029, Greensboro, NC 27420, or call (910) 697-3000 or (800) 737-5223, (also provides monogram and scratch removal service).

Trophies (Old or Previously Issued) —— call the closest chapter of the Boys and Girls Club.

United States Flag (unwanted or unfit for display) —— deliver or mail the flag to the Boy Scouts Council for proper disposal. Girl Scouts and the American Legion will sometimes take flags for disposal.

Watches (Vintage Classic Wrist and Pocket Watches and Small Clocks) and (Vintage Fountain Pens) —— DeMesy & Company, Member Jewelers Board of Trade, 300 Crescent Court, Suite 880, Dallas, TX 75201, call (800) 635-9006 or FAX (214) 871-6777. . . . Not interested in Seiko, Timex, Caravelle, Westclox, Benrus, or Hampden.

PROTECTION AND REPAIR
OF
REAL PROPERTY

Severely Damaged Buildings

If the property has been damaged by a fire, earthquake, flood, etc., immediately call the agent who handles the insurance policy. An adjuster will be assigned to inspect the property as soon as possible. If you do not know who the insurance carrier is, call the county property records department and ask. Make a video or take pictures of the building, inside and out, to establish the amount of damage, and make a list of all damaged items. Do not enter a building that may be unsafe. Before you enter the building, check for structural damage, or wait for a municipal or insurance inspector to declare it safe for entry. If you can safely do it, turn off the water and gas at the main supply line, and the electricity at the main power switch. Be cautious not to walk in standing water if live electrical wires may be present. After it is determined that the building is in no danger of collapsing, you should still use caution when entering. If there is standing water in the building, in addition to being sure there is no electrical threat, beware of foul odors and toxic fumes. Air the building by opening all the windows and doors and wait outside until the odors have dissipated. If you smell gas or see floating oil, do not use any open flames. Use a battery operated flashlight to avoid igniting escaping utility-supplied or other gases. Do not turn on any lights or appliances until an electrician has checked the system for short circuits.

As soon as it is safe, do what is necessary to protect the property from further damage. Cover broken windows and holes in the roof or walls with heavy plastic and plywood to prevent damage from rain. Use two-by-fours and other supporting beams to strengthen damaged walls, floors, ceilings, porches, etc. Be sure to keep all receipts for materials and labor to give to the insurance carrier. Use the "Maintenance and Repair Expense Record" on page R-19. Do not make any permanent repairs until they are approved by the insurer's claims adjuster. Proceed with immediate cleanup measures to prevent health hazards. Perishable items, such as food which is going to be discarded, should be listed and photographed for insurance purposes first. If damage is so bad in the area that regular trash pickup cannot be expected in the foreseeable future, bury perishables in the ground as deeply as possible. Do not drink tap water until it has been declared safe. Flooded basements should be drained and cleaned as soon as possible. Wet furnishings and clothing should be dried in the sun, if possible. Items which cannot be dried quickly will be permanently damaged, if they aren't already. Remove all the finance related papers and valuables to a safe place. For more information write to FEMA Publications, P.O. Box 70274, Washington, D.C. 20024 and ask for the Federal Emergency Management Agency's Publication: *Repairing Your Flooded Home*, or request it from your local American Red Cross, who co-authored it, ask for publication number ARC 4477.

Tidbit: Wet photos or paper-based materials should be dried as soon as possible. Lay photos, image-side-up, on paper towels. If they are muddy, rinse them with cool water first. Use this method for any paper-based materials, such as books, maps, documents, or art works. If you can't dry the items soon, wrap them in freezer paper and freeze them until you can. Mold, which can cause permanent stains, is the greatest threat to paper-based materials. Once the paper products are dry, the Documentation Conservation Center, Andover, Mass., may be able to save them. The process can be expensive. The center will answer questions about specific problems. Call (508) 470-1010.

Protecting Undamaged Vacant Property

If the house of the decedent is now vacant, it is the responsibility of the Administrator to protect the property from damage and, if applicable, to prepare it for sale. The extent of what actions the Administrator takes depends upon the individual circumstances, such as: the neighborhood where the house is located; the current condition of the house; and the intentions of the Beneficiaries as to what they want to do with the house. The first consideration is to protect the property from damage and generally maintain the property until it is occupied by a Beneficiary or a tenant, or it is sold. Start by making a video tape or taking pictures of the entire interior and exterior of the property. Then, evaluate the property, make a list of what costs you believe will be involved for protecting and repairing it, and present the estimate to the Beneficiaries, (and where required to the Courts) for approval, before you spend the money, or you may not be reimbursed for expenses. Use the "Beneficiary Decision Record" on page R-43.

To avoid frozen pipes and the possibility of them bursting:
- Turn off the valves of the outside spigots, insulate them and any vents or openings beneath the house.
- Keep cabinets in the kitchen and bathrooms open so heat can reach pipes.
- Turn off the water main and open a few faucets to relieve water pressure.
- Make sure the heating system keeps working properly. If you cannot do this yourself, ask a reliable friend or neighbor to check on the house twice a day and turn up the thermostat during any severe cold spell. This can prevent pipes in outside walls from freezing.
- Drain water out of any water pipe or fitting that might be exposed to freezing temperatures. After draining pour one-half to one cup of car antifreeze in drains and toilets. If it's not

practical to drain the pipe, wrap it with an inexpensive heating cable, sold at most hardware stores.

To avoid unnecessary repair costs, get the house set for winter:

- Check the chimney for damaged caps, loose or missing mortar, and make appropriate repairs. Clean any obstruction from the flue, and make sure the damper is closed tightly.
- Patch cracks and holes in blacktop paving with a patching material sold for this purpose. Water in open cracks can get under the surrounding pavement where it will freeze, expand, and eventually create a pothole.
- Drain water out of the lawn roller, garden hoses, and spray equipment.
- Connect a plastic downspout extension to the end of downspouts to carry water at least eight feet from the house. This may prevent a flooded basement if a heavy rain should fall while the ground is still frozen.
- Be sure the sump pump, if there is one, is in working order. Pour a pail or two of water into the pit or pump. If the pump doesn't go on, get it fixed.
- Apply a thick mulch to evergreen shrubs around foundations to prevent winter damage and help soil retain moisture. If shrubs are exposed to cold drying winds, protect them with burlap covers. Trim tree branches away from the roof and windows.
- Remove window air conditioners or put weather-proof covers over them.
- Take down removable screens; clean and store them.

To avoid unnecessary repair costs, perform routine general maintenance:

- Clean out gutters and downspouts after the leaves are off the trees. An accumulation of leaves will soak up water and the weight can pull gutters loose. Water in a clogged gutter can also back up under the roof shingles and do extensive damage to the interior of the house. If the possibility of clogged gutters is a continuing problem, either check and clear them periodically yourself, hire someone to do it, or consider installing gutter guards. They prevent debris from collecting in the gutter. Even if debris clings when it is wet, it will be blown off when it dries. Check with your local building supply store or roofer.
- Maintain the furnace and/or air conditioning unit by cleaning or replacing filters periodically (once a month is suggested). You can get filters at hardware and heating supply stores. Check for a maintenance contract and be sure system checks are performed on schedule. If necessary, get the system "tuned up" annually. Keep an outdoor unit free of debris. If a furnace is not working, call the utility company which supplies the fuel to check it before you call a repairman. Many utility companies provide this service for free. The utility company's representative should be able to determine the problem and may correct the problem, if it is minor.
- If you smell gas or the electricity is not working properly; call the utility company, which supplies it, to check the situation. If repairs are needed, the utility's representative may be able to recommend a qualified person.
- Check insulation around doors and windows. If the weather-stripping around doors is damaged, replace it. If the caulking around window frames is damaged, recaulk it. This is as simple as getting a putty knife and some putty or glazing compound. This not only keeps outdoor weather out, but avoids possible water damage to the frames. If you need to replace a door or windows, choose energy-efficient, insulated ones.
- Replace worn out fuses. Before you replace any fuse be sure the ground you are standing on is dry. Keep the hand you are not using close to your body to avoid touching anything.

Start by shutting off the main power supply by shifting the handle on the side of the box to the "off" position. Then, depending upon the type of fusebox: Remove the blown fuse by turning it counter-clockwise -or- pull out the box holding the main cartridge fuses. (Pull the plastic box straight out, then pull the fuse out of the box. Large cartridge-type fuses should be removed with a fuse puller.) Replace the blown fuse with one of the same type and capacity. When everything is back in place, turn the main power back on.

- Remove any clutter from the house, such as piles of old newspapers. Discard all dangerous items such as oily rags, old paint cans, or chemicals. Empty the lawn mower and other gas engines, camping stoves, lanterns, and fuel tanks. These are fire hazards. Contact the local public health department, sanitation department, or fire department for advice on proper disposal.

- Protect appliances against electrical surges by unplugging them.

- Protect the house from water damage by turning off the water supply to appliances such as the dishwasher, clothes washer, and refrigerator, as well as to sinks and toilets. An alternative is to turn off the main water supply to the house. If the house is being sold, do not have the water department discontinue service.

- Turn off the water heater and drain it, if possible.

- Empty refrigerators and freezers. Wash the inside thoroughly and leave the doors open. Be sure to unplug them. Remove mildew from refrigerator gaskets using a cleaning powder or solution that contains chlorine and a soft brush to scrub the crevices in the gaskets. Be gentle or older gaskets will split during cleaning.

- Check all exterior wiring on appliances and lamps for fraying. If frayed, unplug them and put warning signs on them to avoid others plugging them in or get rid of them.

- Make sure everything is as clean and dry as possible. Open all closets and cabinet doors and drawers to allow for good air circulation. To prevent or limit the growth of mildew during hot weather, leave a central air conditioning unit on a high degree setting so it goes on a couple of times a day. Install a timer on window air conditioning units to turn them on once a day for a half hour or so, or have a neighbor do it. Otherwise, ask a neighbor to occasionally open the windows for a few hours, on a dry day, to air out the house and remove dampness. Do not cover furnishings with plastic, it traps heat and humidity, providing a perfect environment for the growth of mildew. If coverings are desired to keep furnishings clean, use cotton sheets, which permit air circulation. To protect clothes, linens, leather goods, etc., store unwrapped bars of deodorant soap with them. Let the bars stand out a few days to dry before packing.

- Avoid insect or rodent infestation by placing ant, roach, and rodent poison traps in inconspicuous places inside the house, or hire an exterminator to administer periodic treatments. Secure the drains of sinks and tubs with stoppers to stop entry.

Tidbit: To prevent a possible tragedy, secure pools and outdoor hottubs from use by neighborhood children. Check zoning regulations to be sure your plan is approved. For more information request a free copy of "Safety Barrier Guidelines for Pools" (CPSC 362) from Pool Safety, U. S. Consumer Product Safety Commission, Washington, D.C. 20207.

To avoid damage from break-ins, secure the house:

Most police departments offer free residential security surveys. While they will not recommend which brands of locks or alarms to buy, they can offer suggestions that are right for each individual house. Here are some security suggestions:

- Indoor lights should not be left on 24 hours. Use timers to turn them on and off.
- Exterior lights, such as floodlights, deter burglars. Arrange them to illuminate all possible points of entry. If they are not motion sensitive or light sensitive, they should be on a timer set to go on at dusk and go off at dawn.
- Keep hedges around decks, patios, porches, windows and doors trimmed, so all points of entry are visible to neighbors.
- Ask a neighbor to park a car in the driveway or in front of the house or to move the decedent's car occasionally.
- Ask neighbors to share their trash, by putting one of their trash bags or cans in front of the house on collection day.
- Ask a neighbor to check for and remove flyers or circulars left at the front door.
- Secure doors with single-cylinder deadbolt locks. A single-cylinder deadbolt, operated by a key from both sides, should be used in doors where there is glass within 40 inches of the lock. Do not leave a key in the interior lock; it defeats the purpose of a double key lock. If service providers, repairmen, or construction workers were given keys, when their services are no longer required change the locks or have the tumblers changed, even if the keys were returned.
- Doors with outside hinges should have internal pins to keep them from being lifted out.
- Doors with window panes should be reinforced with unbreakable glass or iron grill work.
- If doors are damaged, replace them with solid wood or steel-clad doors.
- Electric garage door openers should be unplugged and the door should be padlocked from inside.
- Sliding glass doors and windows can be secured by screwing several pan-head sheet metal screws into the top of the frame. Adjust the screws to take up any slack between the door or window and the frame, so you can just clear the door or window when sliding it. This prevents the doors or windows from being lifted out of the frame. There are also steps to keep the doors or windows from sliding, such as: putting a snugly fitting dowel in the track; or drilling holes through the door or window track and frame, then inserting nails or metal pins; or drilling a small hole at a downward angle in the overlap between the doors or windows and the frame, then inserting a steel pin or heavy nail; or installing keyed locks at the overlap of the frames when the door or window is closed.
- Jalousie windows and doors can be secured by installing heavy gauge metal grating on the inside of the window or door; or by gluing the jalousie slats to the metal clips that hold them; or by replacing jalousies with an entirely different kind of window or door.
- Awning windows can be forced open if they are not tightly closed. If possible, remove the crank handle to increase security. Be sure to put it where you can find it.
- Double-hung windows can be reinforced with just two nails when both parts of the window are closed. Drill a hole at a slightly downward angle in the upper corner of the lower sash extending into the lower corner of the upper sash. Drill this angled hole on both the left- and right-hand sides of the double-hung window and then insert nails.
- Bolt down in-window air conditioners.
- Skylights, roof lights, vents leading under the house, etc. should be sealed and reinforced with metal bars or heavy screening.
- Drapes or shades should be left slightly open. A house looks deserted if they are drawn and closed. Garage windows should be covered with shades or blinds and be reinforced with extra locks or bars.
- Ladders or tools left outside or in an unlocked shed can be used by burglars to gain entry.

■ Install an alarm system to protect against break-ins as well as fires. There are various types of alarms, each with its own strengths and weaknesses. Before buying one, consider your objectives and the cost. Alarm systems can also be rented. Since the house is vacant, there is little point to having an alarm which can only be heard in the house. Therefore, the alarm system should either sound outside, be monitored, or both. Experts suggest that if you choose a monitored system, make sure it is monitored by a person within the state, not by a machine out of state. If you don't want to spend the money for an alarm system, signs and decals warning of an alarm system or neighborhood watch can be purchased at many building supply stores and placed on doors and windows to help deter burglars. However, decals will do nothing for a fire. Smoke detectors are inexpensive, but be sure they can be heard outside the house if they should go off. Remember to check the alarm system batteries periodically. An electrically powered security system should have an auxiliary source of power, such as a battery pack. Call the county or police department to find out if the alarm system must be registered and, if so, if the installer has properly registered it. To allow access to the house in the event of an emergency or to repair a faulty alarm system; give the password to the neighbor who has the house keys. Be sure the neighbor understands how the system works, to keep it in proper working condition. Get permission to give that neighbor's name and phone number to the alarm company.

- **Choosing a security system company:**
    - Contact the Better Business Bureau, neighbors, or local police department. Look in the Yellow Pages under the headings: BURGLAR ALARM SYSTEMS AND MONITORING, FIRE ALARM SYSTEMS, SECURITY CONTROL EQUIPMENT - SYSTEMS & MONITORING, or SMOKE DETECTORS & ALARMS.
    - Ask each company contacted for the names of customers and call them to determine their satisfaction with the system.
    - Have each company survey the property and offer written detailed quotes on the installation.
    - Compare the maintenance or service contract offered by each.
    - Before signing, the contract should be carefully reviewed by you or your attorney.

Property Managers

Throughout this section, we mention asking friends or neighbors to perform some services to help protect the property. If you are not able to rely upon friends and neighbors, you may consider hiring a **Property Manager**. These agents usually offer two types of service. One is to protect vacant property; the other is to supervise the rental of property. In either case, before the property manager takes over, the owner and agent should make an on-site written inspection of the property.

■ The **protection service**, also called a "Home Security Program" consists of:
- Checking a vacant home at least once every two weeks (daily during freezing weather).
- Informing local police and fire departments that the home is under his or her care, and providing a local contact in case of emergency.

- • Issuing a statement, usually bimonthly, to owners with comments and recommendations, such as for repairs.
- • After repair work is approved by the owner, the property manager will obtain estimates, hire the contractor, and supervise the repairs.
- ■ The **rental service** consists of:
  - • Qualifying tenants:
    - ♦ Having potential renters complete a "Potential Rental Application";
    - ♦ Requiring potential renters to supply references and checking their references;
  - • Working out the rental agreement;
  - • Suggesting the appropriate amount for rents, fees, and deposits;
  - • Collecting all rent payments, fees, and deposits;
  - • Transmitting all documents and funds, minus the property manager's fee, to the owner;
  - • Taking care of evictions and other legal matters;
  - • Regularly inspecting the vacant rental properties; and occasionally driving by the property, when it is rented, to check on its condition;
  - • Providing an inspection checklist to the tenant, to be filled in and returned within a couple of weeks, when the property is rented and again when it is vacated;
  - • Conducting a final inspection, after a tenant moves out, checking for damage and evaluating the need for repairs and cleaning. Also, making sure the water isn't running and appliances are turned off;
  - • Checking that utility bills are paid and then refunding the balance of the tenant's security deposit.

Locating a Property Manager

Some property managers operate through real estate sales offices, while others are independent. Therefore, if you are listing the home for sale, ask your realtor if the company offers this service, otherwise:
- ■ Ask your real estate agent, attorney, bank loan department, friends, or neighbors for a recommendation.
- ■ Look in the Yellow Pages under the headings: PROPERTY MAINTENANCE, PROPERTY MANAGEMENT, and REAL ESTATE MANAGEMENT.
- ■ Contact a major organization for property managers, such as the Property Management Association of America, 8811 Colesville Road, Suite G106, Silver Spring, MD 20910 or call (301) 587-6543, and ask for a referral to a member in the area.

Hiring a Property Manager

Before contacting a property manager, decide what services you want performed. When you call a prospective agent, describe the location, size, and condition of the property. Use the "Hiring Interview Sheet" on pages R-39 and R-40. Then:
- ■ Ask for a list of the services the agent will perform and how often;

- Ask when and how inspections of the property are conducted and how often a written report is issued. Ask to see a sample inspection report;
- If and when repairs are needed; ask who will arrange for and who will perform the repairs. Be sure only licensed, bonded, and insured contractors are employed;
- Ask for a schedule of fees for the agent's services, including routine services and special services, such as renting the property or supervising repairs;
- Ask what kind of liability coverage the agent carries; be sure to see the policy or other proof of coverage. Call the insurance company to confirm coverage;
- Ask for credentials, state licensing (Call the professional regulation department of the state, to determine if licensing is required.), membership in professional organizations, and local business licenses. Check with the appropriate agency to be sure the agent is current, and if there have been any complaints or sanctions against the property manager;
- Sign a management agreement. Review the contract carefully, or have it reviewed by an attorney, to be sure it provides for the services you want and conforms to relevant state laws.

Home Inspections

Signs of Possible Trouble, Damage, or Improperly Working Systems:

- **Furnace** — soot streaks around registers; discolored (orange) pilot light; fan motor vibration or squealing; smell of gas; or thermostat not operating.
- **Water heater** — cracking or popping noise; signs of rust at bottom of tank.
- **Air conditioner** — outside unit not operational; high noise level; runs continuously; thermostat not operating; overgrown landscaping around outside unit.
- **Plumbing** — any sign of galvanized steel pipe combined with copper pipe; sediment build-up around faucets (usually green); low water pressure; flooring, ceiling, or walls are discolored near or below water sources.
- **Dishwasher** — rust on rack seams and tub bottom; door does not close properly; flooring near dishwasher is discolored.
- **Disposal** — bottom of unit shows signs of rust; signs of water leaking under the sink; trips circuit breaker continuously.
- **Ovens and Stoves** — inoperative stove and oven clocks; missing dials and knobs indicate poor maintenance.
- **Doors** — warped or jammed.
- **Pool Equipment** — cloudy water; rusty pool heater; bubbles in water near supply line outlet; stains or streaks on filter tank.
- **Roof** — Indoors, the signs of a leaky roof are: cracked paint, flaking plaster, peeling wallpaper, or discolored areas near wall and ceiling joints. Outdoors, the signs of a leaky roof are: blistering shingles; fraying, warping, and curling shingles; cracked, loose or missing tiles or shingles; loss of shingle surface granules indicating wear and possible loss of water proofing; damaged sealing around roof installations, such as solar units, vents, chimneys, skylights, etc. This inspection is best done by a professional, and should be done if the roof is 10 to 15 years old.

Professional Home Inspections

If you do not feel competent to do the checks just discussed, you may want to hire a professional **Home Inspector** to do them for you. Although inspections may not be necessary for newer homes, it is advisable with an old home, especially if you are not familiar with its condition. There are two major reasons to have the home inspected. One is to avoid damage by making needed repairs. The other is to avoid surprises when the house is sold and a required inspection performed. If problems are found, the buyer will usually want the repairs completed before the sale closes. The **Inspection Report** should contain analysis of the structural condition of the roof, walls, ceilings, floors, doors, windows, and crawl space, along with the condition and adequacy of the heating, plumbing, electrical systems, and insulation. Realistically a home inspection cannot guarantee that future problems will not arise, only that no problems are currently evident. A routine home inspection usually does not include information on specific appliances, pools or spas, insect infestation, environmental hazards, or underground storage tanks. Inspectors qualified to do these inspections, will usually charge extra for them. Inspectors who are not qualified, will probably recommend contacting someone who is. This may include:

- A specific appliance or home system (such as an alarm system) is best inspected by the manufacturer's certified repair technician or a qualified service contractor, to evaluate the product and determine its condition. Check for existing service or warranty contracts which may afford these services for free.
- Pool inspections should be performed by a competent company that has expertise in pool construction, service, and maintenance; and is up-to-date on the code requirements of the municipality. Aspects of the pool or spa and related equipment, seen from ground level, ordinarily does not uncover leaks.
- Although home inspectors look for, and point out, termite damage, they may not be qualified to determine if there are termites present. A licensed pest-control or extermination service should be contacted to perform this inspection. (This is often required to get a mortgage. The buyer will pay to have one done just before closing.)
- A radon test can be purchased in many hardware stores and the testing instrument sent to a laboratory listed on the box. This is not usually a spot test, but one performed by exposing the testing material to the conditions in the house over a period of time. The expertise is in the reading of the test results by the laboratory. For a free brochure on radon and a coupon to purchase a test kit, call the Environmental Protection Agency's Radon Hotline (800) 767-7236.
- The local water supplier will usually perform a free water analysis of the tap water to check for contaminants or will refer you to a laboratory which can perform the tests.
- Underground storage tanks should be inspected by the builder, supplier, or a certified engineer.

Most states do not have regulations for home inspectors; those that do will give qualified inspectors the designation of a State Certified Home and/or Building Inspector, and should have a professional license or certification number in addition to a business license. The department that regulates professionals in your state can tell you if home inspectors must be certified and if the particular inspector's license is current. If your state does not regulate home inspectors, you must rely upon membership in professional organizations to indicate some level of competency, such as membership in the state's association of building inspectors or in a national organization.

Locating a Home Inspector

When looking for a home inspector, avoid anyone who is referred by, or otherwise connected with, companies or individuals who do house repairs.

- The American Society of Home Inspectors (ASHI) can suggest members in your area; write to the ASHI at 85 W. Algonquin Road, Arlington Heights, IL 60005, phone (708) 290-1919 or (800) 743-2744. The ASHI sets standards of practice for its members. You can request a copy of its standards for $4.
- Ask your real estate agent, attorney, bank loan department, and friends or neighbors for a recommendation.
- Look in the Yellow Pages under the headings: BUILDING INSPECTION SERVICE, HOME INSPECTION SERVICE, or INSPECTION BUREAUS.

Hiring a Home Inspector

Before contacting an inspector, decide what you want inspected. Use the "Hiring Interview Sheet" on pages R-39 and R-40. When you call a prospective inspector, tell the reason for the inspection, the square footage of the home, and whether it is a detached home, a duplex, condominium, etc. Then:

- Ask for an estimate of the amount of time the inspector would expect to spend inspecting the property. (A detached house usually takes one and a half to two hours);
- Ask for an estimate of the cost of the entire inspection. (About $350 for the average-size house);
- Ask for a list of the services or checks that will be included in the inspection;
- Ask if the inspector performs any additional inspections you may want done and the cost of those additions;
- Ask how the inspection is conducted. You want to find an inspector who actually walks on the roof, gets in the crawl space under the house (if possible), tests appliances, and estimates the age of electrical components;
- Ask prospects to show you examples of inspection reports;
- Ask if you will be allowed to accompany the inspector during the inspection;
- Find out what kind of liability coverage the inspector carries; be sure to see the policy or other proof of coverage. Call the insurance company to confirm coverage.
- Ask for credentials, state licensing (if applicable), membership in professional organizations, and local business licenses. Check with the appropriate agency to be sure they are all current and if there have been any complaints or sanctions against the inspector.

Preparing the House for Sale

If the house is to be sold or rented, the better the house looks, the more money you are likely to get for it. Before putting the house on the market, get it into the best possible condition.

Exterior and interior painting are the cheapest, most profitable improvements you can make. Also be sure to clean and repair everything, so all your buyer must do is turn the key in the door to move in. If necessary, install new landscaping and new carpeting so the house looks fresh and inviting. New lighting fixtures and ceiling fans can make the house more attractive at minimal cost. If the kitchen appliances are old, installing a new refrigerator, dishwasher, stove, and possibly a trash compactor, garbage disposal, and built-in microwave oven, can bring this most important room up to date. If a house is damaged, it could be sold as a fixer-upper at a greatly reduced price from the current market value of a similar house in good repair. Of course, a deciding factor is the availability of cash to pay for the repairs, either from the Estate or insurance. All repairs should be carefully considered by the Administrator and the Beneficiaries and, if required, obtain Court approval.

Tidbit: Alcohol or acetone, which is in many commercial cleaners, can dissolve vinyl and leave it tacky. To protect vinyl-coated shelves, clean them with a mixture of soapy water and a little vinegar.

Making a Plan

If the decision has been made to remodel or rebuild a damaged home, the first step is to determine the exact design you want to use for each room. You can start finding design ideas by buying or borrowing books on interior design and touring new homes and recent remodeling projects. Look for features you can adapt to your remodeling. Then get a blank sheet of one-quarter-inch graph paper and work with a scale of one square equals one foot. Use a tape measure to measure the room you are going to do the work on. Translate the measurements into a diagram of the room. Be sure to include features that will affect your design, such as placement or size of walls, windows, doors, and plumbing and electrical outlets. Once you have a complete diagram of the room you can start designing the project. Visit suppliers to find out what is available. Be sure to take measurements of cabinets, fixtures, and appliances, so you can determine exactly how they will fit in the diagram and eventually, the room. Consider if the room would work better if expanded into part of another room. It is important to determine the exact dimensions, materials, extras, etc., including the manufacturers, brands, colors, and model numbers of what you want. If you have access to a computer, there are many specially designed computer programs available to help you in designing the room. Two major considerations before you decide to remodel rooms which are not damaged are: on average, a kitchen renovation will return 74 percent of its cost if the house is sold immediately, about 65 percent for bath remodeling; and that the remodeling should not make the house too expensive for the neighborhood.

With a design plan taking shape, you must decide whether you have the experience, time, and knowledge to do the job yourself or if you need help. If you are going to hire professionals, you need to determine if you need the professional skills of an architect, general contractor, remodeling contractor, engineer or certified kitchen designer, as well as subcontractors, such as painters, plumbers, electricians, and carpenters. Unless the job is small, or you have considerable experience, you will probably have to hire at least one of the professionals listed.

If You Decide to Do-It-Yourself:

Save time, effort, embarrassment, and money by checking your local building code and ordinances before starting any work. Some or part of your project may require that the work be done by licensed professionals. Failure to do this can result in fines, having to tear out your work, and paying to have it redone by a professional. If you decide to do the job yourself with help as needed:

- Decide at what points you will need professional help that will be most practical and least costly. Draw up a schedule for the job and when you will need each professional to do his or her part;
- Obtain and post necessary permits and arrange for any required inspections;
- Gather the needed materials;
- Hire and schedule all subcontractors to fit in with your schedule and theirs, and with the scheduled inspections. If you must deal with several workers, consider hiring a general contractor, especially if the project is sizable. A competent contractor has a thorough knowledge of the building process and is experienced at hiring, handling, and scheduling various subcontractors or workers. In addition, a contractor can usually get materials and labor at lower cost, and often can make a profit without charging much more than you would pay if you were your own contractor.

Tidbit: Check all painted surfaces for lead before doing any sanding or scraping.

Tidbit: Many resilient floorings and flooring adhesives installed prior to the early 1980's contained asbestos. This asbestos is perfectly safe when left in place but tearing it up will send some of it into the air unless precise Environmental Protection Agency abatement procedures are followed. The wisest choice may be a vinyl-over-vinyl installation as long as the existing floor has no serious problems.

Contractors

Locating a Contractor

After you decide exactly what type of professionals you need to complete the work, seek recommendations from:

- Friends and neighbors who have recently had similar remodeling jobs done;
- Insurance agents and appraisers;
- Building supply stores usually have contractors on call to install the products they sell. Major chains will stand behind the work.
- Look in the Yellow Pages of the phone book under the appropriate titles: ARCHITECTS, BATHROOM REMODELING, BUILDING CONTRACTORS, CARPENTERS, CONCRETE CONTRAC-

TORS, ELECTRIC CONTRACTORS, CONTRACTORS EQUIPMENT & SUPPLIES - RENTING & LEAS-ING, CONTRACTORS - FILL, CONTRACTORS - GENERAL, HEATING CONTRACTORS, HOME BUILDERS, HOME IMPROVEMENTS, KITCHEN CABINETS & EQUIPMENT - HOUSEHOLD (includes remodeling contractors), MASON CONTRACTORS, MECHANICAL CONTRACTORS, PAINTERS, PAINTING CONTRACTORS, PAVING CONTRACTORS, PLUMBING CONTRACTORS, ROOF CONTRACTORS, VENTILATING CONTRACTORS, WATERPROOFING CONTRACTORS, etc.

Hiring a Contractor

Have at least three contractors come to the house to make written estimates or bids. Note every point of agreement reached with each individual contractor and be sure it is included in the written contract you sign with the contractor you decide to hire. If you are not sure about the wording or content of the contract, bring it to your attorney for review. For really major jobs have the attorney draft the contract. Use the "Hiring Interview Sheet" on pages R-39 and R-40.

■ Present each contractor with your design and a list of desired materials. This will allow each contractor to make an estimate which is itemized enough so you can compare them. The estimate should give a detailed list of the materials to be used, and payment methods. Assuming all bidders have the same information, bids should be within 10 to 15 percent of each other. Beware of someone willing to undercut the competition.

■ The industry standard is to schedule payments in thirds; one-third before the work starts, one-third half way through, and the final third when the job is complete. The payment schedule of the contractor should be similar to this. It is also wise to hold back 10 to 15 percent from the final payment to be paid 30 days after the work is complete. This gives you time, after the project is completed, to look over everything very carefully before making the final payment.

■ Consider price, but also look carefully at which bids are the most professional and which include specific pricing and a timetable. Ask if the contractor is willing to pay a penalty if the work is not completed on time. Have this put in the contract.

■ Inquire about what other duties the contractor will and will not be responsible for, such as arranging for cleanup and removal of debris from the premises, both on a daily basis and after the job is completed.

■ The contractor should have a business street address, not just a post office box and telephone number. Kitchen and bath specialists should have a permanent location with a showroom and a good reputation with banks and suppliers.

■ Ask how long the person has been a contractor and how long the contractor has been in business in your area. The majority of contractors go out of business within three years.

■ Ask for names and addresses of previous (some older and some recent) and current customers. Call them. Ask if they are pleased with the work and if they would hire the contractor again. Also ask if you can see the work the contractor did. It is a good idea to inspect work which is both completed and in progress. Check each job for quality of workmanship and materials.

■ Since you will be working closely together with the contractor and crew, personality is another important factor. You should feel comfortable with the contractor and be able to communicate easily. The contractor should speak in language you can understand, should be

113

willing to explain exactly what work is involved, and should show evidence that he or she is listening to what you say. Misunderstandings can lead to problems.

- Ask if the contractor has liability insurance, workers' compensation, and, for larger projects, if they are bonded. Liability insurance covers any damages to the house caused by the contractor or natural disasters while the work is in progress. Workers' Compensation covers injury to the workers while working on the property. Bonding protects you against losses if the contractor should go out of business in mid-project. If the contractor does not have these coverages, you may be liable for any damages or injuries. Be sure you see copies of the insurance policies, or other proof of coverage, before you sign a contract and write down the names of the carriers, along with the policy numbers.

- Be sure the contractor is properly licensed, to do the type of work you require, with the state, as well as the county and city, where applicable. Most often, a certified license means the contractor has passed a state examination. Check licensing requirements with the department that regulates professionals in your state and the local building inspectors office. After you choose a contractor, but before you sign a contract, ask to see the licenses, copy the numbers, and check with the state's professional regulation department, to be sure the contractor is properly and currently licensed. Find out if the contractor is licensed for the entire state or for a specific county or city, how long the contractor has been licensed, what type of work he or she is licensed to perform, whether the contractor has complaints against him or her, and if the contractor has been disciplined or prosecuted. Usually the Building & Zoning or Building and Permitting Department of the county or city, will also have this information. The contractor should also have a local business license or permit to conduct a business from either the county or city.

- Check with the Better Business Bureau for any complaints about the contractor.

- If the contractor is a member of a professional organization, contact it and ask if the contractor is a member in good standing, if the contractor has ever been disciplined, and if there are complaints against the contractor. A major organization is The National Association of Independent Contractors, call (800) 982-7285.

- The contractor should be familiar with local building regulations and codes and be willing to obtain the necessary work permits and schedule necessary inspections. The contractor should provide copies for your review and records. Permits must be posted on site before work starts.

- Make sure the contractor guarantees all materials and workmanship. Compare the length of time the work and materials are covered, and the type or extent of coverage provided by the warranties. Before you sign a contract get the warranties in writing.

- Ask how the contractor handles problems if they arise, and if the contractor will request written approval before making changes or substitutes in materials and workmanship. This affords you the option of negotiating a lower price, if appropriate, or refusing the change.

Never Hire a Contractor Who:

- Asks you to obtain the permit. Operators who are not certified cannot obtain permits.
- Tells you a permit or inspection isn't required, unless you check with your city or county and confirm that these are not required.

- Wants to work under a verbal agreement. There should always be a written contract.
- Does not have proof of insurance.
- Shows only a business license and not a professional license.
- Requires payments be made in cash or checks made payable to an individual instead of a company.
- Requests full payment up front.

Signing a Contract

The final contract should include all the points which you and the contractor have agreed upon during the interview and anything else you have been able to negotiate. The contract should include:

- Start up and end dates for the job. Avoid an open-ended contract. Penalty for not completing the work on time, if applicable.
- Complete description of the project, including a complete list of all materials to be used, along with their size, color, weight, model, brand name, and quantity. Be sure the materials to be used are specifically spelled out.
- Financial arrangements should be clearly stated, including: total price, amount of down payment (if any), schedule of payments, and cancellation fee (if any).
- Provisions for changes: how they will be made.
- Terms of any warranties: should state whether they are "full" (all faulty products must be replaced, repaired, or your money returned) or "limited" (restrictions must be listed); plus the name and address of the contractor, manufacturer, or distributor honoring the warranty.
- Local building code or permit restrictions and fees involved.

Monitoring the Work

Once the work has started, it is important to monitor the work as it progresses. The sooner you spot a problem, the sooner you can deal with it.

- Meet with the contractor to iron out possible problems, i.e. dumpster, building material storage, bathroom for workers, etc.
- Set up periodic (usually weekly) meetings, to review the past period, and what is to be done in the coming one.
- Check progress daily; if things are not going as planned, find out why.
- Before any changes in the project are made, get both the price and nature of the change in writing.
- Do not hire a subcontractor in the middle of the project. You want the contractor responsible for the entire job.
- After the job is completed, the contractor should sign a lien waiver, or release of lien and notarized affidavit, meaning all subcontractors and suppliers have been paid and you are released from your obligations. If the contractor does not pay the subcontractors and suppliers for the project, you can be held liable for the bills.

Terminating a Contractor

If you are dissatisfied with the work that is being done and are unable to renegotiate your contract satisfactorily, you may want to terminate the contract. Move cautiously. Consider if you will have enough money to pay someone else to complete the work even if you are not able to get the money back from the original contractor. If you decide you can afford to fire the contractor and find somebody else to finish the work, it is wise to hire an attorney to handle the termination. Most contracts protect the contractors more than homeowners. The most common problems arise when a contract does not specify a timetable or completion date, or when there is no cost breakdown included in the contract. In order to end the contract in a way that releases you of your obligations, you need sufficient proof that the contractor has taken more than a reasonable time to complete the job or has failed to do the work as agreed. An outside expert may be able to help you prove it. If you cannot prove your case, you'll end up owing money to two contractors instead of one. Experts differ on whether you should get another contractor to work on the house before the agreement with the first contractor has been terminated.

TRANSFER AND SALE
OF
REAL ESTATE

In this chapter, we are presenting information to acquaint an Administrator with some of the main points which should be considered when selling real estate property. Since this sale involves signing a number of contracts, we suggest you read Chapter 8, "Basic Contract Definition" before you proceed. Of course, this is not intended to substitute for the advice of an attorney. See Chapter 15, "Hiring An Attorney."

SELLING REAL ESTATE PROPERTY

If it is determined by the Beneficiaries or the Court that the residence or other real property owned by the decedent should be sold, it is the duty of the Administrator to sell the property. Throughout the process of selling a house or other real estate, you will be asked to sign many contracts. Unless you are very familiar with the state's contract laws and the state's real estate laws, it is wise to have all contracts reviewed by your attorney. The main purpose for this review is because every clause in a contract represents an opportunity, for either the buyer or the seller to file a lawsuit. When reviewing a contract, a good real estate attorney will look for two things: all the things that are on the piece of paper, and all the things that are not. The attorney can also explain any terms in the contract which you may not understand. You may even want the attorney to handle negotiations with the buyer or the buyer's attorney. Experts advise real property sellers to bring an attorney aboard in the beginning. Ask the attorney to accept a flat fee with the understanding that an hourly fee will be paid if unforeseen problems arise. Never pay a percentage of the sale price of the property. The attorney does the same amount of work whether the property sells for a lot or a little. Every document that anyone expects you to sign, the attorney should see first. If title insurance is purchased through the attorney, ask for a fee reduction in consideration of the fee paid to the attorney by the title insurer.

Real Estate Sale Methods

When you have decided to sell real property, be sure to review all documents associated with the property. If it is located in a regulated community, be sure to check carefully for clauses which may affect the sale. Some property owners' associations require the property be sold through the association or they may require approval of new owners. Once you have determined the restrictions, if any, which may be applied to the sale, you are ready to decide the method you wish to employ to sell the property. There are three basic ways to sell real estate property: hire a professional to sell it; sell it yourself; or sell it at auction. Our purpose in this section is two-fold. First to present the basics involved in each method of real estate sale, and then to acquaint you with some of the terms and steps involved in real estate transactions.

Tidbit: Most buyers will be interested to know the monthly cost of running the home. It is a good idea to have copies of a year's worth of all utility bills (electric, gas, water, etc.) on display, perhaps on a kitchen counter. Along with property tax bills, trash collection charges, property owners' association dues, and other routine maintenance fees.

Selling Real Estate Property Through a Professional

We thought it would be helpful for you to know the titles of professionals you may come in contact with when selling real estate, along with their basic functions and responsibilities:

- A **"Seller's Agent"** represents the seller only. The agent negotiates price, terms, and conditions most favorable to the seller. The agent is required to present every offer to the seller, no matter how low it is. The agent cannot accept, reject, or negotiate an offer unless instructed to do so. Any private information the seller gives the agent will be kept confidential. Further, the seller's agent cannot reveal the seller's bottom line, say the seller is flexible, or reveal the personal reason for the sale, unless given permission to do so. However, any private information a buyer may give to this agent is not confidential and must be disclosed to the seller. It is not the agent's responsibility to clean, manage, or protect the property beyond locking the door upon leaving the premises. The agent is, however, responsible for any damage resulting from any action he or she did or did not take.
- A **"Buyer's Agent"** represents the buyer only. The agent negotiates price, terms, and conditions most favorable to the buyer. Any private information the buyer gives the agent will be kept confidential. However, any private information a seller may give to this agent is not confidential and must be disclosed to the buyer.
- A **"Dual Agent"** represents both buyer and seller. This may be to either party's exclusion or detriment. The agent will disclose, to both parties, any personal confidences which may place either party at a disadvantage.
- A **"Facilitator/Independent Contractor"** serves as an intermediary to help a buyer and a seller reach an agreement. This person does not represent the interest of either party, but the mutual interest of all parties. He or she will not disclose personal confidences which might place either party at a disadvantage.

The Advantages of Hiring a Professional

There are a few obvious benefits to enlisting the services of a professional. These include access to peer opinion and a networking system through:

- A **"Caravan"** of the realtor's in-house colleagues. They view the property and offer opinions on everything from price to presentation. It is a weekly event.
- A **"Brokers' Open"** is an event for other realty offices to get a preview of the property. It is by invitation only. Lunch is served (a big draw), and while munching, the realtors check out the property in an effort to match it to the right buyer.
- An **"Open House"** allows the general public to view the house, including drive-bys. These are usually most effective when held on a Sunday. Most agents admit these do not do as much to sell the property being shown as they do to help drum up business for the agent.
- The **"Multiple Listing Service"** (MLS) is a list (usually computerized) of homes for sale within a specific area. It gives the home's vital statistics, including: square footage, sales price, and the legal description. The MLS distributes this information to all member agents. It also lets agents know how, or if, they will be compensated if they work with the agent who initially listed the property for sale. Each real estate firm pays a monthly fee to use the MLS and pays for each listing it adds. There can be several MLS vendors within each county. Before a broker lists the property in the MLS, the seller may be asked to sign a form indicating whether the broker can or cannot pay part of the sales commission to a buyer's broker. By listing in the MLS, in addition to working with his or her own agents, a seller should be willing to work with subagents and buyer's agents. To facilitate all these agents showing the property to prospective buyers, a lock-box is placed on or near the front door. The lock-box contains the key to the door. This allows any local real estate agent, with a lock-box key, to get into the house even when no one is home. If there is personal property in the house, it would be wise to insist on an electronic lock-box. It leaves a printed record of which agent last showed the house. This can facilitate a police investigation, if property damage or a theft occurs. The MLS is considered to be the most effective sales tool realty agents have.
- A **"Relocation Network"** shows a prospective buyer in any city, color pictures of homes listed for sale on the network in other cities or states via personal computer (PC). Information from the PC in the office is downloaded into lap-top computers, and then taken to the buyers. This affords the widest base of prospective buyers.
- An **"On-line Listing"** available for viewing by house hunters nationwide on the Internet. Hundreds of local brokers have their own home pages in addition to Web sites with the listings of local and national multiple listing services.

Locating an Agent to Sell the Property

- Ask neighbors which realty company seems to have the best sales results in the area.
- Call a local real estate agent organization or association for reference.
- Look in the Yellow Pages of the phone book, under the headings REAL ESTATE, REAL ESTATE - COMMERCIAL & INDUSTRIAL, REAL ESTATE CONSULTANTS.

Hiring An Agent

The prospective agent should first be interviewed on the phone so you can get a basic idea of the person's experience and personality. If you think the agent is a person you can work with, invite him or her for an interview at the property you are going to list. You do not give a definite promise of listing over the phone and you are not obligated to list with the agent because he or she came to the property. Use the "Hiring Interview Sheet" on pages R-39 and R-40. The information you want to get over the phone includes:

- The length of time the agent has been state-licensed. Check with the State's Department of Professional Regulation to be sure the agent is properly licensed and if there have been any complaints or sanctions brought against the agent.
- The kind, if any, of continuing education courses the agent has taken. A realtor is a broker or agent who is a member of the National Association of Realtors. The first designation a realtor usually earns is a Graduate, Realtor Institute (GRI), which requires 90 hours of study. With more study and/or experience, a realtor can earn the designation Certified Residential Specialist (CRS) or Certified Real Estate Brokerage Manager (CRB).
- If the agent works full- or part-time.
- The length of time the agent has worked in your neighborhood.
- Ask for the name, address, and phone number of the agent's last three sales and the agent's last three expired listings. Then phone and ask those people how long their property was on the market, how well the agent informed them of the process, if they were satisfied or unhappy with the agent, and if they would list property with the same agent again.
- Ask what type of representation the agent offers, and how long the agent has worked with that type of representation.
- Ask how the property will be marketed. Does the agent schedule caravans, brokers' opens, open houses, and list with one or more MLS's or a relocation network? Will the agent also use local "homes-for-sale" handouts, newspaper, television, and radio advertising?
- If you consider it to be advantageous, ask if the company offers **Vertical Integration** by offering services such as, mortgage lending, title insurance, title services, and so on.
- Ask about fees. The standard commission is 6 to 7 percent of the price received for the property. The full commission is almost always paid by the seller. Usually, the agent will split this commission with an agent who finds a buyer. The typical split is 50-50 but may be slightly higher for the seller's agent. This creates a strong incentive for other agents to show the listing to prospective buyers. Consider discount commission agents carefully. Although many are excellent, most do not use the MLS.

When the agent comes to the house, he or she will want to tour the property to evaluate it. Then the agent will sit down with you and discuss the condition, salability, and most likely, selling price. The agent will also prepare and give you a written **Competitive Market Analysis (CMA)**. This form shows recent sales prices of similar nearby property, the asking prices of neighborhood property (your competition), the agent's estimate for the probable sales price for your property, and the agent's recommended asking price. Experts advise sellers add no more than 5 percent to the probable sales price, to allow some haggle room. The agent should also be able to estimate the length of time it will take to sell the property. Even if you are very impressed by the first agent, you should interview at least three so you can compare the CMAs made by each.

Type of Listing

When you choose an agent to sell the property, he or she will require you to sign a **Listing Agreement**. Very basically, the agreement is that the broker will try to find a buyer for the property and that the seller will pay the agent a commission for finding a buyer. There are two primary types of listings:

- With an **Open** or **Multiple** listing, you can contract with any number of realtors to sell the property. Most realty agents refuse to work with an open listing, because the agent lacks control over the sale. An open listing is a written invitation by the seller to one or more realty agents to find a buyer for the home. The agent who obtains an acceptable purchase offer earns the full sales commission but no fee is owed if the seller finds a buyer or if the listing is canceled.

- With an **Exclusive** listing, one realty company is given the exclusive right to sell the property. The majority of residential listings are this type. This listing gives the agent maximum control and incentive. If the property sells during the listing, and in some cases after it expires, the agent receives the commission, no matter who actually found the buyer.

The Listing Agreement

Since the **Listing Agreement** is a legal contract, each clause should be very carefully considered before it is signed. Once you sign a contract with a real estate broker, you are bound by the terms of that contract. So, if you object to a particular clause, ask for it to be changed. Before contacting the real estate broker, consider these usual terms of a contract and the ones you are willing to accept:

- The length of the contract. Although most agents want long listings, experts recommend signing only a 90-day listing. Based upon the agent's performance, when the listing expires, if the property remains unsold, you can rehire the same agent or switch to another. If you sign an exclusive listing for a longer period and then determine the agent is not truly trying to sell the property, contact an attorney. The attorney can determine if you may have grounds to break the contract.
- The agent will receive a commission when he or she finds a "Willing and Able" buyer, even if the seller later decides not to sell the property.
- The agent will receive a commission if anyone finds a buyer during the life of the listing. Even if you find a buyer yourself, unless you specifically reserve the right to find a buyer on your own, you cannot sell the property without paying the real estate commission.
- The agent will receive a commission if, after the listing expires, the property sells to someone the broker had previously brought to see the property or whose name had been given, in writing, to the seller. This is called a **Procuring Clause** provision. Such provisions usually are effective from one month to a year after the listing expires.
- Any additional period of time after the listing expires, and under what conditions the agent will get a commission when the property is sold, even if you or another agent found the buyer.

121

■ The responsibility of the seller choosing to cancel the contract. A seller should be able to cancel the contract at any time. Usually, the seller will be responsible for paying the broker's out-of-pocket expenses and other damages. However, if the cancellation is by mutual agreement, nothing should be owed to the broker. It is important for a seller, who decides to take the property off the market, to notify the agent immediately and offer to reimburse the agent for out-of-pocket expenses, such as money paid for advertising; because under the terms of the listing agreement, if the agent finds a "willing and able buyer," the agent could still be entitled to the commission, even if the house is not sold. Further, if the seller decides not to sell the property after seeing the potential buyers, he or she could be subject to a lawsuit. The refusal to sell to a known buyer could be interpreted to be on the basis of their race, religion, disability, sexual preference, or family status (such as the number of children in the family).

■ Some agents will negotiate the amount of the commission. For example, if the house is sold within 30 days, the commission will be 7 percent; if the sale takes over 90 days, the commission will be 5 percent.

■ The agent is not liable for any damages to the property unless they are the agent's fault.

■ If the prospective buyer forfeits the deposit, it is usually divided equally between the seller and broker. However, the broker's portion should be limited to no more than the amount the commission would have been for the sale.

■ The marketing tools the agent will use: caravans, brokers' opens, open houses, MLS listings or relocation networks, as well as, if and how often, the property will be included in local "homes-for-sale" handouts, newspaper, television, and radio advertising.

■ Consider a clause stating that you will only accept a deposit from a prospective buyer who is pre-qualified for the selling price of the property. Otherwise, you may be tied up while the buyer is trying to find a mortgage. If the buyer does not qualify for the mortgage, you will be back to square one of trying to find a buyer. **Pre-qualified** means the buyer has provided the real estate broker or a lender with financial information and, upon this unverified information, the professional has determined the size mortgage for which the buyer should be able to qualify. **Pre-approved** (sometimes called a **Commitment Loan**) means the buyer will be approved for a specific mortgage program and rate. It includes verification and documentation of income, job, credit, assets, liabilities, and available cash. This approval is given for a limited time (often 30 days), and will depend on a satisfactory contract and appraisal of the house. This costs buyers $300 or more, so they seriously want to buy and will be in a hurry to close, before the loan commitment expires.

■ Avoid embarrassment. Never mention any restrictions on the type of buyer you want. The National Association of Realtors' Code of Ethics and Standards of Practice states a realtor cannot legally discriminate based on race, color, religion, sex, national origin, disability, family or marital status.

For Sale By Owner (FSBO)

Experts warn that sales by owners have a low success level. They point out that it is not as easy to sell a house as it looks, and that most sellers need a lot more knowledge of real estate transactions than they usually have. As you may gather from the bare bones descriptions in this chapter, selling real estate is a time consuming, exacting and complex process. Many metropolitan areas have "For Sale By Owner" companies, which provide assistance or information about the legal process of a real estate sale and often provide an MLS service and other advertising methods to clients. Discount Real Estate Brokerages offer fee-for-service arrangements providing only the support or services a client requests. Before choosing to sell a home or other real property yourself, carefully evaluate your ability to:

- Determine the value of the property in today's real estate market. One method for determining the current market value is to hire a real estate appraiser. Another method is to interview at least three real estate agents and get a CMA from each. Then, average the three CMAs to get an idea of a fair market price.
- Evaluate the current market and estimate how long it will take to sell the property, based upon factors that influence the sale of any property.
- Create, and have copies printed of, a professional looking information sheet or flier: with a description of the property, the highlights of the neighborhood, an accurate floor plan, and a flattering picture of the property.
- Provide ample funds to advertise in the local newspaper, on television, and/or other media available for independent sales in your area. Ask the media representative for help in wording; some phrases can be construed as discriminatory.
- Creating a home page on the Internet with your flier and a few additional interior pictures. The pictures can be scanned in at most small-business support services offices.
- Be available at all times, to answer the phone, respond to inquiries, and go over to show the property.
- Go alone to meet and deal with strangers, whether they have an appointment or just knock on the door and expect to be shown through the house.
- Identify and separate "browsers" from qualified buyers. When prospective buyers call for an appointment you should:
  - Ask what type of house and neighborhood they want and when they want to make the move.
  - Advise that the property is only being shown to pre-qualified buyers. Then ask prospective buyers to bring a letter from a mortgage lender stating they have pre-qualified in the price range of the property.
  - Ask for their names, and for a phone number where they can be reached, in case you have to change the appointment. Then check the name and number in the phone book for authenticity.
  - Advise them that they must show a photo identification (driver's license or passport) before they come in to see the home. When they arrive, write down the buyer's name, phone number, and address, and keep it in a safe place away from the property.
- When showing the property, invite prospective buyers into each room, but do not crowd them or hustle them along; move them through at a gentle pace. If there is personal property in the house, you should never leave a person out of your sight in any room. Try to stand back, and give them an opportunity to discuss their impressions.
- Understand seller financing, second mortgages, contingencies, and other variables that might come up.
- Understand the legal aspects of the sale, including: required inspections, disclosures, title documents, legal descriptions, necessary contracts, funding of new loans, and recording final grant deeds, trust deeds, etc. (The sale process is explained later in this chapter.)
- Be prepared to handle the final walk-through with the buyer and settle any disputes that might arise before closing the transaction.
- Negotiate realistically, being impartial enough to make the right decision.

■ Be sure that the contracts you drew up or purchased at an office stationery store are accepted under state law. If they are not, they may prove to be unenforceable. Experts advise that people who choose FSBO should have a good real estate attorney from the moment they decide to sell. However, if you require too much help with transactions, the attorney may charge as much as an agent's commission. Remember, an attorney will charge a lot more to draw up contracts than to review them. Help is also available from Escrow Services, Title Companies, and Title Insurance Companies that may have an attorney on staff, for real estate closings, escrows, title searches, etc.

Selling at Auction

The main attraction of selling a home through an auction is that it is a fast sale. Therefore, it is the perfect option when a quick sale is needed. Sellers can learn of auctions through real estate agents or auction company advertising. When a seller contacts an auctioneer, a representative will come out, look at the property, and prepare a comparable market analysis. This enables the seller to make an intelligent decision about the form of auction that is best. Auctions can take three forms:

■ **"Absolute"** — where the property is sold to the highest bidder;

■ **"Minimum Bid"** — where sellers set a minimum sales price below which the property will not be sold. If, during the auction, bidding slows, the seller is free to switch to an absolute and sell to the highest bidder.

■ **"Reserve"** — where the seller may reserve the right to reject the highest bid, although some auctioneers are wary of this.

If you choose to sell through an auction, you will be required to sign a contract. The contract includes provisions for the type of auction, commission fees, title and escrow issues, auction date, and the terms of the sale. The home is usually auctioned within 30 to 60 days of the initial contact between the seller and the auctioneer. Buyers must accept the sales contract without any contingencies. However, this does not exempt sellers and auctioneers from their obligation to disclose any defects that could affect the material value of the property before the auction begins. Additionally, buyers can arrange previews of the home before the auction date. They can have home inspectors, engineers, or other evaluators look at the property. Since auctioned homes are sold in as-is condition; once the auction occurs, there are no more inspections. After the bidding, the buyer signs a bid acknowledgment and sets a closing date on the purchase. A ten percent buyer's premium is usually added to the final bid on the house. The closing, generally, is within 45 days after the auction. Typically, prospective buyers bring to the auction a predetermined, certified deposit which buyers risk losing if they don't meet the closing deadline.

The National Association of Realtors' Auction Committee has set forth the following three components as conditions which are favorable to choosing auctions. They suggest a seller consider auction if two of the three components pertain to his or her situation:

- **Market Conditions**: A declining or dull real estate market, or a market where demand and competition are high. If a listing with a real estate broker is about to expire, without any sale in sight, it could be an indicator of a poor market.
- **Seller's Situation**: When the seller needs a quick sale in order to get immediate cash, does not have sufficient funds to keep up carrying costs (e.g., mortgages, taxes, insurance, etc.), or must liquidate an Estate.
- **Property Considerations**: The property has high carrying costs, has equity of 25 percent or more; is vacant; or is difficult to appraise and/or is unique.

Auctioneers are regulated by the Board of Auctioneers, under the State's Department of Business and Professional Regulation. If only the house is being sold, a licensed real estate broker can conduct the auction. However, if the auction includes personal property, an auctioneer's license and auction business license are also required. Contact the appropriate regulator to check if an auctioneer has been disciplined and has a current license.

The Sale Process

Purchase Offer

Since most real estate is sold through agents, we will discuss the process of the sale as if an agent is involved. When the real estate agent finds a buyer for the house, it is customary for the agent to prepare and present the seller with the buyer's **Purchase Offer**. This is usually done on a preprinted form. It includes the selling price and when the home will be available. This is an outline or preliminary agreement. Sellers have three possible responses to an offer: it can be accepted, rejected, or they can make a counter-offer. Be sure you understand every word of that agreement. If you do not understand or like a clause, speak up. Just because it is printed does not mean it cannot be crossed out. Everything is negotiable. If you don't understand something, be sure to consult a real estate attorney before you sign the agreement. If you agree to the terms of the sale, a "Contract of Sale" will be drawn up to give the exact details of the conditions of the sale.

CONTRACT OF SALE

The sale of real estate begins with a sales contract. The **Contract of Sale** is an agreement on the terms by which the seller of property will transfer title to the buyer by means of a deed.

This means that the contract must set out the stated address and the legal description of the property being sold, the purchase price of the property and method of payment, and the kind of deed to be given. The legal description should correspond exactly to the deed, and even if you think you cannot understand a legal description you can certainly check to see if the words and numbers match between the sales contract and the deed. Although accuracy is desirable, if a clerical error or typing mistake is made, but there is no question as to which property was intended to be sold, the contract usually cannot be canceled.

Before signing a contract for the sale of real property, you should consider carefully the terms under which you are selling the property. The contract makes you responsible for the accuracy of the information in the contract and <u>for insuring that the house and surrounding property will be in the same condition at closing as when the contract of sale was signed</u>. Both the buyer and seller can cross out or add any item they have agreed to in bargaining.

If a dispute arises after the closing, such as a misrepresentation for failure to disclose defects, the legal remedies are rescission of the sale or monetary damages. The difficulty is proving the seller was aware of the defect and failed to disclose it. If the buyer can prove intentional fraud, he or she may also be entitled to punitive damages, interest, and reasonable expenses. Sellers have several possible defenses to a specific performance lawsuit. They include inadequate consideration; consent obtained by fraud, mistake or misrepresentation; unfair practices, and unreasonable hardship.

Contract Terms to be Considered - Contingencies

A **Contingency** is a provision included in a real estate purchase agreement that must be satisfied for the transaction to close. The contract should provide a procedure for satisfying each contingency. There are basically two methods of considering a contingency to have been met, either passive or active. With the passive method, a contingency is deemed to be satisfied, unless the party who benefits from the contingency notifies the other party, in writing, that the contingency is not being removed. In this case silence is considered approval. The active method provides that all contingencies must be approved or disapproved in writing. This method is usually preferred because it eliminates any doubt about the status of a contingency. If either the buyer or seller cannot remove a contingency within the time specified in the contract, they must ask for an extension, and be prepared to make some concessions in exchange for the extension. Any extension should be in writing. When contingencies cannot be satisfied, the contract is usually canceled. If this happens, a **Release of Contract** form must be signed by both the buyer and seller in order to make the cancellation final. Most contracts imply or state that good faith efforts will be made by each party to satisfy each contingency. The last lines of the contract usually allow the nondefaulting party to bring a lawsuit for "specific performance and damages" against the party who breaches the contract. The parties may bring a lawsuit even if the contract does not provide for one. **Your signature on the Contract means you have read it, agreed to its terms, and have received a copy of it.**

Contingencies the Seller Might Include in the Contract

Some of the contingencies the seller, or government regulation, may place upon the buyer in order for the sale of the property to go through are:

- Specify the total sale price the buyer must pay.
- Specify the deposit amount, or **earnest money**, required to bind the bargain. A seller should never accept a deposit check from the buyer made out directly to the seller. It should be made out to, and held in, the real estate agent's trust account, a title company's trust account, or the trust account of the seller's attorney. A deposit should only accompany a signed contract.
- Whether or not the buyer must **refinance** (get a new mortgage) or will **assume** (accept the responsibility for the balance of) the existing loan.
- Whether or not the seller will agree to pay some points on the new mortgage. A **Point** (equal to one percent of the loan interest) is a charge assessed by the lender as a loan origination fee, or as a way to prepay interest, reducing the interest rate at which a loan is amortized. **Amortization** is the orderly payment of a mortgage, usually by paying monthly installments until the debt is repaid.
- State the date of **Closing**. When the title will be transferred to the buyer, usually by means of a warranty deed, in exchange for the buyer performing his or her part of the bargain.
- Require that the buyer get mortgage financing within a specific number of days, often 30 or 60 days. If the buyer cannot get a mortgage within this time, he or she must ask for an extension in writing or be considered in breach of the contract. The seller may require a concession in exchange for an extension, such as an increase in the deposit amount.
- If the buyer makes the purchase contingent upon selling their home; a clause should be included allowing the seller to accept another offer if this contingency cannot be removed within a specified time (48 to 72 hours) of notification of the new offer.
- If the seller is going to carry financing, he or she might include approval of the contract by his or her attorney or accountant, or approval of the buyer's financial documents.
- Specify the buyer will pay loan costs, which are the expenses for the services required in obtaining a loan, often including appraisal fees, attorney fees, survey fees, and loan commissions.
- Specify who will pay costs which are usually the responsibility of the seller or buyer, but may be shared or paid by either, depending upon the agreement of the parties involved. These include: certain closing costs (typically paid by the seller); owner's title insurance or abstract (typically paid by the seller); the loan underwriting fee (typically paid by the buyer but paid by the seller for FHA or VA loans); roof, termite, and other inspections (Typically, the first inspection is paid by the buyer. However, if the seller disagrees with the result of the inspection, he or she pays for a second inspection. If there is still no agreement, a third inspection may be paid for on a 50-50 basis.); property owners' association approval fees; transfer and assumption fees (typically split between buyer and seller).
- If the seller forgets something of value in the property, the buyer will return it.
- The remedies the seller may require if the buyer breaches the contract. Usually this will be loss of the buyer's deposit, but may also allow for a lawsuit for monetary damages incurred by the seller because of the breach. These damages may include carrying costs (e.g., mortgage payments, taxes, insurance, etc.) paid by the seller while waiting for another buyer. If

the property is eventually sold for less than the breaching buyer's contracted price, the damages will be the difference between the two prices or specific performance (buyer must buy the property). Further information on legal remedies is available from your real estate attorney.

Contingencies the Buyer Might Include in the Contract

Some of the contingencies the buyer or government regulation may place upon the seller in order for the sale of the property to go through are:

■ The seller is required to make **Disclosure** (tell) to the buyer of anything about the property that may affect its value, including defects that may or may not be readily apparent and those the seller should have known about. A defect or dangerous condition deliberately concealed by the seller, or by the real estate agent, could be the basis for legal action. Some disclosures are required by local ordinances, and state and federal laws. A few states have adopted the seller disclosure form, which the National Association of Realtors is promoting. The disclosure form is a checklist the seller must complete to attest to the soundness, or lack thereof, of the property in question. Disclosure requirements may also include such things as informing the buyer if the property is in a flood zone, or if there is a problem with the title.

■ The contract should specify the number of days the seller has to make these disclosures, as well as a time period for the buyers to investigate the ramifications of the disclosure, and approve or reject, the contingency.

■ That the property pass inspections demanded by the buyer, such as: a general inspection, pool inspection, radon testing, etc. In addition to a general inspection, there may be some requirements of the government, and/or mortgage lender, specific to the area where the property is located, such as: roof inspections, termite inspections, flood zone survey, etc.

■ The seller and buyer should negotiate and specify who will make or pay for repairs if inspections reveal defects. The seller can be required to make repairs or agree to split the cost of repairs with the buyer on a percentage basis, or the seller may lower the price of the property to allow repairs to be made by the buyer.

■ That the property be ready by a specified move-in date, and setting forth specific penalties for failure to turn over the property, in proper condition, on that date. Most real estate contracts stipulate that a home must be habitable and swept clean ("Broom Clean" is a term used in some contracts) when it changes possession. Although there is usually nothing in the contract that requires the seller to take everything with him or her or make sure the house is empty, there should not be so much junk that the buyer cannot move in. The buyer could then file a lawsuit for monetary damages, such as motel or hotel bills, and other living expenses incurred, while waiting for the place to get cleaned out, plus any removal and cleaning expenses to make it livable.

■ Provide a **Home Warranty** policy. A home warranty is basically a one year service contract that typically covers the interior plumbing, heating system, garbage disposal, water heater, wiring, central air conditioning, and built-in appliances. Exclusions may include such major items as the roof and building structure. Prices vary depending on the company and the level of coverage. These are often available through real estate agents or other brokers who get a fee for each warranty sale. ERA, Inc., the acknowledged home-warranty pioneer, offers its own program. Home warranties can be purchased by buyers or sellers. Sellers should be careful not to cover appliances and systems that already might be under other warranties. Newer homes may still be under a warranty bought by the builder.

- That the property is properly zoned for the purpose the buyer is intending.
- To what extent the buyer and seller are responsible for making and paying for repairs for damage caused by a fire or other casualty occurring between the time of signing the contract and the closing. The contract should also specify if such casualty will result in cancellation or release of both parties from the contract if repairs are not completed by a specific date.
- A list of the fixtures that are included in the sale. **Fixtures** are those items which are usually sold with the house by prevailing custom or law, as well as items the seller wants to leave, and items the buyer wants the seller to leave. Real estate includes the land and anything attached to it, built into it, or growing from it. A good rule of thumb is that, if you have to use a tool to remove it, it should stay with the house or property. However, the seller can exclude items that would normally be called fixtures, if the buyer agrees. Most sellers specify that appliances are sold "as is" rather than "in good working order."
- That the property or house will be in the same condition at closing as when the contract of sale is signed. (To avoid problems, the seller should change or remove any fixtures he or she does not want to sell with the property before showing the house.)
- Which appurtenances are included with, or will be reserved from, the sale. An **Appurtenance** is anything that goes along with the land: privileges, rights, and improvements that belong to the principal property. This may include such things as:
  - Mineral, water, and timber rights;
  - An easement or right of way on the property; or
  - Use of an easement on someone else's property.
- Provisions for satisfactory title review.
- The seller is required to provide the buyer with an affidavit that the property is not encumbered. Property is **Encumbered** when it has been used as collateral for a debt or loan, or when a contractor or supplier places a lien or claim against the property title. The debt must be paid off before title to the property can pass to a new owner.
- Claims for money owed for recent repairs may not have been filed yet against the title. Therefore, if any repairs have been made within a certain period before the closing (90 days in some contracts), the seller must give the buyer lien releases or waivers from each contractor and supplier involved with the work.
- Be willing and able to pay typical expenses of the seller, including: the real estate agent's commission; their own attorney's fees; recording fees to clear title; satisfaction of existing mortgages, certified liens, and special assessments; purchase documentary stamps (if required); and a computer update of the final abstract.
- Pay a pro-rated portion to the date of closing on usual carrying costs (e.g., water and sewer fees, fuel oil or heating oil, property taxes, income from any rental property, etc.).
- Provide a **Lot Survey**, showing the perimeters and actual size and position of the property. If you cannot find the original survey, or the name of the firm that did the survey, contact the mortgage company and ask them to check its records for the survey. If you cannot find the survey firm in the phone book, call the local "Surveyor's Association" and ask them who has the records of the original lot survey firm. A repeat survey is usually less expensive than a new one.
- The seller will release the buyer from the contract and return part or all of the deposit, if the buyer either cannot get financing or get it at a particular interest rate.

- The seller will furnish a "Good and Merchantable Title." The contract will usually give the seller a choice of furnishing an abstract or title insurance as proof of this. (These terms are explained later in this chapter.)
- The contract of sale will stipulate the type of deed to be supplied. It should normally call for a Warranty Deed, unless there are unusual circumstances, of which both parties are fully aware. (Deeds are further explained in this chapter.)
- The remedies the buyer may require if the seller breaches the contract. Usually this will be cancellation of the contract and return of the deposit, but may also allow the buyer to force the seller, through a lawsuit, to deliver the deed (called specific performance), as agreed in the contract, and/or to pay damages. Damages may include the cost of living caused by the breach and, if the buyer has to purchase another home at a higher price, the difference in the prices. Until the lawsuit is settled, a notice of *lis pendens* is usually recorded against the title. A **notice of *lis pendens*** warns prospective buyers that the title to the property is in litigation. If someone buys the property, it is done subject to the outcome of the lawsuit. Further information on legal remedies is available from your real estate attorney.

Final "Walk-Through" and Product Warranties

The final **Walk-Through** is the inspection by the buyer to be sure all work agreed upon is done and the property is in the condition promised in the contract of sale. It is done within seven days before closing, but should leave enough time to allow the seller to remedy any problems. Buyers may ask for operating manuals and warranties for appliances, etc., and for the names and numbers of repairmen and trades people who have maintained the property.

Individual Product Warrantees

Most products are sold with a short term warranty to protect the purchaser against loss caused by defects. Often, the purchaser buys an **Extended Warranty Contract** on the product, to provide protection against defects that surface after the manufacturer's warranty has expired, to provide periodic maintenance of the product, or provide repair when a breakdown occurs. When a covered product is sold or transferred, whether as an individual item or included as a real estate fixture, the contract, if it is transferrable, should be given to the new owner. If there is an extended warranty on any personal property of the decedent, read the contract carefully to determine its coverage and terms. Among the provisions to note are:

- The length of the service contract coverage;
- Exactly what repairs and maintenance will be performed;
- The actual provider of the service (the manufacturer, retailer, charge card, or an independent third party);
- If the product must be taken to the service center or if it will be serviced on the owner's premises;
- If the contract is valid if the product is moved to another location; or
- If the contract is valid if the product is transferred to a new owner.

Deeds and Titles

A Deed

A **Deed** is a legal document by which title to real property is transferred from one owner to another and for designating how the property is owned. See Chapter 5, "Property Ownership." Every deed identifies property by describing its location according to surveyors' points on an area map. The most common ways of doing this is by "Lot and Square" or "Metes and Bounds." Some deeds, and many other documents, will use the street or road address as well. Learn the identifying numbers and make sure that whenever your property is described, these numbers are used. To have legal status, a deed must be filed at the county recorder's office, usually located in your county courthouse. These offices keep ownership records for all land in the county.

Recording

Recording a deed is simply a matter of going to the County Recorder's Office, registering the title and paying a fee, usually a nominal amount. The idea of recording is to give notice to all the world of the current status of any piece of real property. Information about real property that is filed at the County Recorder's Office is public record. The county clerk keeps the record books, containing every transaction involving any piece of real estate in that county; and maintains files for the papers documenting the transactions. These will include deeds, mortgages, and other liens. If someone does not record a transaction, such as putting a lien on a piece of property, the law varies from state to state, but that person may lose his or her rights to assert a lien against subsequent owners because he or she failed to give notice of those rights by recording them. These record books are set up alphabetically in two basic ways, so that you can look up the property under the name of the **Grantor** (the one selling or otherwise disposing of a piece of property), or in reverse, under the name of the **Grantee** (the one acquiring the piece of property).

Warranty Deed

The type of deed most often used for real estate transfers is called a **Warranty Deed** which guarantees, or warrants, certain promises as to the conveyance, from the seller to the buyer. It makes the seller responsible for what are called "warrantees of title." This type of Deed makes a "grant and warrant" that:
- The seller has good title to the property and the right to sell it;
- The property is free from **Encumbrances**. This means there are no claims on the property such as mortgages, trust deeds, liens, or outstanding taxes, except those expressly set out in the deed;

■   The covenant, or promise, of quiet enjoyment, meaning the buyer is assured he or she will not be thrown out by someone with a better title. Any buyer suffering from a broken promise (**Breach of Warranty**) down the line, can go back to each former seller to enforce his or her rights.

Quitclaim Deed

A **Quitclaim Deed** is completely different from a warranty deed, in that a quitclaim deed promises nothing. A quitclaim deed is saying "If I have any interest I am conveying it to you." It puts the buyer on notice that the seller is not claiming to have good title, or any title. Whatever interest the party has in the property is unconditionally transferred, along with any outstanding liens or debts attached to the property. A quitclaim deed is often used to clear up a cloudy title. The Administrator of an Intestate Estate may ask all the remote and unlikely but possible Beneficiaries to sign a quitclaim deed. The quitclaim deed can also be used to surrender the decedent's claims to the property, so it can be transferred to a new owner or co-owner. The Administrator of an Estate can use a quitclaim to transfer property from the deceased person to the named Beneficiaries, by surrendering the decedent's claims to the property. It can also be used by a surviving spouse if the property was jointly owned, to surrender the deceased spouse's rights to the property; or by a successor Trustee to transfer property from the Trust to a Beneficiary. The first owner surrenders (quits) any claims to the property.

Quiet Title Deed

When all payments have been made on real estate by someone who does not have a deed; he or she can file a **Quiet Title** action to get clear title to the property. The action requires completion and submission of specific legal forms according to the requirements of the particular state, and presenting documents that prove who made the payments. Advertisements are placed in legal publications to notify deeded owners of the action. If they do not respond, or if they contest the action, the Court will hold a hearing and can authorize the transfer of the title. The entire process takes a few months. Once the party gets the Court's permission, he or she can apply for a deed. The Administrator of an Estate would be responsible for obtaining title if the deceased person was the party making payments. The property can then be transferred to the Beneficiaries, or sold. An attorney is your best bet for this type of action.

Good and Merchantable Title

The seller of property is required to prove that he or she possesses a **Good and Merchantable Title**. This means that the property conforms to the promises made in the deed by the seller. Good and merchantable title shows, by either abstract or title insurance that the seller has the right to sell the property as described and can convey good title to it. The seller must show that there are no defects in the chain of title, down to him or her, since any defect is a **Cloud on the Title**. Lending institutions often require a title search or title insurance before granting a mortgage on the property. Lenders usually suggest a title company who may also act as the closing agent for the bank and buyer. Often an attorney will do the same work and provide representation for about the same fee. If you need more information, contact your attorney, the County Recorder's Office, a title company, or real estate agent.

Chain of Title

The **Chain of Title** is the historical record of all transfers of ownership of a piece of real property. It lists all recorded titles, in the order they occurred, and how the deed to the property was passed from one owner to the next. If a transfer or sale was not recorded, it is called a "break in the chain," and would be considered "outside of the Chain of Title." You can check the ownership by reviewing the previous transfers of the title at the County Recorder's Office, or ask the recorder to send you a property profile that shows the current status of the title. Recording a deed secures title. Court cases have shown that someone outside the chain of title may not be the owner of property. Recording is also important for securing title insurance. A title insurance company will not issue a warranty deed if it thinks the title has a cloud, such as someone claiming title who is not shown on the chain of title.

Abstract

An **Abstract** is a written history of a real estate parcel's chain of title. When an abstract is prepared, it goes all the way back to the original land grant or deed from the government. It shows the continuity of ownership, through the record of sales and purchases, mortgages, or other claims against the property.

Title Insurance

Title Insurance means an insurance company is promising that the title is clear and will make good if the title is not. The seller pays for the insurance, because it is his or her duty to guarantee good title. A straight title policy does not guarantee that the property is free of liens and encumbrances. It is important that you know exactly what risk you are insured against and if the insurance will cover the cost of any loss. The average policy contains numerous exceptions, so there are many problems which title insurance does not cover. Since the terms of the policy can often be negotiated before it's purchased, it is wise to have the policy reviewed by an attorney familiar with title insurance. This can prevent the insurance company from making too many exclusions and leaving you with virtually no insurance. In most states a title insurance policy is given far more frequently than an abstract. The usual cost of title insurance is 0.5 percent of the purchase price. Some of the occurrences which could result in the loss of the title, and which the title insurance should cover are:

- **Break in the Chain of Title**, which could be caused by two titles being recorded to different owners at the same time. This can include: a forged signature on the deed, a missing heir, a deed signed by a minor or a person of unsound mind, a defective foreclosure, or errors in indexing and copying.

- An exercise of **Eminent Domain** which is the right of a local, state or federal government, needing a piece of property for a public improvement (e.g., building a road, dam, school, etc.), to force the owner to give it up for a fair market price. If a government agency is trying to force a sale of the property, get an appraisal of the property's value from a licensed appraiser. See Chapter 9, "Valuing Property."

- Through **Adverse Possession** (also known as **Notorious Possession** or commonly **Squatter's Rights**), which allows someone who has occupied a piece of property for a specified number of years to claim that property as his or her own. Even if a person has a deed and title to the property, if someone else resides on it for a state-specific length of time (typically 5 to 20 years), uses it exclusively, continuously, openly, and without denying that someone else is the owner, that titled owner may not have a right to the land. Claims of adverse possession do not necessarily extend over the entire property. For example, a person who uses a part of another person's property every day for the required length of time can claim rights to that part (e.g., a path through another's field, a shed in another's yard, or another's half of a shared driveway). In that event, the person obtains a limited legal right, called an **Easement**, to that part of the property. A titled owner can protect his or her property by signing an agreement allowing the person use of the property for only a limited time, but specifying at the end of that time, all rights to the property remain with the titled owner.

- Through a **Forced Sale**, where property can be taken and sold. This occurs when the owner violates the terms of a loan, causing its cancellation. Then the person or institution holding a lien on the property through a "Trust Deed" (explained later in this chapter) or other loan, can force the sale of the property to collect the money. The state and federal governments can do the same to collect outstanding taxes. Under most laws, the owner must be notified of a sale and be allowed to pay. Some laws allow the owner to buy the property back within a specified time, if the taxes or debt are paid off. This points out the importance of the Administrator making payments on any mortgages or liens which may be held against the property, as well as being sure tax payments are current.

Transfer of Title

To transfer title of a piece of real estate, someone with legal authority (Administrator, Trustee, joint tenant with right of survivorship) must prepare, sign, notarize, and record a deed listing the new owner(s) to transfer title of the property to them. The type of deed which must be used, depends upon whether or not guarantees are required when the property is transferred. **In many states, upon the death of the owner of property in joint tenancy, title automatically is vested in the surviving joint tenant or tenants. The filing of a death certificate evidencing the death of a joint tenant, recorded in the chain of title record, will usually establish title**

in the surviving joint tenant(s). For real estate owned by a Living Trust, the successor Trustee transfers property to the Beneficiaries by preparing, signing, and recording (in the county recorder's office) a deed from him- or herself, as Trustee for the Living Trust, to the specified Beneficiaries. No Court or other administrative action is required. However, real estate owned solely by the decedent, or as tenant in common with others, will necessitate Probate Proceedings whether the decedent died with or without a Will. An Administrator may not execute a deed without the Court's permission. To transfer the property to a co-owner or Beneficiary:

- Locate the existing deed.
- Purchase a blank quitclaim or grant deed form (either will do) at an office supply store in the state where the property is located. Required language can vary slightly from one state to the next. If possible, use a form in general use in the state where the real property is located. To be absolutely sure, it may be best to have the deed prepared by an attorney.
- Deed the property from the decedent to the new owner(s). Be sure to use exactly the same form of the deceased person's name on the new deed that was used on the old one.
- Delete (cross out) any language on the deed form that relates to a sale. A transfer is not a sale.
- Type all technical information (such as the legal description of the property) on the new deed exactly as it appears on the old one. Beware of typographical errors!
- Sign the deed in front of a Notary Public.
- Record the deed with the County Property Recorder of Deeds for the county in which the real estate is located. Before you actually take the deed in, call and ask:
  - How many copies you need;
  - If there are any local or state transfer taxes applicable to transfers to Beneficiaries. Usually there aren't but it pays to check;
  - What is required to apply for homestead exemption, if applicable;
  - Do any special transfer forms have to be completed, and if they are available at that office. A few states require additional paperwork.

Trust Deeds and Mortgages

A **Trust Deed** (sometimes called **Deed of Trust**) does not transfer property to a new owner. Instead, a piece of property is posted as collateral for a loan or mortgage. A **Mortgage** (the pledge of property as security for a loan) or **Deed of Trust** lien must be filed with the county clerk who keeps the deed book, and is added to the record of that property. If a lending company has a deed of trust on the property and cannot collect loan payments, it can force the sale of that property to collect the debt. A deed of trust allows the lender to almost instantly snatch back the property, without the rules that control foreclosure. This is allowed in a number of states. Under **Default**, i.e. the mortgage is not paid for a specified time, the mortgage holder may be able to issue a **Notice of Acceleration**, calling for payment of the entire amount due. If this happens, it might force you to lose the property or refinance it. In other cases, a foreclosure action can be brought by the mortgage holder according to state statute. A **Foreclosure** action allows the mortgage holder to take and sell the mortgaged property. If the foreclosed property sells for less than the amount of the remaining mortgage, the Estate can be held liable for the difference. If the property has a second mortgage on it and payments to the primary mortgage lender are missed, the second mortgage lender will probably step in, make the missing payments and then immediately begin foreclosure. Therefore, it is important to keep up the mortgage payments on the property. When the **Equity** (the owner's value in a property, determined by the difference between its current fair market value and any encumbrances) on the property is very low or non-existent, an Administrator may consider allowing the lender to foreclose on the property. This action should be carefully considered and discussed with the Beneficiaries, the attorney, and possibly with the Court.

Before real estate is sold or transferred, the mortgage should be carefully reviewed by you, or an attorney, for restrictive clauses. If you cannot find the mortgage, ask the lender for a copy of both the mortgage (or deed of trust) and the promissory note. One restrictive clause is the **Due-on-Sale** clause. This provides for the loan to become due if the property is sold or transferred; in other words, the loan is **Non-Assumable**. Most mortgages today are not assumable by, or transferrable to, a new owner. Therefore, it is necessary to arrange for the existing mortgage to be paid off when the title is transferred at the closing of a property sale, and the new owner to arrange for his or her own financing. The attorney will usually handle the mechanics of this transaction. However, when property is transferred, under certain circumstances, lenders are prohibited from enforcing these clauses. A due-on-sale clause cannot be enforced:

- When a homeowner dies and a relative inherits the residence and occupies it (he or she does not have to qualify to assume the existing mortgage);
- When a surviving joint tenant or a surviving spouse who held title as tenants by the entirety receives ownership title upon the death of the other tenant; or,
- When the property is transferred into a Living Trust, or other Trust, for the owner's benefit, as part of his or her estate plan (the lender is entitled to a copy of the Trust Agreement).

If your lender demands loan payoff under the above circumstances, write and explain the circumstances, insist the lender provide you with a copy of the loan documents with the due-on-sale clauses, and ask the lender to justify why they believe the clause applies to your circumstances. When there is no due-on-sale clause, the lender cannot call the loan when title is transferred. If the lender does not back down from enforcing a due-on-sale clause, contact an attorney.

Another clause which is frequently used in mortgages is a **Due-on-Encumbrance** clause. This provides that the loan becomes due if the borrower places a junior loan, such as a second mortgage, on a property. If the lender demands loan payoff under the due-on-encumbrance clause because the Administrator or Beneficiary gets a second mortgage or similar encumbrance; and, if loan payments are current and the interest rate is at or above today's interest rates; write to the lender, point this out, and try to reason with the lender. If this fails contact an attorney. Often due-on-encumbrance clauses are not enforceable.

Providing Clear Title

In order to receive **Clear Title**, all encumbrances must be cleared. This means arranging for all mortgages and liens to be paid off before title is transferred. This is required by law in most states when property is sold. However, when property is transferred to Beneficiaries, it is not necessary to pay off encumbrances, unless required in the Will or Trust. If not paid off, the mortgage, lien, or other encumbrance passes, along with the title upon sale or transfer of the property. This also applies to car loans. In states which have state death taxes, tax liens (legal claims) may be imposed on all of a deceased person's property, and title cannot be transferred until the lien is removed. Removing the lien may involve posting a bond, filing a final inheritance tax return, or otherwise satisfying the tax authorities that taxes will be paid. To release these tax liens, locate and contact the governmental agency that imposed them and see what is required to release them. To determine the agency, check the real property records at the County Real Property Recorder's Office. See Chapter 7, "Property Transfer Breakdown," Taxes; Consent To Transfer Form (Release from Inheritance Tax Lien.

Renting to a Buyer

If a potential buyer wants to move into the house before the sale closes, consider the following points:

- The buyer might not get the mortgage, even if it looks like a sure thing. Be aware of state laws regarding the eviction of tenants.
- The buyer may discover real or imagined defects in the home, and demand that they must be fixed before completing the purchase.
- The seller is responsible for insuring the house. Check with the insurer to be sure the Homeowner's Insurance Policy provides adequate and appropriate coverage for the property while it is occupied by tenants. See Chapter 18, "Insurance and Insurance Agents."
- Have the buyer-tenant sign an "Occupancy Prior to Close of Sale" rental agreement. It is like a lease but clarifies it is the buyer's duty to maintain the house after moving in. Ask your real estate attorney to prepare the agreement.

Domestic Help

If the deceased person used the services of a housekeeper, gardener, etc., it should be discussed with the Beneficiaries, and perhaps the Court, as to whether or not to continue using their services.

If it is necessary to hire domestic help to keep up the appearance of vacant property, it is important to check with your accountant, or the Internal Revenue Service and the state's taxing authorities, to determine if, and to what extent, you are responsible for paying taxes as an employer. They can also supply the appropriate forms and instructions for filing them. Be aware that even if the IRS concludes that a worker is an independent contractor, a state revenue authority may reach a different conclusion. Usually, independent contractors take responsibility for their own taxes. A person is generally considered an independent contractor if he or she has a local business license, an IRS Employer Identification Number (EIN), brings his or her own tools, and works for more than one employer, such as the once-a-week cleaning help or gardener. But if you are the only employer, you may be responsible for paying employment taxes. These include: Federal Income Tax Withholding, Social Security (FICA), Unemployment Insurance Tax, and State equivalents. Whichever determination you make about whether or not you are an employer, you have to be ready to offer evidence and make arguments to support your position. If you are continuing to use the services of the same domestic help as the deceased person, check what the decedent did in the past. If he or she was audited in the past and his or her treatment toward domestic help was not challenged, they can be treated the same now. You can save yourself the decision by hiring domestic help through an agency who employs such workers to do work for others. They handle all employment related taxes and insurance. Be sure you check that the people they send are bonded, and that the company carries Liability Insurance and Workers' Compensation Insurance.

Depending upon state law, you may also be responsible for purchasing Workers' Compensation Insurance (WC) for a domestic employee. **Workers' Compensation** protects you in the event the worker is injured on your property. Although Workers' Compensation is mandated by government statute, the insurance is purchased from private insurance companies. Even if the worker is an independent contractor, if he or she does not carry his or her own Workers' Compensation Insurance, you may consider buying this insurance. Check with the carrier of the homeowner's insurance policy for advice. If it does not sell WC coverage, look in the Yellow Pages, under the heading INSURANCE for a company that does.

If you have decided the domestic workers are employees, call the local Internal Revenue Office and ask for the Employer Workshop schedule. Or get a copy of its publications: IRS Pub-937 "Employment Taxes and Information Returns" and IRS Pub-15 "Employer's Tax Guide." Additionally, to assure you are in compliance with Wage and Hour Regulations, request the *Handy Reference Guide to the Fair Labor Standards Act*, and, for other regulations, the *Small Business Handbook: Laws, Regulations, and Technical Assistance Services*. Both publications are available from the Consumer Information Catalog, Pueblo, CO 81009. To help you keep track of the employee(s)'s hours and wages use the "Payroll Calculation Record" on page R-17 and the "Employee Expense Record" on page R-18.

Tidbit: If you are planning on requesting a credit check on a potential employee, you must have the person's written permission in advance. See Chapter 27, "Living On a Reduced Income," Credit Report, for the addresses of credit reporting agencies. Written permission is also necessary to request a criminal background or medical records check. In many states, these records can only be accessed by a private investigator. See Chapter 20, "Locating Missing Beneficiaries."

BASIC INVESTMENT INFORMATION

This section is dedicated to familiarizing you with the manner in which investment property may be held. Because investment products are so varied and, in some cases, very complicated, we are limited to giving you just a very basic introduction to the world of investments. We do not intend this to be investment advice, but only to enable you to recognize a piece of paper that represents an investment, and to familiarize you with the documents or instruments involved in investments. It is important to remember that investments rarely are stagnant; the value of investments fluctuates. Sometimes this fluctuation is slow and sometimes it is very rapid. Additionally, there are some investments which have expiration dates. In some cases, ignoring these dates can result in a staggering loss of money. Brokers or investment advisors are your best sources for additional and more detailed information about any investment. They should be notified of the death as soon as possible, so that current investment positions can be reviewed, and recommendations discussed and evaluated by the Administrator and the Beneficiaries.

Understanding Investment Ownership Documents

Proof of the ownership of an investment may be represented by an ornate document called a "Certificate," by a "Confirmation Slip," or by a periodic "Brokerage Statement."

Types of Ownership

Investment **Certificates** (proof of ownership) are usually issued, in either what is known as a **Street Name**, or in the name of the owner(s). A few investments, such as bearer bonds, are issued in the name of **Bearer**, which means they are owned by whomever possesses or "bears" them. When investments are issued in "Street Name," the broker retains possession of the certificates in the owner's (individual, Estate, Trust, IRA, etc.) depository account. When a security is held in street name, the dividends, benefits, and communications (such as financial reports and proxies) from the issuer are usually sent to the brokerage firm. The brokerage then deposits all dividends and other distributions in the owner's account. All communications are mailed to the owner who, when required, signs and returns them to the brokerage, who passes them along to the issuer. Investments held in street name may be in either a "Cash" or "Margin" account.

Cash Account:

A **Cash** account is one in which the owner owns all investments in the account outright. In other words, the owner deposited enough cash in the account to cover the total cost of the investments purchased through the account.

Margin Account:

A **Margin** account means some investments in the account have been purchased with money borrowed from the brokerage firm. The investments in the account are used as collateral. For this reason, only investments held in street name can be margined. An account can usually be margined for up to fifty percent of the account's value, or less if required by the brokerage firm. It should be noted that not all investments are considered marginable. If the value of the investments in a margin account falls below a minimum standard, the account owner is subject to a **Margin Call**. When a margin call occurs, the brokerage will require the owner to deposit more cash, or completely owned marginable investments, into the account; or the brokerage will sell investments in the account to reduce the amount of margin. In a quickly falling market, the broker may sell the investments without notifying the owner. With either a cash or margin account, the owner can request earnings be retained in the account or sent to him or her. However, if the margin in the account is very high, any earnings received will usually be kept in the account to reduce the margin.

Certificate of Ownership

When an investment is registered in the name of the owner, a **Certificate** is issued in the person's name. Investment certificates, which are registered and issued in the name of the purchaser (individual, Estate, or Trust), are either mailed to the owner when purchased, or can be left with the brokerage to be held in its safe. A purchaser may request that an investment certificate be put in his or her name, whether it is bought through a cash or margin account. However, these types of purchases must be paid for in cash and cannot have any margin attached to them. All dividends, benefits, and communications (reports, news releases, split-issues, and proxies) will be sent to the owner directly from the investment issuer, and all owner responses are mailed directly to the issuer. When an answer is required to a communication, such as a proxy, the issuer or the brokerage, will usually include a self-addressed, stamped envelope with the correspondence.

Confirmation Slips

Regardless of what name an investment is registered in, the brokerage firm will issue a **Confirmation Slip** and mail it to the owner whenever an investment transaction is made. The confirmation serves two purposes: first, to allow the owner to check that the transaction was executed according to his or her instructions; and second, when an investment is liquidated, the buy and sell confirmations are compared, and the difference is used to determine the amount of capital gain, or loss, for tax purposes. The confirmation states:

- The date of the transaction;
- The date of settlement (When money is actually transferred. This can vary from stocks which settle in three business days, to futures which settle the same day.);
- The name of the account owner or investment trader, and the account number;
- The name of the broker who handles the account (optional);
- The name, address, and phone number of the brokerage;
- The name of the investment issuer (company, government agency, commodity, etc.);
- The type of investment (common stock, preferred stock, warrant, bond, etc.);
- The type of transaction (bought or sold);
- The quantity of the investment (number of shares, number of futures contracts, etc.);
- The cost of one unit of the investment;
- The total cost of the investment (quantity of the investment multiplied by the cost of one unit);
- The commission (fee) charged by the broker for making the transaction. (Bonds, limited partnerships, new issues, and other products such as back-end-loaded mutual funds do not set forth the commission on the confirmation slip. If you want to know how much money the broker is making for handling the transactions, call and ask. If the broker gets annoyed, or refuses to provide the information, consider changing brokers.); and
- The total cost of the transaction (total cost of the investment plus the broker's commission and, in certain cases, tax on the transaction).

In most cases an investment is bought and later sold. Therefore, by matching up buy and sell receipts, you can determine which investments are still owned. There is one exception to this concept. It occurs because of what is called a short sale. A **Short Sale** is accomplished, for example, when an investor asks the broker to borrow a particular number of shares of a particular stock from another investor's street name account and sell them. The investor does this believing the stock's value is going to fall. If the investor is right, when the stock's price hits the lower price the investor buys an equal number of shares of that stock. The shares are then returned to the account from which they were borrowed. In this case the sell receipt will be dated before the buy receipt. This is important to note, because if the decedent was in a short position and the price of the stock begins to climb, there is the potential for unlimited loss. Eventually, you will have to buy the correct amount of the investment, at whatever price it is available, to replace the borrowed investment.

Account Statements

When investments are held in street name and for some cash accounts, the brokerage firm will send a **Statement** of the account periodically (usually monthly for active accounts, or just for months when activity occurs, or quarterly, for dormant accounts) to the owner. The statement includes the following information:

- The date the statement was prepared and the period of time included in the statement;
- The name of the account owner, and the account number;
- The name of the broker who handles the account (optional);
- The name, address, and phone number of the brokerage;
- A list of all transactions (sales or purchases of investment instruments) made through the account during the statement period;
- Current investment positions. (A list of the investments currently held in the account including: the name of the investment, type of investment, quantity owned, and the current value of each.);
- Amount of cash in the account which is not currently invested;
  - **Note:** Most brokerage firms automatically move cash from the investment account into some form of interest bearing account periodically. This is called a **Sweep**. The contract with the broker usually states how often it sweeps accounts.
- Interest on cash retained in the account;
- Amount borrowed (margined) from the brokerage to buy investments;
- Interest charged for the margined amount;
- Amounts of any cash or check withdrawals, and deposits made by the owner;
- Dividends and other cash payments received from investments;
- Any miscellaneous activity in the account; and
- The total value of the account.

Both confirmations and statements should be carefully reviewed upon receipt, to be sure they are accurate. Statements should also be compared to confirmations, to be sure all investments are properly listed. The "Investment Statement Reconciliation Slip" on page R-44, can be used for this purpose. The statement will not include investments if the certificate is in the owner's possession. If there is an error on a confirmation, or discrepancy between a confirmation and a statement, notify the broker immediately. Statements are often hard to understand. If you have any problem determining the meaning of anything on the statement, don't be embarrassed to ask the broker to help you. If the broker won't help, ask for the branch manager.

Open Order Confirmation

An **Open Order** is represented by a confirmation slip, sent by the broker to an investor who has placed an order which was not yet executed. The reason for non-execution may be that the investment could not be traded at the price the investor ordered; or it could be to confirm that a stop loss order is in place. A **Stop Loss Order** is an order to liquidate a position if it reaches a certain price. When the price of the investment reaches the specified price, the broker will execute the order. If the price of the investment is moving so rapidly that the broker is unable to liquidate the position at the specified price, the order will be executed at the best price available. A stop loss order has two uses: one is to limit loss, if the investment goes in the opposite direction from the one anticipated; and the other is to protect a profit while keeping the position, in hopes of a bigger profit. When an open order is canceled, a similar confirmation slip is sent to confirm the **Cancellation**.

TYPES OF INVESTMENTS

In this segment, we are presenting brief outline descriptions of the most common forms of investments. They are by no means in-depth descriptions, nor a complete list of all the investments or the many variations available. There are enough books and periodicals available to educate and advise investors about investment products and the strategies which can be used with them. Our intention, when writing this segment, is to give a novice the ability to recognize that an investment exists and to alert you to investments with the potential for loss if they are ignored. Our descriptions are over-simplifications, so if you are not familiar with the workings of a particular investment you should seek professional advice before taking any action.

Bonds

A **Bond** is an I.O.U. from the issuer. The issuer can be the U.S. Government, a state, county, city, foreign government, or a domestic or foreign corporation. There are two basic types of bonds. With the first type of bond, when the bond is issued, the issuer agrees to pay back (**Redeem**) the full amount (known as **Par Value** or **Face Value**) borrowed at a specific time, called the **Date of Maturity**. Securities are not redeemable before maturity unless, by the terms of their issue, they are **Callable**. Investors are informed at the time of purchase if the securities are subject to call. The earliest call date should be listed on the bond. Between the time a bond is issued and redeemed, the issuer agrees to pay interest to the owner of the bond. Generally interest payments are made twice a year. Most also have a book-entry, or automatic, interest-paying system. However, there are still a few who require the owner of the bond to send in a coupon, which is usually attached to the bond, to claim the interest.

The second type of bond is an **Original Issue Discount** (OID) Bond, which is sold at an amount lower than the face value. Instead of making interest payments to the holder, interest is accumulated or **Accrued** during the life of the bond, so at maturity they pay the face value. Most of us are familiar with OID bonds in the form of U.S. Savings Bonds, which are sold at a price well below the face value payable at maturity. Bonds can be issued for various lengths of time and may be called by various names depending upon the issuer and their terms.

143

If the owner of a bond wishes to sell it before the redemption date, the bond is offered for sale on what is called a **Secondary Market**, through investment brokers. The price at which the bond will be sold is determined by the current interest rate and the time remaining until the bond's maturity. When prevailing interest rates rise, bond prices fall and vice versa. Therefore, in order to remain a competitive investment, the selling price of the bond in the secondary market will change to make the yield equal, or approximate, to current interest rates. The difference between what a bond is selling for and its value at maturity is called the **Discount** or **Premium**. After the date of maturity or call date many bonds stop paying interest. Therefore, it is important to check this date. Bonds, which have registered owners or are held in street name, are registered with the issuer and when the date of maturity arrives, the issuer will usually send a notice to the individual or brokerage to whom the bond is registered.

Bearer Bonds

However, **Bearer Bonds** held in certificate form are not registered in anyone's name and the issuer has no record of who owns them. Therefore, it is necessary to send in a **Coupon** to request interest at specified times. If owners don't present their interest coupons, they can miss half a year or more in interest. Additionally, bearer bond owners will not be notified of a redemption. If the decedent left bearer bonds you have a few options:

- If you want to remain anonymous, copy down the bond numbers and check with the transfer agent to make sure they haven't already been called. Then check again every six months.
- Carefully check the current "Redemption Notices" listed in the Tuesday issues of *The Wall Street Journal*.
- Take the bonds that are approaching their first call date to an investment broker or banker, who will monitor them for you. They hear about calls as soon as they are announced. They may charge a small annual fee for maintaining the bond.
- Send the bonds back to the transfer agent with a request that the Beneficiary, Estate, or Trust be registered as the owner. There is no charge for this service. Since they are the same as cash, they should be sent by Registered Mail with a return receipt requested, and insured for their total value (face value plus pending interest payments). Keep a list of the bond numbers.

Corporate Bonds

Corporate bonds can range from very short-term instruments, called **Commercial Paper**, which becomes payable in 270 days or less; to **Notes**, which generally mature in 10 years or less; to **Bonds**, which do not mature for 30 years. Corporate instruments are traded through investment brokers. To find out more about a particular bond, check the most recent edition of either *Moody's Bond Record* or *Standard & Poor's Bond Guide*, available at the library. Bonds are rated by these companies. The rating reflects the issuer's credit reputation, and the anticipated ability of the issuer to redeem the bonds at maturity. Each guide explains its rating system.

Government Mortgage Bonds

Collateralized Mortgage Obligations (CMO's) are in effect, serial bonds. CMO's are giant pools of home mortgages backed by government agencies, like the Government National Mortgage Corp. (Ginnie Mae) and Federal Home Loan Mortgage Corp. (Freddie Mac). The broker can supply both a prospectus and a sensitivity analysis (which calculates the estimated principal repayment speed if interest rates were to rise or fall).

U.S. Treasury Securities

The Treasury issues three types of marketable securities: **Treasury Bills** (T-Bills) are short-term obligations that mature in three months, six months, or one year, T-bills are sold as "Original Issue Discount" securities. **Treasury Notes** are medium-term obligations, issued with a term of at least one year, but not more than ten years. **Treasury Bonds** are long-term obligations, issued with a term greater than ten years. Both notes and bonds bear a stated interest rate and the owner receives semi-annual interest payments. A registered security is held in **Book-Entry** and is represented by an engraved certificate or other receipt on which the owner's name and taxpayer identification number is printed. Book-entry securities may be held on the records of a Federal Reserve Bank or Branch which operates the Treasury/Reserve Automated Debt-Entry System (TRADES), or by the Department of the Treasury, Bureau of the Public Debt, in the **"Treasury Direct"** Book-Entry Securities System, which makes interest payments by direct deposit to the owner's designated account at a financial institution. Although the Treasury no longer sells securities in the name of "the bearer," there are still some around. Interest on bearer securities is paid by means of interest coupons attached to the security. On the date the interest is due (this date is printed on each coupon), the coupon is detached from the security and can be presented at any Federal Reserve Bank or Branch, the Bureau of the Public Debt, or most commercial banks for payment.

When originally issued, Treasuries are sold through an auction process. Securities held in Treasury Direct are paid at maturity by direct deposit, unless the purchaser has elected to reinvest the proceeds of the maturing securities into new securities. The only way to stop a previous reinvestment order is to request it. The cancellation request must be received no later than twenty (20) days prior to the maturity date of the bill or note to ensure processing.

The Treasury is not involved in the sale, trade, or pledge of previously issued securities maintained in the "Treasury Direct" system. Instead, these functions are carried out in the secondary (commercial) market, at prevailing market prices through financial institutions, brokers, and dealers in investment securities. Therefore, registered securities must first be transferred to the commercial book-entry system. Before requesting the transfer, arrangement must be made for the sale, trade or pledge with the financial institution receiving the securities. A request for transfer must be received not later than twenty (20) days before an interest payment date, or the maturity date of the security. Registered securities may not be sold, or have ownership transferred, without the written assignment of the registered owner or representative. An assignment form is printed on the back of the security.

Treasury securities may be redeemed at maturity for face value at any Federal Reserve Bank or Branch, or by mailing them to the United States Treasury, Bureau of the Public Debt, Securities Transactions Branch, 1300 C Street, S.W., Washington, D.C. 20228, or call (202) 287-4113. Registered Mail should be used when mailing registered certificates, and Bearer securities should be insured for protection against loss. An alternative is to give the securities to your broker who will handle the redemption. Additional information may be obtained by calling or writing to the nearest Treasury Direct Servicing Office or Federal Reserve Bank or branch, or by writing to the Bureau of Public Debt, Dept. F, Washington, D.C. 20226, or call (202) 287-4217 or (800) 366-3144, the Smart Exchange hotline to change certificates to computer.

U.S. Savings Bonds

Banks usually handle the transactions of **U.S. Savings Bonds** as a public service. Savings Bonds are not transferrable and may be issued with a change in registration only under certain limited circumstances. An owner, or person entitled to act on behalf of the owner, can apply for bond reissue, using forms available at most banks. The bank will either request transfer, or redeem them for you; or will verify your signature on each bond, your authority to act, and put a seal on each bond. Then you can mail the bonds to the Federal Reserve Bank in your area, marked Attention: Savings Bonds Division (ask the bank representative for the address) to carry out the transaction. Some banks will limit the amount they will redeem at any one time to $1000. If this is the case, just bring that amount for redemption at the appropriate intervals, determined by the bank. Be sure you understand the tax consequences of a change in bond ownership or redemption before you request it.

If Savings Bonds are registered in co-ownership form, either co-owner may cash in the bonds at any time, so there is no need for the surviving co-owner to re-register, unless they wish to name or change a Beneficiary. A surviving named Beneficiary automatically becomes owner of the bond upon the death of the original owner(s). In order to redeem the bond, the Beneficiary need only present a certified copy of the registered owner(s)'s Death Certificate(s). Savings Bonds must be held for at least six months after the issue date before they can be redeemed. When they have passed their final maturity dates they cease to earn interest.

E and EE (which replaced E) Series U.S. Savings Bonds are bought at large discounts with a stated maturity date. Although the interest received during the year is exempt from state and local income taxes, it is subject to all federal taxes. For income tax purposes, interest may be reported annually as it accrues, or reporting may be deferred until the bond is cashed or reaches final maturity. However, the tax-deferral status of the accrued income can be extended by exchanging E or EE bonds for HH bonds, instead of cashing them in at maturity. HH Bonds pay interest to investors through checks issued twice a year.

Tidbit: Maximize the value of bonds by choosing when you redeem them. Interest on U.S. Savings Bonds is calculated and credited in most cases every six months. If redeemed before the interest is credited, the interest accrued since the last posting is lost. The bank should be able to supply this information, or write to the Superintendent of Documents, P.O. Box 37194, Pittsburgh, PA 15250 and request the latest "Table of Redemption Value for E Bonds" (TRVE) or "Table of Redemption Value for EE Bonds" (TRVEE), an annual subscription is $5. Another consideration is the percent of interest each bond is earning, compared to interest rates paid by other investments. Complete information on each bond is on the United States Savings Bond Consultant (a DOS program), for $29.95, from Union Information Services, call (800) 717-2663.

U.S. Savings Bonds that have been lost, stolen, or destroyed can be replaced, free of charge, by writing to the Bureau of the Public Debt, Savings Bonds Operations Office, Department of the Treasury, 200 Third Street, Parkersburg, WV 26106-1328. Give as much information as you can about when the bonds were purchased, who purchased them, the purchaser's Social Security number, the denominations of the bonds and/or any other information you may have. The department will search its records and send a list of bonds in that name. You can request a form PD1048 "Application for Relief" from your local bank, nearest Federal Reserve Bank, or the U.S. Treasury to make a claim to have them reissued. They will have the same serial numbers as the lost bonds. The process usually takes six to eight weeks, but can take months if a lot of research is required. For more information call (800) 4US-BOND or write to the Public Affairs Office, U.S. Savings Bonds Division, U.S. Department of the Treasury, 800 K Street, N.W., Washington, D.C. 20226, and request any of the following publications: "Question and Answer Book," "Questions and Answers On The Education Bond Program," "Table of Interest Accrual Dates," "Guaranteed Minimum Rate Chart," "U.S. Savings Bonds — Buyer's Guide," "Tables of Redemption Values," or "Current Market — Based Rate Announcement."

Stocks

Stocks represent a **Share** of ownership in a company. The number of shares owned is represented by a **Stock Certificate**. Transactions are ordered through stock brokers, but the actual trading of the stock is done on three major exchanges, the New York Stock Exchange (NYSE), American Stock Exchange (AMEX), and the National Association of Securities Dealers Automated Quotations (NASDAQ) Composite Index Market. Additionally, very small issues are traded via "pink sheets" (named after the color paper they're printed on) or the "Bulletin Board" (a computerized version of the "pink sheets") listing of stocks and market makers. Included under the general heading of "Stock," and sold on these exchanges, are: Common Stocks, Preferred Stocks, certain Funds, Warrants, Limited Partnerships, American Depositary Receipts, Units, Real Estate Investment Trusts (REIT), and more. All of these investments are bought and sold through stock and bond brokers.

Because these investments represent ownership, shareholders have certain rights. One of these is a vote on company affairs. Instead of everyone who owns a share in a company attending the company's yearly Stock Holders' Meeting, a **Proxy** (a form authorizing one person to vote for another) is sent to each shareholder. Along with the proxy, information is sent about when the meeting will be held, and the subjects to be voted upon. This information corresponds to the items to be voted upon on the proxy. The shareholder, or his or her representative, checks off his or her choices, signs, and mails the proxy back. It is counted when the vote is taken at the meeting. Any proxies you may receive need to be signed by you, with your Administrative title, and promptly mailed, either to the brokerage or the issuing company. Ask the broker if you are not sure how to complete the proxy.

Another right is to receive a proportionate share of the profit earned by the company. This is usually done through payments of cash **Dividends**. However, sometimes a dividend is given in the form of additional shares of stock. Occasionally, in order to lower the price of a share of the stock to one the company believes will be more attractive to more investors, the company will declare a stock split. A **Stock Split** means that, for every share an investor owns, he or she will receive a specific number of additional shares. This would be expressed as a 2 for 1 split, which means the owner would receive one additional share of stock for every share owned; a 3 for 2 split, which means the owner would receive one additional share of stock for every two shares owned; etc. On the other hand, if the price of a stock has declined, and the company wants to adjust the price upward to allow it to continue trading on a certain exchange, the company can declare a **Reverse Split**. In this case, shares are returned to the company and a specified fewer number of shares will be returned to the shareholder. This would be expressed as a 1 for 2 split, which means if there were two shares owned before the reverse split, the shareholder now owns one share; a 1 for 10 split, which means if there were ten shares owned before the reverse split, the shareholder now owns one share; etc. There is no change in the value of an individual's holdings, just in the price of each share.

Another benefit of ownership is receipt of stock shares in subsidiaries of the company in which shares are held. This is called a **Stock Spin-off**. This can occur when a company decides to make a part of its company into a separate company. The owner of the original company's stock would receive a proportionate number of shares in the new company, as well as retaining all of the original stock. It may also occur when one company buys another and chooses to allow it to continue trading under its own name. On the other hand, when a company acquires another company through a **Takeover**, the company may choose to issue stock in its company in exchange for shares of the company acquired. This may also occur through a **Merger** or joining of two or more companies into one new company, which will redeem the outstanding shares of the companies involved for shares in the new company. These occurrences may not produce a confirmation slip; instead, the only proof may be a sentence on the periodic broker's statement; or the absence of the stock certificate named on a confirmation, and the presence of a stock certificate not mentioned anywhere. Look for a notation made by the owner on the purchase confirmation for the missing stock.

Tidbit: Limited Partnerships and REITs issue information statements each year to report earnings. This information is used to complete Income Tax Partnership Tax forms which are filed with the shareholder's regular income tax. These must be filed by the **Partners** (everyone who has shares). The statements are usually sent out annually in mid-March. Additionally, both have liquidation dates. When this occurs, or when the shares are sold, there will be more partnership statements and tax forms.

Since stocks are listed by abbreviations, called **Symbols**, you might not be able to recognize a listing in the newspaper. To find out which market the stock is trading on and its symbol, you can look up the name of the stock in the *Standard & Poor's Stock Guide* (available from a broker or in the Public Library). If it is listed there, it is an ongoing business and the stock should be readily tradable. The *S & P Guide* also rates the listed stocks. If you cannot find the stock, it may be because it has lost its identity through name changes, takeovers, mergers, acquisitions, liquidations, or bankruptcies. You can ask your broker to research it. Many brokerage houses will check a stock for you free, providing extensive research isn't required. If the broker cannot find the stock, or you want to research it yourself, start by looking through the following publications at a University or Public Library: the *Financial Stock Guide Service* (Financial Information, Inc., of NJ) which lists stocks from 1927 on, tells if the stock is still active; any successor companies; and which transfer agent deals with it. The *Guide* includes the *Directory of Obsolete Securities* which lists obsolete stocks. For certificates issued before 1927, look in the *Robert D. Fisher Manual of Valuable and Worthless Securities* (R. M. Smythe & Co. of NY). Another option is to write to the Secretary of State where the company was incorporated. They will track the company stock (a fee may be charged for this service). If the certificate is genuine, the current company must redeem it and pay any dividends that have accumulated over the years. If the company no longer exists and there is no successor, don't throw it away; it may still have value as a collectible.

If you have determined the stock is worthless or obsolete, you can contact a broker dealing in Antique Stock Certificates. The broker can help you find their value, if any, as a collectible. When seeking a quote, send a photocopy of the certificate along with your name, address, and a self-addressed, stamped envelope for a reply. Never send the actual certificates; you may never see them again. Among the brokers who specialize in old certificates are: George LaBarre Galleries, P.O. Box 746, Hollis, NH 03051 and Bond and Share Society, $^{C}/_{O}$ R. M. Smythe & Co., 26 Broadway, New York, NY 10004-1701, phone (212) 943-1880 or (800) 622-1880. You may also include a self-addressed, stamped envelope for information about annual membership and its newsletter for Scriptophilists (collectors of Stock and Bond Certificates). If you do not feel like researching a stock yourself, R. M. Smythe & Co. also researches stocks for current value, as does Stock Search International, in San Diego, CA, at (800) 537-4523. Contact them and ask for current charges for research, and what percentage they charge for any value recovered. They may also make a bid to buy the certificate.

Convertible Instruments

Convertible Instruments include such things as Warrants, Units, and Convertible Bonds. These instruments all have expiration dates, at which time there may be some type of conversion into the associated stock. It is critical that the investor understands the call provisions and knows the terms of conversion to the underlying stock.

Commodity Futures Contracts

Commodity Futures Contracts are contracts that establish a price level now for items to be delivered later. The ever-expanding list of commodities includes agricultural products, metals, petroleum, financial instruments, foreign currencies, and stock indexes. Futures must be closely monitored because of their volatile nature. Therefore, investors, called **Speculators**, usually utilize the services of a professional trading advisor, establish a fully managed trading account, or participate in a futures trading pool, which is similar in concept to a mutual fund. Also, because of the great potential for loss, the broker is required to give a new trader a **Prospectus** (risk disclosure statement) for Securities Futures and Options Trading, and have the investor acknowledge, in writing, that he or she has read the prospectus and understood it.

A **Futures Contract** is, very basically, a contract to buy or sell a certain amount of a commodity on a specified date. To purchase the contract, the investor pays a small fraction of the value of the commodity. It is like putting a deposit on an item in a store lay-away program; it shows good faith that you want to purchase the item. The value of the contract fluctuates up or down with the price of the commodity. So, a contract owner is subject to the exact same dollar gain or loss as if they owned the actual commodity. Futures are traded through margin accounts. Minimum margin requirements for a particular futures contract at a particular time, are set by the exchange on which the contract is traded. The margin requirement is typically about five percent of the current value of the futures contract. The investor deposits sufficient funds in the account to purchase the contract, which is called **Initial Margin**. If the price of the contract is giving the speculator a profit, he or she does not need to add more funds to the initial margin. However, if the contract is giving the speculator a loss, he or she will be required to deposit additional funds to the margin account to meet the "Maintenance Margin Requirement Minimum," even if the contract is still owned. Futures have a daily cash settlement feature, so the broker can demand immediate deposit of additional funds (a **Margin Call**) to bring the account back to the level of the initial margin. If the funds are not delivered timely in the manner (personal check, cashier's or certified check, or wire transfer) required by the Margin Agreement, the broker will sell the contract at whatever the current price is and the loss will be sustained by the investor. Speculators often use stop orders to limit their losses.

There are two types of Futures Contracts: those that provide for **Physical Delivery** of a particular commodity or item, and those which call for a **Cash Settlement**. The month during which delivery or settlement is to occur is specified in the contract. For example, September - Cocoa, July - Natural Gas, December - Eurodollar, etc. The month, day, and year of "delivery" is specified on the confirmation.

The vast majority of futures speculators do not intend to make or take delivery, but to realize a profit by buying or selling offsetting futures contracts prior to the delivery date. Someone who expects a futures price to increase would purchase futures contracts in the hope of later being able to make an offsetting sale of the contracts at a higher price. This is known as **Going Long**. Conversely, someone who expects a futures price to decline would sell futures contracts in the hope of later being able to buy back identical and offsetting contracts at a lower price. The practice of selling futures contracts in anticipation of lower prices is known as **Going Short**.

If a person is in a "Long" position when the delivery date occurs, he or she will own the commodity. Usually this will be in the form of a negotiable instrument (such as a warehouse receipt) that evidences the holder's ownership of the commodity at some designated location. If you allow delivery to occur, the Estate will be the proud new owner of the commodity; and as the Administrator, you will have to figure out not only how to pay the total cost of the commodity, but depending upon the commodity, may be trying to figure out how to sell tons of an agricultural product, such as pork bellies, corn, oats, etc., before it rots. If you just received a million dollars worth of U.S. Treasury Bonds, you may be in a lot of financial trouble. The only way to avoid delivery is to liquidate the position, by making an offsetting trade prior to the delivery date. Even if this means taking a loss, unless you know what to do with the commodity, it probably will not be near the loss that will be sustained if you take delivery. Conversely, if the delivery date occurs while a speculator is in a "Short" position, he or she will be responsible for delivering the correct amount of the commodity, which can be equally as troublesome and costly. For more information, request "Understanding Opportunities and Risks in Futures Trading" from a broker, or request it from the Consumer Information Catalog, Pueblo, CO 81002.

Options

Options are available for many stocks, as well as commodity futures contracts and indexes. An **Option** represents a right, but not the obligation, to buy **Call Option**, or sell **Put Option**, a certain amount of the particular stock or commodity contract, at a specified price, called the **Strike Price**, at any time during the life of the option. The value of the option rises and falls in proportion to the price of the underlying stock, commodity, or index. Options have specified **Expiration** dates, at which time the rights granted in the option end. The month, day, and year of expiration is specified on the confirmation. Option buyers limit their risk of loss to the price paid for the option, called the **Premium**, plus the broker's fee for the purchasing transaction. Options trading can be confusing, because it not only has its own vocabulary, but also its own arithmetic. Basically one option represents the right to buy or sell 100 shares or contracts of the underlying stock or commodity. After an option is bought, the owner has three choices:

- To allow the option to "Expire" worthless. This is done if the option price doesn't move or has gone down. In this case the owner loses the premium, plus the broker's fee for buying the option. There are no transaction fees for expiration and no confirmation issued.
- To "Exercise" the option. The buyer of a "Call" option exercises the option by purchasing the underlying stock or futures contract from the option writer, at the lower option strike price, and selling it at the current higher market price or keeping it in hopes of future profit. The buyer realizes a profit if, upon exercise, the underlying stock or futures price is above the option strike price by more than the premium paid for the option, plus transaction fees. The buyer of a "Put" option exercises the option by purchasing the same amount of the underlying stock or futures contract at the current lower market price and selling it to the option writer at the higher option strike price. The seller realizes a profit if, upon exercise, the underlying stock or futures price is below the option exercise price by more than the premium paid for the option, plus transaction fees. Since there is rarely much difference between the profit that would be received exercising the option and the profit realized by selling the option itself, options are rarely exercised.
- To "Sell the Option" for a profit, if the value of the option goes up. This is the usual reason why speculators buy an option. The vast majority of option traders have no intention of exercising the option.

Option Writers or Grantors

An option is originated by an individual, called a **Writer** or **Grantor**. The sole reason for writing options is to earn the premium paid by the option buyer. If the option expires without being exercised (which is what the option writer hopes will happen), the writer retains the full amount of the premium. If the option is exercised, the writer must deliver as required by the option. Therefore, depending upon the movement of the underlying stock, futures contract, or index, the writer of an option has potentially unlimited risk. An option writer can **Close** or **Offset** his or her position by buying an option which is exactly the same as the one he or she sold. For more information, request a copy of "Characteristics and Risks of Standardized Options" from a broker.

Mutual Funds

A **Mutual Fund** is created when a group of investors pool their money to be invested by experts in various investment instruments. They invest in all of the instruments we've discussed, and more. Some are very specific as to the investments they make, such as only environmentally friendly companies, or Treasuries; others invest in a mixture of instruments. Since there are presently in excess of five thousand mutual funds, the variety is virtually endless. Mutual funds are traded as **Shares**. The value of a share is established by the value of the investments the mutual fund owns, plus the cash on hand, plus the value of dividends and/or interest it receives from its investments. The value of the shares decreases after the fund pays its annual capital gains dividend to the shareholders. This occurs at a set time specified in the mutual fund contract. All funds charge an annual management fee. Many also charge a sales commission, which can be called different things, depending upon how the buyer is expected to pay the commission. A **Front Load** is a straight percentage deducted from the original investment; a **Deferred Sales Charge** is a percentage charged if the investor sells the shares within a specified number of years; and a **No-Load**, where no sales commission is charged and shares are bought directly from the fund. Individuals can buy, sell or transfer their shares in the fund through a broker or by calling the fund's toll-free 800 number, which is listed in the Funds Information Packet and, for most, in *The Wall Street Journal*, along with the current price. For more information, write to the Investment Company Institute, 1401 H Street, 12ᵗʰ Floor, Washington, D.C. 20005-2148 or call (202) 326-5800 or go online to *info@ici.com* and request its free booklet called "An Investor's Guide to Reading the Mutual Fund Prospectus." The ICI is a mutual fund trade association.

Dividend Reinvestment Plans

Dividend Reinvestment Plans (DRIPs) allow investors to buy additional shares of the same company or mutual fund by reinvesting dividends, rather than receiving them. Most also allow shareholders to periodically buy additional shares by sending in cash payments.

Tidbit: Investment brokerages offer free booklets to their customers, explaining the investments in which they deal. These publications, prepared by the Exchanges, offer an in-depth explanation of the investments, as well as some insight into trading strategies.

INVESTMENT BROKERS
AND
BROKERAGE ACCOUNTS

We suggest that if you are not acquainted with financial investments or investment ownership documents, you read Chapter 13, "Basic Investment Information," before you read this chapter.

Dealing With a Broker

In order for an investment or securities broker to make a trade on your behalf, you must open an account with the brokerage firm. This is not a complex procedure and only takes a short time to fill out the forms. Call the brokerage you are going to deal with, and make an appointment with a broker to open the account. To save time and trouble, explain why you are opening the account and ask what documents and information you should bring with you. During the meeting, the broker will guide you through the process and help you make decisions about the type of account that best suits your needs. If the investments are included in probate property, you must first open an **Estate Account** and have the investments transferred into it. When it is time for distribution, the titles of the investments are transferred into the name(s) of the Beneficiary(ies). If you have found an investment certificate and are using the account to sell an investment or transfer its title, it would probably be a cash account. However, if you are opening an account for the Estate or Trust, you will have to consider what type of account you wish to open, and how you want the account to function. Your choice may be determined by the type of account the decedent had. Because debt cannot be transferred to the Beneficiaries (except for a mortgage on real estate), if investments in the decedent's account are margined, it will be necessary to sell investments, or put cash into the account to pay off the margin. Be certain to read and understand all of the literature and agreements you receive from the broker before you sign anything. You should clearly know your rights and obligations, as well as the rights and obligations of the firm with which you are dealing. The broker can provide you with literature, prepared by the Exchanges, about each type of investment. If the broker is out of these publications, write to the Exchange and request them. The addresses for the major Exchanges are listed in the box on page 159.

Always retain full control over your Account, so that your broker must notify you of any trades <u>before</u> they are executed. The one exception to this rule is trading in the commodity or futures market, in which, because it is very volatile, positions may have to be closed quickly to avoid loss or realize a gain. In this case, the time it takes for the broker to ask your permission to close a position might result in a considerable loss of money. **Unless you have specifically given your Broker discretionary power over your Account in writing, he or she should not be making trades, without direction from you.**

It is most important, especially if you decide to give the broker some discretion over an ongoing account, to put your investment philosophy in a letter, sign it, and give it or mail it (by Certified Mail, with a return receipt request) to the broker. The letter should clearly state what discretionary power, if any, the broker is to have. Also include the goals of the investments, i.e. growth, income, or both, and the degree of risk with which you are comfortable. Be sure to keep a copy of the letter. If you are not sure the investments in your account match the statement goals and risk tolerance you gave the broker, get a second opinion from an accountant, financial adviser, attorney, or someone else experienced in investment products. If you determine that the broker is ignoring your instructions, find a new broker. Remember, you can always change brokers if you are not satisfied or are uncomfortable with your current dealer.

Changing Brokerage Firms

Transferring an account from one brokerage firm to another is not difficult, providing the investments in the account are all commonly exchange-traded stocks, bonds, mutual funds, partnerships, etc. An uncomplicated transfer should be completed in about 10 business days through the Automated Customer Account Transfer System, known as Acats, to which all major brokers belong. All that is necessary is to fill out a new account agreement and transfer request form at the new brokerage firm. With the transfer form you must include a list of all investments, usually done by attaching the latest statement from the old firm. If there is a cash management account at the old firm, withdraw the money from the account <u>before</u> you begin the transfer process, either by writing a check, or having the old firm issue a check. Margin will be transferred with the account. Be aware that any open or stop-loss orders will automatically be cancelled upon transfer. They must be given to the new broker if you still wish to have them in place. Some brokerage firms charge a $50 exit fee to cover the cost of paperwork, but the new brokerage firm may pay all or part of the exit fees.

The transfer may become complicated if there are investments in the account which are not readily transferable. The new broker can advise you of which investments will transfer and which will not. Investments which will not readily transfer are in-house mutual funds or other proprietary products that can't be transferred through Acats. This leaves you with the task of deciding whether to keep the old account open and leaving these investments in it while moving the rest -or- selling them and moving the cash to the new brokerage, perhaps to buy new investments. In some cases, selling these investments before a specified date can result in charges that run as high as 6% of the asset. Therefore, it is important to understand all aspects of the investments and consequences of their sale. The investment advisors at both the new and old firms should be consulted for information and assistance in making the decision. Before transferring an account to a new brokerage, be sure it is the brokerage firm you are dissatisfied with, and not just the broker who is handling your account. Most firms have many brokers working for them. If you do not like your particular broker, you may first want to ask for another broker in the firm to handle your account. This would not delay trading or cost any fee.

Trading Through a Brokerage Account

Once you have opened an account with the brokerage, the broker will be able to execute any order you issue. Often these trades or transfers can be requested when the account is opened. When placing an order with a broker to execute a transaction, you should specify:

- Type of transaction, i.e., "buy" or "sell";
- "Quantity" to be traded;
- Name of the "company or security" you want to trade in;
- "Price" at which you want the trade to be made. Before giving the broker a price, you should ask for a **Quote** (the current trading price) of the item. The broker will usually give you two prices. One is the **Bid** price which is the price at which individuals are willing to buy the investment (this will be the lower price); the other is the **Ask** price which is the price at which individuals are willing to sell the investment (this will be the higher price.) Most often, the difference between the two prices is a small fraction. If there is a significant difference between the number of buyers and number of sellers, the broker will add a couple of other numbers indicating this difference. If you do not understand, ask for an explanation. After you know the current trading price, you can designate the price at which you want to trade. This designation can be given as:
  - A specific price (You can state the "Bid" or "Ask" price, any price in between, or another price, depending upon which direction you believe the price will go. The broker will trade at the specified price or one that is more favorable to you. However, it never hurts to add the phrase "Or Better" to the price request. A broker should never trade at a less favorable price than the price you quoted unless authorized.);
  - A range price (This permits the broker to trade within a specified range, above or below a specific price. Usually the range is one-eighth or one-quarter. For example: 25 give or take an eighth.);
  - "At the market" (This is an order to make the trade at the first opportunity, at whatever the price is at that time. This is a dangerous order if the price of the investment you are trading is moving rapidly. It should only be used if you are desperate to make the trade at

any cost. Don't be surprised if the broker refuses to take an order like this. The broker may insist you give a limit.);

■ "When" to execute. Unless otherwise stated, a transaction will be executed as soon as it is received. However, an immediate transaction is not always possible. An investment cannot be sold unless there is someone who wants to buy it at the specified price; conversely, an investment cannot be bought unless there is someone who wants to sell it at the specified price. Therefore, a limit is usually placed on the amount of time the order will be good. These limiting designations are:

  • A <u>day order</u> (If the transaction is not executed before the close of the market that day, it is cancelled.);

  • A <u>week order</u> (If the transaction is not executed before the close of the market on the last business day of the week, it is cancelled.);

  • <u>Good until canceled (GTC), or open order</u> (The transaction may be executed at any time until you give an order to cancel it. Be aware that if the order is still open when a dividend is realized, the price you quote will automatically be adjusted downward when the dividend is paid, in a fraction amount approximately equal to the dividend paid.);

  • <u>Stop-Loss</u> (A stop-loss order is usually given to protect a profit on an investment which is expected to grow in value. It is used as protection from excessive loss if the investment price starts to drop instead of rise. The execution price is usually set two or three points lower than the current price of the investment. The trade will only be executed if the price of the investment starts to fall and reaches this preset price.);

■ When selling a portion of an investment which was purchased in different quantities and prices and bought at different times, designate the purchase date of the portion of the investment being sold;

■ Request that the broker repeat your order on the phone, if the broker does not automatically do this;

■ With some investments, the broker may ask if this transaction is to "open" or "close" a position. A position is "opened" when an investment is acquired and "closed" when the investment is liquidated.

■ Review the confirmation as soon as it is received to be sure the correct trade was made.

■ If you are selling an investment registered in the name of the owner, the certificate of ownership must be brought or mailed to an investment broker. If the investment is in street name, the broker has the certificate.

■ Keep a log of all conversations with the broker. Note any suggestions the broker makes, and the orders you place.

Locating a Broker

The type of broker you must use depends upon the type of investments which are in the Estate, whether or not you need investment advice, or if you just need to transfer investments to the Beneficiary. <u>Unless expressly granted the right to do so under the Will, an Administrator has</u>

no right to invest the assets of the Estate without the written authority of the Court. Should the Administrator do so and sustain a loss, the Administrator is held personally responsible. Before looking for a broker, you should determine what kind of account you need to open and what services you will need. Answering the following questions can assist you in the choice.

- What type of account did the decedent have?_____

- If the decedent had margin on the account, you must open a margin account in order to transfer the stocks. Do I want to open a cash or margin account?_____

- If I am opening a cash account, do I want the investments registered in the name of the Estate, Trust, Surviving Joint-Owner, or in Street Name?_____

- If investments will be registered in the name of the Estate, Trust, or Surviving Joint-Owner. Do I want the certificates mailed, or held by the brokerage? _____

- Do I want the benefits of the investments (dividends, splits, etc.) sent to me, or retained in the account?_____

- To what address do I want certificates, financial reports, proxies, etc. mailed?

_____

- What type of investments am I dealing with?_____

_____

_____

- Do I need a broker to just transfer titles, take orders for investments I choose, or one who can provide investment advice?_____

If the deceased person dealt with a broker on a regular basis, or had a margin account with a broker, it is usually the easiest and best decision to open the Estate Account with that broker. However, if you do not find evidence of a broker or you do not, for whatever reason, care to deal with that broker, you need to find a broker.
- Get the names of brokerage firms and brokers from friends who have similar investments;
- Ask professionals (doctors, lawyers, accountants, etc.) who handles their investments;
- Look in the Yellow Pages under the heading: STOCK AND BOND BROKERS (this listing includes full service brokers), COMMODITY BROKERS, and FOREIGN EXCHANGE BROKERS.
- Check with the local Better Business Bureau for complaints against the company.

Choosing a Broker

Experts suggest you interview a minimum of three brokers. There should be no charge for an interview. Depending upon the reason you are opening the account, how much contact you will be having with the broker, and how much control the broker will have over investments, choose which points below should be covered in an interview. Use the "Hiring Interview Sheet" on pages R-39 and R-40.

■ Ask how long the brokerage firm has been in business. Experts suggest a ten year minimum.

■ Ask how long the person has been a broker, and how long he or she has been with the firm. Look for at least three years experience.

■ Ask what training and experience the broker has.

■ Ask yourself if this broker's approach to the market and personality are compatible with yours. You want to feel comfortable asking questions and feel satisfied with the answers.

■ Ask what government or industrial regulatory organization's supervision to which the firm is subject. If you are told this particular area of investment isn't subject to regulation, take that explanation for whatever you think it is worth.

■ Ask what mechanism the firm uses to resolve disputes equitably and inexpensively, such as arbitration, mediation, or a reparation procedure, either through the company or a regulatory organization.

■ Ask if the broker or the firm has ever been disciplined by any regulatory agency.

■ Ask if they have lost a lawsuit, complaint, or arbitration.

■ Satisfy yourself that you are dealing with a reputable firm by checking on whether the firm or person is properly registered, and whether they have a regulatory history. Violations of exchange rules can result in substantial fines, suspension or revocation of trading privileges, and loss of exchange membership. The regulatory agencies will provide information on firms and brokers that they have taken disciplinary action against; they may not tell about a pending investigation. For the names and addresses of the regulatory agencies, see the box on page 159;

■ Ask the range of their services. Be sure they are able to deal in the investments you are interested in trading. These include: Stock and Bond Broker; Options Broker; Mutual Funds Broker; Tax-Free, Municipal and Government Securities Broker; Commodity Broker; Foreign Exchange Broker; etc. Also, if you need advice on investments, be sure they provide investment advice in the area in which you are interested and to the extent you require. Different firms offer different services. Some, for example, have extensive research departments and can provide current information and analysis concerning market developments, as well as specific trading suggestions. Others tailor their services to clients who prefer to make market judgments and arrive at trading decisions on their own. Still others offer various combinations of these and other services.

■ How often does the broker issue statements of the activity on the account? Only when there is activity, or on a schedule, whether or not there was activity?

■ Be sure the brokerage firm is a member of The Securities Investor Protection Corporation (SIPC). The SIPC insures every member investment broker-dealer in the United States and its territories automatically. This is not insurance to pay account holders for losses from individual investments. It insures accounts if the firm should fail. Each separate account is protected for as much as $100,000 in cash or $500,000 in securities, with a limit of $500,000 for the two combined. The protection does not include commodity contracts, commodity options, or unregistered investment contracts. Before investing with any broker, check the stability of the institution. Ask to see the firm's latest annual or quarterly report. Although all accounts are insured, your money may be tied up for a long time if the institution should fail. Be sure not to put or keep more than $500,000 in any one account, unless the account is in-

Major Exchanges
and
Regulatory Associations

- The **National Association of Securities Dealers** (NASD), contact the nearest regional office (listed by name in the White Pages) or the national headquarters at 1735 K Street, N.W., Washington, D.C. 20006-1506, Attn. NASD Public Disclosure Program, or call (202) 728-8039, or (800) 289-9999. The NASD is an industry self-regulatory organization and the best single source of information. They can tell you whether a broker or firm has been the subject of any disciplinary proceeding, if there are any civil or criminal judgments against them, or if they have lost arbitration awards. If you are dissatisfied with a broker's services, you can file a written complaint with the NASD at 33 Whitehall Street, New York, NY 10004, or call (212) 858-4000;

- The **North American Securities Administrators Association** (NASAA), 1 Massachusetts Avenue, N.W., Suite 310, Washington, D.C. 20001, or call (202) 737-0900. The NASAA can provide the address and phone number of your state's securities regulatory agency. You can also request a copy of the free bulletin, "How Older Americans Can Avoid Investment Fraud and Abuse." Your state's securities commission can tell you how many charges have been filed against a firm, if any;

- The **U.S. Securities and Exchange Commission** (SEC), Public Reference Room, 450 Fifth Street, N.W., Mail Stop 11-2, Washington, D.C. 20549, or call (202) 942-8088. The SEC is a federal regulatory agency. Also, you can write to its Office of Consumer Affairs, or call (800) 732-0330 or (202) 942-7040, and request a free copy of its booklets, "Investigate Before You Invest," "Invest Wisely: Introduction to Mutual Funds," and "Invest Wisely-Advice From Your Securities Regulators";

- The **New York Stock Exchange** (NYSE) Sales Practice Unit, 20 Broad Street, 22nd Floor, New York, NY 10005. The NYSE is at 11 Wall Street, New York, NY 10005, phone number, (212) 656-3000;

- The **American Stock Exchange** (AME) Hearings Dept., 86 Trinity Place, 12th Floor, New York, NY 10006, phone number, (212) 306-1000;

- The **National Futures Association**, 200 W. Madison, Suite 1600, Chicago, IL 60606-3447, phone (312) 781-1300. The National Futures Association (NFA) is a congressionally authorized, self-regulatory, industrywide, member organization which exercises regulatory authority over Futures Commission Merchants, Introducing Brokers, Commodity Trading Advisors, Commodity Pool Operators, Leverage Transaction Merchants, and Associated Persons. The NFA has the responsibility for registering persons and firms that are required to be registered with the **Commodity Futures Trading Commission** (CFTC), a federal regulatory agency. To verify if a firm is properly registered with the CFTC, and/or is a Member of NFA, and be advised of complaints and actions, if any, against the member firm; call the NFA Information Center at (800) 621-3570 [within Ill. (800) 572-9400]. You can also request a number of publications, including *Buying Options on Futures: A Guide to Their Uses and Risks*;

- The **Commodity Futures Trading Commission**, 2033 K Street, N.W., Washington, D.C. 20581, call (202) 254-6367 for complaints only, or (202) 254-8630 for information.

sured for a higher amount through private insurance purchased by the broker. Check with the broker if this is a consideration.

- Ask for three client references, so you can check with them.
- Ask for a sample commission and how it is determined. To allow for a proper comparison be sure to use the same hypothetical trade for each broker. Some brokers use a set rate, some base it on the dollar amount of the transaction, some base it on the number of shares, some combine dollar amount and number of shares, and in most cases, the rate varies depending on the type of security traded. Compare their fees with those of several other brokerages. There may be a considerable difference between the fees charged by discount and full-service brokers.

If you are going to be relying upon the broker for financial or investment advice, you may want to know the answers to the following questions, so you can determine their track record:

- How does the broker choose the investments he or she recommends? If the investments, such as a particular stock, are pushed by the company, they may become temporarily artificially inflated.
- Ask for the last 5 stocks the broker recommended and how they performed. Double check the performance in the newspaper. You can find back issues in the Public Library.

Managed Accounts

Most large brokerage houses offer fully managed accounts commonly called **Wrap Accounts**. With a wrap account, you get the services of a professional money manager, who creates a portfolio of stocks and bonds and takes care of all the trading. Most managers charge an all inclusive flat fee, usually a small percentage (typically 3 percent) of the value of the account. Some may charge a combination of fee and commission. Some may charge only a commission on trades. Wrap account sponsors (which include brokerage houses, mutual funds, insurance companies, and banks), usually give performance data to investors quarterly, which makes comparisons among competing accounts difficult. For more information call The International Association for Financial Planning, at (800) 945-4237, and ask for its free brochure, *How to Evaluate a Wrap Fee Program*. If you are opening a wrap account, you may want to add some further questions:

- Ask for the annual fee and if any transaction commissions are charged in addition to the fee.
- Look closely at the firm's performance record. Ask for documentation of its performance record, sometimes called a **Disclosure Document**. A disclosure document is a prospectus-like document containing information about the investment advisors, their experience, as well as their current and previous performance records.
- Watch for conflicts of interest. Review other accounts and watch for excessive, or very little, trading. With a flat fee, based on the value of the account, some managers make excessive trades to build the value of the account or do nothing and just collect the fee. With a commission for each transaction, the manager may be influenced to make excessive trades. Excessive trades can cause excessive capital gains and increase income taxes. Remember, taxes decrease the overall value of the income derived from the account.

- Ask the broker or manager if he or she will send you a photocopy of the yearly statement, issued by the brokerage, of the total dollar value of gross commissions he or she received on your account.

Protect Yourself — Be Alert

Regardless of what type of account you have, you should get the answers to the following questions for any recommended investment:

- How much risk is involved? Evaluate if the risk is within your comfort zone. As the Administrator of an Estate, or Trustee of a Trust, you should refrain from speculative or high risk investments.
- How long will the money be tied up? -or- How long is the average holding period for this investment? Evaluate if your inability to liquidate the investment sooner would cause you inconvenience.
- How can I sell or liquidate the investment? If the investment is not traded on an open exchange, your money may be tied up for a long time while trying to locate a willing buyer.
- How much compensation will you receive if I buy this product?
- What makes this an appropriate investment for my objectives?

Warning Signs

The major indicator of a reputable investment firm is that it encourages clients to ask questions, to obtain as much information as possible about an investment, to clearly understand the risks involved, and to be entirely comfortable with any investment decision they make. Avoid or discharge any investment broker or advisor who:

- Uses high-pressure sales tactics aimed at making you invest before you have assembled all pertinent facts, and can make an informed decision.
- Wants a quick decision on an investment opportunity.
- Makes bold "promises," such as unusually high yields. **Remember, if a deal sounds too good to be true . . . it is.**
- Offers investments which are not traded on a regulated exchange. Although some bona fide investments are and some aren't traded on a regulated exchange, fraudulent investments never are. Only careful investigation can distinguish the true nature of an unlisted investment.
- Says an investment is without risks. All investments, other than a government security, involve some degree of risk.
- Asks you to buy on the basis of trust and will not provide written information on the investment. Refuses to give you documents, such as a prospectus or risk disclosure statement, containing specific information about the investment. Reluctance to put anything in writing may be an indication the dealer is afraid of running afoul of postal authorities or providing material that, at some point, might become evidence in a fraud trial.

161

- Offers an investment only if you will promise to keep the deal quiet, or refuses to explain the investment proposal to some third party, such as an attorney, accountant, investment advisor, or banker.
- Makes enticing offers with little to back them up or describes them in vague terms, which are left undefined.

It is important to continuously monitor your investments and to be alert for any telltale signs that things aren't quite the way they should be. If you become suspicious or overly uncomfortable with an investment you have made, and if you are unable to totally resolve your concerns, the best thing you can do is try to get out of it. Demand your money back, accompanied, if necessary, by threats to contact authorities. See the box below. Danger signs include:

- The person who sold you the investment suddenly becomes inaccessible or is continuously tied up on the telephone, busy with clients, out-of-town, or does not return your calls.
- Accounting statements, or other documents you were promised, do not arrive.
- Money that was supposed to have been paid to you is not received, and instead of checks, you get excuses.
- Answers to your questions are vague or different from what you had been led to expect.

FRAUD INVESTIGATORY AGENCIES

If an investment sounds suspicious, check with the appropriate agency. Fraud is against the law in every state of the nation. So:

- If you believe a fraud is being committed, contact the private, non-profit National Fraud Information Center, P.O. Box 65868, Washington, D.C. 20005, by phone (800) 876-7060, or go online to *http://www.fraud.org* or by e-mail *NFIC@internetmci.com* Also, notify the office of the State's Securities Administrator, the State's Attorney General, and the local Public Prosecutor.
- If the mails are used in promoting or operating a phony investment scheme, the Federal Postal Inspectors want to know. Contact the Postal Inspector at your local Post Office, listed under the United States heading in the Blue or White Pages, or write to the United States Postal Service, Chief Postal Inspector, 475 L'Enfant Plaza, S.W., Room 3021, Washington, D.C. 20260-2100, phone (202) 268-4298, or call the Postal Crime Hotline (800) 654-8896.
- Fraud involving any form of interstate commerce is also of interest to the Federal Bureau of Investigation. Contact the local agency listed under the United States heading in the Blue or White Pages, or write to the Federal Bureau of Investigation, Justice Department, Ninth Street & Pennsylvania Avenue, N.W., Washington, D.C. 20535, or call (202) 324-3000.
- The Federal Trade Commission has jurisdiction over advertising, franchises, and business opportunities. Write to the FTC, Sixth Street & Pennsylvania Avenue, N.W., Washington, D.C. 20580, or call (202) 326-2000. For information go online to *http://www.ftc.gov*
- Deals involving interstate promotion of land sales are regulated by the Federal Department of Housing and Urban Development. Send a letter to the Housing and Urban Development Dept., Interstate Land Sales Registration, HUD Building, 451 Seventh Street, S.W., Room 9160, Washington, D.C. 20410, or call (202) 708-0502 or the HUD Fraud Hotline (800) 347-3735.
- Cyberfraud should be reported to the National Consumers League's Internet Fraud Watch on the Web at *http://www.fraud.org* or by e-mail *NFIC@internetmci.com*

Investment Arbitration Services

■ **New York Stock Exchange** (NYSE), 11 Wall Street, New York, NY 10005 — (The NYSE is a private industry group that regulates its members.)

■ **National Association of Securities Dealers** (NASD), 2 World Trade Center, New York, NY 10048 — (The NASD is a private industry group that regulates its members.) To request an arbitration kit, write to the National Association of Securities Dealers, Arbitration Dept., 33 Whitehall Street, 8ᵗʰ Floor, New York, NY 10004, or call (212) 858-4000. For the location of an office in your area, look in the White Pages under the same name.

■ Office of Consumer Affairs, **Securities and Exchange Commission** (SEC), 450 Fifth Street, N.W., Washington, D.C. 20549, or call (800) 732-0330, or go online to *http://www.sec.gov* (The SEC is an agency of the U.S. government.)

■ **National Futures Association** (NFA), 200 West Madison Street, Suite 1600, Chicago, IL 60606-3447, or call (800) 621-3570 [within Ill., (800) 572-9400] for a free copy of "Arbitration: A Way to Resolve Futures-Related Disputes," which explains the Arbitration Program and how it works.

Arbitration for Security Disputes

All investments involve risk, because they are influenced by the national economy, world events, false reports put out by issuers, etc. Brokerage firms have no control over these factors, and cannot be held liable for losses incurred simply because the value of investments they made went down, provided they acted in good faith. However, depending on the state, a broker may be liable if his or her actions show negligence, misrepresentation, nondisclosure of material facts, breach of contract or obligation, breach of fiduciary duties, or excessive trading (called **Churning**). Currently, most contracts with brokerages require arbitration, instead of Court proceedings, to settle disputes.

It is important for you to have a written statement, filed with the broker, to prove that the broker was clearly advised of your investment goals and financial circumstances. If the broker makes unauthorized trades, recommends unsuitable investments, or is careless in executing orders, you should take action. Begin by discussing the problem with the broker and ask for a written explanation. Also, notify the office manager, and the firm's compliance officer (brokerage will supply the name and address) in writing. If you do not get satisfaction, take the complaint to the State's Department of Professional Regulation or Consumer Affairs Department (listed in the Blue or White Pages of your phone book under the name of your state). If you are not seeking monetary damages, but want to report what you determine to be an abuse, use the address in the box above, to contact the appropriate regulatory entity. This will result in an investigation and, possibly, disciplinary action against the broker. If you have incurred a loss and want to pursue monetary damages, you may want to bring the case to arbitration. However, in cases where the claim is for less than $10,000, there are cheaper, simplified procedures, either through the company or outside mediation, that resolve cases quicker. Remember, if you lose an arbitration, you will not be able to sue later. It may be wise to speak to an attorney who practices securities law to determine if arbitration is appropriate, or if a lawsuit should be brought and, if appropriate, to represent you at either proceeding.

If you decide to go to **Arbitration**, start by sending a written complaint, describing the events and damages requested, to the Director of Arbitration of the appropriate agency, listed in the box on page 163. If the case is accepted for arbitration, the accused party, typically a broker and/or securities firm, is advised of the complaint and a date is set for the arbitration hearing, usually about a year from the date of filing. At the hearing, which normally lasts about two days, both sides present arguments, usually to a panel of three arbitrators. The plaintiff must demonstrate that the broker intentionally or negligently mishandled the account, not just show that money was lost. The panel makes a decision which may include a monetary award for the investor. Fees for the arbitration procedure are based on the amount of damages. Decisions are final and binding for all practical purposes. Grounds for appeal are very limited.

Mediation

In **Mediation**, a third party tries to help the disputing parties reach an equitable agreement. If you want to try mediation first, ask the brokerage if they use a mediator, or contact your own, they are listed in the Yellow Pages, under the headings ARBITRATION SERVICES or MEDIATION SERVICES. If you cannot find a listing write to the American Arbitration Association, 140 West 51 Street, New York, NY 10020-1203 or call (212) 484-4006. There are no standards for mediators. Their training may range from individuals who observed a few mediations to former judges. The process is typically confidential and the participants are free to go to arbitration or Court if they can't agree to a mediator-assisted settlement. Decisions are not binding.

HIRING AN ATTORNEY

Unless an attorney was named as a Personal Representative, Executor, or Co-executor in the Will, the Administrator is free to choose his or her own counsel. Before looking for an attorney, you must decide to what extent you are going to use the attorney's services. This decision should be based on the complexity of the Estate, requirements of the Probate Court (laws or regulations of the county in which the Will is being probated), the potential for problems, and the time, knowledge and ability you have to handle the various aspects of settling the Estate yourself. This would include understanding all the intricacies of the state's estate laws and regulations, obtaining and learning to complete the court forms and petitions, presenting formal estate inventories, etc. This is likely to be difficult in all but the most simple of Estates and would depend on how helpful the Court Clerk is in providing forms and information. Keep in mind, any mistakes can cause delays and hopefully just a little embarrassment. Serious mistakes could result in a lawsuit if your judgment is determined to be reckless and causes significant loss to the Estate. Of course, unexpected problems may arise which will change your needs as you go along.

By accepting the duties of Administrator, you have already accepted legal responsibility to oversee the Probate process, and make sure all court papers and tax forms are completed and filed in a timely fashion. You have the choice to hire professionals to perform all of the duties involved, or choose to perform some, or all, of the duties yourself. Hopefully, reading this book has given you some insight into what is involved and will help you to evaluate your individual situation and needs for assistance.

If the Estate is simple, or an attorney is needed only to transfer title or close on real estate, a sole or group practitioner who is experienced in that area would be appropriate.

On the other hand, if the Estate is complex, or seems likely to go to trial, you may need a sole practitioner or a group with a partner, who is more specialized and is an experienced trial lawyer.

In each matter, you must determine how much control you wish to exercise, and how much discretion you wish to allow the attorney to exercise.

Fee Structures

Regardless of the fee structure agreed upon, be sure the contract for services includes a statement clearly stating who will absorb the cost of bringing another attorney in to complete the task, if for some reason the attorney is not able to complete the case.

Percentage Fee

If the Estate must go through the formal probate process, the fee will usually be a **Percentage** of the Gross Estate, and be set by the Court according to state law. This percentage is most often split 50/50 between the Administrator and the attorney. Some states also allow an hourly rate for the attorney in addition to the percentage. (If the Administrator is also a major Beneficiary, he or she may waive the fee, which is subject to income tax.)

If Probate will be very simple (no Court appearances), involves only a simple title transfer or closing on real estate, the Estate has just a few assets with large value, or you are going to perform most of the property evaluations and transfers, you can negotiate with the attorney for a lower percentage, an hourly charge, or a flat fee for services. The charge to handle the Estate will then depend on the reputation and experience of the attorney, the amount of time involved in preparing and filing probate forms, and the extent of management and disposition of the Estate property. Be sure the percentage agreement states:

- The percentage to be charged;
- The work the attorney will perform;
- If filing fees or other costs are included or additional;
- That you will receive itemized bills for expenses.

Hourly Fee

If you just need some points of law explained, answers to questions surrounding the Estate, help or advice in transferring trust property, establishing a trust for a child, or if the Estate is subject to bringing or defending a lawsuit, you may want to negotiate an **Hourly Basis** agreement, which is the number of hours worked times the hourly rate agreed upon. Be sure the agreement spells out:

- The hourly fee for work done by the attorney;
- The lower hourly fees for work done by assistants, such as secretaries and paralegals; so you will be charged at their hourly rates, not at the attorney's fee;
- The minimum billing time for partial hours, i.e. one-tenth of an hour, quarter of an hour, etc. This can make a significant difference. Be sure to time phone calls and meetings. Write out questions to ask and keep notes of all consultations to lower the cost;
- That the attorney send an itemized bill to you each month. The bills should describe: the work done, who did it, and for how long;
- That the attorney will notify you when fees exceed a certain predetermined amount, (based on an estimate of the number of hours it will take to work on your case);
- If filing fees or other costs are included or additional;
- That the attorney will require permission for any research that takes more than two hours. (The less experienced or specialized the attorney, the higher the research fees are likely to be.);
- That your expressed consent is required for such things as overtime pay for assistants, meals the firm provides, and faxing (when mail would do);
- That you will receive itemized bills for expenses.

Flat Fee

If you have a particular routine task, such as drawing up a Will or Trust Agreement, or simple transfer of a real estate title, you can usually come to a flat fee agreement. A **Flat Fee** is a set rate that the attorney charges for a particular task, no matter how long the task takes. Of course, if any unexpected complications arise, your lawyer will probably want to renegotiate the fee. Be sure the agreement specifies:
- The exact dollar amount of the fee;
- The task that will be accomplished;
- If filing fees or other costs are included or additional;
- That you will receive itemized bills for expenses, if charges are incurred in addition to the flat fee.

Contingency Fee

If the Estate is involved in, or will be bringing, a lawsuit where a monetary award is sought, an attorney may agree to a contingency fee. **Contingency Fees** average 33 percent of the award and are paid only if the case is won. The fee only covers the attorney's fees, not the cost of filing fees, hiring expert witnesses, copying costs, etc., which must be paid by the Estate, win or lose. In the agreement be sure to spell out:
- A sliding scale percentage, based on the specific dollar amount of the award. The higher the dollar amount, the lower the percentage you may be able to negotiate;
- A sliding scale percentage based on when the case is settled. A lower percentage if settled before trial, higher if you go to trial, and higher still if you go to appeal;

- Whether the fee will be based on the gross award, or after expenses have been deducted;
- That you will receive itemized bills for expenses.

Selecting An Attorney

Locating the Appropriate Attorney

Before you can hire an attorney, you need to make a list of possible candidates that best fill the requirements you have set. The following is to help you compile that preliminary list. They are listed in order of what is considered the most desirable way to find an attorney.

- If the decedent was enrolled in a Pre-paid Legal Plan, read the agreement to determine what services the attorney(ies) will provide. If you determine that they are not appropriate for the current situation, ask for a refund of the unused portion of the pre-paid contract;
- Contact the same attorney who wrote the Will or Trust Agreement;
- Ask a friend, business associate, or professional (your doctor, accountant, clergyman, or a trust officer at your bank) for referral. If the recommended attorney does not handle your particular needs, he or she may refer you to an attorney who does. Usually, an attorney will not accept a case outside his or her ability, because they can be held liable;
- Look in the Yellow Pages of the phone book, under the heading ATTORNEYS. Most will list their specialties and will discuss your needs and their fees over the phone. Call a number of them before asking for an appointment;
- Call the State Bar Association. Most offer an Attorney Referral Service, usually giving three names of attorneys that have reached the top of the rotation list. (This doesn't guarantee any particular expertise, because any attorney is allowed to sign up if he or she possesses the requisite amount of malpractice insurance and agrees to basic rules.);
- The Courthouse Law Library, University Law Library, and some Public Libraries, have the multi-volume publication, *Martindale-Hubbell.* It lists attorneys in the U.S. by state and city, gives field of expertise, representative clients, and reputation in the community. *Martindale-Hubbell* is not a list of all attorneys. In fact, listed attorneys pay a large fee for the privilege;
- The National Legal Aid And Defender Association, 1625 K Street, N.W., 8th Floor, Washington, D.C., call (202) 452-0620 will refer qualified individuals to a local office.

Hiring An Attorney

When you have determined exactly what you want an attorney to do, you are ready to call a few and state what services you need. You do not have to make an appointment during this phone call. Use the "Hiring Interview Sheet" on pages R-39 and R-40. After you evaluate the information from the call and check the attorney out, you can call back for an appointment with the one you finally choose.

■ Ask what the attorney would charge to perform the stated services. Fees are negotiable, so shop around for the best balance of fee and experience.

■ Ask for a free initial consultation, so you can meet the attorney and determine if the attorney is sensitive to your needs and has a compatible personality. You do not want an attorney who talks over your head or in legalese, talks down to you, or specifically discusses other clients' cases.

■ Ask for references, unless you already know satisfied clients. The attorney should be experienced in estate settlement or the area of law for which you need assistance.

■ Ask how long the attorney has been practicing the particular type of law in which you need assistance. Also ask how many cases of the same type he or she handles annually.

■ Check with county and state attorney organizations, such as the State Bar Association, for information regarding complaints against the attorney and if the attorney has been disciplined.

■ Avoid an attorney whose fees or time estimates are much higher, or lower, than the others.

■ Avoid an attorney who will not draw up a written contract, in clear language, which specifies the details of your agreement for services.

■ Be sure the attorney carries a malpractice insurance called an **Errors and Omissions Policy**. This covers the attorney when injury, loss, or damage results because of a dereliction from professional duty or a failure of professional skill or learning. Keep in mind, as in medicine, the attorney does not guarantee results.

■ The attorney will usually require a retainer. A retainer is a partial payment of the fee which you have agreed to pay, made to show good faith. The retainer may also include an expense account to pay for costs of the case, filing fees, and the like. The receipt should state the use for the money. No more than partial payment for fees should be required up front. Additional payments are made as the work proceeds, or full payment is made when the work is completed.

■ Above all, **NEVER** sign a contract or other form you have not read or do not understand.

■ Request copies of every paper and keep them.

Points To Remember

Ethical Behavior

You should expect, and accept nothing less than, ethical behavior from your attorney. If, after you start working with an attorney, you are not satisfied, you should consider dismissal. Some signs that should make an alarm go off is an attorney who:

■ Seems too busy to put much effort into your case;

■ Guarantees to win your case;

- Shoots down your suggestions and doesn't offer alternatives;
- Pushes for costly and time consuming litigation when it seems unnecessary;
- Spends days researching matters that are barely relevant to your case;
- Does not keep you informed about the progress of the case;
- Does not give you copies of all important paperwork.

Dispute Settlement

If a dispute over a change in the fee or management of the case should arise, try negotiating with the attorney. Write an objection, request justification for the change, or offer a compromise if you think it is fair. If, after an honest attempt, you cannot reach an agreement, call your State Bar Association for information about the availability of arbitration in your area and fees. An **Arbitration** panel consists of lawyers and lay people. They will examine the work that went into your case, and work out a settlement between you and the attorney. It is binding and the attorney must abide by it, as must you. If you decide on arbitration, tell your attorney. If the attorney refuses to arbitrate or refuses to accept the decision of an arbitration panel, you can choose to take the attorney to Court. If the amount in dispute is within the small claims court dollar limit in your area, you can sue your lawyer in that Court. If the amount is higher, go to a higher Court. Of course, this will involve hiring another attorney and more expense.

TAX PREPARATION
AND
TAX PREPARERS

Meeting the Requirements Of Taxing Authorities

The Internal Revenue Service, as well as the state, county, and city taxing authorities, will hold the Administrator responsible for filing tax forms and for paying the taxes that are due. If there are any problems, it is you they will come after. So, even if you hire a professional to complete the tax forms, it would be wise for you to check with the IRS and other taxing agencies to determine your responsibility. If the Estate is subject to a particular tax, request the appropriate instruction publications for that tax from the taxing authority and read them, so you know yourself what tax forms are required and when. See Chapter 7, "Property Transfer Breakdown," Taxes for more information.

If you enjoy working with numbers, you can usually cut the cost of tax preparation by preparing the returns yourself then bringing them to a professional for review. Usually an accountant will charge far less to review a return than to prepare it. This is true even if they must redo the return because most of the work is already done. Bring all of the backup documents with you, so the accountant can compare them to the return. The most common mistake made by taxpayers is not taking all the deductions to which they are entitled. This is the reason why a professional's opinion is so valuable.

Qualified Tax Preparers

Any bookkeeper or tax preparer can call themselves an accountant but NOT a **Certified Public Accountant** (CPA) unless licensed by the state. CPA's must complete five years of college and pass a statewide exam to receive state licensing, they are regulated by the state's department of professional regulation. CPA's may only practice in the state where they are licensed unless another state offers reciprocity.

Whatever you determine the tax preparation requirements are, be careful when looking for a tax preparer to choose a professional that is qualified to both prepare tax returns and, not only accompany, but also to represent you, before the tax authorities if the return is audited. The IRS will only allow a taxpayer to be represented by an attorney, a CPA, or an enrolled agent or enrolled actuary. An **Enrolled Agent** or **Enrolled Actuary** is a person who is required to meet continuing educational standards, has passed the IRS Special Enrollment Examination, shown expertise in tax matters, and is licensed directly by the federal government. An accountant will have a **Treasury Card,** as proof of his or her credentials. Keep in mind that IRS licensing is separate from state licensing. If there is a State Income Tax, the preparer should also be licensed by the state to represent you at an audit. Contact the state's department of revenue to learn its requirements. Although a CPA or attorney may usually represent you, some have been disbarred by the IRS. They may still practice as a CPA or attorney, respectively, but cannot represent you before the IRS. Accountants who are either unlicensed or are not enrolled agents may charge less, but since tax laws are complicated, it would not be wise to hire anything less than a qualified tax preparer even for the most simple Estate.

Other Services Offered by CPA's

Depending on your needs, a CPA can provide a number of other services. For individuals, the CPA can develop tax-planning strategies and some provide financial planning services. See Chapter 17, "Financial Planners," for more information. For businesses, CPA's can perform audits and reviews of accounting systems and recommend improvements; determine the value of the stock of a private corporation; consult on business problems and ways to improve the use of resources; and provide compilation services for special studies to facilitate mergers, acquisitions, or loans.

Selecting an Appropriate Tax Preparer

Before you hire an accountant, you need to make a list of possible candidates that best fill the requirements you have set. The following is to help you compile a preliminary list.

Locating a Qualified Tax Preparer

- If the deceased person used the services of a CPA or an enrolled agent, this is the most obvious choice, because this tax preparer would have knowledge of the decedent's financial history.
- If you have hired an estate attorney, he or she will probably have the taxes done by the CPA he or she usually works with, or do the taxes him- or herself.
- Ask your attorney, banker, or insurance agent; these professionals can often suggest a few names.
- Call the Association of Certified Public Accountants to get a list of members in your state. Look in the White Pages for the Association under the name of your state.
- The American Institute of Certified Public Accountants (AICPA) is a nationwide professional group with state chapters. Look in the White Pages under the name of your state, or write to the AICPA, 1211 Avenue Of The Americas, New York, NY 10036-8775 or call (212) 596-6200, or (800) 862-4272.
- Call The National Association of Enrolled Agents, at (800) 424-4339, or (301) 212-9608, or write to them at 200 Orchard Ridge Road, No. 302, Gaithersburg, MD 20878, for a list of enrolled agents who are IRS approved to represent taxpayers.
- Contact the National Association of Enrolled Federal Tax Accountants at P.O. Box 59-009, Chicago, IL 60659-0009, or call (312) 463-5577, who will refer you to members in your area.
- Look in the Yellow Pages of the phone book under the headings ACCOUNTANTS and ACCOUNTANTS-CERTIFIED PUBLIC.

Hiring an Accountant

When you have determined exactly what you want an accountant to do, you are ready to call a few and state what services you need. Use the "Hiring Interview Sheet" on pages R-39 and R-40. You do not have to make an appointment during this phone call. After you evaluate the information from the call and check the accountant out, you can call back for an appointment with the one you finally choose.
- Ask the accountant how much experience he or she has with estate tax preparation;
- Ask for names of clients you can call for references;
- If the tax preparer is an attorney or CPA, ask if he or she will be able to represent you in the event of an audit, both before the IRS and state taxing authority, as appropriate. For other accountants, ask if they have a current Treasury Card from the IRS and state equivalent, if applicable;
- Ask what kind of continuing education he or she has taken;
- Ask which professional organizations he or she belongs to, and check with the organization for current membership status and complaints against the member;
- Ask about charges. Normally accountants bill by the hour, though sometimes they charge flat fees or minimums. Many firms charge more for work performed by a partner and a good deal less for work done by a junior accountant or a data-entry clerk. Big firms typically

charge more for their services and handle primarily business clients. Smaller firms charge less and focus on individuals;

- Interview the candidate you like the best. Personal chemistry is also important;
- If the tax preparer is an attorney or CPA, check with the state's department of professional regulation or licensing board to be sure he or she has a current license. They may also be able to advise you of complaints which have been lodged against the professional.

FINANCIAL PLANNERS

A **Financial Planner's** function is to review all the aspects of a client's finances and guide them in decision making. A good planner can take charge of the total financial plan and coordinate a team of professionals to implement the plan. The planner will help clients to formulate a budget, help in investing a lump-sum pension distribution or inheritance, plan tax strategies, evaluate insurance needs and policies, update estate planning, provide investment risk management to meet present and long-term needs, and evaluate retirement plans and investments. Although a planner who is not also a securities broker will hesitate to pick specific investments, he or she can offer a second opinion on a significant investment move to be sure it is in line with the client's goals.

While some states do provide for licensing of financial planners, in many states "Financial Planner" is a title anyone can use. On the other hand, the designation of Certified Financial Planner (CFP) from the Certified Financial Planners Board of Standards, means a planner is a professional who has taken courses and passed examinations in numerous financial-planning topics and meets experience and ethical criteria. The Board is a national trade organization whose aim is to protect the public by making certain those who earn the CFP designation are well qualified.

Many financial planners are individuals with professional credentials in other fields, such as investment brokers, attorneys, CPA's, and insurance agents. These professionals have taken additional training to enable them to give financial planning advice. Often these professionals stay in their original professions and sell some of the things they advise. For instance, an investment broker would make trades on your behalf, an attorney would draw up and execute documents, a CPA may do the taxes, and an insurance agent may sell you an insurance policy. These planners may charge a fee for their services, but offset (lower) the fee with income they derive from the sale of the other services they provide for you. Look at compensation carefully. A planner who works only for a set fee may do very little investing, while a planner who receives commissions might do excessive trading or product buying. These professionals usually concentrate in a particular field and restrict their advice to that field. They may not examine your entire financial situation. On the other hand, some financial planners have pooled their individual specialties and work as a team, in firms devoted exclusively to financial planning. They do not sell financial products or services, but they do refer clients to firms that make them available. These planners charge a straight fee for their time and often lower fees for services provided by staff members. See the box on page 177 for the names, addresses, and phone numbers of major organizations.

If the planner charges fees for advice on securities investment, he or she must register with the United States Securities and Exchange Commission (SEC). After paying a registration fee and filing a completed "Application for Investment Adviser Registration" (ADV) report to the SEC, an adviser receives the title of Registered Investment Adviser (RIA). Therefore, RIA is not a credential but a yearly renewable registration. Part II of the ADV form is available to clients. Ask the advisor to send his or her brochures and a copy of his or her Form ADV to you. It provides a great deal of useful information on the planner's services, education, experience, fees, and operating methods. Look for an investment adviser with advanced financial degrees.

Avoid any financial planner who wants power of attorney or full discretionary power over the money. Discretionary power means that the planner is free to buy and sell securities or other products for you, without consulting you regarding each decision. Don't invest in anything unless you really understand it. Educate yourself enough to be an informed participant. Be inquisitive and skeptical about the planner's suggestions and don't be pressured to invest immediately, or in something that is clearly out of line with your goals. See Chapter 14, "Investment Brokers and Brokerage Accounts," for more information on cautious investing. Reading Chapters 1 through 5, plus Chapters 18 and 19, and Chapters 24 through 28, of this book, and considering the information in relation to your own situation, should help you to determine what assistance you may need to formulate and execute a suitable financial and estate plan.

Disputes with Financial Planners

It is important, if you give the planner any control over investments, for you to have a written statement, filed with the planner, clearly advising of your investment goals and financial circumstances. A financial planner may be liable if his or her actions show negligence, misrepresentation, nondisclosure of material facts, breach of contract or obligation, or breach of fiduciary duties. If the planner makes unauthorized investments, recommends unsuitable investments, or is careless in executing your financial plan, you should take action. First, discuss the problem with the planner and the firm's management and ask for a written explanation. If you do not get satisfaction, take the complaint to the regulatory organization in which the planner is a member; and, if appropriate, the State's Department of Professional Regulation or Consumer Affairs Department (listed in the Blue or White Pages of your phone book under the name of your state). If you have incurred a loss and want to pursue monetary damages, you may want to bring the case to arbitration, mediation, or file a lawsuit. For more information see Chapter 14, "Investment Brokers and Brokerage Accounts," <u>Arbitration</u> and <u>Mediation</u>.

Financial Planning Professional Organizations

The following are professional organizations who provide training and testing for members or require CFP designation.

- The **International Association For Financial Planning** (IAFP), 2 Concourse Parkway, Suite 800, Atlanta, GA 30328, call (404) 845-0011 or (800) 945-4237 to get a list of five financial planners who have qualified for the groups "Registry" in your area. Also request its free booklets, *Consumer Bill of Rights* and *Consumer Guide to Financial Independence.*

- **Institute of Certified Financial Planners** (ICFP) offers advice, a free booklet on selecting a planner, and will give the names of three members with the CFP designation in your area. Call (800) 322-4237. You can also write to the ICFP at 7600 E. Eastman Avenue, Suite 301, Denver, CO 80231, and request its publications: *Financial Planning: A Common Sense Guide for the 1990's,* "How to Manage Your Financial Resources: Creating a Spending Plan You Can Control," "Your Children's College Bill: How to Figure It . . . How to Pay For It," and "Avoiding Investment and Financial Scams: Seeking Full Disclosure is the Key."

- **National Association of Personal Financial Advisors** (NAPFA) is made up of fee-only planners. The NAPFA does not require its members to undergo any type of testing or certification. However, members must meet some education requirements and have at least three years of experience. Call (800) 366-2732 for referrals and a useful interview form.

- **American Institute of Certified Public Accountants** gives the designation of Accredited Personal Financial Specialist (APFS) or Personal Financial Specialist (PFS), to CPA's who have completed financial planning courses, passed tests sponsored by the Institute, and have met experience criteria. Call (800) 862-4272 to ask for names of CPA's in your area with the PFS designation, or to check on their designation.

- **American Society of CLU and ChFC**, 270 S. Bryn Mawr Avenue, Bryn Mawr, PA 19010, phone (610) 526-2500, awards the designation of Chartered Life Underwriter (CLU) and Chartered Financial Consultant (ChFC) to insurance agents and planners who have satisfactorily completed courses and passed examinations in various insurance areas. A CLU can plan and provide insurance where necessary. A ChFC has completed additional educational courses at the American College to provide financial planning. Call (800) 392- 6900.

- The **Association of Investment Management and Research** (AIMR), 5 Boars Head Lane, P.O. Box 3668, Charlottesville, VA 22903, call (800) 247-8132, or (804) 977-6600. The AIMR gives the designation of Chartered Financial Analyst (CFA) to those who have completed a three-year program focusing on investment analysis. Many CFA's are professional securities analysts and money managers. The AIMR publishes the *AIMR Standards of Practice Handbook,* as well as study guides.

Locating a Financial Planner

It is important to work with a planner who does business with clients in roughly equal circumstances to yours. Increasingly, planners are specializing in one area, such as retirement, investments, or estate planning. Therefore, you should look for one who provides the services you want. Look for candidates who possess professional credentials, a broad mix of education, and have several years of experience providing financial planning.

- Ask for a recommendation from a trusted friend, attorney, insurance agent, or accountant familiar with the planner's work;
- Call planner associations for names of local members. (See the box on page 177.);
- Check the Yellow Pages under the headings FINANCIAL PLANNERS and FINANCIAL PLANNING CONSULTANTS.

Choosing a Financial Planner

When you have determined exactly what you want a financial planner to do, you are ready to call a few and state what services you need. You do not have to make an appointment during this phone call. After you evaluate the information from the call and check the financial planner out, you can call back for an appointment with the one you finally choose. Use the "Hiring Interview Sheet" on pages R-39 and R-40. The following questions should allow you to gain the information you need to determine if a particular planner is the right one for you:

- How long has he or she been doing financial planning in this community?
- How many financial planning clients has he or she worked with?
- Ask for the names of at least three clients. Call each and ask if the planner has delivered what was promised, what they did not like about the planner, and if clients believe they got their money's worth.
- What services does the planner provide? Keep in mind your particular needs.
- What professional designations does he or she have, and to what professional organizations does he or she belong? Call each organization to check the planner's credentials, and ask if there have been any complaints about the planner. The planner's credentials should be appropriate to the services you are seeking, and the services the planner intends to provide.
- What are the planner's fees? Does the planner offer full disclosure of fees and commissions up front and in writing? Planners may charge fees of $1000 to $2000 to evaluate a person's finances and make recommendations. Most will also provide targeted advice at hourly rates. Reject anyone who won't tell you exactly how, and how much, he or she is paid.
- Most planners will spend a half-hour with someone to get acquainted, free of charge. During this interview, the planner should discuss your needs and problems; how he or she can help; how long it will take; and what it will cost. Request a free interview with the planner, to see if personal chemistry is there. If he or she is not addressing your concerns or using professional jargon, try another planner.

Learning Financial Planning Techniques

Courses and seminars about financial planning may be available through cooperative extension service programs of your local college or university. Also watch for free seminars on financial planning, estate planning, and money management conducted by brokerage firms, insurance companies, and others. You create no obligation by attending.

INSURANCE
AND
INSURANCE AGENTS

General

All insurance policies have limitations and exclusions. An insurance company does not stand behind what an agent says; it stands behind what is written in the actual policy. It is up to you to review the policy carefully, to learn what the limitations are, and if they are acceptable to you. If you determine that the exclusions and limitations are unacceptable, you can pay more to gain the coverage, either by purchasing a **Rider** (amendment) to an in-force policy or by purchasing a separate policy to cover the particular risk. If the coverage is not available through one insurer, contact another insurance carrier who may have a policy with more suitable terms. Almost all types of insurance have a deductible of some sort. A **Deductible** is the amount of the loss the insured is required to absorb, or pay, before the insurance company will start paying benefits. Most policies offer deductibles of varying amounts. As a rule, the higher the deductible, the lower the **Premium**, or cost of the policy. To determine the best arrangement for you, ask for quotes of the same coverage with each deductible, from different companies. The cost of the same coverage can vary widely between companies. Be sure to select a deductible you can afford.

No matter how good the coverage of a policy you purchase appears; the policy is worthless if the insurance company is not in business, or unable to pay, when you need the benefits. Commercial insurance rating services, such as: A.M. Best & Company, Moody's, Standard & Poor's, and Duff & Phelps, rate the claims-paying ability and financial strength of insurance companies. Each uses a different rating system, so read the rating system information in each book. You can find these rating publications in the Public Library. For more information about insurance in general, and life insurance in particular, write to the American Council of Life Insurance, 1001 Pennsylvania Avenue, N.W., Washington, D.C. 20004-2599. Among its publications is "A Consumer's Guide To Life Insurance"; this pamphlet is also available from the Consumer Information Catalogue, Pueblo, CO 81002. For answers to general questions about various insurance matters, referral of consumer complaints to appropriate agencies, and to request consumer brochures: Call the Insurance Information Institute's National Insurance Consumer Hotline (800) 942-4242. Additionally, each state has a department of insurance or insurance commission, which licenses insurers to operate in the state and takes complaints about registered insurance companies and agents. Consumers are welcome to contact the agency to find out about complaints filed against insurers and to request general information brochures about all types of insurance. Look in the Blue or White Pages under the name of the state.

Homeowner's Insurance

Homeowner's insurance offers three types of coverage. The first is to provide payment to rebuild the house, garage, and out-buildings if they are destroyed or damaged. Second, to replace the contents of the home when they are damaged or destroyed. Third, to protect the homeowner from loss when someone (other than an occupant) is injured while on the property. However, it is not that simple. Each part of the policy must be examined carefully to determine if the coverage it provides is sufficient.

- **BUILDING:**
  - The coverage should be "guaranteed replacement," and sufficient to rebuild the home at the current price of materials and labor.
  - What types of destruction or damage are not covered by the policy? Most will exclude some natural disasters, such as floods, earthquakes, or landslides. In areas prone to these risks, separate policies are offered to cover losses.
  - Most policies only guarantee to pay to rebuild the home to the building code standards to which it was built before the destruction. If the building codes have changed since the home was built, this policy will not pay the extra costs of bringing the building up to current code. However, for an additional premium, the insurance companies do offer a "building code endorsement" to cover the added cost of rebuilding to code.

- **CONTENTS:**
  - There are two basic types of coverage. The first pays only for the "depreciated value" of the contents. This means that if your property is stolen or destroyed, the insurance company will pay you the "current value" of each lost item before it was destroyed. The loss of your five year old 25 inch television would probably be worth $25. The alternative is "replacement value" coverage, in this case, you would receive enough money to purchase a new item equal to the one that was destroyed. You would have a new 25 inch television. Keep an inventory of all contents in a safe place away from the property.

- **LIABILITY:**
  - Typically, liability coverage might be $100,000 per injury. Depending upon the condition of your property, the number of people who enter it, and the risk from pets, etc., you may want to increase the amount of this coverage. Check the policy for exclusions. If you determine that you need coverage for a particular excluded risk, ask if it can be included in a rider for an extra premium. If you have substantial assets to protect, you may consider a multi-million dollar "umbrella" policy. This would afford protection against claims of fault for damages against you regardless of the place or cause. This coverage costs just a few hundred dollars a year.

Tidbit: Insurance companies will not knowingly insure a vacant home. Therefore, if the house is going to be vacant, it may be better to keep the current homeowner's policy, even if it is inadequate coverage than risk loosing all coverage. Be sure to make payments on time.

Condominium

In a condominium, the association's insurance policy will usually cover repairs to damaged walls in the unit that support the building structure, as well as the electrical wiring and plumbing inside the walls. However, the condominium owner will need insurance to cover everything else, including non-supporting walls, kitchen and bathroom appliances and furnishings, and all personal property, such as furniture and clothing, and perhaps even the floor covering (rugs, tile, etc.), as well as liability coverage for inside the unit. The best way to protect yourself is to understand exactly what is, and is not, covered by the association's policy and then arranging to get the coverage you need.

Renters

People who rent a house or apartment need renter's insurance. These policies protect renters when they lose personal property (furniture, clothes, etc.). The policy the owner of the dwelling buys will only cover damage to the building, not the loss of the renter's personal property. If the insurance provided by the property owner does not provide adequate liability insurance, you may also want to buy liability coverage.

Automobile Insurance

Automobile insurance is divided into different coverages depending upon state law. While each state mandates certain types of insurance and sets minimum standards of coverage for each protection, it is usually wise to buy protection higher than the minimum required by the law.

- **Liability** insurance affords protection when your car causes harm to someone or something else.
- **Medical** payments coverage provides for doctors, hospitals, and surgical expenses for injuries to individuals.
- **Collision** coverage covers the cost of making repairs to your car.
- **Comprehensive** coverage takes care of damage to your vehicle caused by a non-collision type accident, such as an act of God or vandalism.
- **No-fault** coverage applies to any loss to you no matter who is to blame.
- **Uninsured motorist** coverage protects you from loss when you or your property have been injured by a liable, but uninsured, driver.

181

Life Insurance

If the surviving spouse has dependent children, it would be wise to consider investing in insurance to be sure the dependents are provided for in the event of the surviving spouse's death. Since experts disagree as to how much life insurance is adequate, it may be a good idea to consult an insurance agent, who is also a financial planner, to determine the amount and type of insurance that would best fit your needs. See Chapter 17, "Financial Planners." Insurance needs depend upon your age and earnings, income from investments, Social Security and other benefits, amount of savings, family status, debts, expenses, the number and ages of your dependents, and inflation. Other considerations are whether to maintain an identical standard of living, providing for day care expenses, maybe sending children to private school, college and graduate school, unexpected medical or other costs, and the financial status of the guardian who will care for the children. Do you want the insurance proceeds to be sufficient for the income from investments to provide for the dependents needs and then give them the principal when they are of age; or should the principal be spent over the time it is needed?

Children and individuals with no dependents may not need life insurance or only enough to cover funeral and burial expenses.

In addition to insuring your own life, you may also insure the life of another person if you have an "Insurable Interest." This means you can, for instance, insure the life of a person who owes child support, so the children will be provided for in the event of the support payer's death. You cannot insure the life of a stranger or someone in whom you do not have any insurable interest.

Life insurance policies fall into two broad categories: term-life and cash-value. Policies are available in many combinations of these two basic categories. The best combination for you depends upon your circumstances.

- **Term-life** policies pay benefits only after the insured dies. Term-life insurance is purchased for a specified number of years, usually between 1 and 20. If the insured dies during the term of the policy, the beneficiary(ies) named in the policy receives the specified **Death Benefit**, which is the face-value of the policy. After the "term" of the policy ends, so does the insurance coverage, unless the policy is renewed or a new policy bought. If you decide to purchase term insurance, it is wise to purchase a "guaranteed renewable" policy. This coverage costs a bit more, but it will enable you to continue your insurance to age 65 or 70 without taking a new physical examination, even if your health deteriorates. The cost of term-life is based upon the age of the insured at the time of purchase or renewal, and premiums rise as the insured ages.
- **Cash-value** policies (known as whole-life or universal-life) are part insurance and part savings that build up value. The insured pays a fixed annual premium to keep the policy "in force" (active). The cash-value is placed in a "reserve" (also called the investment or savings). The reserve grows, tax-deferred, and after a number of years, the policy can become paid-up and no further premiums will be required. The insured can access the money in the reserve through low interest loans or the policy can be cashed out by the insured after a specified number of years and/or reaching a specified age. After the insured dies, the beneficia-

ry(ies) named in the policy receives the specified death benefit, less any outstanding loan amount and interest.

Because a term-life policy will only pay benefits upon death, the cost of coverage is considerably lower than the cost of a cash-value policy. In fact the difference can be up to 10 times more for a cash-value policy than for a term-life policy with the same benefit. In view of this, insurance agents sometimes suggest clients purchase term-life insurance and invest the cash difference between the premium for the term-life and an equal benefit cash-value policy. However, making regular investments, when not required, takes discipline which most of us do not have. The agent may even suggest terminating an existing cash-value policy to facilitate the purchase of a high benefit term-life policy. Many experts do not agree with this strategy. If you are considering termination of a cash-value policy, before you take action, carefully read your policy to determine the projected interest rates, conversion options, and surrender fees. Also, contact the National Insurance Consumer Organization (NICO) at P.O. Box 15492, Alexandria, VA 22309. The NICO will analyze the rate of return you would have to earn investing the difference to beat the rate on a proposed or existing policy. Standard & Poor's (212) 208-1527 will tell you its safety ratings on most life insurance companies for free.

Life Insurance Rate Comparison Shopping Services

The cost of life insurance can vary significantly. To assist buyers, service organizations have formed to give purchasers comparative pricing information, among them are:

- **InsuranceQuote** (800) 972-1104 — will compare costs for you and may even arrange for the purchase of a policy.
- **LifeQuote of America** (800) 521-7873 — will compare costs for you and may even arrange for the purchase of a policy.
- **SelectQuote Insurance Services** (800) 932-2210 — will compare costs for you and may even arrange for the purchase of a policy.
- **TermQuote Services** (800) 444-8376 — will compare costs for you and may even arrange for the purchase of a policy.
- **Quotesmith** (800) 556-9393 — for a comparison list of up to 150 life insurers, including the insurers' financial stability. The current cost of the report is $15.
- **Insurance Information Inc.** (800) 472-5800 — will find the lowest cost insurance policy from about 550 insurers in its program. The current cost is $50.
- **Fee for Service** (800) 874-5662 — which receives its fee from the insurance companies, will refer callers to flat fee per-hour insurance brokers for advice on the type and amount of coverage you need. They will also compare costs for you, and act as the broker for purchasing the policy. Call (800) 808-5810, its Wholesale Insurance Network, which sells policies of the 10 insurers they represent. You must know the exact type of insurance needed.
- **LifeRates of America** (800) 457-2837 — will compare costs for you to find the three lowest rates from all the top-rated insurance companies.

In addition to determining the type and amount of coverage which is best for you; two additional options should be considered when buying a policy. They are:

■ An "accidental death benefit rider" which pays more if you die in an accident. Consider if this bonus is worth the additional premium in view of the fact that you will need the same coverage no matter how you die.

■ A "waiver of premium rider" which pays your premium if you become disabled. Experts suggest long-term disability insurance is preferable.

Among the categories of term-life policies is **Mortgage Life** insurance. As the name suggests, when the homeowner dies, the insurance company pays off some, or all, of the remainder of the mortgage on the decedent's home. Mortgage life insurance is usually purchased through the lender when the mortgage is granted. It is an optional coverage and is not required by the lender. The loan officer usually receives a commission for selling the policy. Before purchasing mortgage life insurance, it might be wise to compare the premium with the cost of a term-life insurance policy with the same amount of coverage. See the box on page 183, for a listing of agencies which provide comparisons of life insurance policy costs.

Accelerated Life Insurance Benefits and Viatical Settlements

Individuals suffering from a terminal illness, and sometimes their spouse or caregiver, often are not able to work. The lack of income can result in the loss of the ability to pay for the basic needs of life. In this case, an existing life insurance policy can be a financial life saver. While life insurance is usually purchased for the benefit of survivors; it will not benefit anyone if the insured cannot afford to pay the premiums and the policy lapses. An individual who is diagnosed with a terminal illness and advised of a specified limited life expectancy can receive a portion of his or her own existing life insurance policy's death benefit to help make the person's remaining time more comfortable. Qualified individuals may receive an **Accelerated Benefit** from their life insurer. Over 200 life insurance companies offer accelerated benefits to individuals with a life expectancy of less than 6 months, some less than one year. Insurance companies pay anywhere from 25 to 95 percent of the death benefit.

An alternative to receiving an accelerated benefit is to seek a viatical settlement. A **Viatical Settlement** is simply the sale of life insurance benefits to a third party. This provides a source of badly needed funds for a "viator" (insured) with a life expectancy of less than 36 months. A viatical settlement is usually 50 to 80 percent of the death benefit of the policy. The percentage that will be paid depends upon the life expectancy of the insured. When the insured dies, the insurance company pays the death benefit to the viatical company. For a list of viatical companies call the National Viatical Association at (800) 741-9465 or the Viatical Benefits Foundation, Inc. at (800) 871-9440 for information and referrals. For a free 66 page booklet "Every Question You Need To Ask Before Selling Your Life Insurance Policy," call the National Viator Representatives, Inc. at (800) 932-0050.

Although severe financial stress is the usual reason a terminally ill individual will seek an accelerated benefit or viatical settlement; it is not a requirement for receiving benefits. The benefits can be sought to enhance the quality of life or to fulfill a life-long-dream. The companies will require a professionally prognosed life expectancy. Be aware accelerated benefits and viatical settlements are subject to income taxes; while benefits paid to Beneficiaries are tax free. For information about the financial, legal, and tax consequences, write to the Federal Trade Commission, Public Reference Branch, Room 130, Sixth Street and Pennsylvania Avenue, N.W., Washington, D.C. 20580 or call (202) 326-2222 and request a copy of its free brochure.

Annuities

An **Annuity Contract** is an insurance policy which provides guaranteed regular (usually monthly) payments to the owner of the policy, of a specific amount, for a specified number of years, or for life. It is basically a **Retirement Income Plan**. It can be provided as a pension plan through an employer or can be purchased by an individual directly from an insurance company. Some policies make provisions for a joint annuity to the annuitant's spouse. Most contracts end with the death of the main annuitant (and the spouse in a joint annuity). However, some will continue payments, or make a lump-sum payment, to a named beneficiary, upon the death of the annuitant. Monthly payments made to the joint, or survivor, annuitant may be lower than the payment made to the annuitant. Usually, the greater the monthly benefit for a joint or survivor annuity, the lower the annuitant's benefit will be. Annuities are also available through mutual funds. For additional information, see Chapter 25, "Employer Health and Pension Benefits."

Health Insurance

When purchasing health insurance, like any other insurance, you should review the policy, as stated in the General section above. Also, refer to Chapter 24, "Social Security, Medicare, and Medicaid" and Chapter 25, "Employer Health and Pension Benefits." Look in the Yellow Pages under the heading HOSPITALIZATION, MEDICAL & SURGICAL INSURANCE for listings of independent agents and companies who sell health insurance policies. Health insurance policies are available for individual coverage or family coverage. Before buying a policy consider your anticipated health care needs and the amount of money you can afford to pay both for premiums and for health care services when they are received.

There are three basic categories of major medical or catastrophic care coverage available from private insurance companies. They are:

■ **TRADITIONAL INDEMNITY:**
  • The insured pays a specified premium (usually monthly) for coverage. Traditional indemnity insurance usually carries the highest premiums and deductibles. The insured has the freedom to choose any doctor, or other health care provider, clinic, or hospital to provide care. The majority of plans pay 80 percent of doctor and other medical service bills,

and 100 percent of in-hospital bills; the insured is obligated to pay the balance. It is important to read and understand the coverage provided in the plan:

*   The meaning of the wording in these policies. Some policies will pay 80 percent of the "actual" charge. While others will pay 80 percent of the "usual and reasonable" or "reasonable and ordinary" charge for services. This simple turn of a phrase can mean a significant difference in the amount the insured must pay for services. The insurer determines the amount of the charge which is "usual and reasonable" — this amount may be hundreds of dollars less than the actual charge.
*   The total dollar amount of out-of-pocket expense the insured must pay before the insurance will pay 100 percent of the bills incurred.
*   The percentage of each type of medical service the insurance will pay.
*   Any medical condition or service which is excluded from coverage. Many companies will not pay benefits for pre-existing conditions, organ transplants, or procedures the company deems to be "experimental" or "unnecessary."
*   The maximum benefits which will be paid over the insured's life-time.

■   **PREFERRED PROVIDER ORGANIZATION (PPO):**

●   Individuals insured under a PPO plan choose their primary care doctor and specialists from a list of doctors who belong to the plan's network. The network typically includes other service providers, such as laboratories, radiology clinics, pharmacies, hospitals, etc. The insured is free to take advantage of any of the services provided by network members at will. However, if the insured goes outside of the network to other providers, the plan may pay part of the bill, or none of the bill. For example, if the PPO pays 80 percent of the bill for the services of a provider inside the network; it might pay only 60 percent of the bill for services provided outside the network. PPO premiums are typically lower than for traditional indemnity insurance, because the providers in the network agree to limit their charges for services to the amount allowed by the PPO.

■   **HEALTH MAINTENANCE ORGANIZATION (HMO):**

●   An individual, who joins an HMO, picks a primary care doctor from a roster of physicians who have negotiated with the insurance company to manage a patient's health-care needs for a set price. If the patient needs to see a specialist, who is part of the plan, the primary care doctor has to arrange for it, and often must get approval from the home office. The downside of an HMO is limited choice for the patient of health care provider. The up side is expenses for health care is limited to a known amount, namely the premium and the set minimal co-payment, such as paying only $5 for a visit to the doctor or for filling a prescription. Before joining an HMO, determine if it has been accredited by the National Commission for Quality Assurance (NCQA). The NCQA is a private agency that conducts comprehensive examinations of HMOs and determines whether they are worthy of accreditation. Commission teams review systems to make sure patients do not get too much or too little care. They examine physicians' credentials and medical services that aim to prevent health problems. For information about a particular HMO, write to the National Committee for Quality Assurance, 1350 New York Avenue, N.W., Suite 700, Washington, D.C. 20005, or call (202) 628-5788.

When determining whether or not to join a PPO or HMO, consider the answers to these questions:

- If you become ill in another state, or wind up in the emergency room of a hospital not covered by the plan; what coverage is provided?
- How many of the plan's doctors have certification from peers in their specialty?
- How thoroughly is the company checking the member doctors' qualifications?
- What is the procedure if you have a complaint? For example, if an HMO worker denies your physician's request for a specialist; what can you do about it?
- How many doctors, hospitals, and other providers are in the plan? What specialties do they offer?
- Are a sufficient number of providers near your home or job?
- Is the doctor you want as a primary caregiver accepting new patients? Just because doctors are listed in a pamphlet, does not mean they are currently accepting new patients.

An individual choosing traditional indemnity or preferred provider insurance may determine the need for a medical supplemental policy to help pay for the deductible and **Co-payments** (the portion of the medical bill not paid by insurance) of the major medical policy. When purchased to supplement Medicare, a supplemental policy is called a Medigap policy. When buying a supplemental or Medigap policy be careful not to buy duplicate coverage; both policies most often will not duplicate benefit payments when you make a claim. There are three basic types of supplemental insurance, with many choices within the basic structure:

- **TRADITIONAL INDEMNITY:**
  - Some policies pay a specified percentage of the cost of each service covered under the policy. It may also pay part or all of the deductible. Often this insurance will pay 80 percent of the 20 percent co-payment. Be careful not to get a policy that pays 80 percent of the expense. Other policies pay a specified dollar amount for each service received by the insured. Read the policy carefully for exclusions from coverage and conditions of coverage.

- **SPECIFIC DISEASE INSURANCE:**
  - This type of insurance usually pays a specific dollar amount for each treatment required to treat a specific disease, such as cancer. The policy will not pay for any treatment not directly related to the cancer, even if the ailment is indirectly caused by, or would not be suffered if not for, the cancer.

- **DAILY BENEFIT INSURANCE:**
  - These policies pay a daily pre-determined specified dollar amount for each day the insured is a patient in the hospital. Some include coverage for a stay in a rehabilitation center or nursing home. Often the policy will pay double benefits for time spent in an intensive care unit. Some policies pay only if the hospitalization is due to an injury; while others include illness. Some pay the benefit from the first day of hospitalization, others may not start paying until the third day of confinement.

Every state runs a free health insurance and long-term care insurance counseling program for seniors. These programs can help you determine the coverage that best suits your individual needs. For more information contact your area agency on aging or the state's department of insurance. Additionally the state's department of insurance provides an array of information on health insurance, including consumer guides on HMOs specifically and health insurance generally. The guides are free of charge.

Long-Term Care Insurance

Long-term care insurance usually provides for a daily benefit amount to be paid when the insured requires long-term care, either in a nursing home or in his or her own home. The cost of the coverage is based on the age of the insured when the policy is purchased and the benefits included. Chapter 24, "Social Security, Medicare, and Medicaid" and Chapter 26, "Providing Care for a Dependent Adult Survivor," may help you choose the type and extent of coverage you want to purchase. The terms to consider when purchasing a policy include:

- The policy's definition of the circumstances which qualify the insured to receive benefits.
- The types of services included in the coverage. Services can range from care provided by professionals, such as nurses and physical therapists, to custodial care (assistance with eating, bathing, dressing, walking, etc.) provided by a nurse's assistant. Will benefits be paid for custodial care even when professional care is not required?
- Are benefits paid only for care provided in a nursing-home or other skilled nursing facility, or is care provided in your home covered? What are the benefit limitations, if any, of the type of care provided in the home? Some policies cover home care, but only after you receive care in a nursing home.
- What waiting period is acceptable? This is the number of days after qualified care has begun before the policy will pay benefits. The longer the waiting period the lower the premium.
- The amount of the daily benefit that will be paid by the insurance company when you are receiving qualified care. Does the benefit increase with inflation? Take into consideration the expected income from Social Security, pension, etc., which will go toward paying nursing home costs.
- Carefully read the exclusions. Some policies do not provide coverage for certain illnesses, injuries, or pre-existing conditions. Be sure the policy covers care for Alzheimer's disease.
- Under what circumstances can the insurer cancel the policy? It is not wise to buy a policy that is not guaranteed renewable.
- Will the policy premium remain level, or will it increase as you age, or with the rate of inflation? Consider your ability to continue to pay the premium after retirement when income is lower.
- The number of years the benefits will be paid.
- Does the policy have a nonforfeiture option? This allows individuals to collect some reduced benefit if they stop making payments after a number of years.

The following pamphlets may assist you in choosing the appropriate plan:
- "A Shoppers Guide to Long-Term Care Insurance" from the National Association of Insurance Commissioners, 120 W. 12th Street, Suite 1100, Kansas City, MO 64105, or call (816) 842-3600.
- "Before You Buy: A Guide to Long-Term Care Insurance" from AARP, 601 E Street, N.W., Washington, D.C. 20049.
- "A Consumer's Guide to Long-Term Care Insurance" from the Insurance Information Institute, 110 Williams Street, New York, NY 10038 or from its National Insurance Consumer Helpline (800) 942- 4242.

Disability Insurance

Disability insurance provides for the replacement of income in the event that the policyholder, because of illness or injury, is no longer able to work. The premium for a disability policy is typically between 2 and 3 percent of the insured's annual salary. If you work part time, have just started a new business, have a heart condition, or work in a high risk occupation, the cost of disability insurance may be excessive, or you may not be able to get it at all. Individuals covered by disability policies through their employers should read them carefully for exclusions and the amount of replacement income they offer. It might be wise to purchase a supplemental disability policy to close the gaps in coverage, or to raise the amount of income you will receive if you become disabled. Typically, disability policies replace no more than 60 percent of lost income. Even with a supplemental policy, total benefits are usually limited to about 80 percent of the insured's salary. Individuals who are not covered by disability insurance through their employers can purchase an individual policy directly from an insurance carrier, or get group coverage if offered through their alumni or professional organizations. The main points to consider when reviewing a disability policy are:

- Gain a full understanding of the policy's "definition of disability." Some policies pay benefits if you are unable to engage in your usual occupation. With this type of coverage, you will not be forced to take a job you might not like and which may not pay nearly the same salary as your usual occupation. You receive benefits even if you might be able to work in another occupation. Other policies pay only if you are totally disabled or impaired to the point where your are unable to perform any job.
- Consider the "elimination period" you can accept. This is the waiting period between the onset of the disability and the time benefits begin. The waiting period can be a few days, or can be extended to 90, 180, or 365 days. Consider how well you will be able to support yourself with savings and investments during the waiting period. The longer the waiting period, the lower the premium.
- Does the policy provide benefits to age 65, if so, will benefits be lower, or is a longer waiting period required before benefits begin?
- Under what circumstances can the insurer cancel the policy?
- Does the policy offer level premiums to age 65, or will the premium be raised as you grow older?
- Check for the complexity of filing a claim, including what proof of disability will be required, how soon after the onset of disability the claim must be filed, and how you can obtain the required documents.
- Is a disability caused by a progressive illness such as multiple sclerosis, diabetes, arthritis, Alzheimer's disease, etc. covered?

Choosing an Insurance Agent

If you already have a particular type of insurance and you are satisfied with the service the insurance carrier has been giving you, contact the company's agent to discuss the coverage.

If you do not have an insurance carrier, or your carrier does not offer the particular insurance you want to purchase, you will have to find an insurance agent. There are two basic types of insurance agents: one that works for a particular insurance company; and one who works as an independent agent, offering policies from a number of insurers. Unless you have the time to evaluate the coverage and costs of policies offered by a number of companies, your best bet is the independent agent. Look in the Yellow Pages of the phone book under INSURANCE for both insurance companies and independent agents. You should also have your agent review your coverage from time to time (experts suggest every three years) and advise you about changes in the insurance field and their effect on your coverage. When you call to make an appointment, be sure to establish that the company or agent can offer the type of insurance you want. Consultations should be free unless you are contacting the agent as a financial planner. At the consultation, you should evaluate not only the product offered, but also the agent. Talk to more than one agent or carrier. Compare the prices and explanations given by one with another. Things to consider include:

- The length of time the agent is willing to spend:
  - Listening to your situation;
  - Determining what type of insurance will best fill your needs;
  - Finding the appropriate insurance plan; and
  - Looking at insurance products that fit the needs of the plan;
- An independent agent should only recommend products from top insurance companies;
- The agent should be up-to-date on:
  - Tax laws regarding the products;
  - The products themselves; and
  - The trends or new products of the insurance industry;
- An agent should be willing to divulge his or her commission on each product, and be willing to lower it by selling combined policies;
- The agent should make you feel comfortable, should not talk down to you or use language that is very technical, and should be willing to explain every aspect of the product you are considering until you fully understand it. If, instead of an answer to a question, you hear "trust me" — Run;
- The agent should not push for an immediate decision to buy the coverage, but should encourage you to review the policies and make an informed decision. However, if you regret the purchase of insurance, the Federal Trade Commission's "Cooling Off" rule provides that consumers have three business days to cancel a contract without penalty. In addition, most states have laws requiring a free look at insurance policies for a minimum of ten or as many as thirty days without penalties;
- An agent should not just tell you that you are covered, but should point out, in the policy, the clause which provides each type of coverage and show the extent of the coverage. If it is not specifically stated as coverage in the policy, you probably are not covered for it;
- You should review all exclusionary clauses; these can effectively reduce some coverage to nothing;
- The price of the same type of coverage can vary from one company to another. If the agent is suggesting a more expensive policy, he or she should be able to clearly demonstrate the added benefit provided by it;
- The agent should be able to give you information about the financial stability and rating of the insurance company issuing the policy.

FINANCIAL INSTITUTIONS

Before opening an account with a bank, savings and loan association, or credit union, consider what type of account or banking services you will need. This Chapter discusses some areas of consideration.

Federal Account Insurance

Banks or Savings and Loan Associations

Be sure the institution is a member of The Federal Deposit Insurance Corporation (FDIC) which insures accounts in both banks and savings and loan associations through two separate funds, the Bank Insurance Fund and the Savings Association Insurance Fund, respectively. It is through these funds that the federal government currently insures each account for up to $100,000 in the event the institution should fail. However, in some cases, separate accounts (including private and employer sponsored pension accounts) in the same bank, depending on how the accounts are titled, can be added together and considered one account and the $100,000 insurance limit will be for all accounts combined. Remember that different branches of the same institution are still the same bank. The only way to have more than $100,000 insured in one institution is to have each account under a different combination of names according to FDIC guidelines. The best way to be absolutely sure each account is fully insured is to limit the amount in each institution to $100,000. Accounts in separate institutions owned by the same person or entity are insured separately. When depositing funds into an account, remember that interest payments will raise the total in the account. Always be sure the institution, and the instrument you are investing in, are insured. Mutual funds and annuities bought through banking institutions are not currently included in FDIC coverage. For more information regarding the rules, pick up an FDIC pamphlet at your banking institution, or request a free pamphlet outlining deposit insurance, by writing to the Office of Consumer Affairs, FDIC, 550 - 17th Street, N.W., Washington, D.C. 20429, or by calling the FDIC's office of consumer affairs at (800) 934-3342. It also has a pamphlet on rules and regulations for living trusts. If you have a complaint about a federal savings bank or savings and loan, call the United States Treasury's Office of Thrift Supervision consumer hotline (800) 842-6929.

Credit Unions

The National Credit Union Administration (NCUA) charters, supervises, and examines all federal credit unions and oversees the National Credit Union Share Insurance Fund, which insures individual member's deposits up to $100,000 in the event of a member credit union's bankruptcy. This insurance covers all federal credit unions and is available to state credit unions. For more information, ask the credit union for a copy of "Your Insured Funds," or request the booklet from the NCUA, 1775 Duke Street, N.W., Alexandria, VA 22314-3428 or call (703) 518-6300.

Note: To protect your bank account and credit cards from fraudulent use:
- Never give your credit card number, bank account number, Social Security number, or P.I.N. (Personal Identification Number) to a stranger. Only give your account number over the phone or online if you have initiated the contact and know the office is legitimate; never to someone who has contacted you, no matter who they say they represent. Your bank or credit card issuer knows your account number. They may ask you to verify your number but should never ask for your account number or P.I.N.
- Never give your ATM or credit card P.I.N. to anyone. Do not write your P.I.N. on your ATM or credit card or carry a written copy with you. If you forget the number, the issuer will let you pick a new one.
- Notify your bank immediately if you discover unused checks are missing. Your bank can stop payment on the numbers of the missing checks.
- Carefully store unused and cancelled checks, as well as receipts containing your ATM or credit card numbers, or P.I.N. Destroy cancelled checks and receipts before discarding.

Determining the Stability of the Institution

Although all accounts are insured if the institution should fail, the money may be tied up for a long time. Therefore, it is wise to determine the stability of the institution. This can be done by dividing the institution's loans by its deposits. If the figure is above 70 percent, it is a very aggressive bank and perhaps you should look elsewhere. If loans are 50 percent or less, then it has a better chance of meeting minimum standards, providing it has an adequate cushion of liquid assets. Other conditions which should be considered signs for caution are a high percentage of construction loans in comparison to mortgage loans, or if repossessed assets are more than half of the net worth. To check the financial stability of a bank, thrift or credit union, call the Bauer Financial Reports, Inc., a research firm specializing in evaluating the financial soundness of banks, thrifts, and credit unions providing free star-ratings, from zero to five stars, with five being the best. For information call (800) 388-6686.

Comparing Institutions

Interest Rates

Compare interest rates offered by the financial institutions. Many local newspapers print a comparison of interest rates offered by local institutions in the "Business" section. If this is not published in your area, call the institutions you are considering. What you should compare is the annualized yield of the various accounts. Annualized yield is the actual interest rate paid at the end of a full year. The difference in yield depends upon the frequency of "compounding" (how often interest is added to the account). To illustrate: Two accounts are each paying 7 percent. One compounds annually (also called **simple interest**); the amount of return at the end of a year is 7 percent. The other account compounds quarterly; the actual annualized yield is 7.2 percent, because the earned interest is deposited each quarter, and with compounding, the interest earns interest. The more frequent the compounding, the higher the yield. Compounding can be done daily, weekly, monthly, quarterly, or yearly.

Services and Charges

Compare services offered and charges imposed by the financial institutions. The differences can be meaningful. This information can be found in ads placed by the institutions in newspapers and magazines. The personnel at the institution are usually well equipped to counsel you about the various types of accounts and services their institution handles. Most institutions have pamphlets outlining them. Some points to consider are:

- Does the institution offer the type of accounts and services you require? If you need a safe deposit box and it does not have them, you may consider transferring an account to an institution which does. Most institutions will not let you open a box unless you have an account there.
- Compare the maintenance costs of each institution you are considering. Our record sheet, "Financial Institution Comparison Sheet," on page R-34, can help you. To use the sheet, fill in the applicable monthly charges for each account or service you need. A blank space was left in each section for any account or service we did not think to include.
  - **Monthly Service Charges** can usually be avoided by maintaining a minimum balance in the account. Determine if you will be able the keep this amount in the account, or if you will end up paying the fee each month. If maintaining the balance will be no problem, you would probably want an interest paying account. However, if you are going to be paying the monthly service charge each month, it may be better to get an account which does not charge for service and does not pay interest and has no minimum balance requirement. Unless you maintain an extremely high balance, the amount of interest received usually does not equal the service charge.
  - **Transaction Fees** can add up if you write a lot of checks or make a lot of deposits. Compare your anticipated monthly per-transaction fees to a flat service charge and pick the one which would be least expensive for you.

- **Combined or Package Accounts** offer account-holders advantages if you deposit a specific amount in specific accounts. Some offer a free safe deposit box if you have a checking and passbook account or Certificate of Deposit there. Compare the cost or benefit of these combined accounts with individual accounts in the same or another bank. Often, these combined accounts pay a lower interest rate or charge higher fees to offset the cost of the free benefits.
- **Debit, Check, or ATM Cards** offer the owner of the account the ability to withdraw funds directly from the account. It is the same as writing a check. Some institutions charge for this service. Charges may include a monthly fee to have the card and/or a transaction fee when the card is used.

Tidbit: To help balance your checkbook, use the "Bank Statement Reconciliation Worksheet," on page R-45.

Tidbit: This is an example of a check written in a manner to prevent alteration.

Note:
- Never write a post-dated check.
- To avoid a check being cashed by someone other than the payee to whom you are writing the check; never leave the "Pay to the order of" line blank. Avoid writing a check to "Cash," even if you are writing the check to yourself.
- To prevent a person from altering the amount of the check:
  - The amount of the check in words should begin as close to the start of the line as possible. See what a difference a "Sixty" can make if you leave the space for it:

    Sixty Three Hundred and Twenty-Five 00/100
  - Always extend a line from the end of the words to the end of the line. Put the cents amount over 100 as close to the end of the words as possible. See what a difference a "Thousand" can make if you leave the space for it:

    Three Hundred and Twenty-Five Thousand 00/100
- If the check is written to pay a bill, always include the number of your account with the company, to be sure the payment is properly credited.
- Never sign the check until you have filled in all the blank spaces on the check.

LOCATING MISSING BENEFICIARIES

When the whereabouts of a Beneficiary is unknown, the Administrator should make a diligent search for them. The sooner the search is begun, the sooner the probate process can proceed, and the sooner the property can be distributed to the Beneficiaries. In order to prevent undue hardship to other Beneficiaries, when all reasonable efforts have been made to locate a missing Beneficiary have failed, their share of the property can be deposited by the Administrator with the Probate Court. Then, at the end of a state-prescribed period of time, most commonly seven years, if no one who is legally entitled to inherit the property appears, the property goes to the state. The Administrator has two basic choices of ways to find a missing Beneficiary. You can either:

■ Hire a private investigator to search for the person. If the attorney or your friends, neighbors, or professional associates cannot suggest an investigator; look under the headings COLLECTION AGENCIES, DETECTIVE AGENCIES, INVESTIGATORS, MISSING PERSONS BUREAUS, or PROCESS SERVERS, in the Yellow Pages; or call a national search agency, such as: (800) U.S.SEARCH, Tracers International (800) 872-2377, or The Nationwide Locator (800) 937-2133. Do not hire a professional on an hourly basis. Only agree to a flat fee, which should be less than $200 for a data base search, less than $1000 for an extensive search; or,

■ Take some steps to find the person yourself. The following information can help you conduct your own search.

Conducting Your Own Search

The Social Security Administration maintains the largest database of people in the United States. It includes everyone who has a Social Security number, and current addresses on all people who are working, disabled and receiving benefits, or retired and receiving benefits, even if they live outside of the country. Additionally, they maintain a record of all individuals whose death has been reported to them. Unless the person you are trying to find is homeless or purposely hiding, their current or a fairly recent address should be in the database. As a humane service, the Social Security Administration, and the Internal Revenue Service, will use the information in their databases to forward letters from Estate Administrators and attorneys, to otherwise unlocateable Beneficiaries. The local office of the Veterans Administration will check its computer for family members of deceased veterans who are receiving benefits, or received a burial award, and will forward a letter to them. To find someone in, or retired from, the military, write to the appropriate branch of the service at:

- CNC Military Records Bureau, U.S. Marine Corps, Washington, D.C. 20380;
- The Navy Locator Service, 121, Washington, D.C. 20370;
- Commander, U.S. Army Enlisted Records and Evaluation Center, Fort Benjamin Harrison, Indianapolis, IN 46249;
- Air Force World Wide Locator, Randolph Air Force Base, San Antonio, TX 78150.

Therefore, locating a missing Heir or Beneficiary may be as simple as writing a letter. The local Social Security Administration office will accept a letter written to the person you are trying to contact. It should be enclosed in an unsealed, stamped, envelope with the name of the person, you wish to contact on the front. This envelope should be enclosed in another, unsealed envelope, with a letter addressed to the Social Security Administration explaining the reason why you are trying to contact the person, and your personal or legal relationship either to the decedent or the person you are hoping to contact. Be sure to include all identifying information you may have about the person to allow the Social Security Administration to locate the right person. The letters must be hand delivered, not mailed, to the local SSA office.

Since the person you are trying to locate will be getting money or other property, he or she will probably want to be found. So, the letter should be enough to get a response. However, if there are hard feelings, he or she may not want to contact you directly. Therefore, you may want to use the name and address of the attorney or the Probate Court as the return address on the envelope and in the letter. The Social Security Administration's representative can check the national computer database for a listing of the person while you are there and advise you if the person is listed as dead or alive. The SSA is not permitted to give you any information if the person is alive, so do not put anyone on the spot by asking. Just be assured that the SSA will forward the letter and then it will be up to the potential Beneficiary to respond. Of course, if the inside envelope is returned as undeliverable, you will have to decide what further action to take.

When the Missing Beneficiary is Deceased

On the other hand, if the person is listed as deceased, the SSA representative can pass this information along to you. If the person is deceased, be sure to ask for a printout of the person's record and take it with you. The reason for getting a copy of the record is to give you the information you will need to obtain a certified copy of the Death Certificate, required by the Court to prove the Beneficiary is deceased. The record contains abbreviated labels for the information it contains. Including:

- The name of the beneficiary;
- If the benefits are based on another person's work record, the name of that person;
- SSN — the Social Security Number of the person upon whose work record the benefits are based;
- BENREF BOAN — the Social Security Number upon which benefits were based;
- ZIP — the five- or nine-digit zip code for the person's last known address;
- BIC-A — the full name of the person upon whose work record benefits are based;
- DOB — the beneficiary's date of birth; and
- BDOD — is the beneficiary's date of death.

In most cases, if the Beneficiary is deceased, his or her children or grandchildren may be legally entitled to receive the inheritance. The first step to finding these potential Beneficiaries is to ask the SSA representative to check for other relatives, such as a spouse, dependent child, or a disabled child, who may be receiving benefits under the same Social Security number. If a spouse or other dependent is alive, you may want to write another letter and ask the SSA to mail it to them. If the spouse is also deceased and there are no surviving dependents listed, ask for a printout of the spouse's record.

If both the missing Heir and spouse are deceased, and their descendents (children, grand-children, etc.) are entitled to inherit, you may be able to determine their existence or locate them, through Probate Court records. Some of the documents involved in an Estate which was probated will be available as public record. Since probate takes place in the county where the person was domiciled, look on the SS record for the Zip Code. Call the Clerk of the Court. Explain why you are calling. The clerk may send a request for information form just from the phone call or may require a written "request for information." In this case, be sure to ask how to address the envelope. The clerk will send a list of the documents available to the public. Review the list and choose the documents, which contain the names and addresses of the Beneficiaries at the time the probate proceedings took place, or of the Administrator and attorney, who may be able to help you contact them. Since the documents or forms used in each court system vary, the names of the documents may not be familiar to you. Either call the Clerk of the Court again, and ask what each document includes, or ask your attorney. There will be a fee for copies and, possibly, a research fee. Keep in mind that if both spouses are deceased, researching the probate of the last to die might be more rewarding, because most spouses hold all property jointly, and the first spouse's Will was probably not entered into probate.

If the person was given up for adoption, you can register with the birth state's Adoption Reunion Agency and The Soundex Reunion Registry, P.O. Box 2312, Carson City NV 89702, phone (702) 882-7755. Both accept names of adoptees and biological relatives, and try to match them to facilitate reunions.

Getting an Agency's Address and Phone Number

The quickest way to get the address of an agency located outside of your area is to call and ask for its address. If you know the state, and city or county, you can call Directory Assistance for any long-distance phone number by calling (900) 555-1212. They can provide any domestic number for 75 cents and any international number for $1.99. Ask for the number for the agency you want to contact. If you are not sure which agency has the information, ask for the number of the State, County, or City Information Desk. Call the information desk, explain what information you are seeking, and ask for the name and phone number of the agency which maintains the records. Then call the agency. Explain the reason for calling; they will either offer to send the proper request form, or give you an address so you can write and ask for the request form. **Do not send any money or documents with this first inquiry, unless instructed to do so.** If all you have is the Zip Code, call or go to the Post Office and ask for the city, county, and state represented by that Zip Code. Birth and death records are usually kept by the State or Territory in its Office of Vital Statistics (or similar designation), located in the State Capital. It may also have marriage and divorce records, although these are usually maintained in the county where the event occurred. Another method for obtaining the mailing addresses of agencies which have vital records is to request a 22 page guide on how to obtain certified copies of birth, death, marriage, and divorce certificates, titled *Where to Write for Vital Records - Births, Deaths, Marriages, and Divorces.* It was published by the National Center for Health Statistics, within the U.S. Department of Health and Human Services, and is available through the Consumer Information Catalog, Pueblo, Colorado 81002. A quicker method is to call the Federal Information Center at (800) 688-9889, and ask for the address of a particular State's Office of Vital Statistics.

General Rules for Requesting Information or Documents

Since most agencies require all requests for information or documents be on its official request forms, do not expect anything more from your initial contact. The vast majority of government agencies charge a fee for certified copies of documents or research. Along with the official request form, you will also receive a schedule of fees and instructions for requesting the document or information. Whether you are contacting an agency on the phone or in a letter, be sure to provide the following information:

- Your name;
- Your relationship to the person you are trying to find, or to the decedent, and/or your official title;
- What information or document you want from the agency;
- The reason why you are trying to locate the person or information, or why you need the document you are requesting; and
- All the information you already have about the person. You must provide the best and most complete information you can about the individual. Be sure the spelling of the name is exact, including the middle and/or maiden names.

Sometimes a non-existent record can be just as helpful as an existing record. For instance, when a search for a record is requested, it is most often to look for the record of a person who is known to exist. However, a search of birth records can also be used to establish that no child was born to a couple or individual during a particular period of time in a particular state.

If you visit the office in person, the clerks will tell you how to do a search. Do not ask for the original of a document. That is always kept in the agency's records. Therefore, what you request, and what the agency will issue, is a **Certified Copy** of the certificate. The following are the offices to contact:

- **State Office of Vital Statistics** — Certified copies of birth or death certificates and in some states, marriage and divorce records. If separated or divorced, ask when and where the papers were filed. Divorce records would include information of whether a woman took back her maiden name or a name from a former marriage.
- **City or County Registrars Office** — at the local courthouse, usually maintains marriage licenses, which contain the names of both spouses and of their parents, plus the couple's ages, birthplaces, and addresses at the time of marriage. They also maintain the Divorce Records and Adoption Records. Some states maintain these records; therefore, to save time it is best to call and be sure you are dealing with the correct agency before you write.

- **Appropriate Foreign Consulate or Embassy** — to obtain birth certificates or other documents from their country.
- **U.S. Department of State, Passport Services** — contact the Correspondence Branch, in Washington, at (202) 647-0518, for birth certificates of Americans born in other countries.
- **County Probate Court** — Certain documents involved in the probate process can provide the name and address of the attorney and the Administrator, as well as Beneficiaries.

Before You Start

Before you can find anyone, you must make sure you are looking for the right person. This means having his or her exact name, with the correct spelling, including middle or maiden names. Since many people may have the same name, it is a necessity to provide some additional information to identify the person, such as the place, date, and year of birth, or at least his or her approximate age, Social Security number, names of parents, etc. If you are not sure of the person's name, or the information you have about him or her, start your search by asking relatives and friends what they know about the person. Each bit of information or document you collect gives you a little more information and a better chance of obtaining other documents and more information. The "Search Record," on page R-31, was provided to help you keep track of the contacts you make and the information you gather.

If you have no other avenue for obtaining basic information, you can check a census record from 1920 or before at the National Archives, or your local Public Library may have a copy. For later years you can write to the U.S. Department of Commerce, Bureau of Census, Personal Census Search Unit, P.O. Box 1545, Jeffersonville, IN 47132 or call (301) 457-2794. It is not permitted to give much information. It will, however, only in the case of death, provide the name, age, place of birth, and citizenship status of the occupants of a specific supplied address. Information will be given only to the following individuals:
- The parent, child, husband, wife, brother, or sister of the deceased person upon presentation of a certified copy of the Death Certificate;
- The Beneficiary of the deceased person upon presentation of proof of the identity of such Beneficiary; or
- The Administrator or Executor of the Estate upon presentation of a certified copy of the Letters of Administration or Letters Testamentary.

Finding the New Address

If a person has moved recently, the following agencies and publications may be able to help you catch up with him or her:
- **United States Postal Service** — although it will usually not give out a new address, the USPS will forward a person's mail to him or her for at least six months after he or she moves. Address a letter to the person at the old address. Write on the envelope "Important - Please Forward." If you want to know where the letter was delivered, send it by Certified or

Registered Mail with a "Return Receipt Requested," and specify it to show the address and to whom it has been delivered. Also, indicate a "Restrictive Delivery," requiring delivery to the addressee only. If you are not on good terms with the person you are trying to locate, you may want to use the attorney's, or Court's, return address on the envelope.

- **The *Criss-Cross Telephone Directory* or *Polk Directory*** — lists telephone numbers in numerical order, giving the name of the party, address, and occupation. It also lists addresses in the same manner. Check the Public Library research section in the county where you are searching for a copy. If you have a prior address, a neighbor may have information about the person's present whereabouts. Be prepared to give your name and the reason for trying to make contact. Do not expect the neighbor to give you the new phone number or address. Instead, ask the party to contact the person you are seeking, and ask him or her to call or write to you, the attorney, or the Court. Ask if you can check back in a few days to find out if contact was made.

- **Telephone Directory**, or call information — "411" local or (900) 555-1212 nationwide, for the county in which a person is located, if you have a name.

- **Nationwide 800/888 Information Line** — This is useful when you know the person is a member of a large organization which has an 800 or 888 number. Call (800) 555-1212, and give the name of the agency, organization, association, business, etc. If they have a listed 800 or 888 number, the operator will be able to give you the number. The agency, organization, etc., may provide the name and address of members, or offer to contact them for you. If you are not sure of the name of the organization, etc., look through the *800/888 Directory*, at the local library. This directory is arranged in categories, like the Yellow Pages.

- **County Voters Registration Office** — may give you the name, address, and telephone number, if the person is a registered voter.

- **State Motor Vehicle Bureau** — request any vehicle registration, or driver's license, in the person's name. Include date of birth or approximate age, if possible. This information is not available to the public in some states.

- **Utility Companies** — if the person moved within the same area, the company that provides water, electricity, gas, etc. may have the new address.

- **Board of Education** — if records were sent to a new school or college, or the records were sent to a bonding company or employer, they may have the new address.

- **County Property Appraiser, Clerk, or Records Office** where deeds are recorded — If a person recently sold real property, he or she owned, the records may include the name of the title company or local abstract company who participated in the sale, or the name of the new owner, the mortgage company or other lien holder, who may have the current address. Also, in some states, an alphabetical list of property owners' names is maintained. If the person you are seeking lived in a rental, the landlord may be able to give the new address, or supply the name and address of the moving company who assisted in the relocation; which may have the new address.

- **Municipal Criminal Courts** — keep traffic tickets on microfilm; you may find out a person's current address and where the violation occurred.

- **County or City Business License Bureau** — if the person is self-employed, or owns a business, he or she must have a city and/or county business license. These offices can supply the name and address of the business, and the name of the owner.

- **State Department of Professional Regulation** — will have the name and business address of all professionals operating in the state. Regulations for which professions require registration vary by state.

SHIPPING ESTATE PROPERTY

If you have items which must be shipped to another location, start by measuring and weighing (if possible) each item or box. Then, call package shipping companies, such as the United States Postal Service (USPS) or United Parcel Service (UPS), to find out their package size and weight limits. If the item is too large or too heavy to be shipped as a package, you may have to decide whether to hire a moving and storage company, or use a rental truck and move it yourself. Another option is to look in the Yellow Pages, under PACKING & CRATING SERVICES or DELIVERY SERVICES. Most make deliveries locally, within the state or a few counties, while others deliver countrywide. In addition to properly packing the objects, most will insure the items and many will also arrange for shipping. Establish a file for all packing, moving, or shipping papers and receipts. You can use the "Miscellaneous Expense Record," on Page R-24, to keep track of the expenses.

Professional Moving Companies

If you have decided to use the services of a moving and storage company, reservations must usually be made at least one month prior to the time you want the item moved. It is also a good idea to call a couple of days prior to pick-up and confirm. Government regulation of moving companies depends upon whether the move is across state lines (**Interstate**), or the move is within the state (**Intrastate**).

Interstate Moves

Interstate moves are regulated by federal laws administered by the **Interstate Commerce Commission (ICC)**. The nationwide regulations, which affect both the moving and storage companies and their customers, include:

- Interstate carriers are required by law to give you a copy of the ICC pamphlet "When You Move: Your Rights and Responsibilities," and a copy of the company's most recent "Annual Performance Report," showing the percentage of its total moves which resulted in a loss or damage claim in the previous year, and how quickly the carrier handled the claims.

- Movers are required to prepare an **Order of Service**, a work order showing the terms of the initial agreement for services. If any changes in the planned move are made, a new Order of Service should be issued. Keep a copy of this form.

- An estimate of the cost of moving the property is made by a sales representative, usually at no charge. The cost of an interstate move is based on the weight of the items to be moved, the distance of the move, plus the cost of additional services performed and materials used. An estimate can be:

  - **"Binding"** — which means the mover guarantees the price before the move;
  - **"Non-Binding"** — which means the final charge will be determined after the shipment is weighed. The result is that no matter what price was quoted, there is no ceiling on your final cost. (To avoid **Weight-Bumping** insist on meeting the driver at the scales before your property is loaded. Be present again for the reweigh after the goods are loaded. If you believe your shipment has been weight-bumped, notify the van line or its agent. The carrier will either request a reweigh, or do a weight analysis from the inventory, at no extra charge.); or,
  - **"Hybrid"** — such as **Guaranteed** or **Customer Benefit** estimates, which let you pay either the binding estimate or the actual cost of the move, whichever is lower.

- You are legally bound to pay the estimated price, plus ten percent of any additional charges, at the time of delivery. Any balance over this amount must be paid within 30 days. If you refuse to pay, the mover has the right to refuse to unload your items from the van and place them in storage at your expense.

- Interstate movers are required to offer three kinds of coverage in the event that your property is damaged or lost. These are:

  - **Limited Liability** — coverage is free and you must sign for it, but you collect only 60 cents per pound for each lost or damaged item, no matter what it is worth.
  - **Added-Value Protection-Liability** — usually equals $1.25 per pound and costs $5 for every $1000 of coverage. If goods are lost or damaged the mover will pay the full replacement cost, less depreciation, of all items, up to the limit of coverage.
  - **Full-Value Protection** — though plans and costs vary, this liability usually is calculated at $3.50 per pound. With full-value protection, goods are repaired, replaced, or reimbursed at today's prices. You can keep the cost down by including a deductible in your coverage.

- The burden of proof, when a claim is made for loss or damage of property, rests with the customer. Therefore, it is important to accurately record the condition and value of each item before it is moved and, when it arrives at its destination. On an interstate move, you have nine months after the date of delivery to file a claim. The company must acknowledge the claim within 30 days and pay, decline, or offer a compromise within another 120 days.

■ If you have an unsettled dispute with an interstate moving company, you can receive a claim form and more information by writing to the Interstate Commerce Commission, 12th Street and Constitution Avenue, N.W., Washington, D.C. 20423, or calling (202) 927-5500.

Intrastate Moves

Intrastate moves are not subject to ICC regulation. However, most states have regulations governing local moves and require licensing of qualified moving and storage companies. Call the state's public service commission or transportation department for regulatory information. If the state does regulate intrastate moves, ask if the mover you plan to hire is licensed.

■ Estimates for local moves are generally based on hourly charges, plus services and materials. A non-binding estimate can result in unlimited overcharges, if the time required for the move is grossly underestimated.

■ Licensed movers are usually required to demonstrate the ability to settle claims and show proof of adequate liability insurance. An unlicensed carrier usually has no procedure for settling claims.

■ If you have an unresolved problem with an intrastate mover, you may have to file a lawsuit in Small Claims Court. Other options are to report the problem to the State Attorney General's Office, the State Consumer Protection Office, and the local Better Business Bureau.

Choosing a Moving and Storage Company

Finding a Mover

■ Ask friends, neighbors, and acquaintances who have moved recently for recommendations.

■ Real estate agents, or relocation managers of large companies, may be able to recommend a reputable mover.

■ Call local or national trade groups for referral to a member company near you. Two of the best known national associations are:

• The National Moving and Storage Association is the oldest industry trade group. Write to 11150 Main Street, Suite 402, Fairfax, VA 22030-5066, or call (800) 538-6672.

• The American Movers Conference, write to 1611 Duke Street, Alexandria, VA 22314, or call (703) 683-7410.

Hiring a Moving and Storage Company

Get three to five estimates from different moving companies. Use the "Hiring Interview Sheet" on pages R-39 and R-40. For best results, always ask for a discounted move, but insist the sales representative write down the services included. Then you can compare the weight, distance, or hourly charges. Also, be sure the estimate includes an itemized list of the services and supplies with their cost. The more detailed an estimate is, the easier it will be to compare the estimates. A mid-point bid is usually the best one to accept. A really low bid may mean unskilled workmen and/or inferior materials. Before signing a contract:

- Check if the mover has a business address and a phone number in the local phone book. Then visit and check out the facilities. Ask for the name of an agent you can contact with questions.
- Ask for three recent customer references and call them.
- Check with the local Better Business Bureau and Chamber of Commerce, to find out how many, and what kinds of, complaints were lodged against the mover during the previous year.
- Before buying additional liability protection from the mover, check the homeowner's insurance policy, or ask the insurance agent if the property insurance covers the property during the move. If the move is not covered by the homeowner's insurance, ask if the company offers special moving insurance.
- Ask the mover about claim procedures. Specifically, how to file a claim and how long it would take to be reimbursed.
- Require the mover show you written proof of the type and extent of liability coverage the mover carries. If the company does not have adequate liability insurance for loss or damage, a small-claims lawsuit will be the only option to recoup your losses.
- Require the mover show you written proof of Workers' Compensation Insurance, or you could be held liable if a worker is injured during the move.
- State in writing, on the initial order for service, that you will accept only company trained labor and that the company is not to use a substitute hauler. You have the right to refuse entry to your home to any person you find offensive.
- Request a written list of all services that could result in additional charges. This information may be included in the van line's literature. Be sure to read it carefully; the carrier can charge extra for any service or item not specified in the original estimate. Get an agreement, in writing, that any additional services will be approved in advance because, if the service is performed, you must pay for it.
- Specify, in writing, the form of payment the mover will require. Many companies require cash, a money order, or certified check, while others may accept traveler's checks or credit cards.
- Review the contract thoroughly and make sure all blanks are filled in before you sign it.

Rental Trucks

Arrangements for a truck or trailer rental should be made a month in advance, if possible. Things to consider before contracting with a rental company are:

- Rentals are based on the truck's capacity in cubic feet, not just its length. Will the company help you estimate the size of the truck or trailer you will need?

- Compare prices on trucks, including: mileage rates, overtime charges, drop-off charges.
- If the vehicle you hire turns out to be too small, is the company's fleet large enough to allow you to rent a larger vehicle immediately?
- Does the company also rent dollies, pads, and packing cases? Compare their costs.
- Does the company provide guidelines on how to pack cartons and the van?
- Can you hire workers through the company to do the packing of cartons or vans?
- Will the company provide guidelines to help you inventory the items you will be moving?
- Read the contract carefully. Be sure all the particulars are stated in the contract and that there are no blank spaces before you sign it.

The Actual Move

Whether you are shipping one item or a houseful of furnishings, the same basics apply.

Shipment Pick Up

- Be sure someone is at the house when the moving truck arrives to pick up the shipment and stays until it leaves.
- If the movers will be present for an extended period of time, arrange for the care of pets and small children; both can be distracting.
- Before loading, the driver will give you a **Bill of Lading**, which specifies the complete information about the move, including: the dates of the move, the property to be shipped, services to be performed, and estimated cost. This is your contract. Don't sign it until you agree to everything it says. To avoid delays, make sure you and the driver have a copy at all times. If the property is being shipped to someone else, copy the bill of lading, and mail the original to the receiver.
- Your best protection against loss or damage claims is an inventory that spells out what items are being moved and their condition prior to shipping. The driver should inventory the items you are shipping. Watch as the driver does the inventory, to be sure everything is included. Do not sign the driver's inventory unless you agree with the description of the property. Some drivers exaggerate scratches and nicks to protect against later damage claims. If you disagree on any descriptions, note your exceptions on the inventory sheet. Make sure you are given a copy of the inventory. If the property is being shipped to someone else, copy the **Inventory Sheet** and mail the original to the receiver. If the driver does not inventory your goods, do it yourself before the property is loaded on the truck and give the driver a copy. Use the "Tangible Personal Property Inventory and Sale Record" on page R-2.
- Before the van leaves, check that all items you want to ship have been loaded.
- Give the driver exact directions to the house or storage facility where the shipment is to be delivered and give the driver your phone number, or the phone number of the recipient, in

205

case they need to contact someone for further directions, get permission to do something which will add to the cost of the move, or to announce their arrival time.

Shipment Delivery

- Be sure someone is at the destination location when the van arrives to avoid charges for delay of unpacking, or possible storage charges.
- The recipient of the shipment should supervise the unloading and unpacking. One person should stand by the front door, inventory in hand, to check off items as they are unloaded. Another person should either unpack or supervise the unpacking, checking each box, crate, and item carefully for damage, especially to breakable or valuable objects.
- Make sure any damaged or missing items are noted in writing, on both your copy and the driver's copy of the inventory. Failure to make these notations will make it virtually impossible to win a liability claim. Therefore, **DO NOT** be rushed or intimidated into signing before everything has been thoroughly checked.

Packing

Precautions

To ensure that items arrive at their destination in the same condition as when they left, before any item is packed, crated, or loaded on a van, be sure to:
- Photograph each object to establish its condition and value. This is especially important for valuable or breakable pieces.
- Have antiques appraised.
- Remove anything from drawers, cabinets, or appliances that might break, spill, or stain.
- Label each box with its contents or a number which corresponds to its individual inventory record. If you are shipping items to different destinations, be sure you clearly mark the destination on the boxes as they are packed. It will save time when checking for damage, if the boxes containing breakable items are clearly marked.

Packing Choices

Another consideration is whether you are going to have the items packed by the movers, a packing and crating company, or do it yourself.

If you choose to have the items packed by the movers:

- Movers will charge for packing and unpacking your property in boxes and crates, and will also charge for the packing materials they use. This charge is in addition to the cost of the move. If the move is insured, the company will have to pay to replace any item they packed that is lost or damaged.
- Special packing is available for valuable items or antiques, at an additional charge.
- If you pack poorly, the movers will repack and charge for it.
- Watch the movers as they pack to be sure each item is placed in the correct box and added to its inventory. This also is a theft prevention method.

If you choose to have the items packed by a packing and crating company:

- They will pack each item according to guidelines set forth by the shipping companies.
- Charge for the materials used as well as their service.

If you choose to pack the items yourself:

Depending upon how many items you are shipping, you can save hundreds of dollars if you pack yourself. However, be aware that moving and storage companies as well as package shipping companies, probably will not pay for breakage in cartons you pack.

- Give yourself enough time to pack items properly and place them according to destination, in an area where they will be protected and undisturbed until they are shipped.
- Appropriate packing materials and self-packing information are available from most truck rental agencies and moving and storage companies. According to your needs, you can purchase or rent cartons, padding, clean paper, and tape, or you can use strong cardboard boxes from a grocery or liquor store, and newspapers.
- Doors, drawers, and lids of furniture, or appliances, should be taped or tied shut in a manner that will prevent them from opening when the object is moved.
- Remove legs from tables, chairs, and other furniture, where possible.
- Electrical cords should be rolled or folded and taped to the item they power.
- To protect breakables, line the bottom of the box with wads of crumpled newspaper, and wrap each piece in pages of newspaper. Reinforce boxes with professional packing tape on both the bottom and top. Pack the heaviest items in the bottom of the box and add crumpled newspaper between the layers to pack cartons tightly.
  - Do not stack plates, but stand them on edge.
  - Pack water glasses, mugs, etc. right side up.
  - Place stemware upside down in a partitioned box. Stems should be wrapped separately before wrapping the entire glass. Bubble wrap is suggested.
- Lamp shades should be wrapped in clean (non-printed) paper in their own cartons. Pack the lamps in a separate carton.
- Stand mirrors and pictures in boxes and wrap each in clean (non-printed) paper with corrugated cardboard between each one, or use bubble wrap. Crisscrossing the glass with masking tape adds protection.
- Remove disks from computers and insert the cardboard moving disk, or an old disk, into the drive. Use the original packing carton, and materials, if available. Data files should be backed-up on disk or tape and stored in their original containers.

■ Remove the ink cartridge from laser and dot matrix printers. Insert a piece of paper in the platen to secure the print head for a pin printer. Use the original packing carton, and materials, if available.

■ Remove all tapes, records, and CDs from audio and video equipment. If there is a "transport screw" (usually located under the unit) tighten it. Detach all removable parts and secure lids and trays with tape.

■ Consider waiting to hand deliver irreplaceable family photos or precious heirlooms.

Safely Moving Heavy Objects

Before moving a heavy or large item, plan exactly the route you will follow, giving careful thought to the size and weight of the object.

■ Measure the object, as well as doorways, stairwells, elevators, and passageways; then determine if the object will fit through them and the best way to move the object through them.

■ Whenever possible, push rather than pull.

■ Putting newspapers, cardboard, or blankets on the floor under a large object makes it easier to push.

■ Lift and carry objects with the strength in your legs, not your back. To accomplish this:
  • Stand with your feet apart, knees slightly flexed and one foot forward;
  • Lower your hips to the level of the surface supporting the weight you plan to lift by flexing your hips and knees;
  • Keep your back straight and head erect. Do not rotate your spine, instead shift the position of your feet to turn;
  • Carry objects as close to your body as possible;
  • Wear a back-brace.

■ Don't overestimate your ability to move large or heavy items; get help if needed.

■ Use a dolly or hand cart, if necessary.

■ Give consideration to the path you or the movers will take from the house to the van. Arrange for the shortest route possible. Then remove all obstacles from the route. If necessary, arrange for use of the elevator.

DEALING WITH THE GRIEF

Bereavement is defined as "loss through death." Grief, or mourning, is defined as the behaviors and processes associated with bereavement. Grief is necessary for recovery and growth. It is a normal and adaptive process, allowing the affected person, eventually, to get on with life. Grief is a normal feeling that can show the depth of our love and loneliness for a departed loved one. It is not a weakness. Although grief is a universal experience, every person responds to the death of a loved one differently. In fact the same person may respond differently from one loss to another. There is a great amount of individual variation. Of course, the most devastating of all is the loss of a person with whom life is intimately shared, such as a spouse or a child. These losses can be overwhelming, because the survivor's world has collapsed. Life is forever changed, and so is the bereaved person. Many people are surprised by the intensity of their emotional reaction to the death of a loved one, especially when they thought, because the departed suffered from a long terminal illness, they were well prepared for the loss.

The customary memorial service is an important time for the survivors. Family and friends gather together to bid farewell to the one who has died and to comfort each other. The sharing of memories, the laughter and tears, remind us of our mutual love for the deceased person. The ceremony is our way of completing the relationship. It's a time to freely express our feelings of sadness and grief. However, it should be remembered that, although these observances provide a form of closure, they do not mark the end of grief or the need for comfort.

The Four Phases of Grief

The experts have defined four phases of grief. Although they generally follow one after the other, some people move back and forth between them. The important thing is to get through all four stages. If a person does not work through the grief, he or she will have problems coping with life.

The first phase of grief begins immediately after the loss and may last up to a few weeks. The survivor experiences shock, numbness, and disbelief. Other common symptoms include crying, sighing, throat tightness, and a sense of unreality. Sometimes a person becomes paralyzed by grief, unable to take an interest in anything. He or she is scared and confused.

Phase two is characterized by preoccupation with the decedent and a yearning to recover the lost person. The survivor frequently re-examines the past relationship, including conflicts, disagreements, and unresolved anger. Emotions can fluctuate wildly, from intense sadness to anger, or to guilt. Dreams of the deceased person may be intense and vivid. Weakness and fatigue are also common.

Disorganization and despair characterize the third phase. Sadness persists, along with feelings of emptiness and loss of interest in usual activities. During this phase, the survivor accepts the permanence and the fact of loss.

Phase four involves resolution and reorganization of behavior. The bereaved person regains interest in normal activities, resumes usual tasks, sets new goals, and establishes new social contacts. Occasional feelings of sadness, emptiness, and crying spells may occur, but less frequently than before and with less intensity. Past events with the deceased person can be recalled with some pleasure.

The "normal" period of mourning is about two years; however, it is not unusual for phase four to stretch out a decade, or even a lifetime. It is important to realize that the bereaved person never really gets over the loss, but through proper grief, can adjust to living with it. By living each day as it comes, and disregarding tomorrow's possible burdens, the bereaved person will come to realize that the pain of grief will probably last longer than he or she hoped, but not as long as he or she feared. The basic goal of the bereaved person is to pass through the phases of mourning, by dealing with the feelings and emotions, accepting the reality of the loss, and readjusting to a new environment. If phase one or two extends beyond several months, or is characterized by social isolation or alienation, compulsive overactivity without a sense of loss, severe depression or loss of health, it may signal the need for professional help. See the box on page 216 for listings of Psychotherapy Referral Services.

Factors Which Affect the Grief and Healing Process

The grief and healing process can be more difficult for those who lack a support system, those in poor prior physical or mental health, those who are addicted to drugs or alcohol, those with severe financial difficulties, and those under 65. The mourning process may also be affected by the circumstances of the death, including the deceased person's age, the suddenness of the death, and the type of death. Feelings and emotions can be complicated by bewilderment, betrayal, anger, and a lot of unanswered questions when the death was a result of suicide, or was sudden or brutal. If the person was killed, whether on purpose or by accident, grief may be put aside by overwhelming feelings of anger, thoughts of revenge, or attempts to see justice done.

If the loved one suffered hard and long before the death, feelings and emotions are complicated by guilt. Sorrow over the loss is mixed with relief that the suffering is over. The death has brought the wanted peace and rest to the departed loved one, as well as the survivors. In these situations, feelings of relief are normal. There is no reason to be ashamed of these emotions. At first, memories of the loved one's suffering and deterioration are intense. In time, they will fall into perspective. Other memories will become more vivid. The bereaved person will be able to look at a whole life, and remember the good times and the bad times, the faults as well as the wonderful qualities that made it so hard to say good-bye.

Feelings Commonly Associated With the Grieving Process

Grief overwhelms the brain, resulting in the following common conditions. They may take up to two years to pass completely. Because this is such a confusing time, experts suggest that major life-style changes, such as moving, should not be made until at least a year after the loss.

- Being angry with doctors, nurses, and him- or herself, for not doing enough.
- Being angry at God, the deceased person, and friends for being left alone.
- Experiencing a change in appetite and/or sleeping habits.
- Experiencing aches, pains, weakness, and lethargy.
- Feeling that no one understands what he or she is going through.
- Feeling that friends should call more, or call less; talk longer, or talk less.
- Being unbearably lonely, depressed, or crabby.
- Crying for no apparent reason.
- Being obsessed with thoughts of the deceased person.
- Being forgetful, confused, uncharacteristically absent-minded, unable to concentrate, comprehend, or remember, and, at times, panic-stricken.
- Feeling guilty about things he or she has, or has not, done.
- Compulsive activity, in an effort to avoid the grief, by doing such things as going to the store every day; buying things he or she doesn't need; constantly calling friends and talking about everything but his or her feelings; attending every social event, or joining clubs and participating in any activity he or she can; wanting to sell everything and move, etc.
- Not wanting to attend social functions, and avoiding anything that he or she used to enjoy, and that might, for a minute, allow the bereaved person to forget the lost loved one, or the pain of the loss.

We All Need Help

Working through grief cannot be done alone. It is not a weakness to need help during this emotionally devastating time. A strong belief in the power and mercies of God, or a higher pow-

211

er, can bring courage and strength to the bereaved person. Many find quiet times reading the Psalms comforting. However, prayer should not lead to isolation or convey the attitude that he or she must maintain a stiff upper lip, because this is the worst way to facilitate the mourning process. It is important for a grief-stricken person to be in a setting of caring, warm, and compassionate people, who realize how tremendous the loss has been, who encourage the bereaved person to talk, and are willing and able to be good non-judgmental listeners; a setting where feelings and fears can be expressed, and talked through, healthy tears shed, and memories and anecdotes of the lost loved one shared.

Because grief causes such deep psychological pain and, often, physical symptoms, the newly bereaved person is often unable to cope with the ordinary activities and stresses of everyday life, much less be able to handle the added paperwork necessary to administer the Estate of the deceased person. Because of the confusion and fright during this time, the bereaved person is in no condition to make decisions, or even go places, alone. It takes time to make the adjustment to doing everyday things for him- or herself again, or in some cases, for the first time. The load can be lightened by caring friends and relatives, who can be counted on to be there for the bereaved person, to help with whatever he or she has to do; to accompany him or her wherever he or she has to go, visiting with him or her, and joining the bereaved person in social activities. Keep in mind that the healing process cannot be rushed and each person must proceed at his or her own pace.

Be aware that holidays and significant anniversary dates can be difficult for a grieving person. All involved should consider and discuss where, and in what manner, these events should be observed. Often changes, sometimes radical, from the usual traditions are helpful. It should be understood that a person in mourning is often not up to preparing big dinners, being around crowds, shopping for presents, or sending greeting cards. Others find comfort in the familiar and want to do his or her usual tasks. Each person should be guided by his or her own needs, and what the person is comfortable doing, without the pressure of doing what is "expected" of him or her. Some find it comforting to give a gift, he or she might have given to the deceased person, to a charity in memory of the loved one.

Mutual Self-Help Groups

Living in a highly mobile society, a bereaved person may be far from those family members who can best understand his or her pain and best offer support. However, the need to express feelings, and have stability and support remains constant. To avoid isolation and provide an understanding atmosphere at a time when it is most needed, **Mutual Self-Help Groups** for grieving individuals were formed.

Participating in a mutual self-help group for the bereaved is considered the best way to resolve loss because of the special bond among people who share the same experience. Knowing that someone else truly understands one's feelings, by virtue of having "been there," brings a sense of relief. Groups provide emotional support, by reassuring the bereaved person that he or she is not alone, and that his or her feelings and emotions are common and natural. They provide a friendly, confidential atmosphere of compassion and open acceptance, where members are encouraged to share their sorrows, fears, and frustrations. Groups discuss topics of mutual concern and experiences, and offer practical advice in dealing with problems common to all members. This allows the bereaved person to view his or her problems more objectively, and find effective coping strategies.

Each local group determines its own programs and meeting schedules. Typically, groups hold regular meetings in church halls, public buildings, or other no-rent or low-rent facilities. Smaller groups meet in a member's home. Dues, if any, are minimal, usually $10 to $15 yearly. Programs for meetings can include group discussions, visiting speakers, and other activities that inform the members and help to build their confidence. Newsletters published by both parent organizations and local groups report information about the group's concerns. Some groups maintain a "hotline," so that those in need will have constant access to an understanding listener.

Finding the right Mutual Self-Help Group in your area:

- Call local hospitals, health and social-service agencies, or your house of worship.
- Look under the specific group's name in the White Pages of the phone book. One local organization is **Hospice, Inc. Bereavement Program**.
- Call the **Grief Recovery Hot Line** at (800) 445-4808, noon to 8pm EST, Mon. to Fri.
- Some newspapers announce local meetings or social events of self-help groups.
- Look in a directory of Mutual Self-Help Groups, such as *The National Directory of Bereavement Support Groups and Services*, which can usually be found in Public Libraries. Or, contact either the: **Self-Help Clearinghouse**, St. Clares-Riverside Medical Center, Denville, NJ 07834, (201) 625-7101 which publishes *The Self-Help Source Book*, listing 500 national organizations; or the Self-Help Center, 1600 Dodge Avenue, Suite S-122, Evanston, IL 60201, (312) 328-0470, which publishes in conjunction with the American Hospital Association the *Directory of National Self-Help/Mutual Aid Resource*.
- There are also many self-help books about grief available in libraries and bookstores. They often provide comfort and enlightenment to readers, as well as listings of mutual help groups. Here is a sampling of comforting publications:
  - *Widowed*, by Dr. Joyce Brothers, (Ballantine);
  - *Afterloss: A Recovery Companion for Those Who are Grieving*, by Barbara Hills LesStrang (Thomas Nelson Publishers);
  - *Seven Choices: Taking the Steps to New Life After Losing Someone You Love*, by Elizabeth Harper Neeld (Delta); and
  - *Life After Loss*, by Bob Deits (Fisher-Books).
- Contact one of these national groups for referral to a local group or, if they do not have a group in your area, they will provide information on organizing one:
  - **AARP, Widowed Persons Service**, 601 E Street, N.W., Washington, D.C. 20049, phone (202) 434-2260 — acts as a clearinghouse for referral to help. The Widowed Persons Service is a national outreach group with branches in 75 cities. All members are volunteers and widowed themselves. Most branches locate the newly widowed person either

by a post-card request from the widowed person (a relative or friend), or through the obituary columns. Eight weeks after the death, a volunteer writes to the widowed person, telling a bit about him- or herself and asking if the newly widowed person has experienced any of the difficulties common to the widowed. This is followed up with a phone call and, if desired, with a visit. The volunteer's main job is to listen. However, they are prepared, if asked, to give advice on everything from selling the house, to learning how to go out alone at night. Send a postcard to request its booklet "On Being Alone."

- **The Compassionate Friends**, P.O. Box 3696, Oak Brook, IL 60522-3696, phone (708) 990-0010 — peer support for bereaved parents.

- **Theos Foundation**, 1301 Clark Building, 717 Liberty Avenue, Pittsburgh, PA 15222 phone (412) 471-7779 — peer support for the widowed and their families.

- *alt.support.grief* — an online service providing a warm, friendly and sympathetic environment 24 hours a day for the bereaved to share their feelings, experiences, and advice with others who are grieving.

WHEN A CHILD IS ORPHANED

Like adults, children need to come to terms with death and the grief that accompanies it. Young children should be given the truth in gentle, basic terms, about the death. If it is a new experience for them, explain what will occur at the wake, visitation, funeral and burial. Answer all questions simply, but make sure you understand the question the child is really asking before you answer. Children often believe they are in some way responsible for causing or, at the least, not preventing the death. Even if they do not express these feelings, you should do your best to dispel them. Share your own feelings of grief with the child, and your tears, and the need for a hug. This is not the proper time for a stiff upper lip or being strong.

Unfortunately, when a child loses his or her family, he or she must often be relocated to live with a guardian and a new family. Moving time is difficult for any child; it can cause anxiety and, sometimes, depression. It is not easy to leave friends and activities, and the familiar surroundings of home, school, and neighborhood. Add to this the trauma of being orphaned, and it can be overwhelming. The guardian should recognize the difficulty a child may have in dealing, not only with the loss of his or her parent(s), but also with making new friends, adjusting to new teachers, becoming familiar with the new neighborhood and school and, maybe, most difficult of all, trying to find his or her place in a new family situation.

It is expected that all of this will cause depression in the child. Temporary problems, such as a slight slump in grades, or an occasional angry outburst, are quite normal. However, if these problems are pronounced, the child is excessively withdrawn, seems totally unaffected by the loss, or is taking more than six months to make the adjustment, seek professional help. Talk often with teachers, who can evaluate the student's progress and spot problems before they get out of hand. If a problem is noted, first check into school resources, such as guidance counselors, psychologists, and social workers; or talk to your family doctor and ask for suggestions for professional help. If none of these sources are fruitful, contact one or more of the organizations in the box on page 216. The members of the new family should do their best to be understanding of the trauma the child has suffered. This does not mean that the child should be treated differently from other children in the family. Inappropriate behavior should be corrected just as it is with the other children. A child cannot feel like a member of the family if he or she is not treated like a member of the family.

Psychotherapy Referral Services

The following national mental health organizations, some of which have local chapters in major cities, can refer you to therapists in your area. Ask for two or three referrals, so you will have a choice.

Call:

- The **National Mental Health Association**, (800) 969-6642.
- The **Suicide Crisis Referral Line**, (800) 292-8553.
- The **American Association for Marriage and Family Therapy**, (800) 374-2638.

Write:

- The **American Psychiatric Association**, Division of Public Affairs, 1400 K Street, Suite 501, Washington, D.C. 20005, send a postcard.
- The **American Psychological Association**, Public Affairs, 750 First Street, N.E., Washington, D.C. 20002-4242, enclose a self-addressed, stamped envelope. Also request a free copy of its publication, "Finding Help: How to Choose a Psychologist."
- The **National Association of Social Workers**, 750 First Street, N.E., Suite 700, Washington, D.C. 20002, enclose a self-addressed, stamped envelope, phone (202) 408-8600 or (800) 638-8799.

Just as with any grief-stricken person, the child needs to talk about the person(s) he or she has lost, and his or her feelings and problems. It is important for the child to communicate his or her feelings. If this option is denied or the child is unable to open up, he or she may act out instead. Talk with the child often, try to encourage him or her to express his or her feelings, but don't push. Talk about school, or movies, or other things the child is comfortable discussing. Just let the child know you are ready to listen when he or she is ready to talk. As with adults, the purpose of talking is to help the bereaved child to sort out his or her feelings. Be careful to be understanding, and not to be condemning of the child's feelings, no matter what they are. It would be comforting for the child to keep in touch with old friends. If possible, allow the child to visit with them. If distance prohibits this, let the child phone old friends, and also provide stamps and writing material, so he or she is encouraged to write to them.

One thing anyone with an overwhelming loss needs is to recapture a sense of control. To this end, it is helpful to allow the child as much control over his or her situation as possible. Some simple things you can do is allow the child either to pack or direct the packing of whatever he or she wants to take from his or her own room and from the rest of the house, at least to the extent the child's age permits. Remember, the child is in grief, with all the confusion, anger, fear, and indecision of an adult, maybe more. So, if possible, do not rush the child into entering, or going through items in, the home. Until the child is emotionally able to go into the home, assure him or her that the things in the home will not be removed or sold until he or she has had a chance to get what he or she wants. As much as possible, help the child in making decisions as to what to take from the home. Of course, children need their clothes, toys, school books, etc., which anyone can retrieve and bring to them. Older children should be asked for permission to retrieve these items or they may perceive it as an invasion of privacy and further loss of control. If possible allow the child to choose the color of the paint, curtains, linens, etc., for his or her new room, and to use former room furnishings and wall decorations, if desired.

Keep in mind that children, even teenagers, may not appreciate the sentimental value of some items. Therefore, if you believe they are leaving behind things they might later want, take them for the child. Some children will totally reject the idea of taking anything from the home. This is not an abnormal reaction. The child may be too angry or hurt to want anything that will remind or connect him or her with the past. If a child reacts this way, you may want to take things from the home you think are, or will be, important to the child. Then, pack and store them until a later time, when the child may want them. When it seems appropriate, such as when he or she expresses regret that everything is gone, tell the child you kept some items. Allow the child to decide when to go through the boxes. Be sure to keep items which were special to the parents or child, such as: mementos, awards, photographs, pictures, family videos, family heirlooms, jewelry, etc. Although it may be too painful for the child to see them now, in time, he or she will probably treasure them, and be very grateful that you kept them.

Choosing the Right School

Finding a School

In most areas, children attending public school, will be assigned a school according to their residence. However, if there is a choice of public schools, or the child is going to attend a private school, the following are suggested methods for finding the most appropriate school.

- If you are not familiar with the schools in the area, talk to neighborhood parents to get a feel for what each school has to offer.
- Visit each school you are considering. If it can be arranged, let the student visit prospective schools with you. Make appointments, in advance, to meet with administrators, teachers, and counselors to determine the philosophy and expectations of the school.
- Tour the building and evaluate the facilities.
- Discuss with the child his or her academic, athletic, and social interests, and determine the importance of each, to ensure most of the child's needs will be met. Then, write a list of questions before you go.

Points to Consider

The United States Office of Education's booklet, "Choosing a School for Your Child," suggests consideration of these factors:

- **What does the school offer?**
  - Basic curriculum;
  - Elective and special education classes;
  - After school care (if needed for younger children);
  - Extra-curricular activities (these are important in building self-esteem and making new friends);
  - School buses, or, is the school easily accessible with public transportation.

- **School Philosophy:**
  - Whether traditional or alternative;
  - Rules of discipline and methods of disciplinary action;
  - Method used to measure a student's progress (grading);
  - Regarding homework;
  - Method of informing parents of attendance and progress.

- **Proof of results:**
  - Ask to see test scores for the past few years. If the scores have been declining discuss this with the principal;
  - Check the attendance rates for both students and teachers;
  - Ask about drop-out rates;
  - Ask about positive signs, too.

- **Tour the Facilities:**
  - Do classrooms have adequate lighting, ventilation, spacing between desks, and furniture?
  - Do they have adequate and appropriate equipment, machines, books, tools, etc. to fulfill the student's academic and social interests?
  - Do they have adequate physical education facilities to accommodate the student's activity interests?
  - Is there at least one large room or auditorium for performances and meetings?
  - Evaluate the dining facilities and menus.
  - Evaluate dormitory facilities and rules, if applicable.

- **Staff:**
  - How many teachers are required to teach outside their field?
  - How many students are in an average class, and the maximum number of students allowed in a class?
  - Are there aides in the classroom?
  - Is individual tutoring by teachers or student-to-student programs available? (This can be helpful to students in transition.)
  - How accessible are student counselors, psychologists, social workers, and a nurse?
  - How often are teachers available to discuss the student's progress?

- **For Pre-School:**
  - Are surprise visits by parents and guardians encouraged?
  - Are criminal background checks done on all staff members?

When you have made a decision as to the school the student will attend, ask what information the new school requires. Give the old school plenty of time to transfer records. If possible, obtain a copy of the child's records from the old school. (You may also want to collect medical records from doctors and dentists.) This is particularly critical for mid-year transfers, when precious time can be wasted waiting for records to arrive. If it is near the end of a term, you may want to keep the child in the old school until after the grade is completed, if appropriate living arrangements are possible. In any case, be sure the teachers and administrators are aware of the child's recent loss, and ask to have frequent meetings to discuss their opinion of the student's overall behavior, and his or her academic and socializing progress.

Other Considerations

Choosing a Summer Camp

In addition to the traditional camps offering water sports, hiking, and fun, there are a number of specialty camps offering a wide variety of programs, including: archeology, computer skills, electronics, entrepreneurship and free enterprise, environmental conservation, grief and mourning, languages: French, Spanish, etc., law, marine biology, oceanic engineering, robotics, scuba diving and sailing, special needs, survival skills for college-level classes, weight loss, writing skills, and more. Enrollment in these camps is often limited; so start your search early and submit the child's application as soon as possible.

- **To find out what camps are offered:**
  - Check with the child's school guidance counselor for information about local camps.
  - Check with the local YMCA, YWCA, Boys and Girls Clubs, churches, etc.
  - Look in the Yellow Pages under the heading CAMPS.
  - The American Camping Association is a national clearinghouse that accredits about 2,000 summer camps. Its guide to camps is available currently for $16.95, call (800) 428-2267 for information, or look for it in the school's library.
  - For teenagers, check with colleges and universities for summer programs of interest to the student.

- **Considerations for finding an appropriate camp are:**
  - Use the same criteria as for finding the appropriate school, with a few additions:
  - Is the camp accredited? If not, why not?
  - Check the credentials and academic qualifications of the instructors who will be teaching specialty programs.
  - Few camps offer financial aid. Will financing be a problem? Be sure to include additional costs of field trips and supplies.
  - Is the camp age appropriate?
  - How often are the campers taken on field trips?
  - What type of field trips?
  - What type of transportation is provided?
  - In case of injury, does the camp have adequate and appropriate insurance coverage?

Choosing In-Home Help

When you need to hire a person to live-in, or to take care of the child in your home on a daily basis, it is most important to choose wisely. This means taking your time to find the right person. Before beginning the interview process, list your specific needs. Then outline the exact duties you want performed; the personal qualities you are looking for in the caregiver, including methods of discipline; the hours expected to work; the number of months or years the person's services will be required; and the salary you can afford to pay. Then, formulate questions that will allow you to determine the candidate's ability to meet your needs. See Chapter 12, "Transfer and Sale of Real Estate," for information about employee tax and insurance responsibilities. See Chapter 8, "Basic Contract Definition." For additional help, call (800) 634-6266 and request a free copy of "Nanny News." The International Nanny Association (INA), (609) 858-0808, is a placement service, ask for its brochure "A Nanny For Your Family." To receive information about the Au Pair in America program, call (800) 727-2437. For agencies who provide in-home sitters and nannies, look in the Yellow Pages under the heading CHILD CARE SERVICES. While interviewing potential candidates, keep in mind a second choice who may be able to take over if your first choice does not work out, or when the caregiver must take time off. When you have chosen a candidate, check his or her references carefully. You may even wish to hire a professional investigator to do a background check, before you hire the caregiver. Above all, do not hire anyone unless you are completely comfortable with him or her. When you are satisfied with your choice, draw up, or have an attorney draft a contract. The contract should clearly state your expectations of the caregiver, as well as what the employee can expect of you as an employer. Include a method for problem solving, and what behavior on the part of each party will constitute grounds for separation. Some parents are hiring companies which provide rented surveillance systems to monitor in-home child caregivers, look in the Yellow Pages under the heading SECURITY for companies such as Nanny Watch and Babywatch.

Child Support From a Non-Custodial Parent

When a non-custodial parent is court ordered to pay support, but is not meeting this obligation, the handbook on child support enforcement may help. For a copy of "Kids, They're Worth Every Penny. Handbook on Child Support Enforcement," published by the Department of Health and Human Services, is available from the Administration for Children and Families, Office of Child Support Enforcement, 370 L'Enfant Promenade, S.W., Washington, D.C. 20447, phone (202) 401-9373, or through the Consumer Information Catalog, Pueblo, CO 81009.

Custodial Grandparents

Grandparents, who must care for their grandchildren, can receive information about community resources available to provide emotional, legal, and other support, by contacting: the AARP Grandparent Information Center, Social Outreach and Support, 601 E Street, N.W., Washington, D.C. 20049, phone (202) 434-2296; Grandparents as Parents, P.O. Box 964, Lakewood, CA 90714, phone (310) 924-3996; or the National Coalition of Grandparents, 137 Larkin Street, Madison, WI 35705, phone (608) 238-8751.

Chapter 24

SOCIAL SECURITY, MEDICARE, AND MEDICAID

Social Security Administration

The Social Security Administration (SSA), within the U.S. Department of Health and Human Services, is responsible for administering two income benefit programs: Social Security Benefits (SS) and Social Security Income (SSI).

Social Security Benefits

Social Security benefits are funded through contributions to Social Security and Medicare Taxes, made when a person is working, either through payroll deduction, or payment of the self-employment tax. The funds are then used to pay the worker and his or her dependents a monthly benefit when the worker retires, becomes disabled (has a severe physical or mental condition which prevents him or her from working and is expected to last, or has lasted, for at least 12 months or is expected to result in death), or dies. The amount of Social Security benefit a person and his or her dependents will receive is based on the person's contributions to the fund during his or her working years, not on the individual's financial need. Beginning this year the government will require electronic direct depositing of payments into new recipient's bank accounts. Direct deposit will be required for all payments by August 1997.

The amount of the benefit a person is entitled to receive from Social Security is based on the average he or she earned over a 35-year work history, and is ordinarily figured on a formula that pays 90 percent of the first $310 to $426 of the person's average monthly earnings, plus 32 percent of the next $1,556 to $2,141, and 15 percent of amounts over $1,866 to $2,567. If a person did not work a total of 35 years, the unworked years are averaged in as zero earnings. Credit is given under our system for work done in 16 other countries, including: Austria, Belgium, Canada, Finland, France, Germany, Ireland, Italy, Luxemberg, the Netherlands, Norway, Portugal, Spain, Sweden, Switzerland, and the United Kingdom. For more specific information, contact the embassy of that country in Washington, or the consulate in your city, or call the SSA Hotline, (800) 772-1213.

Supplemental Security Income (SSI)

Supplemental Security Income (SSI) assures a minimum monthly income, currently up to $687, to people with limited income and resources, who are 65 or older, and for blind or disabled people of any age. These benefits are not earned, but based on need, and are funded from general revenues. Since SSI is based on need and not contribution, applicants must disclose all their income and property to demonstrate that they meet the requirements. The amount of property an individual or couple may own, excluding their home, car, personal effects, and household goods must be very low. Depending upon the circumstances, a person or family may be eligible to participate in more than one welfare or benefit program. For instance, recipients of SSI may also receive SS benefits, if they are eligible for both.

A person in need should apply for all benefits for which he or she may qualify, and which are available in the community, including SS, SSI, Aid to Families with Dependent Children (AFDC), Food Stamps, Worker's Compensation, Medicaid, etc. Then, if eligibility is established under more than one program, the person may choose whichever program is most beneficial to the family's needs. The decision should not be made until all determinations are made and all the facts are available. The personnel at the Social Security Administration, or a county social worker, can provide information about available options and can help with the decision. Check the senior hotline in your area for how to apply for various government programs, including nursing home care.

Social Security Survivor's Benefits

The following is a very basic guideline of who may be eligible for survivors benefits. As with all government regulations, these are subject to change and interpretation. Do not base your decision to apply or not apply, upon the information we have supplied here. Even if you think you will not be eligible, apply anyway, in writing. Let the agency determine your eligibility. If benefits are denied, you can appeal (but you can only appeal a written determination.)

- The current and life long surviving spouse. This may include a spouse who, in good faith, believed he or she was married, but who, because of some defect in the ceremony or procedure, or because of a failure to dissolve a prior marriage, was in fact, not married. The deemed good-faith spouse can collect benefits, as well as the legitimate spouse, but only if he or she is living with the primary beneficiary at the time of application. Additionally, common-law marriages are sometimes recognized as legitimate marriages, if the man and woman presented themselves to the public as a married couple.

■ For step-families, a second spouse may be entitled to collect Social Security benefits, based on a retired worker's earnings record, if the new spouse is over 62; or is younger, but takes care of the deceased person's child under 16 (or over 16 and disabled). He or she must apply for the benefits — they're not automatic. Also, either the marriage must have lasted at least one year when the survivor applies for benefits, or the couple must have had a child entitled to collect Social Security benefits based on a retired worker's earnings record.

■ A second wife or husband can apply for widow's or widower's benefits if he or she is over 60, or under 60 and disabled, but the marriage must have lasted at least nine months before the worker died, or a shorter marriage has to have ended by accidental death, or the couple must have had a child together.

■ Divorced widows or widowers may be entitled to the same benefits as the surviving spouse, if their marriage with the deceased person lasted at least 10 years before the date the divorce became final, and did not remarry before age 60 (or if they remarried before age 60, they may be eligible after that marriage ends). The 10 year rule doesn't apply if the deceased person's children aged 18 or under, are with that spouse. A former spouse can get benefits under the same circumstances as the surviving spouse.

■ Once survivor's benefits have begun, remarriage after age 60 does not terminate benefits.

■ Children who are unmarried, up to age 18 (19, if attending high school full time); or children disabled before age 22 for as long as they are disabled.

■ Under certain circumstances: grandchildren, great grandchildren, and dependent parents 62 or older may be eligible for payments.

■ A lump-sum death benefit is available, if applied for within two years after the death of a working individual. This benefit is payable to an eligible surviving widow, widower, or eligible child upon presentation of the worker's death certificate.

A widow or widower who is 65 or older and already receiving benefits, will continue to receive the total amount of his or her own benefit, plus as much of the deceased spouse's benefit that would bring the total amount up to the amount of the higher recipient's full benefit, if the deceased spouse was over 65 at death. The end result is one check a month in the amount equal to the highest benefit possible.

Considerations Before Making
An Initial Application
For Social Security Benefits

A survivor who is under age 70 and is not currently receiving Social Security benefits should first consider his or her entire economic picture, including: whether benefits will be based on his or her own work history or the deceased spouse's work history; his or her current earning capacity; the effect applying for benefits at this time would have on finances now and in the future. The survivor can meet with a Social Security Administration representative, who will calculate the benefit, and discuss options before he or she actually applies for benefits; or call the Social Security Administration Hotline at (800) 772-1213. They will calculate the highest benefit the survivor can receive, and what option the government will choose. If you decide to apply, insist on filing a written application. This establishes a right to the correct grant from the date of the original application and will generate a written decision, which can be appealed. A verbal decision cannot be appealed.

As of this writing, when a person is working and receiving Social Security benefits, he or she must file estimates of earnings and file an "Annual Report of Earnings" to report all wage or self-employment income for all months prior to the month of his or her 70th birthday. These excess earnings may also effect benefits received by your dependents.

- A person 70 years of age or older, may earn as much as he or she can, without any effect on his or her Social Security benefits.
- A person between the ages of 65 and 69 is allowed to earn up to $12,500 a year without penalty. But, for each $3 earned above the current $12,500 annual limit; $1 will be deducted from his or her Social Security benefits. The earnings limitation goes up each year.
- A person under age 65 is allowed to earn $8,280 a year without any effect on his or her benefit. However, for every $2 earned over the current $8,280 annual limit; $1 will be subtracted from his or her Social Security benefits. The earnings limitation goes up each year.

A widow or widower can start receiving SS survivors benefits as early as age 60, and even at 50, if disabled. However, they will not be full benefits. At age 60 (or 50 and disabled) the benefit will be only 71.5 percent of the late spouse's full retirement benefits. Benefits are reduced proportionately by the number of months still left before age 65. Once a person starts receiving retirement benefits, he or she receives the same benefit for life. With few exceptions, there are no increases, except for cost of living raises. Benefits are reduced by a fraction of one percent for each month prior to age 65 that benefits begin. This means that if benefits begin at age 62, you would lose about 20 percent of the monthly amount you would be entitled to at age 65. If you begin taking benefits at age 62, you would be ahead of the game for a while, break even at age 77, after which you would start losing. If benefits do not start until age 65, the entitlement is equal to 100 percent of the spouse's benefits.

Because it takes two to three months to process an application, benefits do not start immediately after a person applies for them. If necessary, while waiting you can apply for an "emergency advance." Benefits cannot be paid for any time prior to the time application is made. An exception is that an applicant for Social Security benefits who is 65, may have his or her benefits backdated up to six months, but not earlier than the individual's 65th birthday. Written application should not be delayed simply because a person does not have the information and documents required. SSA personnel can help applicants obtain whatever is needed. When a claim is approved, SSA sends a "Certificate of Award" and a copy of the booklet *Your Social Security Rights and Responsibilities - Retirement and Survivors Benefits.*

Appealing A Decision

A written notice will be sent to an applicant or recipient of benefits each time a decision is made on his or her SS or SSI claim. If the beneficiary does not agree with a decision, he or she has the right to appeal. An appeal must be made in writing and within the time specified on the decision document. Failure to appeal timely (within the time specified on the determination) would make the case ineligible for any review or appeal. If the beneficiary disagrees with the appeal decision, he or she has the right to a higher appeal. Although a person has the right to be represented by a qualified person of his or her choice in any dealings with the SSA, in most cases it is not necessary. However, services of a representative should be used by a person who has a comprehension or communication problem, or if a case reaches the court appeal level. If the representative charges a fee, the amount of the fee is limited, and both the representative and the fee must be approved by the SSA.

Getting the Information You Need

An information kit is available from the Social Security Administration by calling toll-free (800) 937-2000, or by writing to the Social Security Administration, Wilkes Barre Data Operations Center, P.O. Box 7004, Wilkes Barre, PA 18767-7004. The computer will ask for your name and address. The kit includes a Form SSA-7004, "Request for Earnings and Benefit Estimate Statement," which allows you to check your Social Security earnings record. To find out if all Social Security contributions withheld from your paycheck are properly recorded, complete this form, mail it back, and the Social Security Administration will then send your "Personal Earnings Benefit Estimate Statement" (PEBES), which is a listing of employment earnings reported for you and your expected retirement benefits. If you think there is an error, contact your local Social Security office. Look in the Blue or White Pages for the United States Government listings, under the Department of Health and Human Services. Be prepared to show appropriate tax returns or earning statements. Also included in the kit is a postcard to request the forms to apply for a new or replacement Social Security card and information on retirement insurance, survivor insurance, disability insurance, and Medicare. You may also request the benefit calculation formula. See Chapter 7, "Property Transfer Breakdown," Social Security Administration.

The Social Security Administration also provides an information hotline (800) 772-1213, TTD (800) 325-0778 (7 a.m. to 7 p.m., Monday through Friday, regardless of the caller's time zone). A representative will answer individual questions. You may also request Form SSA-7004, "Request for PEBES" and any of the SSA's free publications, including: *Understanding Social Security, Retirement, Survivors, When You Get Social Security Retirement or Survivors Benefits...What You Need To Know, The Appeals Process, Supplemental Security Income*, or *Disability*.

Additionally, forms, applications, and an online version of the Social Security handbook are available online at *http://www.ssa.gov*

Medicare

Medicare is a federal health insurance program, which is overseen by the Health Care Financing Administration (HCFA), within the U.S. Department of Health and Human Services, and administered through private insurance companies, called **Intermediaries**. Between 1996 and 1998 Medicare will centralize administration into the Medicare Transaction System. This system will handle all Medicare billing, pay the provider automatically, and simultaneously bill the patient's Medigap plan for the rest of the bill. Medicare coverage is available for people 65 or older, and people under 65 who have a qualifying disability, or suffer with permanent kidney failure. Medicare coverage is divided into two parts:

Medicare Part A:

Pays benefits for services provided in a hospital or skilled-nursing facility, home health care, and Hospice care for the terminally ill. This insurance is automatically available to all qualified Social Security benefit recipients as a matter of right. It is funded through the Federal Insurance Contributions Act (F.I.C.A.) taxes paid by workers, with matching funds from their employers. Individuals 65 or over who haven't worked long enough to be eligible for hospital insurance can get this protection by enrolling and paying a monthly premium; and

Medicare Part B:

Pays benefits for services provided by doctors, outpatient hospital care, diagnostic tests, durable medical equipment, and related services, such as rehabilitative therapy. This insurance is applied for separately and a premium is paid by the insured, either through a monthly deduction from his or her Social Security check or by sending the payment to SSA if they are not receiving SS benefits. At the same time a person becomes entitled to hospital insurance, individuals who are receiving Social Security or Railroad Retirement benefits are automatically enrolled in Medicare Part B, unless they refuse it. The cost of Medicare coverage is raised periodically.

Medicare does not provide 100 percent coverage at this time. There is a yearly deductible for medical expenses, which must be met each year before benefits begin. When entering a hospital, an initial deductible of a specified amount must be paid. Currently for Medicare Part A the deductible is $736, for Medicare Part B the deductible is $100. After the deductible is met, Medicare pays only 80 percent of the amount considered fair for each covered service; and does not pay for either prescription or non-prescription medications (with few exceptions) outside of the hospital. The amounts not paid by Medicare are the responsibility of the patient. To help meet the expenses of the deductibles and co-payments, Medicare beneficiaries purchase private insurance called a Medigap policy; join a Health Maintenance Organization (HMO), which usually accepts Medicare as full payment for services or charges a small flat fee for each service rendered or medication prescribed; or qualify for Medicaid, see <u>Medicaid</u> on page 229. For more information about Medigap insurance and HMO's see Chapter 18, "Insurance and Insurance Agents." Usually Medigap and Medicaid will require a written determination of Medicare benefits before they will process a claim or pay benefits. Therefore, all medical bills should be submitted to Medicare for a formal determination. If benefits are denied, only written formal Medicare denials can be appealed. Appeals must be in writing to the Medicare insurance carrier who issued the determination. The company's address is on the determination. If an appeal is not made within the time limit specified on the determination, further action is barred.

Whether a person is working or retired, he or she should apply for Medicare two to three months before his or her 65th birthday, because many insurance companies automatically reduce coverage to their customers at age 65. If a person should have the misfortune of illness during this period, he or she may not be covered completely by insurance. In any case, no one should cancel any insurance coverage until he or she has received notification of coverage and the booklets *Your Medicare Handbook* and *Guide to Health Insurance for People with Medicare.* These publications, as well as others, will fully explain the options available to Medicare beneficiaries. They are available at local SSA offices, by calling the SS Hotline (800) 772-1213, by writing the U.S. Department of Health and Human Services, Health Care Financing Administration, 6325 Security Blvd., Baltimore, MD 21207-5187, or go online to *http://www.hcfa.gov*

Tidbit: Medicare, and many private insurance policies, DO NOT extend coverage to care received outside of the United States and its territories. Therefore, before you travel outside the U.S., check coverage offered by your policy. Travel insurance can be purchased through your travel agent. Check the travel policy carefully for exclusions before purchase.

Medicare Home Health Benefits

In addition to providing benefits for hospital stays and visits to doctors, laboratory tests, x-rays, etc., Medicare also currently provides up to 35 hours per week (56 hours in certain circumstances) of free in-home care for patients who require care to aid in their recovery. The service must be ordered by the attending doctor, and either the hospital's social worker or the doctor's office can arrange for the service. The patient must be homebound or have severely limited mobility, either temporarily or for an indefinite period of time, and require some form of skilled care either from nurses or therapists. Along with the skilled care, home health aides are usually provided to assist the patient with bathing and other personal needs. The extent of services offered may be augmented by state or county agencies. Prior hospitalization is not required, only an illness or injury which necessitates skilled services. Skilled nursing care can include certain medication administration, dressing wounds, changing catheters, or observation and assessment of a patient's instable condition. Skilled therapy services may include physical or rehabilitative therapy, such as speech or gait training. Services are provided through a Certified Home Health Agency (CHHA). Its nurse will visit the patient at home and evaluate the patient's condition, the need for service, and whether or not Medicare will pay for the service. For qualified patients, the nurse will draw up a two month care plan. A new plan can be drawn up and care renewed indefinitely. However, if the nurse determines that care cannot be justified under Medicare guidelines, the CHHA may refuse to provide the service because it will not be paid. The patient may, of course, offer to pay for the services personally. The treating physician must certify the need for services and approve the CHHA's care plan. If the CHHA wants to terminate care before you believe it is appropriate, speak to the treating physician. The state's health department or local Area Agency on Aging may be able to answer specific questions about benefits.

Tidbit: Although you are not directly paying for these services, you have the right to be happy and satisfied with the help provided. It is important for the aide, nurse, or other professional to provide appropriate services, act in a caring manner, and be compatible with the patient. If these criteria are not met, call the agency and request the caregiver be replaced.

Nursing Home Coverage

Medicare also provides limited benefits for stays in an approved rehabilitation facility or nursing home. Generally, all Medicare beneficiaries who enter a nursing home within 30 days of a 3 day or longer hospital stay are entitled to coverage of some part of their nursing home care. If the patient's condition warrants care in a skilled nursing facility and Medicare requirements are met, Medicare currently provides full coverage, with no patient co-payment, for the first 20 days. For days 21 through 100, the patient must pay $81.50 per day, with Medicare covering the balance, if any. Beyond 100 days, Medicare benefits end. Even if care received is not payable by Medicare A, some incidental expenses such as x-rays, lab tests, or doctor's visits may be covered under Medicare B. See Chapter 26, "Providing Care For A Dependent Adult Survivor."

Physician Billing Under Medicare

For each service Medicare covers there is an approved fee. Medicare Part B pays 80 percent of the approved fee; the beneficiary is responsible for the remaining 20 percent. Participating physicians contract to accept the amount Medicare approves as full payment for their services. In other words, the provider accepts assignment in all cases. The law limits the amount a physician who does not accept assignment can bill a beneficiary, to 15 percent above Medicare's approved fee. This amount is called the excess charge, or balance billing. Some states have passed stricter limits. Always check the "Explanation of Benefits" for overcharges. If a physician overcharges, ask the doctor's office for an explanation and, if warranted, ask for a refund. Should the doctor believe Medicare's approved fee to be too low, either you or the doctor may appeal to the Medicare carrier. If the appeal is denied, the doctor must pay the refund within 15 days of receiving the decision. If you have trouble obtaining a refund from the doctor, contact the Medicare carrier. The carrier's telephone number and address are on the "Explanation of Benefits" form and in the *Medicare Handbook*. You must specifically request, by phone or in writing, that the carrier write a letter to the doctor informing him or her of a lack of compliance, and suggesting the doctor issue a refund. However, no one can force the doctor to give a refund. For help, contact your Area Agency on Aging office.

The law also requires doctors (whether or not they accept assignment) to submit their bills to Medicare, if the patient requests it, and provides that any phone conversations with the doctor, prescription refills, and medical conferences between the doctor and other professionals, are included in the physician's fee for a visit, and should not create an extra or additional charge.

Any private contracts or "waivers" the patient might have signed to get around these regulations are invalid and are not legally binding. Plus, they will not protect doctors from civil penalties for violating Medicare procedures. This does not include an agreement for the patient to pay privately for services that Medicare will not cover, or for which Medicare may deny payment because the procedure is deemed not reasonable or medically necessary. To be valid, the written agreement must clearly specify the procedure, advise the patient that Medicare is unlikely to pay for the procedure, and be signed by the patient. However, if the amount billed is too high once Medicare has determined the allowable charge, the doctor is obligated to refund any excess paid by the patient.

If you receive bills from a medical service provider for services that were never received call the Medicare Fraud Hotline, (800) 368-5779, or write to the Inspector General's Office, HHS OIG Hotline, P.O. Box 23489, Washington, D.C. 20026, to make a report. To register a complaint concerning the sale or marketing of Medigap policies, call (800) 638-6833. See Chapter 7, "Property Transfer Breakdown," <u>Doctor, Hospital, Medical Bills, and Health Insurance Policies</u>.

Medicaid

Medicaid (MediCal in California) is a federal program partially funded by the HCFA, along with local and state revenues. Although there are federal guidelines, each state designs, formulates, and administers its own program. It is the individual state that sets its own qualifications and benefits. The range of services available may vary by county. Basically, Medicaid provides health care for low income individuals, couples, and families who otherwise could not afford medical care. Medicaid recipients can receive care either at county clinics or through private health care providers, who agree to bill Medicaid for their services. They accept the payment Medicaid makes as payment in full. Medicaid can be used as the only medical care payor, or as a supplement to Medicare or other insurance which may provide coverage. For persons who have both Medicare and Medicaid, Medicaid pays Medicare's deductibles, premiums, and co-payments. Therefore, if you are eligible for Medicaid, you should not buy supplemental insurance, as it will not provide additional coverage.

Federally mandated benefits Medicaid programs must provide are:
- In-patient hospital care,
- Out-patient hospital care,
- Skilled-nursing facility care,
- Doctor services,
- Diagnostic tests,
- Home health care,
- Preventive and medically necessary services.

Optional benefits Medicaid programs may provide are:
- Prescription drugs,
- Dental care,
- Personal or custodial care services.

Generally, Medicaid is available to low income individuals and couples including: SSI recipients 65 or over, those who are blind, disabled, and AFDC recipients between age 21 and 65. As explained above, Medicare provides coverage in a nursing home for only 100 days. After this, the patient is responsible for paying the costs. However, when the patient's funds are reduced to the point where he or she is eligible for Medicaid coverage, Medicaid will pay for the remaining stay, no matter how long. Individuals who do not qualify for Medicaid may meet the requirements for a program that will help pay Medicare premiums, and even provide a plan similar to Medigap insurance, under the "Qualified Medicare Beneficiary" (QMB) program. Application can be made to the local Medicaid office, or call (800) 638-6833.

It is not necessary for an individual or couple to be totally destitute before they are eligible for Medicaid. In general, although they must have a very low monthly income, they are permitted to own a home, household furnishings, a car, and have a few thousand dollars in assets. Therefore, if medical bills are being accrued, apply as soon as you foresee a potential problem paying them. Be sure to tell your medical care provider you are on or plan to apply for Medicaid. If the provider does not accept Medicaid patients, you must find a care provider who does. Applicants for Medicaid have the right to appeal any decision regarding Medicaid eligibility through its office and Medicaid recipients have the right to a hearing regarding any denial of services, prior to authorization for services or an unreasonable delay of prior authorization. If you experience problems regarding Medicaid or county medical services, contact your legal services office for assistance. For more information, contact your state or county welfare office, public health office, social service office, or state Medicaid Office.

EMPLOYER
HEALTH AND PENSION BENEFITS

Employee and Dependent Benefit Protection under ERISA and COBRA

The **Employee Retirement Income Security Act (ERISA)** is administered by the U.S. Department of Labor, Pension and Welfare Benefits Administration. Currently, the law neither requires an employer to offer a pension or health insurance plan, nor does it dictate how an employee becomes eligible to receive benefits or the type or level of benefits the employer may offer. However, it does require certain employers who offer such benefits to conform to standards set forth in the Act. ERISA requires the plan administrator to automatically furnish a **Summary Plan Description** (SPD) booklet within 90 days after a person becomes a participant or beneficiary, or within 120 days after the plan is subject to the reporting and disclosure provisions of the law. The SPD outlines the benefits offered under the plan, rules for how workers become entitled to benefits, and includes the employees' rights under ERISA with regard to the plan.

An amendment of the ERISA is the **Consolidated Omnibus Budget Reconciliation Act (COBRA)**. The law generally covers group health insurance plans maintained by companies who employed 20 or more employees on at least 50 percent of the working days in the previous calendar year. It applies to plans sponsored by private sector employers and by state and local governments. The SPD provided by the plan administrator must explain how to qualify for and obtain benefits under the health plan and include written procedures for processing claims and outline COBRA regulations for continuation of health coverage for qualified beneficiaries after

separation from the company. Complete plan rules are available from employers or benefits offices. There can be charges up to 25 cents a page for copies of plan rules. COBRA does not apply to plans sponsored by the federal government and certain church-related organizations. Federal employees are covered by a law similar to COBRA; contact the personnel office serving their agency for more information on temporary extensions of health benefits.

A group health plan ordinarily is defined as a plan that provides medical benefits for the employer's own employees and their dependents, whether coverage is provided through a self-funded, pay-as-you-go, reimbursement insurance plan, a Health Maintenance Organization (HMO), or combination of these. Medical benefits provided under the terms of the plan and available to COBRA beneficiaries may include: inpatient and outpatient hospital care; physician care; surgery and other major medical benefits; prescription drugs; and any other medical benefits, such as dental and vision care.

COBRA Provisions

Very basically the provisions of COBRA are:
- Qualified beneficiaries have the right to elect to continue coverage that is identical to the coverage provided under the plan. A qualified beneficiary may be an employee, the employee's spouse and dependent children and, in certain cases, a retired employee, the retired employee's spouse and dependent children.
- Once COBRA coverage is chosen you are required to pay for the coverage.
- Employers and plan administrators have an obligation to determine the specific rights of beneficiaries with respect to election, notification, and type of coverage options.
- Upon the death of a qualified employee or retiree, the plan must offer continuing coverage to the qualifying spouse and dependent children for up to 36 months. However, a plan, at its discretion, may provide longer periods of continuation coverage. Additionally, special rules for disabled individuals may extend the maximum periods of coverage.
- Qualified beneficiaries must be offered benefits identical to those received immediately before qualifying for continuation coverage.
- Some plans allow beneficiaries to convert group coverage to an individual policy. In this case you must be given the option to enroll in a conversion health plan. You usually must enroll in the plan within 180 days of when COBRA coverage ends. The premium is generally not at a group rate; the conversion option, however, is not available if you end COBRA coverage before reaching the maximum period of entitlement, or it is unavailable under the plan.
- Specific notice requirements are triggered for employers, qualified beneficiaries, and plan administrators when a qualifying event occurs.
- Employers must notify plan administrators within 30 days of an employee's death, termination, reduced hours of employment, entitlement to Medicare, or a bankruptcy. Multi-employer plans may provide for a longer period of time.
- The health plan must inform qualified beneficiaries, in person or by first class mail within 14 days of receiving information that a qualifying event has occurred, of their right to COBRA coverage.

- Qualified beneficiaries have a 60-day period to accept coverage or lose all rights to benefits. This period is measured from the later of the covered loss date or the date the notice to elect COBRA coverage is sent. COBRA coverage is retroactive if elected.
- COBRA does not prevent an employer from unilaterally changing or even eliminating benefits to all employees and/or retirees.
- For further information on private plans contact the U.S. Department of Labor, Pension and Welfare Benefits Administration, Division of Technical Assistance and Inquiries, 200 Constitution Avenue, N.W., Room N-5658, Washington, D.C. 20210.
- For further information on public sector plans contact the U.S. Public Health Service, Office of the Assistant Secretary for Health, Grants Policy Branch (COBRA), 5600 Fishers Lane, Room 17A-45, Rockville, MD 20857, phone (202) 219-8921, or check the Blue or White Pages for a local field office.
- Publications available from the U.S. Department of Labor, Pension and Welfare Benefits Administration, 200 Constitution Avenue, N.W., Washington, D.C. 20210 include: *What You Should Know About the Pension Law* and *Health Benefits Under the Consolidated Omnibus Budget Reconciliation Act (COBRA)*.

Employer and Union Sponsored Pension Plans

Although there are a number of different types of employer or union sponsored pension plans, they all fall into one of two categories: either a "Defined Benefit" or a "Defined Contribution" Plan. Both of these plans can provide for payment of the pension funds either through a **Life Annuity** (monthly payments for life of a specific amount) or a **Lump-Sum Distribution**. Qualified plans are governed by ERISA and IRS regulations. Under ERISA regulation a plan which provides for benefits to be paid in the form of an annuity, must also provide a "Qualified Joint and Survivor Annuity" (QJSA) for the qualified employee's spouse. However, the non-employee spouse may sign a waiver known as "Spousal Consent" stipulating that he or she will receive nothing if the employee dies before receiving benefits or at any time after benefits start. Plans must follow a rather detailed set of rules concerning these issues.

Pension law is complicated, so we can only advise that you acquaint yourself thoroughly with the pension plan with which you are dealing. The amount of benefits the surviving spouse or other designated beneficiary may be entitled to receive depends upon the plan's rules, as set forth in the **Summary Plan Description** (SPD). It includes the plan's rules regarding who is eligible to participate in the plan; the formula by which benefits are **Accrued** (earned) and when the benefits become **Vested** (non-forfeitable); at what age, and under what circumstances, the employee, surviving spouse, or beneficiary may begin receiving benefits; the type and amount of benefits; who qualifies for benefits; and how survivor benefits will be affected by whether the employee dies before or after he or she has begun receiving benefits. If the SPD and associated documents do not answer all your questions, contact the employer, "Plan Administrator," "Benefits Officer," or similarly designated person for help. ERISA permits the administrator of the plan to charge a specified fee to send copies of the SPD or other documents. For more information request *Looking Out for #2 — A Married Couple's Guide to Understanding Your Benefit Choices at Retirement from a Defined Contribution Plan* and/or *Looking Out for #2 — A Married Couple's Guide to Understanding Your Benefit Choices at Retirement from a Defined Benefit Plan.*

The U.S. Department of Labor, Pension and Welfare Benefits Administration, Washington, D.C. 20210, guarantees the benefits in most employer and union sponsored pension plans, if for any reason they are underfunded or bankrupt. If this problem presents itself, contact it. For more information request "How to File a Claim for Your Benefits" from it, or through the Consumer Information Catalog, Pueblo, CO 81002. The Pension Rights Center publishes numerous booklets. For a list of publications, send a self-addressed, stamped envelope to 918 - 16th Street, N.W., Suite 704, Washington, D.C. 20006, phone (202) 296-3776.

If a surviving spouse is entitled to receive monthly pension checks, the employer should send a "Notice of Withholding on Pension Payments" to him or her. After determining your total income for the year, decide whether or not income tax should be deducted by the employer from the survivor pension payments. Recipients of pension plans have the right not to have federal income taxes withheld from their monthly checks. They also have the right to revoke a federal income tax withholding election at any time. If taxes are not withheld from pension checks and income is sufficient to be taxable, quarterly estimated taxes should be sent to the Internal Revenue Service, as well as the state and city taxing authorities, if applicable. Penalties may be incurred if withholding and estimated tax payments are not sufficient to cover taxes. Retirement program payments made to a surviving spouse or other beneficiary are normally exempt from probate, and, currently, the payments are not included in the decedent's Taxable Estate for Federal Estate Tax or State Death or Inheritance Taxes.

Individually Funded Retirement Plans

An **Individual Retirement Arrangement** or **Individual Retirement Account (IRA)** is a private pension fund set up by an individual to provide money for their retirement years. All the earnings and/or investment gain from property in an IRA is tax-deferred. **Tax-deferred** means income is accrued without being subject to Federal or State Income Tax until the income or funds are withdrawn. Currently, individuals are permitted to invest $2000 per year into an IRA. Depending upon their income, and whether or not they are participating in an Employer sponsored plan, this investment may be tax deductible in the year it is made. **Simplified Employee Plan (SEP) IRA** and **Keogh Plans** are similar retirement plans for the self-employed or small businesses (although the yearly deposit limit is higher). One person may have many separate IRA accounts with various amounts in each. Although there are some restrictions, the property in an IRA may be in the form of a cash account, an annuity insurance policy, or a mutual fund annuity, investment instruments, and certain collectibles. The property in an IRA may be transferred from one financial institution, insurance company, or investment institution to another as many times as desired in a year, provided the transfer is made directly between the institutions. However, the owner may make one rollover of the property per year. A **Rollover** occurs when the owner actually takes possession of the property. Currently, he or she has 60 days to deposit the property in another IRA account in order to maintain its tax-deferred status.

Since IRA's are intended to provide funds for the owner during his or her retirement years, the IRS imposes severe penalties for individuals who withdraw funds prior to reaching age 59 and a half, as well as for those who fail to start required minimum withdrawals at age 70 and a half. However, since IRA's often contain money when a person dies, the owner may name a Beneficiary to receive the property in the account in the event of the owner's death. The money can be paid in a lump-sum or in installments, in the form of an annuity. Any money left in the account at death goes to a named Beneficiary free of probate, but may be included in the decedent's Taxable Estate. For more information, request a copy of IRS Publication 590 *Individual Retirement Arrangements (IRA's)*.

Lump-Sum Distributions

If you have chosen, or are required, to take a total distribution from a pension or retirement plan, be sure to check the rules for the pension plan, as well as the current IRS regulations regarding rollovers into IRA's, and federal and state income tax laws governing treatment of distributions before taking action, or consult an accountant familiar with retirement planning. Do not take too long. Many companies won't allow you to keep funds in the plan indefinitely after the employee or retiree dies, and failure to know how, or if, you can maintain the tax-deferred nature of the funds can result in a taxable distribution. However, it is not necessary to select investments immediately. Because IRA property can be transferred later, you can just open an IRA account with a financial institution and deposit the money in a regular savings or money-market account. Then, take your time to decide, based on investments you already have, which investments to buy and which to sell. To make a tax-free transfer, contact the new custodian of the IRA, who will have you sign papers to open the proper qualified account, and to request transfer of the property from the current plan sponsor or custodian.

A lump-sum distribution probably will put in your hands more money than you have ever had at one time in your life. Therefore, you should probably seek professional help to determine how the money should be invested. Two opinions are usually best. Then use your own judgment to evaluate the information you receive from the professional advisors:

- Most brokerage firms, mutual-fund companies, and insurers have created "Retirement Planning" units that are designed to help its brokers or agents to act as retirement investment advisors. See Chapter 14, "Investment Brokers and Brokerage Accounts."
- Consult with a financial planner. For information on finding a qualified financial planner see Chapter 17, "Financial Planners."

- If you or the decedent worked in a large corporation, contact the human resources department for information about company-sponsored seminars offering financial planning advice.
- Financial experts suggest that recipients of lump-sum pension plan distributions have proposals reviewed by an attorney and an accountant before making a commitment; and
- Avoid an adviser who:
    - Wants you to put all your money into one investment;
    - Spends a minimal amount of time on analysis of your situation and options;
    - Spends most of the time looking at investment choices;
    - Will not discuss how he or she is paid; or
    - Discourages you from getting another opinion.

PROVIDING CARE
FOR A
DEPENDENT ADULT SURVIVOR

If the decedent, before his or her demise, was providing care to the surviving spouse or other person, alternative care and support must now be found for the dependent individual. Choices are limited by the actual needs of the dependent individual, the family situation, the services available in the community, and the financial means of those involved. A meeting of family and supportive friends should be held to discuss the current situation and to make a care plan. Since changes can occur in the condition of the person needing care, as well as the ability of the caregiver to provide care, future meetings will probably be required periodically to re-evaluate the situation. Possible changes and how to handle them should also be discussed at these meetings. Include the individual requiring care in the planning to the extent he or she is able to participate. Considerations include:

- Is the person able to remain at home alone, or is around the clock companionship or assistance required?

- Is a family member or friend willing and able to either move in with the person or have the person move into his or her home? Before making any commitment, keep in mind that care may be required for many years.

  - Is this person willing and able to perform all needed services him- or herself?

  - Are friends or relatives willing and able to provide care for a few hours daily, or weekly, to allow the primary caregiver time for a social life away from the responsibility? Don't forget to provide for an occasional long weekend, plus one or two weeks for a vacation, at least once a year.

  - Will professionals come into the home on a daily or frequent basis to provide personal care? These services may be provided by professionals, either hired privately or provided under a Medicare or Medicaid program (if the person qualifies physically and financially for these services). For more information see Chapter 24, "Social Security, Medicare, and Medicaid."

- Does the person require around the clock professional attention provided by a live-in companion or around-the-clock shifts of home health aides or nurses hired through a service? Listings for these services can be found in the Yellow Pages under the headings: NURSES or HOME HEALTH SERVICES. They usually charge by the hour or shift for the services of their personnel and can be extremely expensive.
- Is it appropriate for the person to move into an assisted living community, a shared housing program, or a nursing home?
- If it is determined to be necessary to gain legal guardianship of the dependent person see Chapter 3, "Trusts."

Tidbit: Regardless of where the person will reside, it is wise to have him or her wear an I.D. necklace or bracelet. This can be invaluable should the person become confused and wander away. The I.D. should include the person's name, condition, and the caregiver's phone number.

Finding the Help You Need

Luckily, help is available in most communities to assist with these decisions. These include:

- A trip to the Public Library to review *The Catalogue of Federal Domestic Assistance.* This is the ultimate source of information about available government programs.
- Contacting a social worker. The social worker can come to the home, evaluate the situation, and provide information concerning care alternatives available through social service agencies and financial assistance programs. The social worker can also provide information about services available from private agencies in the community, as well as alternative living arrangements. Programs available may include: transportation services to doctors and shopping; homemaker services, such as shopping, cleaning and laundering, cooking meals, etc.; adult day care at community centers (providing supervised arts, crafts, and other activities, as well as meals, some offer limited personal care); and home health aides to provide personal care services, such as bathing, dressing, feeding, etc.; and financial assistance. The social worker will either arrange for needed services, give you appropriate forms so you can make an application, or refer you to other agencies. Hospitals usually have a social worker on staff, or the person's doctor can request a county or state social worker visit. Alternatively, you can call the local social service agency, or the State Department of Health and Human Services listed in the Blue or White Pages under the name of the state, and request a consultation with a social worker.
- Call the ElderCare Locator Information Line. ElderCare is a nation-wide non-profit organization. Its purpose is to refer older people and caregivers to local agencies, which assist the elderly with legal counseling, housing, adult day care, home health, rides to doctors, meals delivered to the door, and other types of social services. The ElderCare Locator's toll-free number, (800) 677-1116, is in operation from 9 a.m. to 11 p.m., EST, Monday through Friday. The operator will ask for the name, address, and zip code of the person needing help, and a brief description of the problem or the assistance needed. The same organization also

provides an information and referral service to retirement housing (both assisted and independent living) throughout the country. You can request information by writing to ElderCare Referral Agency, Inc., 14591 Newport Avenue, Suite 202, Tustin, CA 92680 or calling (800) 667-1116 or (714) 581-8100.

- Contact the local Area Agency on Aging, listed in the Blue or White Pages under the name of the state. They act as a clearinghouse for information on programs for the elderly and their families, including: Meals-on-Wheels, the United Way, Family Services of America, Visiting Nurses Association, and the Red Cross.
- Contact AbleData, a program of the U.S. Department of Education, call (800) 346-2742, for help finding products to assist people with disabilities.

As you explore the services available, determine what needs are, and are not, met by the programs offered by the social service agencies. List the needs of the individual and the service that meets that need. Then list the services still required and your financial ability to fill them through private providers.

Individual's Needs:

Social Services Provided:

What additional assistance is needed?

How can these needs be filled?

Geriatric Care Managers

With the increased mobility of our population, and the resulting distance from our aged parents, we have become less able to care for them when they need assistance. This has given rise to a growing field of professionals called **Geriatric Care Managers** (GCM). Their main function is to look in on family members, evaluate their independent-living needs, and arrange for them to receive appropriate services. Where available, care management is offered by public agencies, such as Area Agencies on Aging, usually free or on a sliding scale based on income. Care management may also be available under Medicaid or Medicare, and usually involves no direct cost to the recipient. However, because government social workers are usually very over-burdened, they cannot always provide the level of individualized attention the family may desire. Therefore, an alternative is a private GCM. The fees vary with location and the services provided. During the initial visit, the GCM evaluates the client's physical, functional, social, and emotional condition, then recommends community and private services which can meet the client's needs. Some recommended services may be free, others covered by Medicaid, Medicare, or private insurance, and the client may be totally responsible for the cost of others. If approved by the person who hired the GCM, the GCM will arrange for the client to receive the appropriate services. Services may include visiting nurses, meal delivery, home care, escort service, bill-paying and budgeting assistance, and crisis intervention and counseling, to name a few. When appropriate, the GCM will visit the client on a set schedule, to monitor the client and make regular reports to the distant family. Private GCM's will usually have more communication with the family of the client than one provided by a public agency.

Finding a Geriatric Care Provider

- Ask the local hospital's discharge planner, Area Office on Aging, the Visiting Nurse Association, National Association of Social Workers or your senior center for referrals.
- Send a request for a list of members in the prospective client's area, along with a self-addressed, stamped envelope, to the National Association of Professional Geriatric Care Managers, 1604 N. Country Club Road, Tucson, AZ 85716, or call (602) 881-8008. This is a professional association of independent care managers. It has set voluntary standards of quality and established a code of ethics. Although it requires members to possess a professional degree in a human services discipline and at least two years of geriatric experience, it does not independently verify the members' credentials.
- Look in the Yellow Pages under the title GERIATRIC CONSULTING & SERVICES.

Hiring a GCM

Because the GCM is often given the keys to the home and car, it is important to carefully check references. If a power of attorney or other access to funds is granted, it is prudent to check with the Better Business Bureau and run a credit check or require the GCM to be bonded. You may also consider limiting the amounts of money in any account accessible to a GCM. Use the "Hiring Interview Sheet" on pages 39 and 40. Questions to ask before hiring a private geriatric care manager include:

- What is your experience in geriatric care management?
- Do you belong to any geriatric care managers association?
- Do you have a professional license (social worker, nurse, counselor, etc.)?
- Can you provide references from clients, as well as local organizations (such as hospitals, professional associations, or senior centers)?
- Do you arrange for free, low-cost, or medically insured services when available and appropriate?
- Do you personally provide any of the needed services?
- Do you screen service providers for experience, reputation among other community services, licensing, insurance (including worker's compensation), and criminal records?
- Are you affiliated with any service provider? If so, are you free to recommend competing providers?
- Do you get referrals from any service provider? If so, do you receive a share of their fee?
- Do you carry professional liability insurance? Are you bonded? See proof of insurance or call the insurer to confirm.
- How often do you monitor each service personally?
- Who covers for you when you're off duty?
- How often can I expect routine reports? Written or phoned?
- What are your fees and what do they include (e.g., initial assessment, expenses, etc.)?
- Will you provide a written contract specifying fees and services?

Miscellaneous Assistance Programs for Low Income Individuals and Families

- The County or State **Dental Association** can refer callers to dentists who will provide free care or try to work out a payment schedule for low-income patients.
- The **Pharmaceutical Manufacturers Prescription Drug Indigent Programs** are private programs through which almost every major brand-name pharmaceutical manufacturer provides free prescription drugs to disadvantaged patients of all ages. If you cannot afford a prescribed medication, tell the prescribing physician. The doctor will contact the drug's manufacturer, or its sales representative. The physician is required to state on the phone or, in most cases, on specific written forms, that the patient is indigent. Some programs require that the patient not be covered by private health insurance, Medicare, or Medicaid. The physician then requests the amount of the prescribed medication needed for treatment. The drug will be delivered to the doctor's office to be given to the patient free of charge. For more information write to the Pharmaceutical Research and Manufacturers of America, 1100 15th Street, N.W., Washington, D.C. 20005, phone (202) 835-3400, or call its hotline at (800) 762-4636. If the doctor is not familiar with the program, request an explanation of the program and a directory of the participating pharmaceutical companies.

241

- The **Home Repair/Modification Programs for Elderly Homeowners**, which provides grants for modifications to a home, to make it safe and accessible to the occupant; such as installing ramps and widening doorways, to make it wheelchair accessible. For more information, write to American Communities, P.O. Box 7189, Gaithersburg, MD 20898, or phone (800) 998-9999.
- The **American Association of Retired Persons** (AARP) is an organization open to all individuals 50 or older. It offers a variety of publications which are of interest to seniors. A number of them are mentioned in this book. Members receive its magazine, *Modern Maturity*, and bulletins to keep them informed on law changes which may affect them. They also offer a number of benefits, including group insurance policies for health, auto, home, and mobile homes; a pharmacy program, investments, Medigap policies, travel discounts, and outreach assistance programs in the community. These are manned by volunteers and provide driver education programs, a tax-assistance program, and social support programs including a Widowed Persons' Service and Retirement Options. To request a membership application, write to the American Association of Retired Persons Membership Center, 3200 E. Carson Street, Lakewood, CA 90712. The following AARP publications are free. To order, address a postcard to the publication's title and number, AARP Fulfillment, 601 E Street, N.W., Washington, D.C. 20049.
  - *A Home Away From Home: Consumer Information on Board and Care Homes* (D12446),
  - *CHISS (Consumer Housing Information Service for Seniors): Resource Guide on Accessory Apartments* (D12775),
  - *Selected Retirement Housing* (D13680),
  - *Staying at Home: A Guide to Long-Term Care and Housing* (D14986),
  - *Nursing Home Life: A Guide for Residents and Families* (D13063),
  - *PERS - Personal Emergency Response System Report* (D12905), (A PERS is an emergency call button worn by individuals living alone.),
  - *A Checklist of Concerns/Resources for Caregivers* (D12895),
  - *Making Wise Decisions for Long Term Care* (D12435),
  - *A Path for Caregivers* (D12957),
  - *Caregiver Resource Kit* (D15267).
- The **Family Caregiver Alliance** provides information for caregivers to find emotional support and respite services. Write to 425 Bush Street, Suite 500, San Francisco, CA 94108, call (415) 434-3388 or go online to *http://www.caregiver.org*
- The **National Alliance for the Mentally Ill** provides information, emotional support, and advocacy through local and state affiliates to families and friends of seriously mentally ill individuals. Write to 2101 Wilson Blvd., Suite 302, Arlington, VA 22201, or call (703) 524-7600.
- **Alzheimer's Disease and Related Disorders Association (ADRDA)** is a non-profit organization which offers assistance and information to Alzheimer's victims and their families through about 200 local chapters nationwide. They can refer clients to barbers, dentists, podiatrists, and other professionals, in the community, who make home visits. Request a free copy of its pamphlets: "If you think someone you know has Alzheimer's Disease," "When the diagnosis is Alzheimer's," and "If you have Alzheimer's Disease: What you should know, what you can do." Write to the ADRDA, at 919 N. Michigan Avenue, Chicago, IL 60611, phone (312) 335-8700, or call toll free in IL (800) 572-6037, Nationwide (800) 272-3900, or check the White Pages for a local listing.

- Fraternal and veterans' organizations, the Veterans Administration, local church or synagogue sponsored charitable groups, religious social-service organizations, such as: Jewish Family Services, Protestant Welfare Agencies, and Catholic Charities, as well as occupational unions often provide some services or maintain retirement homes for members and their spouses.

- Organizations and mutual self-help groups dedicated to individuals suffering from a particular disorder and their families. They provide education and help in managing the specific problems associated with the disorder. Look in the White Pages under the name of the disorder such as: the CANCER INFORMATION SERVICE, DIABETES RESEARCH INSTITUTE, KIDNEY FOUNDATION, OSTOMY HOTLINE; look under the word "National" for organizations such as the NATIONAL STROKE ASSOCIATION; look under the word "American" for such organizations as the AMERICAN CANCER SOCIETY, AMERICAN DIABETES ASSOCIATION, or the AMERICAN LUNG ASSOCIATION. Look in the Yellow Pages under the headings: SOCIAL SERVICE ORGANIZATIONS and ASSOCIATIONS.

Alternative Living Arrangements

When a person cannot, or desires not, to live independently, there are a few choices of alternative living arrangements which can be made. These generally fall into three categories: residential communities, shared living arrangements, or nursing homes. The final choice will depend upon the person's physical, psychological, and financial condition.

Residential or Assisted Living Community

First we will discuss **Residential Communities**, also known as **Continuing Care Retirement Communities**. These communities are usually for senior citizens. In these communities, each person has his or her own personal living space. These range from a hotel room, to an apartment, to a connected or separate home. Some have a number of rooms set aside for those who need total care and those who require some assistance with daily living. Others are located near, or include, a nursing home facility, where residents are transferred if and when the need for care arises. Although many residential communities are privately owned and can be quite expensive, some communities offer this type of living facility for low income individuals. Other communities offer financial assistance to residents in private communities.

The main attraction of residential communities is that they offer independent living to the extent the individual is able to care for his or her own needs. These communities are equipped, to varying degrees, to provide assisted living services when necessary. These services may include dining facilities, maid or housekeeping services, scheduled transportation to local shopping and doctors, planned social activities, recreational facilities, emergency alert systems, a nurse on duty, assisted bathing and personal care, medication administration, special diets and, when needed, full assisted care, either on a temporary or permanent basis. These communities are listed in the Yellow Pages under the headings: RETIREMENT APARTMENTS & HOTELS and RETIREMENT & LIFE CARE COMMUNITIES & HOMES. Visit a number of these communities and compare the services they offer to find the best match to the prospective resident's current and future needs.

Before signing a contract, be sure to:

■ Check the financial stability of the community. Ask for a copy of the most recent financial statement.

■ Ascertain that the associated nursing home is properly accredited. See <u>Continuing Care Facilities or Nursing Homes</u> later in this Chapter.

■ Evaluate the cost in comparison to the prospective resident's financial situation. This is best done by a financial planner.

■ Carefully review the contract. This is best done by an attorney familiar with these contracts.
- The contract should clearly state all costs for residency including:
    ◆ Initial cost of entering the community. What portion, if any, of the down-payment will be refunded to Beneficiaries if the resident dies within a specific number of years;
    ◆ The dollar amount of the basic monthly fee. The services included in the basic fee. The length of time these services will be provided for the basic fee;
    ◆ If services will be provided beyond the basic time limit and, if so, the cost of extending services for a longer period of time;
    ◆ The effect of inflation, if any, upon both basic and additional fees;
    ◆ The amount of increase, if any, of the fee if and when the resident requires additional care and is moved to the nursing home;
    ◆ Should a resident's funds become exhausted, will the community accept Medicaid payment and will Medicaid pay for care for the rest of the resident's life? If not, will the resident be required to move out of the community?
- The cancellation terms and conditions of the contract.
- The affect of marriage, divorce, and death.

AARP and the American Association of Homes for the Aging have produced *The National Continuing Care Directory*, published by AARP and Scott, Foresman and Company, 1865 Minor Street, Des Plaines, IL 60016. You can write and ask for a current price quote or place a credit-card order by calling, toll-free, (800) 627-6565. The directory is a state-by-state listing of retirement communities that provide nursing care, and includes the details of services and costs. Another source of information is the magazine "Where to Retire," available at magazine counters and some Public Libraries.

Shared Housing Programs

A second alternative, for a person who cannot live totally independently, is a **Shared Housing Program,** also known as an **Adult Congregate Living Facility** (ACLF). Shared housing provides peace of mind for concerned family members by providing residents with needed assistance, companionship, and as much independence as possible. Typically run by a government or nonprofit agency, nearly all of these programs plan to add housing and residents.

There are two basic types of shared housing: group-homes and match-ups. The purpose of both is to promote independence through interdependence. In a group-home situation, anywhere from three to 16 seniors and/or handicapped individuals live together as an unrelated family in a large house or apartment. Each person has his or her own bedroom and shares common areas, everyone watches out for each other and has a say in running the household. Some programs have a live-in manager, and some include cooking, laundry and housekeeping services, while in others, the residents help each other with these daily chores.

In a match-up program, a homeowner or apartment dweller opens his or her home to someone who needs a place to live, often a college student. The tenant often provides some services, such as cooking and cleaning, in exchange for reduced or free rent. If you're opening your home to a housemate, be sure to check the person's references. See Chapter 23, "When A Child Is Orphaned," Hiring In-Home Help.

In either situation, if a participant requires assistance with personal care, arrangements must usually be independently made with a home health aide, visiting nurse, or other service provider.

If at all possible, find a program that interviews all participants. These interviews are conducted to help find compatible housemates. Before making a commitment to either of these living situations, meet with all the residents. Ask questions and be alert to personality traits and habits that would annoy you. Evaluate the situation in view of your own needs and ability to be flexible and compromise. Each participant should sign a written agreement detailing his or her duties and the house rules. This can eliminate any misunderstandings in advance. Keep in mind that it will take time to adjust to the new living arrangement, but the rewards make it worthwhile. For more information on shared housing and to locate a program in your area, contact your local Area Agency on Aging, or the National Shared Housing Resource Center (NSHRC), 431 Pine Street, Box KC-893, Burlington, VT 05401, call (802) 862-2727.

Continuing Care Facilities or Nursing Homes

The third alternative living arrangement is a **Nursing Home**. Nursing homes are usually privately owned, hospital-like institutions which provide full care to their residents. Although some offer private rooms, most rooms are made for two occupants. Professional nurses are on duty at all times; however, most of the patient care is provided by nurse assistants. A doctor is usually on call for emergencies and usually visits each patient on a scheduled basis. Some provide physical therapy and respiratory therapy for residents and may have laboratory and X-ray equipment on site. Meals are served in a communal dining room or will be served at the bedside, if necessary. A nursing home should also provide daytime and evening social activities, seven days a week, for those residents capable of participating. These may include on-site movies and live entertainment, games, crafts, exercise and academic classes, pet visitations, and even trips to local shopping centers and attractions. Visit all the nursing homes in the community and check out their services. Be sure your choice meets the physical and psychological needs of the prospective resident. To find care facilities in your community look in the Yellow Pages under the headings: NURSING HOMES and INFORMATION & REFERRAL SERVICES-NURSING HOME.

The facility you choose should be accredited. Check for accreditation by writing to the Continuing Care Accreditation Commission, American Association of Homes and Services for the Aging, 901 E Street, N.W., Suite 500, Washington, D.C. 20004-2037, or call (202) 783-2242. They also offer a list of accredited facilities.

Before signing a contract; tour the facility. Be sure to:

- Look for signs of neglect. Take note of whether residents are lying in bed or properly groomed, dressed, and out of bed. Is the smell of urine or body odor present?
- In shared rooms, are the occupants mentally and socially matched?
- Observe the residents. Do they appear to be involved in the activities? Is morale good?
- Visit the dining room at mealtime. Ask either to be served a meal (there might be a fee) or at least to taste the food. Look at a weekly menu; do residents have choices? Do residents appear to be enjoying the food? Are residents, requiring assistance, fed promptly while the meal is still hot?
- Talk to some of the residents, and ask their opinion of the residence. Compare their answers to the image portrayed by management and the brochures.
- Talk to the staff. Are they responsive to your concerns?
- Observe the staff. Do they appear friendly, respectful, and responsive to the residents? Do they knock before entering a resident's room? Are doors closed and/or curtains pulled during personal care to assure privacy?
- Are residents permitted to have their own furniture and wall decorations in their rooms?
- Will the nursing home permit the resident's personal physician to provide care?
- Do residents have access to eye, foot, hearing, mental health, and dental care?
- Are appropriate religious services conducted on the premises? Are residents visited by the clergy?
- Is there a wheelchair and walker accessible outdoor area? Are chairs available?
- Does the nursing home permit an aide, hired by the family through a home health agency, to provide care or sit with the resident around the clock, if desired?
- Does the home provide physical, occupational, or other therapy, appropriate to the resident's needs? If not, will professionals, hired by the family, be permitted to provide services?
- Is the nursing home equipped to handle all manner of a resident's behavior? Will an unruly resident be discharged?
- Obtain a copy of the contract for review by an attorney. Refer to considerations posed in Residential or Assisted Living Community, above.

Medicare, Medicaid, and Nursing Homes

Federal law and regulations govern nursing homes whose residents receive Medicare or Medicaid benefits and require that nursing homes:

- May not charge the patient any deposits or fees for services covered by Medicare or Medicaid. This is true no matter how long Medicare or Medicaid take to pay, or whether the deposit will eventually be refunded.
- May not require a deposit or prepayment to cover co-insurance charges.
- May not require advance payments from patients who are already residents in a facility, to pay deposits or advance co-payments fees that would be prohibited for new patients.
- May not evict, or threaten to evict, Medicare patients because they are unable to pay a co-payment when it becomes due.
- May bill patients for services not covered by Medicare or Medicaid as costs for those services are incurred.
- Must provide a written notice of non-coverage, if a facility believes that Medicare will not pay for services a patient needs; and may not bill the patient for any services prior to such notice.
- Must give patients a written explanation of their right to request that a claim be submitted for a formal determination of Medicare coverage.
- Must send a "demand bill" to the Medicare intermediary for a determination, if requested by the patient, and is prohibited from billing the patient, except for legitimate co-payments as they become due, until Medicare responds to the demand. The Medicare intermediary must respond to the claim within 90 days.
- May demand payment from the patient if the intermediary denies Medicare coverage for any part of a nursing home stay.

If you have any problems with a long-term-care facility, your first stop should be the "Ombudsman." The ombudsman's number should be posted in a conspicuous place. If it is not, call information or your local Area Agency on Aging Office. If you feel pressed to pay a deposit that you consider improper or have already paid one, contact a Medicare advocacy organization, senior legal aid project, or your Medicare intermediary and ask for help in obtaining a refund. These organizations can also assist you if the nursing home fails to provide written notice of Medicare non-coverage, or refuses to send a demand bill on your behalf. Your state or local Area Agency on Aging should be able to refer you to an advocacy group. The Area Agency on Aging is usually listed in the Blue or White Pages of the phone book under the name of the state, county or city. Illegal deposit or pre-payment demands should be reported to one or more of the following agencies: the state agency that licenses nursing homes in your state, call your local or state Department of Health and ask for referral to the appropriate licensing division; a state or local consumer protection agency; or division of the State Attorney General's Office. Urge them to investigate the charges as unfair business practices.

Some states require facilities to make good the fair market value of lost items even if a waiver was signed to relieve them of responsibility. However, if the facility does not insure its residents' property or maintain a fund to make restitution, it would be wise to expand your homeowner's insurance, if you can, to include the property in a nursing home. Ultimately, it is the nursing home's responsibility to protect residents' property. Under federal regulations, nursing homes must take "reasonable preventive measures" against theft and loss. If there is a loss, report it immediately. If you suspect a theft, you can also call the ombudsman available through your state agency on aging or local Area Agency on Aging, the police, and the agency that licenses the facility. It can reflect on the facility's ability to keep its license.

Protecting the Property of a Communal Living Situation Resident

Ask each facility about procedures for preventing loss or theft. The questions to ask include:

- Are meal trays, trash, and the pockets of clothing in the laundry routinely checked for carelessly left items?
- Does each resident have a personal locked space?
- Does the facility have "claim" days, on which unclaimed items are displayed to residents and families?

You can help avoid loss of the property of a resident of a nursing home or other communal residence by labeling all the property the resident brings to the home with the person's name or Social Security number.

- Clothes can be marked with either a laundry marking pen or sewn in labels.
- Shoes can be marked in the same way.
- Dentures, hearing aids, and eyeglasses can be etched by the doctor or retailer where purchased.
- You can engrave the same on radios, TVs, etc., and/or secure them to the wall, if permitted.
- Make copies of family photos before bringing them to the home.
- Be sure a complete list of all items, in detail, is made at the time of admission. If something is brought later, add it to the list. The administrator of the residence should keep one copy, the resident should keep one copy, and a friend or relative should keep a third copy.

LIVING ON A REDUCED INCOME

Financial Assistance - Sorting Out Your Finances

Friends or relatives who are assisting a surviving spouse with financial matters and investments should not force him or her into any investment, financial, or estate planning devices. The owner of the property should completely understand and be totally comfortable with each decision. This may mean leaving all cash in a savings passbook account or C.D.'s. Although they might not be the wisest choice for financial growth or income, they will not keep the surviving spouse up at night. If it is wise to change the title of property, such as setting up a Living Trust, be sure the person understands the instrument totally and is comfortable with the decision.

Living on a Reduced or Fixed Income = Budgeting

The first step in formulating a budget is to determine your current monthly expenses. We have provided a "Budget Calculation Record" on page R-42, for your convenience. This means keeping a careful record of all the bills you pay and all the money you spend. Remember to include yearly expenses by dividing them by twelve. Then, determine if your income from work and/or retirement, and benefits, plus income from investments are sufficient to pay these expenses. Since funds may currently be available from insurance policy proceeds, or lump sum distributions from an employer, or other pension plan, use them to reduce or eliminate outstanding debts. Start by paying off all credit card debts (their interest is usually high). Then, establish a cash reserve in a pass-book savings or money market account sufficient to cover at least three months' expenses. If your income is not sufficient to pay your basic living expenses, apply for government assistance programs. These may include food stamps, housing subsidies, Supplemental Security Income, public transportation discounts, utility company discounts, and more. For more information, see Chapter 26, "Providing Care for a Dependent Adult Survivor," Chapter 24, "Social Security, Medicare, and Medicaid," and Chapter 25, "Employer Health and Pension Benefits." Free or low-cost counseling on debt reduction and consolidation, as well as, effective credit management is available from the Consumer Credit Counseling Service. Call this non-profit organization at (800) 388-2227 for referral to a local office. Although classic wisdom says a bereaved person should not make any major life changes for at least one year after the death, if it is clear that an individual cannot afford to maintain the current residence, a choice to sell it, before it is foreclosed, is a wise decision.

Reverse Mortgages

Senior citizens (age 62 or older), who have equity in their homes, may be able to obtain a **Reverse Annuity Mortgage** (RAM). This is known as a "home equity conversion plan" backed by the Federal Housing Administration (FHA). A "reverse mortgage" is a loan from a bank or mortgage company using your house as the collateral. However, instead of paying you the lump sum of the loan when you apply for the mortgage, a reverse mortgage pays you a monthly income for life. The amount of money you get monthly depends on your age, the value of your home, and how much equity you have in the house. Then, after your death, or when the house is sold, the lender gets back all the money it paid to you, plus interest. Just like any other mortgage, you must also pay closing costs and associated fees. Before choosing a reverse mortgage, you should investigate thoroughly the effect the added income will have upon other benefits you are currently receiving or may be eligible to receive. If you cannot evaluate the possible effects yourself, consult an attorney or financial planner. For more information call the Federal National Mortgage Association (800) 732-6643. For information or to file a complaint, write to the Department of Housing and Urban Development, Office of Single Family Housing, 451 Seventh Street, S.W., Room 9272, Washington, D.C. 20410, or call (202) 708-2700. For a list of lenders who make RAM loans, send a self-addressed, stamped envelope and $1 to the National Center for Home Equity Conversion, 7373 147th Street, W., Suite 115, Apple Valley, MN 55124 and ask for the "Reverse Mortgage Locator."

Credit Report

By law, you are entitled to receive a free copy of your credit report if it has led to a denial of credit, employment, or insurance. Otherwise, credit bureaus charge varying amounts for a report. Knowing what is in your credit report is important, because bad credit can affect your ability to get a loan, a mortgage, or a job. Although few reports contain errors, it is wise to be sure yours is not one of them by reviewing it periodically. If you find an error, the agency has 30 days from the date it receives your complaint to prove or correct the information. You can write to the credit bureaus and request your credit report. With your request, include your full name, current address, and previous addresses going back five years, your date of birth and Social Security number, spouse's first name if married, along with a check for the correct charge, if any, and proof of your current address. Be sure to sign your request. You may want to call first and ask for current charges. Local numbers for credit bureaus are listed in the Yellow Pages under CREDIT REPORTING AGENCIES. The three major credit reporting agencies are:

- **Equifax Inc.**, Information Service Center, Consumer Department, P.O. Box 704241, Atlanta, GA 30374-0241, or call (800) 685-1111, charges $8 per report. However, the report is free if you have been denied credit within the past 30 days.
- **Trans Union Credit Information Co.**, National Consumer Relations, P.O. Box 7000, North Olmsted, OH 44070, or call (800) 851-2674, charges $8 per report. However, the report is free if you have been denied credit within the past 30 days.
- **TRW Credit Data** — TRW Complimentary Credit Report Request, P.O. Box 2350, Chatsworth, CA 91313-2350, or call (800) 682-7654, for one free copy per year of your own credit report. Additional reports cost $7.50 each in most states.

Finding Employment

Jobs for Seniors

The Senior Community Service Employment Program (SCSEP) is a federally funded program, administered by local social service agencies. They can offer part-time (20 hours a week) jobs in government offices and non-profit agencies to individuals 55 or older with limited financial resources. SCSEP is available to single and married seniors who meet the financial requirements. Typically, they offer clerical jobs paying minimum wage. If a person is not interested in these jobs, they will provide help in resume-writing, interviewing, and self-esteem building. Some offer job placement services with private employers, either in regular or federally subsidized jobs.

Displaced Homemakers

The loss of a spouse often leaves a widow (or widower) facing the prospect of finding his or her first job, or re-entering the workforce after a long absence. This is a scary situation for most. They may feel alienated, unskilled, and fear they do not have what it takes to get a good job. Often, their job skills are out of date. Recognizing this need, and ready to help, is the National Displaced Homemakers Network, Suite 300, 1625 K Street, N.W., Washington, D.C. 20006, phone number (202) 467-6346. Through local outreach programs, they offer a variety of services for widowed and divorced men and women who are experiencing trouble entering the workforce. The services include training, education, mentoring, individual counseling, and job placement. Contact them to receive information about local programs, or call the community college nearest you. Many offer similar programs. A couple of publications which may save you some trouble are: *Job Hunting: Should You Pay?* and *Job Ads, Job Scams and 900 Numbers*. They are available free from the Public Reference Branch, Federal Trade Commission, Sixth and Pennsylvania Avenue, N.W., Washington, D.C. 20580. Additionally, information on local job-readiness and training programs, financial-aid options, health insurance rights, and child-support agencies is also available from Women Work: The National Network for Women's Employment, call (800) 235-2732.

251

Educational Grants and Financial Assistance

Federal and state scholarships or grants are available to people of all ages because the law prohibits discrimination. Check with the financial-aid office at the technical schools or colleges you wish to attend to get information about grants and scholarships. Apply for as many as you can; then, if approved, you can choose the one which is most beneficial for you. For information about federal programs, contact the Federal Student Financial Aid Information Centers, Department of Education, P.O. Box 84, Washington, D.C. 20044, phone (800) 4-FEDAID (433-3243), or go online to *http://www.ed.gov* Ask for a free copy of its publication *The Student Guide, Financial Aid from the U.S. Department of Education*, and an "Application for Federal Student Aid." There are also a number of publications in libraries and bookstores on scholarships and student financial-aid. Also, check with the United Student Aid Funds, Inc., 11100 USA Pkwy., Fishers, IN 46038, phone (317) 849-6510 or (800) 824-7044. Never pay a firm to find scholarship funds for you.

Temporary Personnel Agencies

To gain immediate employment and to enhance your chances of obtaining full-time work, try signing up with a temporary personnel agency. Most will test your current skills, some will test for potential, and they can recommend business skill courses you can take to enhance your skills. Some provide training, as well as benefits, such as health insurance and vacations.

When you sign with an agency, you become its employee. When an employer calls the agency requesting a worker for a particular job, the agency calls one of its employees and presents the details of the assignment. When offered a job through the agency, you have the freedom, to accept or refuse the job. Also, as the agency's employee, you are free to leave an assigned job just by notifying the temporary agency. The decision of which job you will accept and when you will leave it is totally yours. You will be offered another assignment when a job is available.

Although all jobs start as temporary positions, they can become permanent. Often employers request temporary workers when their businesses are expanding or when a regular employee is on leave for an extended period. Some employers request temporary workers when they are looking for regular employees. This method of hiring saves the employer the hassle of placing ads in newspapers, conducting hiring interviews, and cumbersome record-keeping. If the employer is pleased with the work of the temporary worker, an offer of regular employment can be made. Often the employer may have to pay the temporary agency a fee for hiring one of its employees.

From the employees perspective, it is an ideal situation. You get to see the work you will be required to do, the people with whom you will be working, and the atmosphere in which you will be working. If you do not like the situation; you can refuse the position. You are still an employee of the temporary agency.

Chapter

28

ESTATE PLANNING
FOR A
SURVIVING SPOUSE

Reviewing all the financial affairs of the decedent presents an ideal opportunity to also review and establish or revise the **Estate Plan** of the surviving spouse. Estate planning allows you to designate your beneficiaries, provide for the management of your assets if you are incapacitated, name a guardian for young children, and eliminate or reduce probate costs and, maybe, Estate Taxes. Although this chapter is primarily directed to a surviving spouse, it may be wise to remind other survivors, who may have named the decedent as a beneficiary, trustee, guardian, etc., that they need to review these designations and make revisions as necessary.

Estate planning tools, many of which we have given you a working knowledge of in this book, include: Wills, Trusts, joint ownership, gifts, sales, family annuities, and other arrangements which are used to accomplish planning objectives. First, as has been previously pointed out, everyone should have a Will to transfer property not included in a probate avoidance device. Second, choose which probate avoidance devices you wish to establish. These include: formal and informal trusts; giving gifts; selling property; buying insurance and annuities; and specifying beneficiaries on bank accounts, insurance policies, etc., as appropriate to the amount of property and the family relationships involved. See Chapter 2, "Wills and Probate," Chapter 3, "Trusts," Chapter 4, "Wills and Trusts Compared," and Chapter 5, "Property Ownership." The existing Will and probate avoidance devices of the survivors, especially a surviving spouse, should be reviewed. If the deceased person was the sole beneficiary, or only joint owner, new provisions must be made to assure the passage of property to a desired beneficiary. We have included in Chapter 7, "Property Transfer Breakdown," statements and questions that should be considered regarding beneficiaries and ways of holding property before contacting the holder of the property of the decedent. Remember, if the sole designated beneficiary of property predeceases you, the property will pass under the laws of intestacy of the state.

253

Providing for Your Health and Financial Well-being

In addition to the legal papers necessary to transfer property to beneficiaries, there is a third consideration in estate planning. These are documents which provide for someone to handle your affairs if you become seriously ill or incompetent and unable to do so yourself. These tools include a Durable Power of Attorney, Joint Ownership, Living Trust, and a Health-Care Proxy. An attorney should draft the Will and formal Trust Agreements to be sure they conform to the legal requirements of the state. Additionally, an attorney familiar with "elder-law" can assist in decisions about what probate avoidance instruments would best suit your particular circumstances. You may also seek help from a financial planner. See Chapter 17, "Financial Planners." There are numerous books, as well as computer software programs, on estate planning strategies that can help you make planning decisions.

Durable Power of Attorney

A **Power of Attorney** is a document which allows whomever you, as the **Principal**, designate as your agent, known as the **Attorney-in-fact**, to do such things as sign tax returns, transfer assets into a trust, and make financial decisions for you. A plain power of attorney gives these powers to an agent, either for a specified period of time, or to handle a specific financial matter and, usually, his or her powers end if the principal becomes incapacitated. However, if you intend the powers to be given to the agent only in the event that you become incompetent and unable to conduct your own affairs, you must execute a **Durable Power of Attorney**. In most states, a power of attorney is durable only if it stipulates it will continue in effect even when the principal is incompetent. There may be other restrictions and qualifiers, which vary from state to state. Although fill-in-the-blank forms are available in stationary stores, it is usually wise to have a durable power of attorney drafted with the help of an attorney.

Even if most of your property is in a living trust, which provides for a successor trustee to handle your financial affairs if you are unable, it is wise to also have a power of attorney as a back-up for property not included in the trust, or if the successor trustee is unable to perform the duties. To avoid confusion, you might consider making the successor trustee the primary agent, and naming a successor attorney-in-fact. Keep in mind that, unlike the successor trustee of a living trust who retains control after the originator's death, the power of the agent lapses (ends) upon your death.

Although a durable power of attorney states that the agent has full discretion over all your assets, or only those you specify, it is not necessarily accepted by all financial institutions. Therefore, it may be necessary for you and the agent to sign a special power of attorney form obtained from brokerages and insurance companies. You may also be required to have the agent sign as a joint owner on your bank accounts and safe deposit boxes, in order to give them access to these. In addition, forms must be signed with government agencies to handle benefits paid through Social Security, Veterans Administration, Railroad Retirement, Etc., in order to have the attorney-in-fact given "Representative Payeeship." This does not mean that he or she can just take over at will. You can have the person of your choice act as your agent to sign the appropriate forms, but if he or she does not know the brokerage or bank account or box numbers, etc., he or she really does not have access. The attorney who prepares a power of attorney should collect the special forms most banks, brokerages, insurance firms, and government institutions provide. If the attorney does not do this, after you have executed the power of attorney, you should deliver copies of it to the institutions that handle your finances and obtain from them a letter saying they will honor the arrangements. This will avoid delays if, and when, the document must be used. If a financial, or other, institution declines to honor the power of attorney because it is not specific enough, the agent will have to go to Court to get an "Order of Guardianship" or sue the institution for specific performance (require the institution to accept the power of attorney).

Be aware that, depending upon the size of the accounts, making an agent a joint owner may cause some income tax problems, so consult an attorney or accountant, before signing the forms. You can undo the durable power of attorney by writing a letter to the institutions saying that the power is revoked.

Bear in mind that, if you become incapacitated while all your property is in your name alone, and if you have not designated someone to manage your finances in a living trust or durable power of attorney; anyone can go to Court and request guardianship for you. See Chapter 3, "Trusts." This has two drawbacks: first, it costs money to go to Court as well as time and trouble; and second, the person appointed as the guardian or conservator of your property may not be the person you would have chosen or trusted, or it may even be a stranger who is a professional conservator.

A durable power of attorney is not only for single people; it is a necessary document for anyone, even your spouse, to handle your individual property and in some cases, your jointly held property. Without a power of attorney, if one spouse becomes incapacitated and the other wishes to sell, transfer, or use jointly owned property (other than bank accounts) as collateral for a loan, he or she cannot do it until a legal representative has been appointed by the Courts to authorize the transaction on behalf of the incapacitated spouse.

Before going to the attorney to have your power of attorney drawn up, you should carefully consider who you want to act as your attorney-in-fact, and alternate agent; exactly what property you wish them to control and its location; and the extent of the power you wish them to have. The attorney-in-fact may be an individual (relative or friend), a professional (attorney, accountant, etc.), or a bank or trust company. Be sure to bring the name, address, and phone number of each financial institution where property is located, and all account or other related identifying numbers. Decide in advance if you wish the agent to have limited or total discretion over the property. Should the agent have the power to make gifts, forgive debts, fund trusts, make elections and disclaimers, etc.?

Living Will

In addition to providing for your financial well-being if you become incompetent, you should also consider appointing someone to make decisions for your physical well-being, in the event you become unable to make them yourself. This can be done by executing a **Health-Care Proxy**, which may include a **Living Will and Durable Power of Attorney for Health**. Regulations vary from state to state, as do the formats of the documents, and some states do not recognize them at all. However, even in states that do not recognize the documents under law, they can be helpful to physicians and the courts in making health care decisions for a patient who cannot speak for him- or herself.

With the health care proxy or durable power of attorney for health, you delegate power to a particular person, persons, or physician to make decisions regarding your medical treatment at any time that you cannot make these decisions yourself. By specifying who will speak for you, this document can avoid confusion when permission is sought for an operation or other treatment, especially if relatives disagree as to the treatment they think you should be given. They are most often used when a person is in the last stages of a painful disease, such as cancer, or in a persistent vegetative state resulting from such things as an accident or stroke. They may also be used when you are not terminally ill but your condition prevents you from making or expressing a decision about the medical care that should, or should not, be given to you.

With a living will you express your desires as a guideline to the agent. You can specifically outline what life saving measures are acceptable to prolong your life if you are terminally ill or injured. Before completing a living will, you should consider what life support you would not want to have to prolong your life when there is no hope that you will ever again be a functioning human being. These measures include, but are not limited to: cardio-pulmonary resuscitation, respirators, artificial feeding (through intravenous, abdominal, or naso-gastric tubes), oxygen, surgery, antibiotics, etc. You can specify at what point in your deterioration you would want these measures withdrawn. It should be stipulated that you would want medications and personal care to limit pain and make you as comfortable as possible. Also, include what measures are to be taken to honor any arrangements you have made regarding organ donation. Women of child bearing age should specify what they would want done, if they are pregnant at the moment of decision.

These documents have become necessary because of the advances in the medical field, which allow doctors to keep people alive under almost any circumstances. Even when there is no quality to the life, the body can be kept alive. Additionally, doctors are legally bound to use all efforts to keep someone alive with life support, unless that person has recorded health care directives in a health care proxy. For further information and forms individualized to your state's requirements, contact Choice In Dying, Inc., 200 Varick Street, New York, NY 10014-4810 or call (800) 989-WILL. It can also supply information about "Do Not Resuscitate" forms. Where permitted by law, these allow the patient's doctor to order that no extraordinary life saving measures be taken by emergency medical technicians or paramedics when they are called to the home.

Tidbit: If you are interested in organ donation:
- Go to your local Bureau of Motor Vehicles, Drivers License Division;
- Contact the Living Bank, P.O. Box 6725, Houston, TX 77265-6725 or call (800) 528-2971; or,
- Request a free Uniform Organ Donor Card by calling (800) 622-9010.

Executing the Documents

All these documents (with the possible exception of a living will) must be signed and witnessed before a Notary Public. If an attorney draws up the documents, they will handle the notarization process for you. However, if you choose to use fill-in-the-blank forms or draw them up yourself, you must go to a Notary Public for the signing. Be sure to check how many witnesses are necessary in your state for the document to be legally binding. It is not necessary for Notaries to read or understand the contents of the documents they notarize. Notaries may want to know what type of document is being placed before them, in case they are later called to testify to its authenticity. In some states they may also be required to testify that you were of sound mind, not under duress to sign, and understood the nature of the document you signed. Therefore, the Notary may ask you some questions to determine your state of mind. Notaries will also ask for identification of all parties signing the document.

Medicaid Estate Planning

Eligibility rules for Medicaid vary widely from state to state. However, as a rule, a single person on Medicaid in a nursing-home can keep only $2000 in cash; a healthy spouse is allowed to keep no more than $68,000. Some assets aren't counted in those totals, and the trick is to move as much money as possible into exempt categories. Of course, the legal and tax aspects of any strategies should be thoroughly investigated before making any transfers of money or other property. The best way to execute these transfers in a manner which would fill your needs, and not cost you, or the beneficiary, unnecessary tax or other repercussions, is to consult a member of the growing industry of elder-law attorneys. These attorneys guide clients in the fine points of **Medicaid Estate Planning**, all of which are perfectly legal. In this chapter, we are giving just a brief overview of some strategies you may consider. Of course, all of this would be unnecessary if a long term health care plan is established by the government.

In most states, a primary residence is exempt and there's no limit on the value. Where this is true, money can be sheltered by paying off the mortgage, remodeling the current house, or buying a more expensive house. Many states do not count household goods, so money can be sheltered by investing in new household furnishings, from appliances to fine art and jewelry. A stay-at-home spouse is also allowed to keep a car, no matter how expensive. This strategy would not help a widowed spouse who wishes to shelter money in case he or she is later in a situation where he or she will have to enter a nursing home; and eventually sell all of the assets to pay for care and then qualify for Medicaid.

Single or widowed individuals must find other ways to shelter their assets. This can be done in a number of ways; the catch is that most states require that some sheltering strategies be completed no less than 30 months before application is made for Medicaid or the transfer of assets will not be recognized. It cannot be left for the last minute. One method of sheltering assets

257

so they can be passed to chosen beneficiaries, instead of being paid to a nursing home, is to establish an irrevocable **Medicaid Trust**. The grantor receives the income from the trust; however, he or she loses control of the property and cannot revoke the Trust. See Chapter 3, "Trusts." Although this method can be used to shelter property the grantor owns, most states require that a nursing home resident's individual income must go toward paying the nursing home bill. A stay-at-home spouse can keep income that comes in his or her own name, no matter how much it is. Other ways a Medicaid estate planner may suggest of conserving money for heirs is to:

- Pre-pay your funeral expenses and buy a burial plot;
- Purchase long-term care insurance. See Chapter 18, "Insurance and Insurance Agents";
- Transfer (give) money directly to your beneficiaries. Of course, that money is then theirs to spend. Often, these gifts are made with a verbal agreement that the beneficiary will use the money for your benefit, if needed in the future. In this case, make the gift to the beneficiary alone, and not in the names of the beneficiary and his or her spouse. Then, instruct the beneficiary not to put the money in a joint account. Additionally, if there is a divorce, the law in most states will let the beneficiary keep the full gift. See Chapter 5, "Property Ownership." Although a gift may consist of appreciated property, such as stock, this would erase the benefit of stepped-up basis on inherited property. See Chapter 9, "Valuing Property";
- Transfer assets under a **Sale-leaseback** or **Gift-leaseback** agreement. This means that a person sells or gives his or her home to the beneficiary but continues to live there, paying rent. If your state provides a "Homestead Exemption" from the property tax of a resident-owner, the benefit may be lost. An attorney's advice can prove very valuable;
- Buy a life insurance policy and transfer ownership of it into an irrevocable "Insurance Trust."

Funeral Pre-Need Plans

The three main advantages of pre-planning are: to prevent emotional overspending by distraught survivors; to allow you to choose the products and services you want; and usually, to "freeze" the costs at today's prices. Most funeral, cemetery, and crematorium directors offer pre-arranged or pre-financed services. There should be no charge for pre-need planning. You can either visit or call two or three providers to compare costs, or you may wish to consider joining a local memorial society. These are nonprofit organizations dedicated to the ideal of inexpensive funerals. For more information, contact the Funeral and Memorial Societies of America, 6900 Lost Lake Road, Egg Harbor, WI 54209, call (800) 458-5563. When you meet with the provider:

- Ask for a price list for the pre-payment products and services offered. Funeral directors are required by the FTC Funeral Rule to make the price list available.
- Compare the prices of the products and services you have selected to find the best value.
- Do not allow anyone to pressure you into purchasing merchandise or services, you do not want or can not afford.

The type of plan you choose depends upon your personal desires. The following is a short list of the types of services available from different providers:

- **Funeral Homes** provide a variety of merchandise and services, from the traditional funeral and burial, to memorial services and cremation. They can also arrange for the shipment of the remains to any other funeral home in the country, or in the world. They have a selection of caskets with a wide variety of prices and burial plans.
- **Cremation Providers**, such as the Cremation Association of North America (CANA) or the National Cremation Society offer cremation services and provide a selection of urns for permanent containment of the cremated remains. The urns may be placed in a **columbarium** (a building or structure with family and single "niche" spaces); or, family plots may be used. Cemeteries often permit the interment of more than one person in an adult space if cremation has occurred. In many cemeteries, there are also specially designed areas for this purpose, which are called urn gardens. In most communities, cremated remains may also legally be scattered as desired, and some crematories provide scattering gardens.
- **The Neptune Society** provides pre-need cremation plans and scattering of the ashes at sea.

Pre-Paying

Although you can pre-arrange without pre-paying, most people do pre-pay for the arrangements they make. Usually, pre-payment is either made in a lump-sum at the time of arrangement, or installment payments are made over a number of months or years, until the total cost of the pre-arranged merchandise and services has been paid. There are no federal regulations, and few states have regulations concerning how companies are to invest or protect pre-need funds. The money paid for pre-need plans can be held in a variety of trust plans or accounts. The most common are:

- An **Individual Revocable Trust** — where a person opens an "in trust for" or "pay on death" account with a bank, naming the provider as the beneficiary.
- An **Individual Insurance Policy** — where a person buys an insurance policy with a face amount equal to the cost of the services and merchandise, then names the provider as the beneficiary upon the death of the owner.
- A **Regulated Trust Fund** — where each member's pre-payment funds are usually placed in a separate fund, to be managed by a trustee until they are needed to pay for services and merchandise.

Before Signing a Contract

Before you sign a pre-need contract, get a copy and review it, to make sure you understand all the terms and conditions of the contract, especially any cancellation and refund policies. If you have any questions, be sure they are answered in writing on the contract. Depending upon the type of plan offered, these are suggested questions:

- If the cost of merchandise and services increases before the need for them arises, does the provider guarantee to assume all risk that the original price, plus interest, will pay for the designated merchandise and services?

- If the bank account or insurance policy is worth more when you die than the services and merchandise requested, what happens to any excess funds?
- Who receives the interest generated by a trust fund?
- Who must pay taxes on that interest?
- Under what circumstances can you cancel the contract?
- What is the penalty for cancelling the policy?
- Under what circumstances is the pre-payment refundable, in part or in full?
- What happens if the funeral home or other service provider goes out of business?
- How portable is the plan? If you move, will a local provider honor the contract for services and merchandise at the agreed price? This is usually accomplished by providers who belong to a trust which is transferrable to other member providers throughout the country, or with a fully refundable plan.

Check the reputation of the provider(s) carefully:

- Call the state's department of professional regulation to be sure they are properly licensed or registered;
- Call the local Better Business Bureau consumer protection office, State Attorney General, or the Funeral Board to see if any complaints have been filed against the provider.

Check the stability of the investment vehicle and institution where funds are placed:

- Life insurance:
  - Almost all states have a guarantee fund which protects policy holders if an insurance company fails. If the program is financed through an insurance policy, check out the insurance company with the State Insurance Commissioner and ask if the state will cover the policy if the company goes broke. See Chapter 18, "Insurance and Insurance Agents," General.
- Trust Accounts or Funds:
  - If funds are placed in a financial institution, be sure they are FDIC insured. See Chapter 19, "Financial Institutions";
  - Some states maintain an enforcement agency to audit and investigate trust funds and have established a guarantee fund, or similar arrangement to pay losses due to fraud, or funeral homes that go out of business; check to be sure your plan is covered.

Whether or not you pre-arrange your services, it would be wise to copy "Information Needed For The Death Certificate" on page R-35, "Memorial and Funeral Arrangements" on page R-36, "Optional Information For Memorial Book or Obituary" on page R-37, and "Achievements" on page R-38, and complete the information, to allow for accurate information when the need arises. This is especially important if no one knows the information and would have to search for records to provide it. For help in filling out these forms, and more information, see Chapter 1, "When A Person Dies."

BIBLIOGRAPHY

Throughout this book, readers have been referred to publications which can afford more detailed information than was presented. The following is a list of source materials, though not quoted, were used as research materials for this publication. Consulting these publications may prove helpful to our readers. We, of course, could not mention all publications available on each subject matter covered, therefore, this list is by necessity brief and no slight is intended toward authors whose works are not listed.

AMERICAN ASSOCIATION OF RETIRED PERSONS in cooperation with the FEDERAL TRADE COMMISSION. *Facts About Financial Planners*, Federal Trade Commission, Office of Consumer and Business Education, 6th and Pennsylvania Avenue, N. W., Washington, D.C. 20580: 1990.
⸺ : *Product Report — Pre-Paying Your Funeral?*, Federal Trade Commission Funeral Rule Statement, AARP, 1909 K Street, N.W., Washington, D.C. 20049: 1988.
AMERICAN MOVERS CONFERENCE (AMC). *Moving With Pets and Plants* and *Guide To A Satisfying Move*, 2200 Mill Road, Alexandria, VA 22314.
AMERICAN STOCK EXCHANGE, INC., CHICAGO BOARD OPTIONS EXCHANGE, INC., NEW YORK STOCK EXCHANGE, INC., PACIFIC STOCK EXCHANGE, INC., AND PHILADELPHIA STOCK EXCHANGE, INC. Characteristics and Risks of Standardized Options: 1994.
FEDERAL EMERGENCY MANAGEMENT AGENCY. *In The Event Of A Flood — Tips to Minimize Loss of Life and Property*, Federal Insurance Administration, National Flood Insurance Program: 1990.
⸺ : and the AMERICAN RED CROSS. *Repairing Your Flooded Home*, FEMA Publications, P.O. Box 70274, Washington, D.C. 20024, or publication number ARC 4477 from the local Red Cross: 1992.
INTERSTATE COMMERCE COMMISSION. *Helpful Tips in Planning Your Interstate Move*, Office Of Compliance And Consumer Assistance, Room 4412, 12th and Constitution Avenue, N.W., Washington, D.C. 20423.
⸺ : *When You Move: Your Rights and Responsibilities*, Washington, D.C. 20423: 1983.
NATIONAL ASSOCIATION OF INSURANCE COMMISSIONERS with the HEALTH CARE FINANCING ADMINISTRATION OF THE UNITED STATES DEPARTMENT OF HEALTH AND HUMAN SERVICES. *1992 Guide to Health Insurance for People with Medicare:* 1992.
NATIONAL FUTURES ASSOCIATION. *Investment Swindles: How They Work and How to Avoid Them*, 200 West Madison Street, Suite 1600, Chicago, IL 60606: 1987.
⸺ : in association with the COMMODITY FUTURE TRADING COMMISSION. *Understanding Opportunities and Risks In Futures Trading*, National Futures Association, 200 West Madison Street, Suite 1600, Chicago, IL 60606 and Commodity Future Trading Commission, 2033 K Street, N.W., Washington, D.C. 20581: 1990.
UNITED STATES DEPARTMENT OF AGRICULTURE with the AMERICAN COUNCIL OF LIFE INSURANCE. *A Consumer's Guide To Life Insurance*, 1001 Pennsylvania Avenue, N.W., Washington, D.C. 20004: 1992.
UNITED STATES DEPARTMENT OF HEALTH AND HUMAN SERVICES. *Where to Write for Vital Records - Births, Deaths, Marriages, and Divorces*, Public Health Service, Centers for Disease Control, National Center For Health Statistics (NCHS), Hyattville, MD: 1992.
⸺ : *Understanding Social Security*, Social Security Administration, Baltimore, MD 21235: 1992.

UNITED STATES DEPARTMENT OF HEALTH AND HUMAN SERVICES. *Social Security Handbook "1993"* (11th Edition), Social Security Administration, Baltimore, MD 21235: 1993.

—— : *Medicare Q& A — 60 Commonly Asked Questions About Medicare*, Health Care Financing Administration: 1992.

—— : *Kids They're Worth Every Penny, Handbook On Child Support Enforcement*, Administration for Children and Families, Office of Child Support Enforcement, 360 L'Enfant Promenade, S.W., Washington, DC 20447: 1989.

UNITED STATES DEPARTMENT OF LABOR. *How To File a Claim for Your Benefits*, PWBA's Division of Public Affairs, Pension and Welfare Benefits Administration, Washington, D.C. 20210: 1994.

—— : *Health Benefits Under the Consolidated Omnibus Budget Reconciliation Act (COBRA)*, Pension and Welfare Benefits Administration, Omnibus Budget Reconciliation Act (COBRA), 200 Constitution Avenue, N. W., (Room N-5658), Washington. D.C. 20210: 1994.

UNITED STATES DEPARTMENT OF THE TREASURY. *Looking Out For #2 — A Married Couple's Guide to Understanding Your Benefit Choices at Retirement from a Defined Contribution Plan*, Internal Revenue Service: 1991.

—— : *Looking Out For #2 — A Married Couple's Guide to Understanding Your Benefit Choices at Retirement from a Defined Benefit Plan*: 1991.

—— : *U S Savings Bonds - Buyer's Guide 1993-1994*, U. S, Savings Bond Division, Washington, D.C. 20226: 1993.

—— : *Information about Marketable Treasury Securities (Bills, Notes, and Bonds) Sold at Original Issue*, Bureau of the Public Debt: 1990.

—— : *Buying Treasury Securities*, Bureau of the Public Debt: 1995.

DEPARTMENT OF THE TREASURY, INTERNAL REVENUE SERVICE. 1993.

—— : Publication 17 *Your Federal Income Tax For Individuals*,

—— : Publication 463 *Travel, Entertainment, and Gift Expenses*,

—— : Publication 525 *Taxable and Nontaxable Income*,

—— : Publication 544 *Sales and Other Dispositions of Assets*,

—— : Publication 550 *Investment Income and Expenses*,

—— : Publication 551 *Basis of Assets*,

—— : Publication 552 *Recordkeeping for Individual's*,

—— : Publication 554 *Sales and Other Dispositions of Assets*,

—— : Publication 559 *Tax Information for Survivors, Executors, and Administrators*,

—— : Publication 590 *Individual Retirement Arrangements (IRA's)*,

—— : Publication 917 *Business Use of a Car*,

—— : Publication 937 *Employment Taxes and Information Returns*,

—— : *Instructions for Form 3903 — Moving Expenses*,

—— : *Instructions for Form 1041 and Schedules A, B, D, G, J, and K-1— U.S. Fiduciary Income Tax Return*,

—— : *Guide to Free Tax Services — Free Tax Help Every Season*.

UNITED STATES DEPARTMENT OF VETERANS AFFAIRS. *Federal Benefits for Veterans and Dependents*, Washington, D.C. 20420: 1992.

UNITED STATES OFFICE OF CONSUMER AFFAIRS. Consumer's Resource Handbook: 1992.

A single copy of publications authored by departments of the United States government is available from the Consumer Information Catalog, Pueblo, CO 81002. Write and request the catalog which lists the publications available, including cost and ordering information. Or go on-line to the Consumer Information Center at *http://www.pueblo.gsa.gov*

INDEX

Accounting Records

and

Worksheets

SAFE DEPOSIT BOX INVENTORY RECORD

INSTITUTION WHERE LOCATED: _____

ADDRESS: _____

BOX NUMBER: _____

DATE OPENED: _____

ITEM DESCRIPTION	DATE	ADDED TO ASSET RECORD	DATE	PROPERTY DELIVERED TO	NOTES

This is a pass through record. Use it to list the contents of the box as things are removed and placed either in another safe deposit box or with similar documents.
Directions: Enter the description of the item, then the date it is listed on the proper asset record and the asset record used. Then list the date the actual property is moved and where it is placed, or to whom it is given.

R-1

TANGIBLE PERSONAL PROPERTY INVENTORY AND SALE RECORD

ADDRESS: _____

ROOM: _____

ITEM NUMBER	PROPERTY	APPRAISED VALUE DATE OF DEATH					TRANSFER OR SALE						FINAL VALUE	
	DESCRIPTION	DATE	PROBATE	NON-PROBATE	VALUE SET BY	DATE	BENEFICIARY	AMOUNT	DEPOSITED TO	NET GAIN		PROBATE	NON-PROBATE
TOTALS:													

This record is used to inventory and keep track of the personal property of the decedent, and, if there is a sale, to record the proceeds from the sale.
Directions: Enter the complete description of the item. When a value is placed on it, by you or the appraiser, enter the date and value and who placed the value and put this value under the appropriate probate or non-probate column. If the item is given to a beneficiary, the beneficiary should sign the form if possible. If the item is sold, enter the amount received and where the funds were deposited. Then place the value received in the appropriate probate or non-probate column. Funds received from the sale of small items should be listed in the final column and identified as Miscellaneous.

R-2

COLLECTIBLES BASIS RECORD

ITEM NUMBER	PROPERTY		ORIGINAL BASIS INFORMATION						PREVIOUS TRANSFER				
	DESCRIPTION	DATE	ORIGINAL COST	RESTORA- TION COST	SOURCE OF FUNDS	TITLE	TOTAL VALUE	DATE	VALUE	APPRAISER	TITLE PRIOR TO	TITLE AFTER
TOTALS:												

This record is used to record the original value, as well as the value at the time of a previous transfer. It is necessary to establish the basis of collectibles, because unlike most personal property who's value depreciates with time, the value of a collectible usually appreciates with time.

Directions: Fill in if, and as appropriate, to each collectible item. After determining the basis, include the item on the "Tangible Personal Property Inventory and Sale Record" on page R-2.

APPRAISER: _____ _____

COLLECTOR: _____ _____

ADDRESS: _____ _____

PHONE #: _____ _____

TYPE ITEMS: _____ _____

FINANCIAL ACCOUNTS BASIS AND TRANSFER RECORD

INSTITUTION	DATE	ACTION	CASH BALANCE	DEPOSITS		WITHDRAWALS			VALUE	
				AMOUNT	SOURCE OF FUNDS	CHECK NUMBER	AMOUNT	DEPOSITED TO	PROBATE	NON-PROBATE
NAME:										
ADDRESS:										
ACCOUNT #:										
TYPE OF ACCOUNT:										
TITLE:										
EXPIRATION DATE:										
NAME:										
ADDRESS:										
ACCOUNT #:										
TYPE OF ACCOUNT:										
TITLE:										
EXPIRATION DATE:										
NAME:										
ADDRESS:										
ACCOUNT #:										
TYPE OF ACCOUNT:										
TITLE:										
EXPIRATION DATE:										
NAME:										
ADDRESS:										
ACCOUNT #:										
TYPE OF ACCOUNT:										
TITLE:										
EXPIRATION DATE:										
TOTALS:										

This record is used to keep track of bank, savings and loan, or credit union accounts which will be transferred or closed.
Directions: Use one section to enter the information for each individual account. Then enter the appropriate information under each column across.

R-4

INVESTMENT BASIS RECORD

INVESTMENT DESCRIPTION	ORIGINAL PURCHASE INFORMATION							PREVIOUS TRANSFER					VALUE DATE OF DEATH	
	DATE	# OF UNITS	COST/ UNIT	NET COST	TOTAL COST	SOURCE OF FUNDS	TITLE	DATE	VALUE	TITLE PRIOR TO	TITLE AFTER		PROBATE	NON-PROBATE
TOTALS:														

The purpose of this record is to establish the basis for tax purposes and determine whether or not the value of the property is to be included in the probate estate.

Directions: Begin by listing the full name and description of the investment. Include any particulars, such as the original issue discount and amortization rate. Use a separate line for each individual purchase of the same investment. If necessary use more then one line.

Then fill in the **Original Purchase Information**, including: the date of purchase, number of shares or units bought, cost per share or unit, the net cost, total cost of the purchase, whose funds were used to pay for the investment, and how the investment was originally titled. The difference between the Total and Net Cost is the Cost of Purchase, (not noted).

If the property was inherited or transferred to another person, trust, etc. after purchase, or from another person to the decedent after purchase; fill in the **Previous Transfer** section listing: the date of transfer, value at transfer, the title prior to the transfer and the title after the transfer.

Then fill in the value of the investment on the date of death under the probate or non-probate column, as appropriate. Then add both of these columns individually.

R-5

INVESTMENT ACCOUNT TRANSFER RECORD

DATE	BROKER	ACCOUNT NUMBER	ACTION	CASH WITHDRAWAL		CASH DEPOSIT		CASH	MARGIN		INVESTMENTS	
				AMOUNT	DEPOSITED TO	AMOUNT	SOURCE OF FUNDS	BALANCE	MONTHLY INTEREST	BALANCE	DELIVERED	RECEIVED
TOTALS:												

This record is used to record dealings with individual brokerages.

Directions: Fill in the names of brokerages and information for each below. Then record all information as indicated above, being sure to include all conversations and any action taken. Under the Investments columns, list the amount and name of the investment as it is transferred from one account to the other or for investment certificates you deliver to the brokerage or receive from them.

BROKERAGE: _____

ADDRESS: _____

PHONE #: _____ BROKER: _____

ACCOUNT TITLE: _____

ACCOUNT NUMBER: _____

BROKERAGE: _____

ADDRESS: _____

PHONE #: _____ BROKER: _____

ACCOUNT TITLE: _____

ACCOUNT NUMBER: _____

BROKERAGE: _____

ADDRESS: _____

PHONE #: _____ BROKER: _____

ACCOUNT TITLE: _____

ACCOUNT NUMBER: _____

R-6

INVESTMENT SALES RECORD

DATE	BROKER	DESCRIPTION OF INVESTMENT	NUMBER OF UNITS	GROSS SALE PRICE	COST OF SALE	NET SALE PRICE	EXPIRED WORTH-LESS	NET GAIN OR (LOSS) SINCE DATE OF:			VALUE	
								PURCHASE	DEATH		PROBATE	NON-PROBATE
TOTALS:												

Directions: Enter the complete name of the investment when it is sold or expires.

Then enter the name of the broker who made the transaction, the number of shares or units sold, the gross amount of the sale, the broker's commission and/or other charge for the transaction, and the net proceeds from the sale in the appropriate probate or non-probate column. Then figure the gain or loss by comparing the sales price with the value at the date of death and, if the property is jointly held, the gain or loss since the investment was purchased. If a loss put in ( ).

R-7

INDIVIDUAL INVESTMENT TRANSFER RECORD

| DATE | INVESTMENT DESCRIPTION | NO. OF UNITS | BROKER/TRANSFER AGENT NAME AND ADDRESS | TITLE TRANSFERRED | | DATE OF DEATH | VALUE | | | VALUE | |
				FROM:	TO:		ALTERNATE	CURRENT		PROBATE	NON-PROBATE
TOTALS:											

The purpose of this record is to record all transfers of individual investments from one account to another and for distribution transfers to beneficiaries.

Directions: Enter the complete name of the investment to be transferred and the number of units to be transferred. If transfer is to multiple beneficiaries first determine the number of shares by percentage due to each beneficiary. Then list the name of the investment, the number of shares to be given to each beneficiary on successive lines and, the name of the respective beneficiary listed under TITLE TRANSFERRED TO. If more than one broker or transfer agent is used, fill in the address for each. Use two or more lines if necessary. List the appropriate value, according to tax and probate requirements, appropriate to the situation.

INVESTMENT INCOME RECORD

NAME OF INVESTMENT:

	DATE	TYPE	DEPOSITED TO	AMOUNT	DATE	TYPE	DEPOSITED TO	AMOUNT	DATE	TYPE	DEPOSITED TO	AMOUNT
JANUARY												
FEBRUARY												
MARCH												
APRIL												
MAY												
JUNE												
JULY												
AUGUST												
SEPTEMBER												
OCTOBER												
NOVEMBER												
DECEMBER												
TOTALS:												

NAME OF INVESTMENT:

	DATE	TYPE	DEPOSITED TO	AMOUNT	DATE	TYPE	DEPOSITED TO	AMOUNT	DATE	TYPE	DEPOSITED TO	AMOUNT
JANUARY												
FEBRUARY												
MARCH												
APRIL												
MAY												
JUNE												
JULY												
AUGUST												
SEPTEMBER												
OCTOBER												
NOVEMBER												
DECEMBER												
TOTALS:												

Directions: Across the top of each section put the name of the investment from which income is received. We suggest you arrange the investments in alphabetical order first. Then look for the month the income is received and fill in the date the income was issued or generated, the type of income (i.e., interest, dividend, etc.), where the funds were deposited (which bank account or brokerage account), and the amount of income.

At the end of the accounting period total the columns. You can either make one sheet for income received by the decedent before his or her death and one for the estate, or divide the total.

R-9

LIFE INSURANCE PROCEEDS AND PREMIUM REFUND INCOME RECORD

COMPANY	DATE	ACTION	PAYMENTS RECEIVED					VALUE	
			BASIC BENEFIT	DIVIDEND	INTEREST	PREMIUM REFUND	DEPOSITED TO	PROBATE	NON-PROBATE
NAME:									
ADDRESS:									
PHONE #:									
POLICY #:									
NAME:									
ADDRESS:									
PHONE #:									
POLICY #:									
NAME:									
ADDRESS:									
PHONE #:									
POLICY #:									
NAME:									
ADDRESS:									
PHONE #:									
POLICY #:									
TOTALS:									

This record is used to note requests sent to insurance companies for payment of life insurance and for refund of premiums from any insurance policy.

Directions: Enter the complete name, address, phone number, and policy number for the policy. Then enter the date of correspondence and in the Action column, the request or response. When benefits are received fill in the appropriate columns across.

BENEFITS RECEIPT RECORD

DATE	COMMENTS	PAYMENT		REFUND		VALUE	
		DEPOSITED TO		SOURCE OF FUNDS	CHECK NUMBER	PROBATE	NON-PROBATE
TOTALS:							

This record is used to note and calculate the BENEFITS received from an employer (such as a death benefit, accrued vacation, etc.), pension fund, or government benefit program.
Directions: Enter the date of payment or refund and then the amount under the appropriate column and note the account to which funds were deposited when paid. Or from which funds were removed to pay back unearned funds. Be sure to enter the name of the source of the benefit in the empty title column top space.

AGENCY: _____

BENEFIT TYPE: _____

ADDRESS: _____

PHONE #: _____

ACCOUNT #: _____

INCOME RECORD

DATE	COMMENTS	PAYMENT DEPOSITED TO	REFUND SOURCE OF FUNDS	REFUND CHECK NUMBER	VALUE PROBATE	VALUE NON-PROBATE
TOTALS:						

This record is used to note and calculate Income from Miscellaneous sources.

Directions: Enter the date of payment or refund and then the amount under the appropriate column and note the account to which funds were deposited when paid. Or from which funds were removed to pay back unearned funds. If all funds are from a similar source label the sheet with that title. If funds are from various sources, label the form Miscellaneous.

AGENCY: _____

BENEFIT TYPE: _____

ADDRESS: _____

PHONE #: _____

ACCOUNT #: _____

R-12

DEBTS OWED TO THE ESTATE PAYMENT RECEIPT RECORD

DEBTOR:

ADDRESS:

PHONE #:

ACCOUNT #:

TYPE OF DEBT & EXPECTATION OF COLLECTION:

BALANCE: OPEN: $ _____ . _____ CLOSE: $ _____ . _____ OPEN: $ _____ . _____ CLOSE: $ _____ . _____ OPEN: $ _____ . _____ CLOSE: $ _____ . _____

DATE	COMMENT	CHECK #	SOURCE OF FUNDS	PAYMENT AMOUNT	PRINCI-PAL	INTER-EST	DEPOSITED TO	PAYMENT AMOUNT	PRINCI-PAL	INTER-EST	DEPOSITED TO	PAYMENT AMOUNT	PRINCI-PAL	INTER-EST	DEPOSITED TO
TOTALS:															

This record is used to keep track of payments received from people and companies who have borrowed money from the decedent or for any other reason owes money to the estate.
Directions: Enter the date of the transaction, any comment, the amount paid or refunded (put refunds in parenthesis). When a payment is received, enter the portion of the payment which represents the principal and the interest, and where the money was deposited. If a refund is issued, note the check number and the source of the funds. If you write a letter, write "letter" in the comment column and the nature of the correspondence under the appropriate Debtor's column.

R-13

REAL PROPERTY BASIS, SALE, OR TRANSFER RECORD

PROPERTY ADDRESS: _____ MORTGAGE COMPANY: 1. _____
LEGAL DESCRIPTION: _____ MORTGAGE COMPANY: 2. _____

ORIGINAL BASIS

DATE	ACTION	PRICE PAID	SOURCE OF FUNDS
	ORIGINAL COST:		
	TITLE:		
	LIST OF UPGRADES:		
	TITLE AT DEATH:		
	ORIGINAL BASIS:		

TRANSFERS OF TITLE

DATE	ACTION OR TITLE	VALUE
	APPRAISED VALUE:	
	MORTGAGE:	
	DISTRIBUTION VALUE:	

SALE INFORMATION

DATE	ACTION	AMOUNT
	TOTAL SALE PRICE:	
	BROKER'S FEE:	
	CLOSING COSTS:	
	DEPOSITED TO:	
	NET SALES PRICE:	

GAIN OR (LOSS) SINCE

DATE OF PURCHASE	DATE OF DEATH

VALUE

DATE OF DEATH	ALTERNATE DATE:

VALUE

PROBATE	NON-PROBATE

FIXTURES AND YEAR OF PURCHASE:
_____ , _____
_____ , _____
_____ , _____
_____ , _____

NEW OWNER/S: _____
PHONE #: _____
BUYER'S BROKER: _____
PHONE #: _____
ATTORNEY: _____ PHONE #: _____

REAL ESTATE BROKER: _____
COMPANY: _____
ADDRESS: _____
PHONE #: _____

This record is used to establish the original basis, if this is required for a surviving joint owner; and to keep track of the sale or transfer of real estate property.
Directions: Use the transfer column to record previous transfers, as well as transfers to a beneficiary. Include mortgages transferred or amount paid, if less than fair market value. This column is also used for transfers to the decedent. Be sure to include title from and title to information. If the property is sold, enter the date and action taken, including such things as hiring a broker, signing the contract of sale, requesting transfer of mortgage, etc. When a sale does occur enter the appropriate amounts.

R-14

MORTGAGE OR RENT PAYMENT RECORD

DATE	NAME OF COMPANY, AGENCY, OR TENANT	AMOUNTS RECEIVED FROM:				FUNDS DEPOSITED TO	AMOUNT OF PAYMENT TO:				SOURCE OF FUNDS	BALANCE	
		MORTGAGE COMPANY	LEASING AGENT	PROPERTY ASSOC.	TENANT		MORTGAGE COMPANY	LEASING AGENT	PROPERTY ASSOC.			PROBATE	NON-PROBATE
	TOTALS:												

COMPANY: _____
ADDRESS: _____

PHONE #: _____ ACCOUNT: _____
FOR PROPERTY: _____
YEAR END BREAKDOWN: PRINCIPAL: $ _____
INTEREST: $ _____ TAXES: $ _____
INSURANCE: $ _____ OTHER: $ _____

COMPANY: _____
ADDRESS: _____

PHONE #: _____ ACCOUNT: _____
FOR PROPERTY: _____
YEAR END BREAKDOWN: PRINCIPAL: $ _____
INTEREST: $ _____ TAXES: $ _____
INSURANCE: $ _____ OTHER: $ _____

This record is used to keep track of all payments or refunds received and all payments made for property.
Directions: Enter the name of the mortgage company, leasing agent, property association, or tenant to whom the property is sub-leased. Then list the amounts received or paid, as appropriate to the situation. Under value probate/non-probate enter the balance of the mortgage due, as appropriate.

R-15

UTILITIES EXPENSE RECORD

UTILITY NAME:

ADDRESS:

PHONE #:

ACCOUNT #:

DEPOSIT:

DATE	NOTE	DEPOSITED REFUND TO	PAYMENT AMOUNT	CHECK #	SOURCE OF FUNDS	PAYMENT AMOUNT	CHECK #	SOURCE OF FUNDS	PAYMENT AMOUNT	CHECK #	SOURCE OF FUNDS	PAYMENT AMOUNT	CHECK #	SOURCE OF FUNDS
			DATE: - - $			DATE: - - $			DATE: - - $			DATE: - - $		

TOTALS

This form is used to record payments to and refunds from utility companies.

Directions: Enter the date of the transaction, the amount paid or refunded (put refunds in parenthesis). Then enter the number of the check used to pay the bill and the account from which funds originated. If refund is received, note account to which the funds were deposited. If you write a letter, write "letter" in note column and the nature of the request under the Utility.

R-16

PAYROLL CALCULATION RECORD

NAME OF EMPLOYEE: _____

EMPLOYEE ADDRESS: _____

EMPLOYEE PHONE: _____

SS#: _____

WORK - TYPE: _____

LOCATION: _____

PHONE: _____

WEEK ENDING DATE	START AND END								WAGE PER HOUR	REGULAR		OVERTIME		GROSS WAGE	EMPLOYEE DEDUCTIONS							DEPOSITED TO	PAYCHECK		
	S	M	T	W	T	F	S		# OF HRS.	WAGE	# OF HRS	WAGE		FED. WITH.	F.I.C.A.					TOTAL		AMOUNT	SOURCE OF FUNDS	CHECK #
	S																								
	E																								

DATE	TOTALS:

This record is used to note and calculate the weekly wages to be paid to an employee. A separate sheet should be used for each employee.
Directions: Enter the week ending date, the time the worker started work each day, and the time the worker ended. If the worker has an unpaid break use 2 or 3 sets of start and end sections per day. Then calculate the number of hours worked. Over 40 hours a week is overtime and paid at time and one-half. Then calculate the deductions to be made from the employees check.
Note: A separate account should be opened with the employer I.D. number for deposit of taxes until they are paid to the appropriate taxing authority, along with the employer's contribution.

R-17

EMPLOYEE EXPENSE RECORD

| DATE | COMMENTS | EMPLOYEE INCOME TAX WITHHELD | EMPLOYEE F.I.C.A. WITHHELD | EMPLOYER MATCHING F.I.C.A. | | | | | | PAYMENT | | REFUND |
										SOURCE OF FUNDS	CHECK NUMBER	DEPOSITED TO
TOTALS:												

This record is used to note and calculate the taxes withheld from the employees pay, as well as the taxes and insurance required to be paid by the employer.
Directions: Enter the date of payment, deposit of employee withholding, or refund and then the amount under the appropriate column. Then whether the funds are deposited or withdrawn from an account. For refunds or employee deposits use ( ) to show the amount should be subtracted, not added, when totalling the column. They are entered as a positive number when paid to the agencies.

AGENCY: _____

TAX / INSURANCE: _____

ADDRESS: _____

PHONE #: _____

I.D. / ACCOUNT #: _____

R-18

MAINTENANCE AND REPAIR EXPENSE RECORD

SERVICE:					
PROVIDER:					
ADDRESS:					
PHONE #:					
ACCOUNT #:					

DATE	NOTE	DEPOSITED REFUND TO	PAYMENT AMOUNT	CHECK #	SOURCE OF FUNDS	PAYMENT AMOUNT	CHECK #	SOURCE OF FUNDS	PAYMENT AMOUNT	CHECK #	SOURCE OF FUNDS	PAYMENT AMOUNT	CHECK #	SOURCE OF FUNDS
TOTALS:														

This form is used to record payments to and refunds from companies or self employed individuals who do lawn care, pest control, cleaning, etc. to maintain or repair estate property.
Directions: Enter the date of the transaction, the amount paid or refunded (put refunds in parenthesis). Then enter the number of the check used to pay the bill and the account from which funds originated. If a refund is received, note the account to which the funds were deposited. For correspondence, write "letter" in the note column and the nature of the letter under the Company. Phone conversations are noted in the same manner.

R-19

MEDICAL BILLS PAYMENT RECORD

PROVIDER	SERVICE PROVIDED	DATE	BILL BALANCE	INSURANCE CLAIMS							PAID BY PATIENT OR ESTATE		
				COMPANY	ACTION	BENEFIT AMOUNT	DEPOSITED TO	DEDUCT. AMOUNT	EXCUSED AMOUNT	BALANCE AMOUNT	SOURCE OF FUNDS	CHECK #
NAME:													
ADDRESS:													
PHONE NUMBER:													
ACCOUNT NUMBER:													
NAME:													
ADDRESS:													
PHONE NUMBER:													
ACCOUNT NUMBER:													
NAME:													
ADDRESS:													
PHONE NUMBER:													
ACCOUNT NUMBER:													
TOTALS:													

This record is used to keep track of Medical expenses incurred by the deceased person before his or her death.
Directions: Enter information as requested. Be sure to enter in the action column who submits forms and who receives benefit checks.

R-20

FUNERAL AND RELATED EXPENSE RECORD

PROVIDER:

ADDRESS:

PHONE #:

CONTACT:

DATE	SERVICE AND/OR COMMENT	PAYMENT AMOUNT	CHECK #	SOURCE OF FUNDS	BALANCE	PAYMENT AMOUNT	CHECK #	SOURCE OF FUNDS	BALANCE	PAYMENT AMOUNT	CHECK #	SOURCE OF FUNDS	BALANCE	DEPOSITED REFUND TO
TOTALS:														

This record is used to keep track of the expenses and payments made in relation to the funeral or other expenses incurred in relation to the disposition of the decedent's remains.
Directions: Enter the date of action, the name of the provider and cost of the service or item under the balance column. Then list the amount of payments made and the source (bank or charge account, or insurance). List the amount of any refunds received, with the account to which they were deposited.

R-21

ESTATE ADMINISTRATION EXPENSE RECORD

DATE	COMMENTS	ATTORNEY FEES	COURT COSTS	FILING FEES	ADMINIS-TRATOR FEES			PAYMENT			REFUND
								SOURCE OF FUNDS	CHECK NUMBER		DEPOSITED TO
TOTALS:											

This record is used to note and calculate the Administrative expenses of the estate.

Directions: Enter the date of payment or refund and then the amount under the appropriate column and note the account from which funds were paid and the check number. For refunds list account to which the funds were deposited.

SERVICE: _____

PROVIDER: _____

ADDRESS: _____

PHONE #: _____

ACCOUNT #: _____

R-22

ADMINISTRATOR'S EXPENSE RECORD

| DATE | COMMENTS | TRAVEL EXPENSES | | | | | | | COPY FEES | SHIPPING/ POSTAGE FEES | OTHER | PAYMENT | | REFUND |
		# OF MILES	COST BY MILEAGE	REAL CAR COSTS	COMMON CARRIER	TOLLS	PARKING FEES	HOTEL/ MOTEL	MEALS				SOURCE OF FUNDS	CHECK #	DEPOSITED TO
TOTALS:															

This record is used to note and calculate the expenses incurred by the Administrator in the performance of his or her duties. You will have to explore whether or not they will be chargeable to the estate or deductible on taxes.

Directions: Enter the amount of expenses as they occur. You can use either the standard mileage rate or actual car costs.

SERVICE: _____

PROVIDER: _____

ADDRESS: _____

PHONE #: _____

ACCOUNT #: _____

R-23

EXPENSE RECORD

SERVICE: _____

PROVIDER: _____

ADDRESS: _____

PHONE #: _____

ACCOUNT #: _____

DATE	NOTE	DEPOSITED REFUND TO	PAYMENT AMOUNT	CHECK #	SOURCE OF FUNDS	PAYMENT AMOUNT	CHECK #	SOURCE OF FUNDS	PAYMENT AMOUNT	CHECK #	SOURCE OF FUNDS	PAYMENT AMOUNT	CHECK #	SOURCE OF FUNDS
TOTALS:														

This form is used to record payments to and refunds of MISCELLANEOUS expenses. Be sure to label this record either miscellaneous or give it a title for a related group of expenses.

Directions: Enter the date of the transaction, the amount paid or refunded (put refunds in parenthesis). Then enter the number of the check used to pay the bill and the account from which funds originated. If refund is received, note account to which the funds were deposited. If you write a letter, write "letter" in note column and the nature of the request under the Company.

DEBTS OWED BY THE ESTATE PAYMENT EXPENSE RECORD

CREDITOR:

ADDRESS:

PHONE #:

ACCOUNT #:

TYPE OF DEBT:

BALANCE:

OPENING: $ _____ CLOSING: $ _____ OPENING: $ _____ CLOSING: $ _____ OPENING: $ _____ CLOSING: $ _____

DATE	NOTE	DEPOSITED REFUND TO	PAYMENT AMOUNT	PRINCI-PAL	INTER-EST	CHECK #	SOURCE OF FUNDS	PAYMENT AMOUNT	PRINCI-PAL	INTER-EST	CHECK #	SOURCE OF FUNDS	PAYMENT AMOUNT	PRINCI-PAL	INTER-EST	CHECK #	SOURCE OF FUNDS
TOTALS:																	

This form is used to record payments to and refunds from credit cards and personal loans from individuals and companies. It does not include Mortgages on real estate.
Directions: Enter the date of the transaction, the amount paid or refunded (put refunds in parenthesis). When a payment is made, enter the portion of the payment which represents the principal and the interest. Then enter the number of the check used to pay the bill and the account from which funds originated. If refund is received, note account to which the funds were deposited. If you write a letter, write "letter" in note column and the nature of the request under the Creditor.

R-25

CHARITABLE CONTRIBUTIONS RECORD

DATE	CHARITY	PRE-DEATH DONATIONS		DONATIONS THROUGH ESTATE			CHECK #	SOURCE OF FUNDS	DEPOSITED REFUND TO	VALUE	
		AMOUNT	TAX-EXEMP	AMOUNT	TAX-EXEMPT					PROBATE	NON-PROBATE
TOTALS:											

This record is to note and calculate charitable donations made by either the decedent before death or by the estate on behalf of the decedent.
Directions: Enter the complete name of the charity; use an extra line for the address if you wish. Then check the tax-exempt status of the donation, the amount of the donation, and the probate status of the donation.

R-26

TAXES: FILING AND PAYMENT RECORD

DATE	TAX FORM	FORM PREPARED BY	AMOUNT OF TAX DUE & BALANCE	PAYMENTS				REFUND			TAX CARRYOVER	
				AMOUNT	CHECK #	SOURCE OF FUNDS		AMOUNT	DEPOSITED TO	NAME OF BENEFICIARY	NATURE OF CARRYOVER	AMOUNT
TOTALS:												

This form is used to record the taxes paid on behalf of the decedent, the estate, or trust. We suggest you use a separate record for each taxing authority (Federal, State, County or City).
Directions: On the line before the record title word "TAXES" put the name of the taxing authority. Enter the form used. Then enter the name of the person who prepared the tax form and the amount of tax due. When payments are made list amount and source of the funds. If a refund is received enter the amount and where the funds were deposited. When distribution is made, if some tax liability or benefit is passed on to the beneficiaries, list the name of the beneficiary, the type of carryover, and the amount.

R-27

CASH FLOW RECORD

FINANCIAL INSTITUTION:
ADDRESS:
PHONE #:
ACCOUNT #:
ACCOUNT TITLE:

DATE	TRANSACTION DESCRIPTION	CHECK #	WITHDRAWAL	DEPOSIT	WITHDRAWAL	DEPOSIT	WITHDRAWAL	DEPOSIT	WITHDRAWAL	DEPOSIT
TOTALS:										

This record is used to keep track of the money spent and received from different bank accounts, charge accounts, or out of pocket expenses.
Directions: Enter the date of the transaction, list the payee or the name of the record where the transaction is recorded, and the check number or the word cash or charge, as applicable. Then enter the amount of the transaction under the proper account title.

ESTATE SUMMARY

ASSETS	VALUE DATE OF DEATH		CURRENT VALUE	
	PROBATE	NON-PROBATE	PROBATE	NON-PROBATE
Totals:				

LIABILITIES	VALUE DATE OF DEATH		CURRENT VALUE	
	PROBATE	NON-PROBATE	PROBATE	NON-PROBATE
Totals:				

ESTATE AVAILABLE FOR DISTRIBUTION	VALUE DATE OF DEATH		CURRENT VALUE	
	PROBATE	NON-PROBATE	PROBATE	NON-PROBATE
Totals:				

Date:_____,____

_____
Signature and Title of Administrator

Date:_____,____

_____
Signature and Title of Preparer, If Not the Administrator

R-29

ESTATE DISTRIBUTION RECORD

DATE	NAME OF BENEFICIARY	DISTRIBUTION			CASH DISTRIBUTION		PERCENT OF ESTATE	SIGNATURE OF BENEFICIARY UPON RECEIPT	VALUE	
		PROPERTY DESCRIPTION	ORIGINAL BASIS	STEPPED UP BASIS	CHECK #	SOURCE OF FUNDS			PROBATE	NON-PROBATE
TOTALS:										

This record is used to note the distribution of property to the beneficiaries.
Directions: Enter the information as appropriate to the Estate.

BENEFICIARY: _____

ADDRESS: _____

PHONE #: _____

R-30

QUICK REFERENCE CALENDAR

JANUARY	FEBRUARY	MARCH	APRIL	MAY	JUNE	JULY	AUGUST	SEPTEMBER	OCTOBER	NOVEMBER	DECEMBER
1	1	1	1	1	1	1	1	1	1	1	1
2	2	2	2	2	2	2	2	2	2	2	2
3	3	3	3	3	3	3	3	3	3	3	3
4	4	4	4	4	4	4	4	4	4	4	4
5	5	5	5	5	5	5	5	5	5	5	5
6	6	6	6	6	6	6	6	6	6	6	6
7	7	7	7	7	7	7	7	7	7	7	7
8	8	8	8	8	8	8	8	8	8	8	8
9	9	9	9	9	9	9	9	9	9	9	9
10	10	10	10	10	10	10	10	10	10	10	10
11	11	11	11	11	11	11	11	11	11	11	11
12	12	12	12	12	12	12	12	12	12	12	12
13	13	13	13	13	13	13	13	13	13	13	13
14	14	14	14	14	14	14	14	14	14	14	14
15	15	15	15	15	15	15	15	15	15	15	15
16	16	16	16	16	16	16	16	16	16	16	16
17	17	17	17	17	17	17	17	17	17	17	17
18	18	18	18	18	18	18	18	18	18	18	18
19	19	19	19	19	19	19	19	19	19	19	19
20	20	20	20	20	20	20	20	20	20	20	20
21	21	21	21	21	21	21	21	21	21	21	21
22	22	22	22	22	22	22	22	22	22	22	22
23	23	23	23	23	23	23	23	23	23	23	23
24	24	24	24	24	24	24	24	24	24	24	24
25	25	25	25	25	25	25	25	25	25	25	25
26	26	26	26	26	26	26	26	26	26	26	26
27	27	27	27	27	27	27	27	27	27	27	27
28	28	28	28	28	28	28	28	28	28	28	28
29	29	29	29	29	29	29	29	29	29	29	29
30		30	30	30	30	30	30	30	30	30	30
31		31		31		31	31		31		31

FAMILY TREE RECORD

This record is used to show the relationship of family members to the decedent. It can be used to assist an attorney or the courts in determining who may or may not be entitled to benefit from the estate. Ask the attorney how extensive the family tree must be, so you are not doing more work than necessary.

Directions: The oldest generation to be mentioned should appear in the left column. Then each generation should be placed in each successive column. Do not place more than one generation in each column. For example: the first column would include the decedent's parents; the second column would include the decedent and his or her brothers and sisters along with their respective spouses. (Place the spouse's name one space below, also show divorces with year of divorce and length of marriage.) The third column would include the decedent's children, nieces, and nephews, along with their respective spouses, etc. Also show the date of death for all family members who have died. Although the final draft should flow down the generations from left to right, it is usually best for the sake of spacing to begin filling in names at the right hand side of the page. We also suggest using scrap paper to plan your work. If needed two or more sheets can be used to show the family.

FINANCIAL INSTITUTION COMPARISON SHEET

INSTITUTION	TYPE OF ACCOUNT OR SERVICE	CHARGES									MINIMUM BALANCE	ANNUAL YIELD
		MONTHLY SERVICE	PER CHECK/ WITHDRAWAL	PER DEPOSIT	PER A.T.M. USE	EARLY WITHDRAWAL	MONEY ORDER	CASHIER'S CHECK	DORMANT ACCOUNT	PRINTED CHECKS		
NAME:	CHECKING ACCOUNT:											
ADDRESS:	PASSBOOK:											
	MONEY MARKET:											
PHONE #:	C.D.:											
NOTES:	SAFE DEPOSIT BOX:											
	TOTALS:											
NAME:	CHECKING ACCOUNT:											
ADDRESS:	PASSBOOK:											
	MONEY MARKET:											
PHONE #:	C.D.:											
NOTES:	SAFE DEPOSIT BOX:											
	TOTALS:											
NAME:	CHECKING ACCOUNT:											
ADDRESS:	PASSBOOK:											
	MONEY MARKET:											
PHONE#:	C.D.:											
NOTES:	SAFE DEPOSIT BOX:											
	TOTALS:											
NAME:	CHECKING ACCOUNT:											
ADDRESS:	PASSBOOK:											
	MONEY MARKET:											
PHONE#:	C.D.:											
NOTES:	SAFE DEPOSIT BOX:											
	TOTALS:											

This sheet is used to compare the accounts offered by various financial institutions.
Directions: Fill in the amounts charged by each institution and then, by adding the individual costs, they can be compared with the cost of package accounts offered by the same institutions.

R-34

Information Needed About the Decedent
for the Death Certificate

Full Name: _____ Maiden Name: _____

Date of Birth: _____ , _____ Place of Birth: _____ , _____

Legal Residence at Time of Death: _____

_____

Length of Residence: _____ Social Security Number: _____ - _____ - _____

Location When Death Occurred: _____

Name of Mother: _____ Maiden Name: _____

    Place of Birth: _____ , _____

    Date of Death: _____ , _____ -Or-

    Current Residence: _____ , _____

Name of Father: _____

    Place of Birth: _____ , _____

    Date of Death: _____ , _____ -Or-

    Current Residence: _____ , _____

Decedent's Marital Status: _____

Name of Spouse: _____ Maiden Name: _____

    Place of Birth: _____ , _____

    Date of Death: _____ , _____ -Or-

    Current Residence: _____ , _____

Marriage: Date: _____ , _____ Place: _____ , _____

If Decedent was a Veteran: _____ , _____ to _____ , _____ Branch: _____

Education: _____

Occupation: _____

_____ .

Memorial or Funeral Arrangements

Funeral, Cremation, or Memorial Services at: _____

Address: _____ , _____ , _____

_____

_____

Pre-Arrangement Documents: _____

Interment At: _____

Address: _____ , _____ , _____

_____

_____

Religious Ceremonies: _____ , Clergy: _____

Address: _____ , _____ , _____

_____

_____

Military Honors - Location of DD - 214: _____

Religious, Professional, or Fraternal Organization Ceremonies: _____

_____

_____

Disposition of the Remains: _____

Special Instructions for Service: _____

_____

_____

_____

_____ .

Items to be Brought to the Funeral Home, if Casket will be Open:

Clothing: _____ , _____ , _____ , _____ ,

_____ , _____ , _____ , _____ ,

_____ , _____ , _____ , _____ ,

General: _____ , _____ , _____ , _____ ,

_____ , _____ , _____ , _____ .

Optional Information for Memorial Book or Obituary

Obituary to be Printed in: _____ , _____ ,

_____ , _____

Survived By:

Name: _____ **Relationship:** _____

    Residence: _____ , _____

Name: _____ **Relationship:** _____

    Residence: _____ , _____

Name: _____ **Relationship:** _____

    Residence: _____ , _____

Name: _____ **Relationship:** _____

    Residence: _____ , _____

Name: _____ **Relationship:** _____

    Residence: _____ , _____

Membership in Religious, Professional or Fraternal Organizations:

_____ , _____

_____ , _____

_____ , _____

Memorial Gift Preference:

_____ , _____ , _____ , _____

_____ , _____ , _____ , _____

_____ , _____ , _____ , _____

Education:

_____

_____

_____

Military Record:

_____

_____

_____

Cause of Death:

_____

_____ .

Achievements

_____

_____

_____

_____

_____

_____

_____

_____

_____

_____

_____

_____

_____

_____

_____

_____

_____

_____

_____

_____

_____

_____

_____

_____

_____

_____

_____.

HIRING EVALUATION SHEET

Name: _____ Position/Profession: _____

Company Name: _____ Phone Number: _____

Address: _____

Referred by: _____

What do I want this professional to do? _____

_____

_____

     Based on the information in the chapter for hiring this type of professional, formulate the questions you wish to ask each professional over the phone, number each question, then write the professional's answers below next to the corresponding number.

1. _____

2. _____

3. _____

4. _____

5. _____

6. _____

7. _____

8. _____

9. _____

What is the fee: _____

How is the fee determined and/or what is included in the fee: _____

_____

_____

_____

_____

Impression of personality and professionalism: _____

_____

_____

Appointment for Interview: Day: _____ Date: _____ Time: _____

Hire: Yes _____ No _____

REFERENCES, LICENSING, ORGANIZATION MEMBERSHIP, AND INSURANCE

Based on the information in the chapter for hiring this type of professional, formulate the questions you wish to ask each reference over the phone, number each question, then write the reference's answers below next to the corresponding number.

Customer Reference 1. Name: _____ Phone: _____

1._____

2._____

3._____

Comments: _____

Customer Reference 2. Name: _____ Phone: _____

1._____

2._____

3._____

Comments: _____

Customer Reference 3. Name: _____ Phone: _____

1._____

2._____

3._____

Comments: _____

Regulatory Agency/Professional Organization Name:_____

License No. _____ Is this person/firm currently licensed or registered? Yes ____ No ____

Phone: _____ Complaints: Yes ____ No ____ Describe: _____

Regulatory Agency/Professional Organization Name:_____

License No. _____ Is this person/firm currently licensed or registered? Yes ____ No ____

Phone: _____ Complaints: Yes ____ No ____ Describe: _____

Insurance Company Name:_____ Policy No. _____

Phone:_____ Is Policy in Force? Yes ____ No ____ Type of Insurance: _____

Insurance Company Name:_____ Policy No. _____

Phone:_____ Is Policy in Force? Yes ____ No ____ Type of Insurance: _____

Insurance Company Name:_____ Policy No. _____

Phone:_____ Is Policy in Force? Yes ____ No ____ Type of Insurance: _____

ACKNOWLEDGEMENT RECORD

NAME OF RELATIVE OR FRIEND	EXPRESSION OF SYMPATHY	DATE			NAME OF RELATIVE OR FRIEND	EXPRESSION OF SYMPATHY	DATE		
		NOTIFIED OF DEATH	SYMPATHY EXPRESSED	THANK YOU SENT			NOTIFIED OF DEATH	SYMPATHY EXPRESSED	THANK YOU SENT

This record is used to note the notification of friends and relatives of the death and to keep track of the expressions of sympathy that are received and when acknowledgement cards are sent.
Directions: Enter the name of the person contacted, the type of expression received, then the date the person was notified of the death, the date the expression described was received, and the date the acknowledgement for the expression of sympathy was sent. We suggest you try to enter names in alphabetical order to avoid confusion. Start with A, leave a few spaces before the next name and then enter B, leave a few spaces and then enter C, etc. Expect to use four to five sheets depending upon the number of people you expect to contact.

R-41

BUDGET CALCULATION RECORD

FOR THE MONTH OF: _____

DAY	NOTES	RENT OR MORTGAGE	HOME INSURANCE	MAINT. OR UPKEEP	HOUSE TAXES	ELECTRIC	GAS & HEATING FUEL	WATER	PHONE	FOOD	DINING & ENTER-TAINMENT	DRUG STORE ITEMS	HOME & PAPER SUPPLIES	CLOTHING SHOES	LAUNDRY	CAR EXPENSE & INSURANCE	MEDICAL EXPENSE. & INSURANCE	MISCELLANY EXPENSE
1																		
2																		
3																		
4																		
5																		
6																		
7																		
8																		
9																		
10																		
11																		
12																		
13																		
14																		
15																		
16																		
17																		
18																		
19																		
20																		
21																		
22																		
23																		
24																		
25																		
26																		
27																		
28																		
29																		
30																		
31																		
TOTALS:																		

BENEFICIARIES DECISION RECORD

DATE	PROPOSAL AND ESTIMATED COST OR BENEFIT	BENEFICIARY — PLEASE READ THE PROPOSAL — THEN ENTER YOUR DECISION, THE DATE, PRINT YOUR NAME, AND SIGN BELOW IT		
		AGREE - DISAGREE - COMMENTS	DATE	PRINTED NAME AND SIGNATURE

This record is used to document the opinions of Beneficiaries upon proposals for any repairs or other major decisions.

Directions: The Administrator should fill in the date, the proposed action, and the estimated cost or benefit. A copy of the record should then be given to each Beneficiary. The Beneficiary should enter his or her decision and any comments, the current date, and his or her signature. If the record is to be used for more than one decision, draw a line across the sheet to clearly separate the proposals, at the end of each proposal, or after the number of spaces needed for all the beneficiaries to print his or her name and sign, whichever takes the most spaces.

INVESTMENT STATEMENT RECONCILIATION SLIP

DESCRIPTION OF INVESTMENT	LOCA-TION OF CERT.	PURCHASE OR ESTATE VALUE					SALE PROCEEDS						MONTHLY CHECK-OFF	
		MARKET	DATE	# OF UNITS	PRICE PER	NET AMOUNT	DATE	# OF UNITS	PRICE PER	GROSS PRICE	COST OF SALE	NET PRICE	1	7
													2	8
													3	9
													4	10
													5	11
													6	12
TOTALS:							TOTALS:							

INVESTMENT STATEMENT RECONCILIATION SLIP

DESCRIPTION OF INVESTMENT	LOCA-TION OF CERT.	PURCHASE OR ESTATE VALUE					SALE PROCEEDS						MONTHLY CHECK-OFF	
		MARKET	DATE	# OF UNITS	PRICE PER	NET AMOUNT	DATE	# OF UNITS	PRICE PER	GROSS PRICE	COST OF SALE	NET PRICE	1	7
													2	8
													3	9
													4	10
													5	11
													6	12
TOTALS:							TOTALS:							

INVESTMENT STATEMENT RECONCILIATION SLIP

DESCRIPTION OF INVESTMENT	LOCA-TION OF CERT.	PURCHASE OR ESTATE VALUE					SALE PROCEEDS						MONTHLY CHECK-OFF	
		MARKET	DATE	# OF UNITS	PRICE PER	NET AMOUNT	DATE	# OF UNITS	PRICE PER	GROSS PRICE	COST OF SALE	NET PRICE	1	7
													2	8
													3	9
													4	10
													5	11
													6	12
TOTALS:							TOTALS:							

Directions: Cut this sheet into three strips. Arrange the strips by account, then in alphabetical order. Use them to compare the investments in the account to the investments listed on the statement.

Bank Statement Reconciliation Worksheet

Balance from checkbook	$_____	Ending Balance shown on bank statement	$_____
Add Interest Credited	+_____	Add other deposits or credits that appear	+_____
Add other deposits or credits	+_____	in the checkbook but not on statement.	+_____
that appear on statement but	+_____		+_____
not in checkbook.	+_____		+_____
Subtotal	$_____	**Subtotal**	$_____
Deduct other charges or debits	-_____	Deduct outstanding checks	-_____
that appear on statement but	-_____		-_____
not in checkbook.	-_____		-_____
	-_____		-_____
Checkbook Balance	$_____	**Current Balance**	$_____

===

Bank Statement Reconciliation Worksheet

Balance from Checkbook	$_____	Ending Balance shown on statement	$_____
Add Interest Credited	+_____	Add other deposits or credits that appear	+_____
Add other deposits or credits	+_____	in the checkbook but not on statement.	+_____
that appear on statement but	+_____		+_____
not in checkbook.	+_____		+_____
Subtotal	$_____	**Subtotal**	$_____
Deduct other charges or debits	-_____	Deduct outstanding checks	-_____
that appear on statement but	-_____		-_____
not in checkbook.	-_____		-_____
	-_____		-_____
Checkbook Balance	$_____	**Current Balance**	$_____

===

Bank Statement Reconciliation Worksheet

Balance from Checkbook	$_____	Ending Balance shown on statement	$_____
Add Interest Credited	+_____	Add other deposits or credits that appear	+_____
Add other deposits or credits	+_____	in the checkbook but not on statement.	+_____
that appear on statement but	+_____		+_____
not in checkbook.	+_____		+_____
Subtotal	$_____	**Subtotal**	$_____
Deduct other charges or debits	-_____	Deduct outstanding checks	-_____
that appear on statement but	-_____		-_____
not in checkbook.	-_____		-_____
	-_____		-_____
Checkbook Balance	$_____	**Current Balance**	$_____

Order Form

================================

What's Left?
Who's Left?

The Layman's Handbook for Estate Property Management
with Accounting Records
and
Survivor's Guide to Personal and Financial Well-Being

================================

Cost: $24.95 plus $5.95 Postage & Handling for the first book, $3.00 for each additional book.
      Discount schedule for quantity orders (5 or more) available upon request.
Sales Tax: Florida Residents please add appropriate Surtax plus Sales Tax.
Guarantee: Unconditional One (1) Year Money Back Guarantee. No questions asked.
Mail orders: Send completed order form plus check or money order to:
      Tristus Publishing Company, 5449 N. State Rd. 7, Dept. 11,
      P.O. Box 26268, Tamarac, FL 33320-6268
Fax orders: Complete order form including credit card information. Fax to (954) 731-5615.
Telephone Orders: Call Toll Free: (800) 414-8457 - Mon. to Fri. - 9 a.m. to 4 p.m. E. T.
      Have your VISA, Discover, or MasterCard ready.

Please Print

Please send _____ copies of *What's Left? Who's Left?* Total Cost: $ _____._____

Name: _____

Address: _____ Apt. #: _____

City: _____ State: _____ Zip: _____-_____

Telephone: (_____) _____

Payment Method: ❑ Check, ❑ Money Order, ❑ Credit Card:
      ❑ Visa, ❑ MasterCard, ❑ Discover

Card number: _____ Expiration Date: _____

Name on card: _____

Signature of card holder: _____

Order Form

What's Left?
Who's Left?

The Layman's Handbook for Estate Property Management
with Accounting Records
and
Survivor's Guide to Personal and Financial Well-Being

Cost: $24.95 plus $5.95 Postage & Handling for the first book, $3.00 for each additional book. Discount schedule for quantity orders (5 or more) available upon request.

Sales Tax: Florida Residents please add appropriate Surtax plus Sales Tax.

Guarantee: Unconditional One (1) Year Money Back Guarantee. No questions asked.

Mail orders: Send completed order form plus check or money order to:

Tristus Publishing Company, 5449 N. State Rd. 7, Dept. 11,
P.O. Box 26268, Tamarac, FL 33320-6268

Fax orders: Complete order form including credit card information. Fax to (954) 731-5615.

Telephone Orders: Call Toll Free: (800) 414-8457 - Mon. to Fri. - 9 a.m. to 4 p.m. E. T. Have your VISA, Discover, or MasterCard ready.

Please Print

Please send _____ copies of *What's Left? Who's Left?* Total Cost: $ _____.____

Name: _____

Address: _____ Apt. #: _____

City: _____ State: _____ Zip: _____-_____

Telephone: (_____) _____

Payment Method: ❑ Check, ❑ Money Order, ❑ Credit Card:
❑ Visa, ❑ MasterCard, ❑ Discover

Card number: _____ Expiration Date: _____

Name on card: _____

Signature of card holder: _____

Order Form

═══

What's Left? Who's Left?

The Layman's Handbook for Estate Property Management
with Accounting Records
and
Survivor's Guide to Personal and Financial Well-Being

═══

Cost: $24.95 plus $5.95 Postage & Handling for the first book, $3.00 for each additional book. Discount schedule for quantity orders (5 or more) available upon request.

Sales Tax: Florida Residents please add appropriate Surtax plus Sales Tax.

Guarantee: Unconditional One (1) Year Money Back Guarantee. No questions asked.

Mail orders: Send completed order form plus check or money order to:

Tristus Publishing Company, 5449 N. State Rd. 7, Dept. 11,
P.O. Box 26268, Tamarac, FL 33320-6268

Fax orders: Complete order form including credit card information. Fax to (954) 731-5615.

Telephone Orders: Call Toll Free: (800) 414-8457 - Mon. to Fri. - 9 a.m. to 4 p.m. E. T. Have your VISA, Discover, or MasterCard ready.

Please Print

Please send _____ copies of *What's Left? Who's Left?* Total Cost: $ _____.____

Name: _____

Address: _____ Apt. #: _____

City: _____ State: _____ Zip: _____-_____

Telephone: (_____) _____

Payment Method: ❏ Check, ❏ Money Order, ❏ Credit Card:
❏ Visa, ❏ MasterCard, ❏ Discover

Card number: _____ Expiration Date: _____

Name on card: _____

Signature of card holder: _____

Order Form

===

What's Left?
Who's Left?

The Layman's Handbook for Estate Property Management
with Accounting Records
and
Survivor's Guide to Personal and Financial Well-Being

===

Cost: $24.95 plus $5.95 Postage & Handling for the first book, $3.00 for each additional book. Discount schedule for quantity orders (5 or more) available upon request.

Sales Tax: Florida Residents please add appropriate Surtax plus Sales Tax.

Guarantee: Unconditional One (1) Year Money Back Guarantee. No questions asked.

Mail orders: Send completed order form plus check or money order to:

Tristus Publishing Company, 5449 N. State Rd. 7, Dept. 11,
P.O. Box 26268, Tamarac, FL 33320-6268

Fax orders: Complete order form including credit card information. Fax to (954) 731-5615.

Telephone Orders: Call Toll Free: (800) 414-8457 - Mon. to Fri. - 9 a.m. to 4 p.m. E. T. Have your VISA, Discover, or MasterCard ready.

Please Print

Please send _____ copies of *What's Left? Who's Left?* Total Cost: $ _____.____

Name: _____

Address: _____ Apt. #: _____

City: _____ State: _____ Zip: _____-_____

Telephone: (_____) _____

Payment Method: ❏ Check, ❏ Money Order, ❏ Credit Card:
❏ Visa, ❏ MasterCard, ❏ Discover

Card number: _____ Expiration Date: _____

Name on card: _____

Signature of card holder: _____